CECIL RHODES
Flawed Colossus

CECIL RHODES
Flawed Colossus

by

BRIAN ROBERTS

W·W·NORTON & COMPANY
New York   London

Printed in the United States of America.

Library of Congress Cataloging-in-Publication Data

Roberts, Brian.
Cecil Rhodes: flawed colossus/by Brian Roberts.
p. cm.
Bibliography: p.
Includes index.
1. Rhodes, Cecil, 1853-1902. 2. Statesmen—Africa, Southern—
Biography. 3. Capitalists and financiers—Africa, Southern—
Biography. I. Title.
DT776.R4R62 1987
968'.04'0924—dc19   87–33282

ISBN 0-393-02575-6

W. W. Norton & Company, Inc., 500 Fifth Avenue, New York,
N. Y. 10110
W. W. Norton & Company Ltd., 37 Great Russell Street, London
WC1B 3NU

1 2 3 4 5 6 7 8 9 0

FOR
THEO ARONSON

Contents

Illustrations

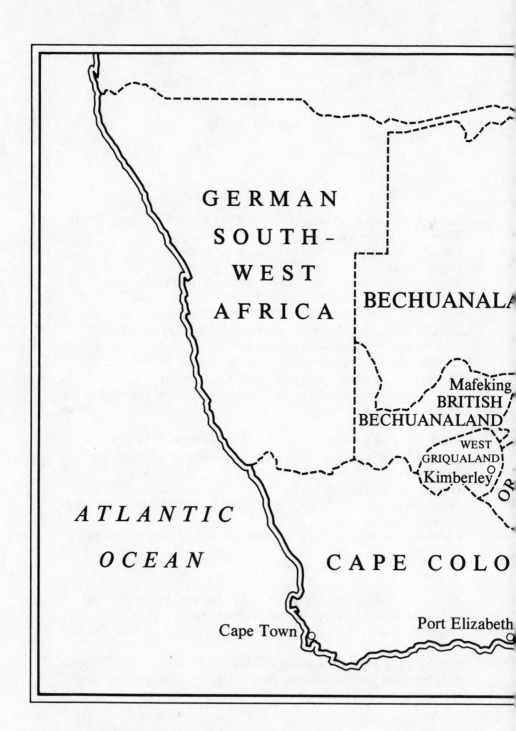

GERMAN
SOUTH-
WEST
AFRICA

BECHUANALA

ATLANTIC

OCEAN

Mafeking
BRITISH
BECHUANALAND

WEST
GRIQUALAND
Kimberley

OR

CAPE COLO

Cape Town

Port Elizabeth

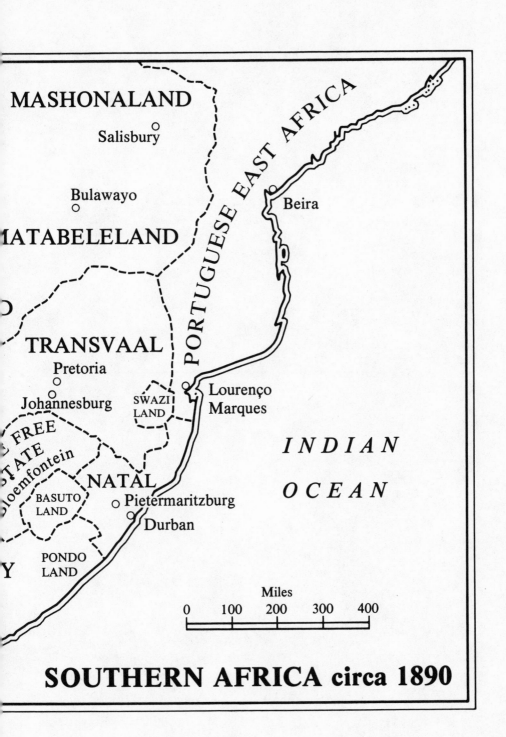

MASHONALAND

Salisbury

Bulawayo

MATABELELAND

PORTUGUESE EAST AFRICA

Beira

TRANSVAAL

Pretoria

Johannesburg

SWAZI LAND

Lourenço Marques

FREE STATE

Bloemfontein

NATAL

BASUTO LAND

Pietermaritzburg

Durban

INDIAN OCEAN

PONDO LAND

Miles

0   100   200   300   400

SOUTHERN AFRICA circa 1890

Author's Note

All biographies must, of necessity, be selective and this book does not pretend to be a detailed account of Cecil Rhodes's wide-ranging political and financial activities. There is no shortage of books on Rhodes as an imperialist and capitalist adventurer who harnessed his huge fortune to promote his dream of Pax Britannica or, as some would have it, to further his quest for personal power. Biographers and historians, apologists and detractors, have subjected his public career to close scrutiny and have judged his actions and motives according to their particular bias. Far less has been written about Rhodes as a man: about his personality, his friendships, emotional attachments, enthusiasms and human weaknesses. While it would be impossible to portray Rhodes without giving due weight to his political and financial intrigues, an attempt has been made here to balance the conventional approach with insights into his character and personal development and so provide a more rounded portrait. This is a biography of Cecil Rhodes, not a history of his times.

Material for this book comes from original research carried out in southern Africa and Britain over a number of years, as well as from previous biographies and recent academic studies. Occasionally it has been necessary to elaborate on certain aspects of Rhodes's career in order to include new, or little known, information but, for the most part, the focus has been kept on the man himself.

I am particularly indebted to Professor Arthur Keppel-Jones's comprehensive and detailed book, *Rhodes and Rhodesia: The White Conquest of Zimbabwe 1884–1902*, and to Professor T. O. Ranger's authoritative *Revolt in Southern Rhodesia 1896–7* for essential information about the Chartered Company's activities in central Africa. My sincere thanks are due to Mr Rob Turrell, of the Institute of Commonwealth Studies, for supplying me with copies of his revealing articles on Rhodes's financial dealings and drawing my attention to other articles on aspects of Rhodes's career. Although the scope of this book allows me to do no more than summarize the findings of these informative articles, they have been invaluable in dispelling doubts about some of Rhodes's more questionable transactions.

xiii

Research over such a long period makes it impossible for me to thank all those who have helped me. I must, however, acknowledge the debt I owe to Mr John A. Flower for copies of Princess Radziwill's letters to his family, to Ms B. Hazell for information from the Natal Archives, to Mrs F. Van Niekerk and Mrs L. Brits of the Kimberley Library, to Ms Leonie Twentyman Jones of University Libraries, Cape Town, to the Curator of the McGregor Museum, Kimberley, and to Mr Graham of the Westgate Public Library, Oxford. A special word of thanks must also go to Mrs Marian Robertson, Mrs Judy Hoare, Mr Andre Bothner and Mrs Muriel Macey of Cape Town and to Mr Keith Killby, Mr R. I. B. Webster, Mr J. E. Malan and Mr Jonathan Kerslake, all of whom assisted my research in a variety of ways. I am grateful to Mr Ian White of Frome for his photographic help and to Mrs S. Bane and the staff of Frome Library for their kind and efficient cooperation at all times.

My final, and undoubtedly my greatest, debt is to Mr Theo Aronson whose expert advice and constructive criticism have, as always, been of immeasurable help throughout the writing of this book.

Brian Roberts
Frome, Somerset
May, 1987

CECIL RHODES
Flawed Colossus

CHAPTER ONE

A Sickly Youth

How long, a member of a fashionable London club once asked the visiting Cecil Rhodes, would he be spending in England?

'Not a moment longer than I can help,' snapped the great man.

Rhodes's answer astonished his listeners. For by this time – the early 1890s – Cecil John Rhodes was widely recognized as one of England's most illustrious and devoted sons. A flag-waving imperialist, a fervent champion of the English-speaking race, the man who was winning Africa for Britain, the Prime Minister of one of Britain's richest colonies, the statesman who had recently informed Queen Victoria that, since their last meeting, he had added 'two more provinces' to her domains, Cecil Rhodes seemed the very personification of all things English.

How then could this dedicated pro-consul of Empire show such contempt for the land of his birth? Why should he be so eager to quit the country to which he had pledged his life's work? These were questions which even Rhodes's close associates – let alone acquaintances in some London club – would not have been able to answer.

There was no simple explanation. For Rhodes believed, and believed passionately, that the British had a mission to civilize the world. Of that there can be no doubt. Throughout his life he proclaimed his faith in the superiority of the Anglo-Saxon race: a faith that was to lead to his being likened to Adolf Hitler. Nor did he make any secret of his own role in furthering British interests.

'I contend,' he had written at the age of twenty-four, 'that we are the finest race in the world and that the more of the world we inhabit the better it is for the human race . . . It is our duty to seize every opportunity of acquiring more territory and we should keep this one idea steadily before our eyes: that the more territory simply means more of the Anglo-Saxon race, more of the best, the most human, most honourable race the world possesses.'

Crude, arrogant and clumsily expressed, this testament, written at a time when his knowledge of other races was minimal, was to provide the basis of Rhodes's life-long philosophy. His belief in the virtues of the Anglo-Saxon race never wavered.

And in Rhodes's heyday – during the last decade of the nineteenth century – there were few of his countrymen who would have disagreed with him. To them his assertions seemed in no way crude or arrogant or clumsily expressed. On the contrary, Rhodes was the embodiment of the imperial ideal; a personification of all the glories of the British Empire.

He was wholly in tune with the spirit of his times. For the late nineteenth century saw the high noon of imperialism. Not only Great Britain, but all the nations of Europe, were expanding, trading, colonizing, establishing spheres of influence and founding empires. This was the age of world powers, of land-hungry visionaries, of aggressive nationalism, of the spread of European civilization. Rhodes was not alone in expounding high-flown theories of racial superiority. Imperialism, far from being denounced, was generally regarded as a noble, romantic, almost mystical creed. Its professed aims of bringing stability, religion and education to the uncivilized areas of the world was seen as entirely admirable.

Of all the manifestations of imperialism, none was considered more important than the Scramble for Africa. Cloaking their national avariciousness in fine phrases, the great – and lesser – nations of Europe were annexing vast tracts of desert, jungle and grassland. In this frantic scramble for African territory, Britain was doing rather better than most. And among those who toiled, explored, or fought beneath the African sun to add lustre to the annals of the British Empire – Gordon, Kitchener, Livingstone, Burton, Speke – none was more illustrious than Cecil John Rhodes. With his grandiose schemes of 'painting the map red', of a Cape to Cairo railway, of spreading 'Anglo-Saxon civilization', Rhodes was regarded as a Colossus, as a man larger than life.

To those who did not know him well, Rhodes had all the glamour of a latter-day Drake or Raleigh. He seemed an amalgam of what they imagined were quintessentially British qualities; they saw him as frank, swashbuckling, buccaneering. His combination of great wealth and personal simplicity, of materialism and mysticism, appealed strongly to the British mind. He could not be judged, thought his contemporaries, by ordinary standards. He was idolized by the public, hailed by London bus drivers and sought after by fashionable hostesses; his admirers ranged from Conservative and Liberal statesmen to radical reformers, future socialists and crusading journalists. Even some of the more cynical of political commentators tended to regard him as a giant among men.

'When all is said,' decided one far from sycophantic contemporary, 'the man who possessed such faith and wrote it in characters of such sprawling bigness belongs to that small company of Englishmen who have really earned the often too lightly conceded adjective "great".'

2

That this Englishman, whose name became a symbol of British imperialism, should sometimes be scathing about his fellow countrymen, about British attitudes and institutions, seemed inexplicable. Some of his criticism may have been prompted by a national characteristic – the Englishman's delight in self-mockery – but not all his outbursts are so easily explained: they were too vehement to be an affectation.

Rhodes's hostility was deep-seated, surfacing only at times of crisis or extreme irritation. It was often in evidence during his visits to Britain. For, apart from his time at Oxford University, Rhodes was not really happy in the land of his birth. He rarely stayed in England longer than was necessary and not until the end of his life – when he wanted a family estate to leave to his brothers – did he think of owning property there. His only settled experience of England was during his childhood and, significantly, that was a period he seemed reluctant to talk about. Little, in fact, is known of Rhodes's formative years. Accounts of his boyhood contain no clues to his later attitudes. For the most part, his biographers have to rely on a few anecdotes vaguely remembered by casual acquaintances, and such stories are seldom informative.

Yet there is reason to think that Rhodes's seemingly conventional upbringing was not as placid as is generally assumed. It could account, in part, for his cynicism in later life, for his distrust of sentimental patriotism and for his reluctance to commit himself openly to emotional attachments. Indeed, were more known of his relationship with his parents, there is much in his convoluted personality that would be easier to explain. As it is, one can only note that the Rhodes family was not without its complexities.

*   *   *

To think of Cecil Rhodes as a child strains the imagination. As an adult he appeared so stolid, so hard-eyed and calculating, that the idea of him as a shy, golden-haired youngster, dressed in a 'plaided frock', nervously clutching his nurse's hand, is little short of ludicrous. Yet this is one of the few glimpses of the knee-high Rhodes to have survived. A schoolmaster who taught his brothers remembered seeing him at a cricket match with the nurse and described how the boy was hit on the arm by a ball. 'I rushed up fearing the bone was broken,' he explained, 'but on testing it found that it was not. I was struck by the delicate frame and small bones, and yet by the Spartan way, almost indifference, with which the child bore pain.' Doubtful in detail, the story is rich in heroic hindsight. This is how Rhodes's admirers liked to picture him – stoical, refusing help, and above human weakness – and a dim memory was revamped to fit the myth.

But there *was* a cricket match. It was played at Bishop's Stortford, in

Hertfordshire: the small town – some thirty miles north of London – where, on 5 July 1853, Cecil Rhodes was born. His biographers claim that his birthplace was the vicarage of the town's Anglican church, St Michael's, but this is misleading. His father, the Rev. Francis William Rhodes, was indeed the vicar of St Michael's, but a year after taking up his appointment, in 1849, he had surrendered the vicarage to the headmaster and boarders of the newly reopened grammar school and the Rhodes family had moved to a semi-detached Georgian house in South Road. It was in this house, half a mile from St Michael's church, that Rhodes was born and grew up.

Little is known of the Rev. Francis Rhodes. He was descended from a Midland family who, in the seventeenth century, had farmed in Cheshire and later drifted south to settle on the outskirts of London, where they had established a successful brick-making business. Francis, born in 1806, had been educated at Trinity College, Cambridge, and, after taking orders, had served as a curate at Brentwood in Essex until he was appointed vicar of St Michael's. By all accounts, he was a strange, somewhat formidable man. Tall, loosely built and intellectual looking, he is said to have been a stickler for discipline and to have possessed 'great individuality'. His servants regarded him as eccentric. Precisely what form his eccentricity took is not known but it seems to have been allied to his domineering manner and puritanical outlook. For all that, he was a courteous and conscientious cleric and his insistence on limiting his sermons to a pithy ten-minute harangue undoubtedly enhanced his reputation as an 'excellent preacher'. He had been married twice. His first wife, Elizabeth Manet, was a young woman of Swiss descent who had died in childbirth two years after their marriage, leaving one child, a daughter; more than nine years elapsed before he married Rhodes's mother, Louisa Peacock.

The second Mrs Rhodes came from South Kyme in Lincolnshire. She was thirty at the time of her marriage, still attractive and far more outgoing than her husband. But her vitality, like that of so many Victorian mothers, was severely tested. The twenty years of her married life were given over to repeated pregnancies and the care of her large family. For, besides inheriting a step-daughter, she had eleven children of her own: nine sons and two daughters. Even so, her concern for individual members of the family was both warm and generous and helped offset the severity of her husband's manner. 'My mother,' Cecil once admitted, 'got through an amazing amount of work: she must have had the gift of organization, for she was never flustered and seemed always to have ample time to listen to all our many and, to us, vastly important affairs.' The close relationship between Rhodes and his mother lasted until the day she died.

The size of the Rhodes family was not unusual for its time, but in

4

other respects the family was far from ordinary. Two of the boys died before Cecil (the fifth son) was born, and of the surviving ten children only two married – Elizabeth, the step-daughter and Ernest, the son born after Cecil. A large family of bachelors and spinsters might be coincidental, but the proportion of eight out of ten seems too high to be entirely a matter of chance. One of Rhodes's biographers has suggested that the boys were too adventurous to settle down but this does not explain their united resistance to marriage. A restless nature does not necessarily prevent a man responding positively to the opposite sex, nor does marriage always require a settled existence. There must have been some other reason why the Rhodes family members remained unmated. Was it an hereditary strain? Or was it, as seems more likely, the effect of their early environment? Environmental influences undoubtedly play an important part in a child's emotional and sexual development and it is possible that a shadow was cast over that crowded English parsonage. Too little is known about these early years for a full understanding of the forces at work in the Rhodes household but there was clearly a lack of intimacy between members of the family. One of the children later confessed that it was 'not the custom' of the brothers and sisters 'to confide in one another', and even their sympathetic mother could not dispel the chilly atmosphere created by their didactic father. Frivolity was frowned upon and idle chatter discouraged. Indeed, Cecil's happiest memories of his childhood centred on his holidays in Lincolnshire, where his mother's sister, Sophy Peacock, allowed him the freedom he was denied at home.

Inhibited the Rhodes children were, and inhibited they remained. Certainly, where sexual matters were concerned, Cecil Rhodes never quite shook off the influence of his father's puritanism. In later life he turned his back on the Church, became an agnostic, involved himself in questionable transactions and spurned Christian ethics but, at the very mention of sex, he would blush and change the conversation.

In this strangely reserved family, Cecil was probably the most stand-offish. He kept himself at a distance and was teased by his brothers who dubbed him 'long-headed Cecil'. The nearest to him in temperament was his sister Edith (who, as an adult, 'dressed like a man, in grey suit, high collar and man's tie and hat' and was noted for her brusque manner) but even she was not allowed to come too close. In later years, when she stayed with him in South Africa, Rhodes was forced to send her packing; his house, he said, was not big enough for both of them – and by that time his house would be very big indeed. Of his two elder brothers, Herbert and Frank, he saw little as a child. These two boys were sent to public schools – Herbert to Winchester and Frank to Eton – and were at home only during the holidays. Cecil was not so lucky.

5

There was a limit to the family funds and he was denied an expensive education. Instead, he was sent as a day boy to the local grammar school.

There was nothing remarkable about Rhodes's school career. His favourite subjects were history and geography and he did well in French, the classics and religious knowledge. Surprisingly, considering his later career, he had difficulty with mathematics. He was a plodder rather than an achiever: the only distinctions he gained were a minor classical scholarship and a silver medal for elocution. He had, it was said, 'the nice agreeable way of speaking which runs in the family'. But this silver tongue did nothing to endear him to his fellow pupils. At school, as at home, he was very much a loner and appears to have made few friends. He was too moody, too touchy and too unapproachable to enter into the rough and tumble of school life. 'A slender, delicate-looking boy . . .' is how he was described, 'possessing a retiring nature, and a high proud spirit.'

Outside school he was happiest roaming the countryside. Left to himself, he could indulge what he described as his 'fantastical' day dreams. Precisely what form these dreams took he did not say but they were unlikely to have been the usual amorous yearnings of a sex-starved adolescent. He had indicated as much when, on reaching puberty, he had inscribed his motto in an album as 'to do or die' and then, true to family tradition, announced his determination never to marry. Nubile maidens played no part in Rhodes's fantasy world. The story is told about a young companion drawing his attention to a pretty girl leaning on a gate. Rhodes did not even look at her; he merely remarked that the farm seemed well cultivated but slackly managed. That was the way his mind worked. People interested him very little, and girls least of all.

The Rev. Francis Rhodes had no time for his son's fantasies. 'My father,' Cecil Rhodes later admitted, 'frequently, and I am now sure wisely, demolished many of my dreams . . . but when I had rebuilt them on practical lines he was ready to listen again. He never failed to put his finger on the weak spots, and his criticism soon taught me to consider a question from every possible point of view.'

Mr Rhodes had his own plans for his sons. He wanted them to follow in his clerical footsteps and saw them becoming 'the angels of the Seven Churches'. But instead of angels they became soldiers, farmers and wanderers. Cecil did toy for a while with the idea of taking holy orders. On leaving school he studied at home under his father and, in a letter to his Aunt Sophy, written shortly after his fifteenth birthday, he explained that he was torn between becoming a clergyman or a barrister. He was more inclined towards the law but thought a clergyman's life was probably the more pleasant. But come what may, he was determined to go to university.

6

It was not to be; at least, not yet. Shortly after leaving school, Cecil Rhodes fell ill. He was sent to be examined by the family doctor, John Edward Morris. On arriving at the doctor's consulting room he was so obviously nervous that Morris advised him to take a walk in the fields until he had calmed down. There is some doubt about the findings of this medical examination but, as a result of it, Dr Morris recommended that Victorian panacea – a long sea voyage. This, in turn, gave rise to a more exciting idea. Cecil's elder brother, Herbert, had recently emigrated to South Africa and was sending home enthusiastic reports about his prospects as a cotton grower in Natal; it was decided that Cecil should join him there.

Cecil never forgot the thrill of being told that he was to go abroad. Late that night, being unable to sleep, he crept downstairs to study a map of southern Africa; he was still poring over the map when dawn broke. The idea of going to a strange land not only promised to improve his health but stirred his sense of adventure. It offered an escape from what he later described as 'the deadly monotony of an English country town'. Only the thought that he might have to postpone his university plans could have caused him regret; but that regret he was forced to swallow. He sailed for South Africa at the end of June 1870, a week or so before his seventeenth birthday.

*   *   *

'Why did I come to Africa?' Rhodes was to say. 'Well, they will tell you that I came on account of my health, or from a love of adventure, and to some extent that may be true, but the real fact is that I could no longer stand cold mutton.'

This was years later, when cynical quips were expected from Cecil Rhodes. It is not to be taken seriously. Rhodes revelled in the myths created by his admirers and often embellished them with a few witticisms of his own. As he well knew, he did not leave England solely to escape the cold mutton of Bishop's Stortford. He left under doctor's orders. The only unanswered question about his departure concerns the nature of his illness.

For a long time it was assumed that Rhodes was tubercular and that, somehow, his illness was cured in Africa. This now seems highly unlikely. Not only was Natal's humid climate unsuitable for anyone with a lung complaint but it would have been extraordinary if, in such a climate, Rhodes had recovered so quickly. For, once he had arrived in Natal, no more was heard about his weak lungs: his later illnesses were caused by a weak heart. This is not surprising. There is reason to think that heart trouble was detected before Rhodes left England; his heart was not thought to be diseased but seriously overtaxed. This may have been why a restful sea voyage was recommended. That, at least, is the conclusion of later research, based on an anonymous typescript which Dr Charles Shee discovered in the Rhodes-Livingstone Museum, Zambia. Entitled simply *Cecil Rhodes*, it provides a more feasible theory of Rhodes's illness.

After studying Rhodes's symptoms, both as a youth and in later years, Dr Shee suggests that he was suffering from 'atrial septal defect', the 'most common congenital deformity of the heart' among adults, known to laymen as a hole-in-the-heart. Difficult to diagnose in the nineteenth century, it nevertheless seems to be confirmed by Rhodes's symptoms. Such a condition would account for Rhodes's recurrent heart attacks, which started when he was young and became more frequent as he grew older, for his tendency to veer from extreme pallor to cyanosis (the bloated, purple-faced appearance which became permanent in the last years of his life), for his repeated fainting fits and for the slow suffocation, through lack of oxygen, which eventually killed him. Certainly Dr Shee's theory is more convincing that the suppositions of Rhodes's early biographers.

*   *   *

The voyage to Natal, which lasted for over two months, proved beneficial to the invalid. It was restful to the point of monotony: the sea was calm, most of the passengers were German-speaking emigrants, and there were few distractions. In a letter to his mother, Rhodes wrote of nightly sing-songs in the deckhouse, of whales, flying fish, porpoises and albatrosses, but he had no real excitements to report. The ship anchored in the Durban roadstead on 1 September 1870 and the passengers were taken ashore by boat. Rhodes summed up his first impressions of Africa as 'very rum' and was probably put out to find that his brother was not there to meet him. He may, though, have known Herbert well enough not to have been too surprised by his absence.

Of the seven Rhodes brothers, Herbert was by far the most erratic. Never able to settle in one place for long and seldom completing any task, he spent his life pursuing an ever-shifting rainbow's end. Flamboyant and reckless, he had none of Cecil's reserve. At school he was described as a born actor, 'clever, volatile, with a face like india-rubber and an extraordinary command of expression.' He was also an irrepressible exhibitionist. 'When I have been out for a walk with the boys,' claimed one of his teachers, 'and we passed an unfinished house, he would run up the ladder and out on a horizontal pole, where, without apparent effort, he would stand unsupported haranguing his schoolfellows.' Such showy behaviour would have horrified the cautious young Cecil.

8

A love of adventure had brought the tall, hatchet-faced Herbert Rhodes to Africa. In the late 1860s he had answered the call of a Land and Colonisation Company which was trying to attract settlers to Natal. The promise of fifty acres of land, with the option to buy a further hundred acres for £120 payable over twelve years, had appealed to Herbert's desire for novelty. He had applied for a farm and was given a free grant of land in the luxuriant Umkomaas Valley, where, against the advice of older colonists, he attempted to grow cotton. His first efforts were far from successful – his crop was attacked by sub-tropical insects and strangled by weeds – but he remained optimistic. He had every intention of trying for a second crop. In the meantime, however, he cast about for an easier way of making a fortune. As it happened, the opportunity presented itself almost immediately.

Herbert's arrival in Natal had coincided with a cataclysmic event in southern Africa. In March 1869, the discovery of a huge, 83½-carat diamond – later known as 'The Star of South Africa' – near the Orange River, inland from Natal, sparked off speculation about the mineral potential of the region. This speculation increased when, towards the end of the year, more diamonds were found along the banks of the neighbouring Vaal River. Soon bands of prospectors began to invade the isolated, sparsely populated region. One of the first organized parties to arrive at the Vaal River was raised in Natal and, needless to say, Herbert Rhodes was among the eager volunteers. He was always ready to try his hand at a new venture.

It was this diamond-hunting expedition that had prevented Herbert from meeting Cecil in Durban. He had, though, arranged for his brother to be lodged with Dr Peter Sutherland, the Surveyor General of Natal, until his return. It was Dr Sutherland who was waiting on the quayside to greet the younger Rhodes brother.

Herbert's absence at this time was to inspire many legends about Cecil's early days in South Africa. He has been depicted as a 'solitary and forlorn' youngster, friendless, alien and unprepared for his new life. This is not altogether true. Friendless and a newcomer Cecil might have been but he was certainly not unprepared. He had, in fact, left very little to chance. With £2000 lent to him by his Aunt Sophy, he was well equipped to set himself up as a farmer. What is more, he had taken the precaution, a month before leaving England, of obtaining a letter of introduction to the Durban manager of the Natal Land and Colonisation Company. Not for nothing was he known to his family as 'long-headed Cecil'.

For all that, he decided to wait for Herbert. Dr Sutherland lived in the Natal capital, Pietermaritzburg, some seventy miles inland from Durban. Here Cecil was made welcome by the Scottish-born doctor and his wife, Jane. They found him a quiet, modest young man, very different from his ebullient brother. Mrs Sutherland was amused by his passion for reading and thought that he had outgrown his strength; her husband was quite convinced that he would end his days as a parson in an English village. Neither of them seems to have expected him to remain long in Africa.

*   *   *

When Cecil Rhodes arrived in Natal, the tiny colony had been open to white settlers for little more than twenty-five years. It was merely one of a complex collection of territories that went to make up South Africa.

Just over two centuries before, the Dutch East India Company had founded the first white settlement in the south-western tip of the African continent, known as the Cape of Good Hope. From here independent-minded Dutch farmers, or *trekboers*, had fanned out into the arid interior. This gradual penetration had developed into a full-scale exodus after the British, in 1806, had taken permanent possession of the settlement and its huge hinterland.

Although many of the Dutch – or Afrikaners, as they became known after inter-marrying with French and German immigrants – had been prepared to acknowledge the rule of the British Crown and remain in what was by then called the Cape Colony, the more republican-minded had trekked northwards in search of independence. In their quest, these tough, reactionary and Calvinistic *voortrekkers* had come up against, and conquered, the various African tribes already settled in the interior. Some of the stronger, more strategically placed tribes had succeeded in withstanding the white incursion and so retained their hereditary lands; but, for the most part, the black man had been forced to submit to Boer or British overlordship. In the south the British remained the dominant force but further inland the *voortrekkers* had established two Afrikaner, or Boer, republics: the Orange Free State and, to the north of it, the Transvaal. The independence of these two republics had been officially recognized by Britain in the early 1850s. By then, the British had created a second colony by annexing Natal – formerly a fiefdom of the mighty Zulu nation – on the eastern seaboard.

Thus, by 1870, South Africa was a hotch-potch of territories made up, not only of the British colonies of the Cape and Natal and of the Boer republics of the Orange Free State and the Transvaal, but of various ill-defined areas peopled by vast African tribes. Huge expanses of the interior were barren, isolated and poverty-stricken. The inhabitants – be they black or white – merely scratched out a living, mainly by stock-farming. Even in the more prosperous southern regions there were few viable industries and the largely rural population depended principally on agriculture. It was not a part of the world that ambitious young men, let alone a sickly bookworm like Cecil Rhodes, could look to for a comfortable future.

But all this was to change. The scratchings along the banks of the Vaal River by men like Herbert Rhodes were to produce undreamed-of results. They were the beginnings of a process which was to transform the economy and politics of South Africa and to lead, after much bitterness and bloodshed, to the unification of the oddly-assorted territories under British control. In this revolutionary process the newly arrived Cecil Rhodes was to play a very significant part: it was a part which neither he nor his Pietermaritzburg hosts could possibly have foreseen.

*   *   *

There is a photograph of Rhodes, taken shortly before he left England. It is a studio portrait and gives one an idea of how he must have appeared to Dr and Mrs Sutherland. Neatly dressed in a braided jacket, with a stiff white collar and a spotted cravat, he looks like a typical middle-class youth. One has seen the face many times before. Pale and unsure of himself, he could be a bank clerk about to start his first job. There is nothing remarkable about him: he has a long nose, a down-turned mouth and a slightly receding chin and, all in all, is rather plain. He would not have stood out in a crowd; there is no hint in his fixed look of his future role in life. The Sutherlands cannot be blamed for mistaking him for one of life's plodders. The dashing Herbert Rhodes, with his aura of derring-do, must have seemed to them a far likelier candidate for setting a continent on fire.

But even Herbert had lost some of his dash by the time he returned from the river diggings. He had found a few diamonds, although not enough to prove worth while. Sorting through gravel was a tedious business and to the easily bored Herbert cotton-growing must have seemed a pleasanter prospect. And so now, with Cecil in tow, he again set off for the Umkomaas Valley. Encouraged by the fact that the next-door farm was having some success, the brothers began planting the cotton seed supplied to them from America. Within a matter of months they had 100 acres of cotton land under cultivation.

The work was hard but Cecil enjoyed it. Despite the hot, steamy climate of inland Natal, he found the outdoor activity invigorating. For the first time in his life he felt free to think, to plan and to act as a man among men. His days in Natal taught him to venerate manual labour; from now on he was to consider men who worked by the sweat of their brows as 'decent chaps'; the rest were dismissed as 'loafers'. When, years later, a friend announced that he wanted to be a writer,

Rhodes was quick to put him right. 'Shouldn't do that,' he scoffed, 'it is not a man's work – mere loafing. Every man should have active work in life.' This was the sort of schoolboyish philosophy that was to guide him through life.

The Rhodes brothers lived simply. They had two huts on the plantation: one they used for sleeping, the other served as a sitting-room-cum-store. Food was cooked for them by an African servant and when this became monotonous they would beg an occasional meal from a neighbour. Primitive as were their household arrangements, they found looking after themselves a chore. One evening they even discussed the possibility of one of them marrying so that a woman could take over the cooking; Herbert suggested that, as the younger brother, Cecil should make the sacrifice. But Cecil, reported Herbert to his parents, did not 'seem to see it'. By and large, they remained good sons of the parsonage. On Sundays they went to church in Pietermaritzburg and occasionally Herbert would take the day off for a game of cricket in the nearby village of Richmond. Distractions were as hard to find in Natal as they had been in Bishop's Stortford.

Cecil never went far from the plantation. He spent most of his spare time poring over the text books he had brought from England. A university education still featured prominently in his plans for the future and this was something he was determined to achieve.

His determination was shared by the only young friend he made in Natal. Henry Caesar Hawkins, a boy of his own age, was the son of a local magistrate: he had come to South Africa with his family after leaving an English public school. Together the two boys read the classics and discussed plans for getting to Oxford without outside assistance.

Life as a cotton grower strengthened young Cecil's self-confidence. He now felt more than capable of making his own decisions. In March 1871 his ego received a further boost when he was left to manage the plantation on his own. News from the diamond diggings prompted Herbert Rhodes to leave Natal for a second time. At the beginning of the year there had been a rush away from the Vaal River to some farms where, it was reported, exciting finds were being made. Herbert waited until March and then, unable to contain himself, went to try his luck at the so-called 'dry diggings'. He would be away much longer this time.

Left to himself, Cecil continued to supervise the cotton picking. Not yet eighteen years of age, he had no qualms about taking on such responsibility. He had learnt a great deal in his six months in Africa and was proud of his new accomplishments. Not least of these accomplishments was his ability to handle the African – mostly Zulu – farm workers. In one of his early letters home he had explained how easy it was to get the 'Kaffirs' to work. A timely advance of wages worked wonders. Such loans were needed to pay the annual hut tax and, in his opinion, this was a good investment. Not only did it secure the farm labour but it helped an employer's reputation.

Rhodes's days in Natal are often cited as the time when he 'came to understand the native'. On a certain level this is probably true. It is equally true, on the same superficial level, that he was given an early lesson in the practice of power. He discovered that men could be bound by purse strings: and the longer the strings, the more securely they were tied – both physically and mentally. Bribery of one sort or another was to play an important part in Rhodes's business dealings.

The cotton crop was an improvement on Herbert's earlier efforts. On 25 May, Cecil exhibited a sample half-bale of cotton at the annual show of the Pietermaritzburg Agricultural Society. His was the only entry from the Umkomaas Valley and it came close to carrying off the top honours. 'Mr Rhodes,' claimed a press report, 'came close behind the winner of the £5 money prize . . . [he] would certainly have taken the best prize had there been the requisite quantity.' Rhodes was to translate this minor triumph into a major symbol. 'Ah,' he would say when warned that something was impossible, 'they told me I couldn't grow cotton.'

Eleven days after the agricultural show, he started negotiating for another farm. Having sent a sample of his cotton home (one wonders what they made of it in Bishop's Stortford) he seemed all set to extend his plantations. He never did. Within a few weeks his plans were entirely changed.

A new bout of diamond fever was sweeping South Africa. The dry diggings were proving richer than anyone expected. The strikes made on two of the farms – Dutoitspan and Bultfontein – had sparked off yet another rush to the fields. More and more men were leaving Natal. In June even Rhodes's earnest young friend, Henry Hawkins, abandoned his books and left for the diggings. 'People out here do nothing but talk diamonds,' Cecil had earlier told his parents. 'Everyone is diamond mad.' That madness now reached new heights.

Even so Cecil remained wary. 'Of course,' he wrote home, 'there is a chance of the diamonds turning out trumps; but I don't count much from them. You see it is all chance. Herbert may find one or he may find one of a hundred carats: it is a toss up. But cotton, the more you see of it, the more I am sure it is a reality. Not a fortune, and not attainable by every one; but still, to one who has a good bit of land, money to start it properly, a fair road, and, above all, a good name amongst the Kaffirs, a very pleasant income.' But he could not ignore the stories that were being bandied about. 'I heard of a fellow,' he admitted, 'who offered his claim for 15s the previous night, the next morning went down and turned out a 70 carat in the first shovelful.' And there was a

Boer who trekked to the diamond fields, found a stone worth £14,000, and trekked out again, all in one day.

It was the astonishing finds on a farm, Vooruitzigt – owned by two brothers named De Beer – that changed Cecil Rhodes's life. The announcement, in the middle of July 1871, of diamond discoveries on a small hillock known as Colesberg Kopje made even the most stable men restless. The stampede which followed these discoveries was called New Rush, and this became the name of the new diggings. Herbert Rhodes was among the first to peg out claims. His luck was instant. In a list of early New Rush returns 'Mr Rhodes of Natal', was reported to have found '110 carats, including stones of 14, 16 and 28 carats.' This was enough to alert even the doubtful Cecil. But he remained calm. Not until the last of the cotton crop had been harvested (and sold for a poor price) did Cecil Rhodes prepare to join his brother at the diggings.

The 400-mile journey to the diamond fields took Rhodes over a month to complete. He left Natal on a pony, riding in front of his heavily laden ox-cart. His luggage reflected his ambitions: alongside an assortment of diggers' tools were stacked volumes of the classics and a Greek lexicon. He still regarded diamond prospecting as a chancy business. If cotton growing had lost some of its attractions, Oxford remained his ultimate goal.

CHAPTER TWO

The Beginnings

'An uglier place,' wrote one early visitor to the famous diamond fields that were to develop into the town of Kimberley, 'I do not know how to imagine.' Situated on a wide, cindery, almost treeless plain, scorched by the unremitting sun and often enveloped in dust so dense that it seemed as though 'the solid surface of the earth had risen diluted into the air,' the diamond fields did indeed present one of the most uninviting spectacles imaginable. Yet they also presented, admitted this same visitor, 'one of the most interesting.'

The 'dry-diggings' consisted of four separate mines. Two of these mines had been dug on adjoining farms, Dutoitspan and Bultfontein, and the other two – Old De Beers and New Rush – were on the Vooruitzigt farm. It was at the most recently discovered mine of New Rush that young Cecil Rhodes established himself in November 1871. Each mine was surrounded by its own camp, with the tents clustered as close to the mine workings as possible. A resolution that New Rush, in contrast to its three older rivals, be laid out in an orderly fashion had been quickly frustrated: in the frantic scramble for claims and living space, all thought of town-planning had been abandoned. Having pitched their tents or positioned their wagons, the diggers refused to budge. Roads were merely dusty tracks weaving haphazardly between the maze of tents. The streets of New Rush, they said, simply followed the course of the wheelbarrows.

Here and there among the sea of tents and covered wagons were a few more permanent-looking structures: wooden or corrugated-iron sheds that served as stores, billiard rooms or even hotels. The only really distinguishable feature of New Rush, and one of which the inhabitants were inordinately proud, was a large open space known as Market Square. Fringed by diamond-buying offices, makeshift shops and canvas-walled canteens, it formed the heart of this higgledy-piggledy settlement. Here meetings were called, announcements made and demonstrations held.

No number of market squares, though, could have transformed New Rush into a town. It remained, at the time of Rhodes's arrival, a primitive camp, lacking even the most elementary facilities. Not only

15

were its inhabitants forced to contend with the blazing heat, the choking dust and the swarming flies, but with an almost complete lack of sanitation. 'Just fancy,' wrote one observer of Dutoitspan in 1871, 'the organic *debris* of 20,000 persons with their belongings, canine, equine, asinine and bovine deposited on the edge of a pan [small lake] without outlet.' And what was true of Dutoitspan was true of New Rush. Not only were the lavatories simply huge open trenches but no attempt was made to dispose of even the most foul-smelling rubbish; the carcasses of slaughtered oxen, sheep and goats were left to rot outside the tents. What with this, and the lack of pure drinking water or fresh vegetables, diseases such as diarrhoea, dysentery and enteric fever were widespread. In addition, many diggers suffered from a form of ophthalmia, caused by the vicious dust storms and the strain of sorting diamonds in the glaring sun.

All in all, the diggings were hardly the most suitable place for a young man of uncertain health. But if Cecil Rhodes did suffer from any of these diseases, he made no mention of them in his letters home. His attention, like that of the entire community, seems to have been focused almost exclusively on the hill known as Colesberg Kopje. 'Imagine,' he wrote to his mother, 'a small round hill at its highest point only 30 feet above the level of the surrounding country, about 180 yards broad and 220 feet long . . . . I should like you to have a peep at the kopje from my tent door at the present moment. It is like an immense number of antheaps covered with black ants, as thick as can be, the latter represented by human beings.'

What these ants were doing was excavating and – at the same time – demolishing Colesberg Kopje. Indeed, by the end of November 1871, these New Rush diggings had reached a depth of some sixty feet and the weekly value of diamonds unearthed was being estimated at between £40,000 and £50,000. Already this mine – which in time, as the 'Big Hole', was to become one of the most famous sights in the world – was awe-inspiring.

'Holding to one of the posts by which buckets are hauled up and down, you crane your neck over the edge, and look down into the gulf. You draw back in amaze, with an exclamation!' runs one breathless contemporary account. 'There is another world yonder, sixty feet below. The crowd is almost as great as that around you. Naked blacks, diminished to the size of children, are shovelling, picking and loading – hundreds of them in that cool, shadowed, subterranean world. They fill buckets with crumbling earth, and endlessly haul them up and down on pulleys. Some are swarming to the surface on rope ladders. There is an endless cry, and laugh, and ring of metal down below. Buckets rise and fall with the regularity of a machine. On top they are detached and emptied in a heap, ready for

16

conveyance to the sieve . . . . The white dry earth is carted off to the outer edge, and goes to swell the monstrous piles that lie there. Upon the surface – so much as is left of it, which is but roadways – what a swarm of busy men!'

Few were busier than Cecil Rhodes. And he became busier still when his brother Herbert, always itching for new excitements, quit the diggings and sailed, after a visit to the Natal plantation, for England. This meant that the eighteen-year-old, and completely inexperienced, Cecil Rhodes found himself in sole charge of three diamond claims estimated to be worth £5000.

Rhodes tackled diamond mining as competently as he had tackled cotton-growing. Before long he could give an expert assessment on the value of a diamond. He learned that the yellow-tinged ones were often deceptive: they had 'a nasty habit of suddenly splitting all over.' On the other hand, every stone had some value: 'the great proportion are nothing but splints,' he reported home, 'but still of even these you very seldom find one that is not worth 5s.'

He became no less of an expert in the handling of African labour. As most of his day was spent at the sorting table, supervising the sifting of the soil – which was spread out on the table and scraped with a flat piece of iron – he was able to keep an eye on his labourers. He needed to. Inevitably, and understandably, there was a brisk trade in illicit diamonds; for the raw tribesmen, the temptations of easily acquired wealth were enormous. The majority of the Africans trekked to the diggings with one purpose in mind – to earn enough money to buy a gun and ammunition; and as the possession of a single diamond was often enough to fulfil these ambitions, a claim-holder needed to be sharp-eyed to prevent the best of his finds being spirited away.

The simple requirements of the Africans presented other problems as well. Having procured his coveted gun, a labourer was liable to head for his distant home, leaving the claim-holder short-handed or, as was often the case, without any workmen at all. When this happened, Rhodes would strip off his shirt and set to work, shovelling soil into bags and hauling them to the sorting tables. It was while engaged in such manual work, claims J. G. McDonald, that Rhodes broke a little finger which, being never properly set, always made it impossible for him to give a proper grip when shaking hands.

By a combination of hard work, efficient management and a shrewd business sense, Rhodes soon established a considerable reputation. Although young, he had no illusions about the way money was made. Unlike his feckless brother Herbert, he did not pin his hopes on one spectacular find. Diamonds had only to continue at a fair price, he told his mother, for a fortune to be amassed. But as it would need at least four years for a claim to be worked out and as he

17

was averaging about £100 a week, he was not thinking in terms of overnight riches.

Reading through Rhodes's letters to his parents, one is struck not only by their eminently practical tone but by their curiously impersonal quality. They read more like company reports or environmental studies than like letters from a youngster to his parents. Bleakly signed 'Yrs C. Rhodes', they contain nothing of an intimate nature; there are few enquiries about the family, no snippets of news about himself. Even allowing for the formality of Victorian family life, they are strange letters for a son to be writing home. Once again one is aware of the gap in personal relationships between the members of the Rhodes family.

But then there was a similar gap between Rhodes and the members of the New Rush community.

* * *

The diggers on the diamond fields were very different from the friendly English-speaking colonists whom Rhodes had known in Natal. A tough, brash, oddly-assorted mob of individualists, they had flocked to the diggings in the early 1870s from every quarter of the globe. James Anthony Froude, the historian, who visited the settlements two years after Rhodes arrived there, described them as: 'Diggers from America and Australia, German speculators, Fenian head-centres, ex-officers of the Army and Navy, younger sons of good family who have not taken to a profession or have been obliged to leave; a marvellous motley assemblage, among whom money flows like water from the amazing productiveness of the mine.'

To Rhodes, they were quite a new breed; utterly unlike the reticent townsfolk of Bishop's Stortford or the worthy pioneers around Pietermaritzburg. Viewing them with suspicion, he held himself aloof. It was during these early days on the diamond fields, he later claimed, that he learned the value of doing a good day's work and keeping his own counsel.

But if Rhodes was chary of the diggers, they were equally chary of him. He just did not seem to fit. He was not a rake or a chancer; nor was he excessively prim or earnest. His contemporaries on the diggings described him as taciturn, abstracted, thin-skinned. He is remembered as: 'A tall gaunt youth, roughly dressed, coated with dust, sitting moodily on a bucket, deaf to the chatter and rattle about him, his blue eyes fixed intently on his work or on some fabric of his brain.' W. C. Scully, said by Rhodes's biographers to have been one of his close friends, seems not, in fact, to have found him very amenable. 'I received several kinds of favours at his hands, but we never became really intimate,' he says.

And the acerbic Louis Cohen – admittedly a biased witness – is in agreement with the rest when he says: 'The silent, self-contained Cecil John Rhodes . . . I have many times seen him in the Main Street, dressed in white flannels, leaning moodily with his hands in his pockets against a street wall. He hardly ever had a companion, seemingly took no interest in anything but his thoughts.'

Most of these recollections of the young Rhodes were written many years later and pictured him through the dazzle of his subsequent reputation. Coloured by hindsight, they attribute his solitary preoccupation to the broodings of a budding genius. But there could be a simpler explanation. A genius is also human and it is possible that Rhodes was just a lonely, sensitive youth, out of his depth, and on guard against a world he did not yet fully understand. He would not be the first young man to try to impress a crowd of self-confident strangers by adopting a pose of silent, inscrutable superiority. Such poses are the refuge of the young introvert. He was, after all, still in his teens.

Yet he should have been able to find some congenial company. His brother Herbert had shared a mess with a group of young men – sometimes known as the Twelve Apostles – which Cecil Rhodes joined and remained with after Herbert's departure. Such messes were common at New Rush and they were usually formed by the 'swells' of the diggings: men who had struck it rich and were able to afford a small measure of luxury. Mostly bachelors, the members of the mess lived in thatched huts or large, well-furnished tents pitched on a rise and protected by a thorn-bush fence. If they were lucky enough to be close to one of the few remaining thorn trees, they would use it as a larder: 'its branches tastefully hung with legs of mutton and other joints of meat [sun-dried meat, known as *biltong*, was popular on the diggings] so that it looks like a very substantial Christmas tree.' The great advantage of living in a mess was that one could share the expenses of food and servants and enjoy the *camaraderie*.

Here, one would have thought, Rhodes could have relaxed and joined in the communal life. But the picture of the abstracted youth persists. That, and something else: more than one of his mess-mates mentions the subtle ways in which Rhodes would draw attention to himself, either by suddenly breaking his brooding silence to offer an opinion or by, just as suddenly, stalking out of the tent without saying a word.

Such behaviour, allied to his outbursts of violent temper, suggests a frustrated personality trying to assert itself as much as it does the vague yearnings of adolescent genius. The two interpretations could, of course, complement each other; it is the age factor which indicates the emphasis. The more one reads of these early days, the more difficult it is to escape the impression of Rhodes as a nervous exhibitionist.

19

But there were times when Rhodes was less moody and more companionable. It was not unknown for him to join in a celebration and even play a part in a practical joke. One friend he made was Charles Dunell Rudd. Like Rhodes, the twenty-eight-year-old Rudd had come to South Africa from England to recuperate after an illness. Rhodes had met Rudd briefly in Natal, but now, finding themselves working adjoining claims, the two young diggers decided to pool their resources. The partnership prospered. Rhodes and Rudd not only worked together in the diggings but devised schemes for improving their capital, including the buying of an ice-making machine from which they supplied diggers with ice-cream and cold drinks.

Starting as a business arrangement, the Rhodes–Rudd partnership blossomed into a firm friendship. If Rudd had one minor fault as a partner it was that he lacked the stomach for the lavish toastings which invariably concluded any business transaction. This was left to Rhodes. And Rhodes, for all his customary reserve, was more than a match for the most hard-drinking digger. This was one of the puzzling things about him: he could drink and swear with the best of them, yet he remained 'unclubbable'.

It may have been because of these drinking bouts that Rhodes later wrote to Dr Sutherland to say he had given up all thought of becoming a village parson. On the diamond fields, he claimed, he had been subjected to too much 'lust of the flesh' to contemplate taking holy orders. Certainly this lust could not have been the one that must have immediately sprung to the good doctor's mind. There was nothing like that about young Cecil Rhodes. Wine, yes; women never. It was another of his peculiarities. To be one of the boys meant having an eye for the girls and here Rhodes drew another anti-social line. He made no pretence about it: women simply did not interest him. Admittedly he was occasionally seen at camp dances, but he went to dance and nothing more. Invariably picking the plainest girls in the room as partners, he was the answer to many a wall-flower's prayer – even if his insistence that he was only dancing 'for the exercise' was somewhat deflating.

'I do not believe,' remarked Louis Cohen, 'if a flock of the most adorable women passed through the street he would go across the road to see them . . . . It is a fact that Rhodes was never seen to give the glad-eye to a barmaid or tripping beauty, however succulent.' Cohen, who could smell out – or invent – any sexual liaison on the diggings, had to admit himself stumped by Rhodes. In a community, he says, where 'every chap had his white or black mate' no woman was 'ever linked with his name'. What could one make of a bloke like that?

If Rhodes did have an interest other than his work, it was his studies. He was still busy on his text books with young Henry Hawkins, who had preceded him to the diamond fields, and he remained determined to go to university. As his religious ambitions dwindled, the attractions of a legal profession became stronger. A university education, he was heard to say, would help him in any career and if he went on to eat his dinners at the Inns of Court, the position of a barrister would always be useful. So he continued to study. The sight of Rhodes seated amid the dust and clatter of the diggings, his attention divided between his labourers and his textbooks, became a familiar one at New Rush.

In time, though, he did find a few like-minded companions. Among them was John Xavier Merriman, son of the Archdeacon of Grahamstown. Some twelve years older than Rhodes, Merriman had recently been elected to the Cape Parliament and was trying his luck on the diamond fields. Lanky and aesthetic-looking, he appeared to Rhodes to be a 'pleasant young fellow' and together they would ride into the veld discussing the classics, history and South African politics. According to Merriman they came to an agreement that the only intellectual pursuit for a colonist was to take an active interest in public affairs. It was an agreement they both took to heart, although with differing results.

Then there was the portly John Blades Currey, Government Secretary to the first Lieutenant-Governor at the diamond diggings. Currey was in his early forties when he arrived at the diggings with his wife and Rhodes formed a lasting friendship with the entire family. Although old enough to be Rhodes's father, J. B. Currey was to be one of the pallbearers at his funeral and his son, Harry Currey, was to become one of Rhodes's private secretaries.

But, welcome as were such friendships, they did little to dispel the image of the solitary young digger that Rhodes had created for himself. When all is said and done, the impression remains of a shambling, shrill-voiced, self-absorbed youth riding about the camp on his Basuto pony, accompanied by his most constant companion – a tail-less mongrel which, it is said, looked more like 'an exaggerated guinea pig' than a dog.

*   *   *

Towards the end of 1872, Herbert Rhodes returned to the diggings after a year's absence. With him he brought his debonair brother, Frank – known in the family as 'the Duke' – who was then awaiting his commission in the Royal Dragoons. The two brothers discovered Cecil in one of the claims with a lawyer, measuring the ground, and threatening to sue a neighbour who, he claimed, was encroaching on his property. The dispute shocked the inexperienced Frank. 'I know,' he wrote home, 'that Father will be horrified at the idea of Cecil going to law.'

21

But the situation was not as alarming as it appeared. Similar rows were constantly breaking out among claim-holders. The deeper the mine was dug, the more precarious the digging became. Originally provision had been made for fourteen roads to run north to south across the mine. These roads, fifteen feet wide, had been cut from the claims – diggers on either side surrendering seven and a half feet of surface soil – and were regarded as common ground: they were essential for carting soil to the sorting tents at the mine's edge. When the diggings were relatively shallow, the system had worked well enough. By the middle of 1872, however, the mine was fifty to eighty feet deep: the roadways between the claims became walls, the walls began to crumble and, not only did digging become dangerous but the demarcation line between claims was frequently in dispute. Young Cecil Rhodes was not one to give away an inch of his property. This was something that his newly-arrived brother quickly discovered. 'Mr Merriman praises Cecil up to the skies,' Frank told his mother. 'He says Cecil is such an excellent man of business; that he has managed all the business in Herbert's absence wonderfully well and that they are all so very fond of him.'

Shortly after Herbert and Frank arrived, Cecil fell ill. He suffered his first recorded heart attack. It was largely a matter of overwork and, nursed by the Currey family, he appears to have recovered fairly quickly. All the same, it was decided that he should have a short break from the diggings. Herbert arranged to borrow a wagon and a span of oxen and, leaving Frank and Charles Rudd in charge of the claims, set off with Cecil on a trek to the north. But the journey was not planned solely as a convalescent trip. Rumours of gold finds were beginning to drift in from the Transvaal and Herbert, ever the optimist, was anxious to investigate them. There was a chance that both brothers would benefit from a couple of months away from the diamond fields.

After jolting along the Missionaries' Road into Bechuanaland, the brothers turned eastwards to the Murchison Range where Herbert expected to find his gold. This lonely trek across the vast stretches of the highveld is said to have marked another turning point in Cecil Rhodes's life. Just as Natal is supposed to have given him a deep understanding of the tribal African, so this journey to the Transvaal is said to have widened his knowledge of the *platteland* Boers. On the scantest of evidence, his more romantic biographers have pictured him outspanning his oxen at isolated farmsteads, being welcomed by the solemn, pipe-puffing patriarchs and their homely wives and drinking in earthy wisdom along with the coffee he was served on the stoeps. Such descriptions are largely imaginary, but they may contain a germ of truth. The Boers were noted for their hospitality and would undoubtedly have put themselves out to entertain a stranger. But how much this helped to conquer Rhodes's prejudices is another matter. It would have taken longer than a few weeks to reach an understanding of a people as complex as the Transvaal Boers and, as the future was to show, there was a great deal about them that Rhodes never did appreciate.

But the journey was not entirely unrewarding. It helped to restore Cecil's health and gave him his first experience of Africa beyond British rule; in the Transvaal, also, he acquired his first property, when he bought a farm of 3,000 acres. As a gold prospecting expedition, however, the long trek proved disappointing. The rumours had been more exciting than the finds and by the time the Rhodes brothers arrived, most of the miners had already moved on.

Even so, Herbert remained undeterred. No sooner had they arrived back at the diamond fields than he was preparing a new venture. This time his rainbow-chasing was to carry him out of Cecil's life. Selling up his share of the diamond claims, he set out on a series of wanderings that were to last another six years and end only in a ghastly accident in which he was burnt to death in his hut in Nyasaland (present-day Malawi) in 1879. It seems tragically appropriate that such a smouldering, fitful life should have ended in a burst of flame. When his death was reported in the diamond fields press, he was remembered for his kindness to his African labourers.

The Transvaal trek helped Cecil to arrive at a decision about his future. The time had come, he felt, to put some of his vague plans into action. Frank was due to return to England and Cecil decided to go with him. He had no hesitation in leaving his diamond interests in the competent hands of Charles Rudd. The partners had earlier discussed the possibility of Rhodes going to university and Rudd, himself a Cambridge man, had readily agreed to look after their joint interests while he was away.

Cecil and Frank Rhodes sailed for England at the end of July 1873. Cecil was twenty years of age and was at last going to Oxford.

*   *   *

Few places on earth could have been less like the diamond diggings than the city of Oxford. Everything – its damp climate, its lush greenery, its ancient buildings, its aura of tranquillity, its sense of tradition, its atmosphere of learning – was in stark contrast to the world that Rhodes had left behind in Africa. There was no echo of the dreaming spires to be found among the corrugated-iron shacks of New Rush. And few Oxford undergraduates were to pursue their degrees in as erratic a fashion as Rhodes. It took him no less than eight years to obtain his pass degree. He matriculated at Oriel

College in October 1873 and did not graduate until December 1881.

For, of course, Rhodes was running two careers in tandem. Despite his faith in the benefits of a university education and his urge to acquire professional status, he remained an active partner in the Rudd–Rhodes enterprise: diamond digger, claim holder and contractor. He was thus obliged to lead an extraordinary double life: a life divided between high learning and high finance, conducted in two continents and involving, it is said, an outlay of some £2,000 in steamship fares alone. This bizarre division of interest and environment, this curious see-sawing from philosophy to materialism, from the cloisters to the mining office, was to have a profound effect in moulding the man who was to develop into the Colossus.

These were to be the formative years of his life. They saw the awkward youth burgeon into the man of destiny. At Oxford Rhodes discovered the philosophical vehicle to which he could harness the fortune he was amassing in South Africa. Each aspect of this double life was dependent on the other: without either, his subsequent career might well have been sterile.

But it was a slow process. At first, Rhodes seemed no more at ease at Oxford than he had on the diggings. Older, quieter, more ponderous than the majority of undergraduates, he nevertheless revealed a streak of boyish brashness that could embarrass those students intent on proving their own maturity. His habit of flinging down a fistful of diamonds to convince his audience of the prospects awaiting an enterprising 'Oxford man' was looked upon as decidedly vulgar.

All the same, it would be a mistake to picture him at Oxford, as have some of his biographers, as a 'shy and solitary spirit', a brooding misfit at odds with his callow contemporaries. He enjoyed his time at Oxford, felt at home there, and made friends. 'He belonged to a set of men like himself,' remembered one of his tutors, 'not caring for distinction in the schools and not working for them, but of refined tastes, dining and living for the most part together, and doubtless discussing passing events in life and politics with interest and ability.' At least two, James Rochfort Maguire and Charles Metcalfe, were to join his African enterprises and remain loyal to him throughout his life.

When set against the true meaning of Oxford in Rhodes's life, factors such as his gaucherie, his insularity, even his lack of academic achievement, become unimportant. For Oxford came to represent something far more significant than a mere course of studies: it gave him – through his reading of Aristotle, Gibbon and Marcus Aurelius – an intellectual stimulus which, in turn, developed into a philosophy of life.

Many years later, at the height of his fame, Rhodes spoke to the journalist W. T. Stead about these years at Oxford. He had been

24

profoundly impressed, he admitted, by Aristotle's dictum about having an aim sufficiently lofty to justify spending one's entire life endeavouring to reach it. At the time, he had no such aim. On his periodic returns from Oxford to the diamond fields, he had been unable to accept the object to which those about him were dedicating their lives. There was surely nothing very lofty in the pursuit of money for its own sake?

And so, says Stead, 'he fell a-thinking'. To what lofty ideal should he dedicate himself? Religion? He had none. Such faith as had survived the rough and tumble of the diamond diggings had been swept away by his reading of that 'creepy' but influential Victorian history of mankind: Winwood Reade's *The Martyrdom of Man*. Faced with this *mélange* of Darwinian theory, comparative religion and literary skill, Rhodes, in common with many of his contemporaries, was very nearly won over to atheism. But not quite. He was willing to give God a fifty-fifty chance of existing. At such odds it might be as well to accept the Deity's existence as a working proposition but it was hardly a firm enough base on which to build his life's work.

What then was the most elevated ideal towards which he *could* strive? The answer, he decided, was a social trinity: Justice, Liberty, Peace. If there *were* a God, then surely it would be on such a cornerstone that He would want human society to be founded. But how was such a society to be achieved?

'Mr Rhodes,' says Stead, 'had no hesitation in arriving at the conclusion that the English race – the English-speaking man, whether British, American, Australian or South African – is the type of race that does now, and is likely to continue to do in the future, the most practical, effective work to establish justice, to promote liberty, and to ensure peace over the widest possible area of the planet.'

Pax Romana was dead; long live *Pax Britannica*! If Stead is to be believed, it was at Oxford that Cecil Rhodes found his light on the road to Damascus. His mission in life was decided.

*   *   *

To later generations, Rhodes's great mission – the spreading of Anglo-Saxon civilization throughout the world – has distinctly sinister connotations. Sickened by twentieth-century manifestations of the theory of racial superiority, Rhodes's critics find his philosophy crude, naïve and arrogant. They see him purely in terms of a power-grasping megalomaniac, of a ruthless racialist. All this is understandable.

It is also unfair. The ingredients of racialism are undoubtedly there and, once launched on his quest, Rhodes was to drift into some very questionable byways but his motivations were far removed from those

25

of later exponents of a 'master race'. The world had much to learn about the brutalities that could distort such concepts. To Rhodes, at Oxford, in the 1870s, it all looked very different. Not only did he regard his crusade as an eminently practical one (to him, the achievements of the English-speaking race were self-evident: a triumph of 'decent chaps' over 'loafers') but he regarded it as an almost divinely-inspired one. His vision was born in an atmosphere of high endeavour.

The 1870s ushered in the golden age of British nineteenth-century imperialism. These were the triumphant years during which that most dazzling of prime ministers, Benjamin Disraeli, was urging his country to greatness. Queen Victoria was proclaimed Empress of India; Britain gained control of the Suez Canal, opening up the way to mastery of Egypt and the Far East; the Transvaal Republic was summarily annexed as a first step towards a great Confederation of South Africa; Disraeli pulled off a major diplomatic *coup* at the Congress of Berlin and brought home his famous 'Peace with Honour' to a country which had already sung itself hoarse with the newly-coined 'jingo' threat to Russia: *'We don't want to fight, but by Jingo if we do, we've got the ships, we've got the men, and we've got the money too'*. And if this jingoism – this blend of national self-righteousness with territorial aggrandisement – was somewhat distasteful, it was certainly infectious. Many a young man succumbed to it.

For several generations the youth of Great Britain – or, at least, the upper-class, public school-going youth – were to be inspired by the quasi-mystical vision of Empire. In the triumphant strains of Elgar, in the battle scenes of Lady Elizabeth Butler, in the poetry of Kipling, in a thousand and one adventure books, the glories of imperialism were trumpeted. The mythology of Empire was full of heroes who had given their lives for Queen and Country. Few homes were without their reproductions of a painting of British redcoats bravely facing the onslaught of primitive tribesmen under a burning sun. The broken square, the jammed Gatling gun, the tattered colours saved, were all scenes guaranteed to set the pulses pounding.

This strident imperialism had been mirrored, in an altogether more idealistic fashion, by that high-minded if unorthodox socialist, John Ruskin. At Oxford, Ruskin's famous Inaugural Lecture, expressing his interpretation of Britain's imperial mission in 'words of unsurpassed beauty', left an indelible impression on an entire generation of undergraduates.

'There is a destiny now possible to us, the highest ever set before a nation to be accepted or refused,' ran the prophet's mellifluous phrases. 'Will you youths of England make your country again a royal throne of kings, a sceptred isle, for all the world a source of light, a centre of peace; a mistress of learning and of the Arts, faithful guardian of time-tried principles? . . . This is what England must either do or perish: she must found colonies as fast and as far as she is able, formed of her most energetic and worthiest men; seizing every piece of fruitful waste ground she can set her feet on, and there teaching those of her colonists that their chief virtue is to be fidelity to their country, and their first aim is to advance the power of England by land and sea . . . . If we can get men, for little pay, to cast themselves against the cannon-mouths for England, we may find men who will plough and sow for her, and will bring up their children to love her . . . .'

What idealistic young Englishman could resist so stirring, so reasonable, so unselfish, and above all, so romantic a call? Certainly not Cecil John Rhodes. In later life he was to admit how much he owed to Ruskin's inspiring message. For despite his eminently practical outlook, his shrewd business sense, his ruthless political manoeuvrings, his often cold-blooded machinations, Cecil Rhodes always maintained something of the idealism of youth. With his personality unresolved, he used the British empire as an emotional outlet, dedicating his entire life to the imperial ideals imbibed as a young man at Oxford.

CHAPTER THREE

Digger and Dreamer

Shortly before Rhodes had left South Africa for Oxford, important changes had taken place on the diamond diggings. At the beginning of January 1873, Richard Southey –a former Colonial Secretary at the Cape – had arrived at New Rush to take up his appointment as Lieutenant-Governor. Southey's appointment was intended as the first step towards granting the diggers a form of self-government which, it was hoped, would end the constant agitation, riots and lawlessness that had plagued the diggings since their inception. As Lieutenant-Governor, Southey was to preside over a Legislative Council composed partly of members elected by the diggers and partly of government nominees.

Before the elections to the Council could be held, however, a decision had to be reached about a new name for the diggings. Griqualand West, in which the diamond fields were situated, was now a British Crown Colony and in London the Secretary of State for the Colonies, Lord Kimberley, was insisting that the camps be given 'decent and intelligible names'. His Lordship, it appears, 'declined to be in anyway connected with such a vulgarism as New Rush' and he refused to accept Vooruitzigt – the name of the farm before it became New Rush – on the grounds that 'he could neither spell nor pronounce it.' What was needed, said Kimberley, were 'English sounding names'.

Southey passed this problem on to the Government Secretary, J. B. Currey, who quickly found names for the various electoral districts. When it came to renaming New Rush, however, Currey proved himself an accomplished diplomat. He made quite sure that Lord Kimberley would be able to spell and pronounce the new name. He called it 'after his Lordship'. The names were officially announced on 5 July 1873. New Rush was no more: from now on it would be known and celebrated as – Kimberley.

The elections for the Legislative Council were held on 25 November 1873. Rhodes, who was then at Oxford, appears to have taken little interest in them. But a relapse in his health, following the death of his mother on 1 November 1873, obliged him to break off his studies and return to South Africa. By the time he reached the diggings, at the beginning of 1874, the Council had already met for the first time and appeared to be functioning well. One of its more important innovations had been to replace the rough and ready diggers' committees – then the most influential bodies on the diggings – with carefully controlled Mining Boards. There had been no open opposition to this new measure; the new governing authorities were able to congratulate themselves on an initial success. 'All,' noted J. B. Currey, 'seemed to be going well.' Only later did it become apparent that the Council chamber was no real reflection of the growing resentment in the camps. The fiery members of the old diggers' committees were even then preparing to hit back. They had been too powerful for too long to accept any high-handed treatment from the newly arrived officials. The apparent lack of opposition to Governor Southey's administration was, as events would show, more ominous than reassuring.

Rhodes remained aloof from any political intrigue. At this stage, he was far too involved in his business concerns to play a public role. The Rudd–Rhodes enterprise required the full attention of both partners if it were to expand. For although Charles Rudd had nursed and improved the business while Rhodes was at Oxford, there was a limit to the enlargement of any diamond digging operation in Kimberley: a ruling by the old diggers' committees restricted the number of claims any digger, or combination of diggers, could own. These restrictions remained in force under the Southey regime which, in a recent proclamation, had disqualified any individual or combination from holding more than ten claims. In effect this meant that any expansion of the Rudd–Rhodes partnership would have to be achieved through subsidiary undertakings: undertakings that would yield a greater profit than their rickety ice-making machine.

As it happened, the answer to their problems literally descended on them shortly after Rhodes's return to the diggings. A disastrous drought in 1873, which lasted throughout the year, was followed in February 1874 by torrential rains. The four mines were quickly flooded. Primitive pumping equipment had to be hastily rigged up to make it possible for work to continue. Rudd and Rhodes were among the first to put in a bid for the pumping operations at Dutoitspan. Together with a young Australian digger, William Alderson – who knew a little about engineering – they obtained a second-hand water-pumping plant which, although badly in need of repair, was sufficiently serviceable for their offer to be accepted. They immediately ordered another plant from the Cape and set to work with the battered pumps, which they hoped would last until the new equipment arrived.

It was very touch-and-go. The pumps were constantly breaking down, fuel was scarce, and there were endless delays in bringing up the new equipment. Things were not helped by Rhodes's notorious absentmindedness. In later years Rudd was fond of telling the story of how Rhodes had almost ruined the new enterprise. Alderson was away and Rudd and Rhodes had been left in charge of the pumps. One night, as Rudd was clearing debris at the edge of the crater, he glanced down and saw that Rhodes, who should have been working the engine, had left his post and was walking up and down abstractedly. Seconds later there was a loud explosion. The boiler had burst: Rhodes had forgotten to supply it with water. They appear to have patched up the plant for, shortly afterwards, it was working well enough for them to make a bid for a contract with the De Beers mine.

By that time, however, events on the diggings had taken a nasty turn.

*   *   *

Discontent among the diggers was endemic and could be traced to many causes. In the early days, squabbles among the various states – the Cape, the Orange Free State and the Transvaal – laying claim to the ill-defined diamondiferous territory, had created hostile factions in the camps. The resulting friction had been cynically exploited by unscrupulous land speculators. Added to this there was the uncertainty which hung over the diamond industry. Periodic booms and slumps plagued the diggings. In 1873 panic had broken out when the familiar yellow soil – in which most diamonds were found – had given way to deeper, much harder 'blue ground' which was thought to be barren. By the time Rhodes returned from Oxford, the so-called 'blue ground scare' had been overcome: 'the diggers,' reported the *Diamond Field* newspaper, on 3 December 1873, 'have gone down into the blue and report the finds are improving.' Far from being barren, the harder ground was to prove highly productive. Nevertheless, confidence had been shaken: many a despairing digger had sold up and left and the population of the fields had dwindled alarmingly. No less discouraging were the climatic conditions. The recent drought, followed by heavy rains, had increased the difficulty of working the mines and made digging more expensive. Import duties imposed by the Cape Colony were causing the cost of living to soar. Now, with the abolition of the diggers' committees, claim-holders felt they were not sufficiently protected – neither physically nor financially – and that the new administration was inefficient if not, as many agitators insisted, downright corrupt.

But the most inflammatory of the diggers' resentments concerned the Africans. For the discovery of diamonds had brought to South Africa the industrial problems of the nineteenth century – the conflicts between capital and labour, the insecurities of the artisans and the unskilled workers, and the rootlessness of the masses. This, in terms of the country's racial composition, meant a sharpening of the divisions between the white and the black man.

Most of the manual work in the mines was performed by the tribesmen who flocked to the diggings. They provided a cheap labour force for which most diggers were grateful. But bitter objections were raised when a few of these Africans were allowed to work their own claims. Many of the early riots on the diggings were sparked off by bigoted diggers who were determined to force the black men out of business. Feelings ran high. 'Nigger,' a new term of abuse – often used by Rhodes – was popularized by American diggers. An illustration of the growing racial tensions was given when a digger asked to be excused from jury duty because 'he hated the nigger' so much that he did not feel able 'to acquit him of anything'. This was the South African interpretation of Europe's 'class warfare.'

The black man – whether self-employed or a labourer – was also thought to be at the root of the industry's greatest evil – IDB (illicit diamond buying). This was the most serious affliction suffered by the diggers and, more often than not, the Africans were held responsible for smuggling stones to the buyers of stolen diamonds. That the poorly paid labourers were merely pawns of devious white men, who reaped the richest rewards, was rarely taken into account. Demands for laws to check IDB and rid the diggings of 'vagrants' featured prominently in the protests by the diggers.

Richard Southey was not the most suitable official to deal with the worsening situation. Staunch imperialist that he was, he was seen by the diggers as an arrogant, self-righteous autocrat. His aloof manner made it difficult for him to deal with agitators. Conscious of the dignity of his office, he tended to dismiss all protests out of hand and to rule by the book. But probably his greatest offence, in the eyes of the diggers, was his undisguised sympathy for the Africans. As Lieutenant-Governor, appointed by the Crown, he considered that it was his duty to protect the interests of all the inhabitants of the diamond fields, irrespective of colour. It would, he once observed, be a 'great injustice' to grant privilege to 'white persons purely because they were white'. Enlightened as such sentiments were, they gained him few friends among the race-conscious mining community.

If Southey was intractable, his opponents – that oddly-assorted collection of fortune-hunters – were implacable. Agitation against his administration mounted. Committees were formed, meetings were called and demonstrations were staged. Secretly the would-be rebels began to arm themselves. At one rowdy meeting, held in the Kimberley Hall at the beginning of 1875, the audience was called upon to take up arms as soon as a black flag was hoisted at the mine. The instigator of this revolutionary move was Alfred Aylward, a huge,

31

black-bearded Irishman who had recently served a prison sentence for wounding a man in a racial brawl. Loud-mouthed and vehemently anti-British, Aylward was one of Kimberley's most flamboyant characters. With his inclusion among the leaders of the protest movement, events began to take an ugly turn.

More meetings were called, seven armed companies were formed, and men paraded the streets shouldering arms. Southey responded by appealing to the Cape authorities for troops.

Things came to a head when, in April 1875, William Cowie, a canteen keeper, was arrested. He was charged with unlawfully supplying twenty guns to Alfred Aylward. This gave the militants the pretext they had been waiting for. While Cowie's trial was still pending, the rebels let it be known that any attempt to carry out a conviction would be resisted by force of arms. The case was heard in the Resident Magistrate's Court in the afternoon of 12 April. Cowie was found guilty and sentenced to pay a £50 fine or, alternatively, serve three months' hard labour. Refusing to pay his fine, Cowie was led from the dock to serve his sentence.

Immediately sentence was passed, things began to happen. 'It was apparent from the noise outside the Court that some movement was on foot,' reported the magistrate. Some movement was indeed on foot. The police acted swiftly. Accompanied by four Justices of the Peace, they hurried Cowie to the nearby gaol. As they approached the prison, they were overtaken by armed diggers. At that moment police reinforcements, armed with rifles with fixed bayonets, appeared at the lower corner of the gaol. It was a tense moment. There were some three thousand people, armed and unarmed, milling about the gaol; if either side opened fire, it would end in mass slaughter.

The situation was saved by the coolness of the magistrate. Despite a revolver being fired close to his head, he agreed to take the rebel leaders to see Southey. Stiff as ever, Southey refused to grant an interview. However, it was agreed to release Cowie on the handing over of a cheque for £50, not to be cashed until the sentence had been reviewed. With that the 'Black Flag Rebellion' fizzled out. Cowie was freed and the crowd dispersed.

There had, in the past, been stormier incidents on the diggings. Riots, tent burnings, canteen wreckings and even an occasional death had resulted from the rabble-rousing of earlier days. But such outbreaks had been spontaneous, ill-organized and short-lived, more a matter of hooliganism than of subversion. The Black Flag Rebellion was entirely different: a planned attempt to defy, or even overthrow, the authority of a British Crown Colony. Although it failed, it produced serious repercussions. Not only were Richard Southey and J. B. Currey sacked but the post of Lieutenant-Governor was abolished and an Administrator appointed. At the end of the year it was also announced from Whitehall that a Royal Commissioner was being sent to Kimberley to report on the financial position of the mining community and to recommend economies.

Cecil Rhodes had kept well clear of the turmoil. He may even have tried to use the crisis to further his own ends. That, at least, is the accusation that was levelled at him during the bickering sequel to the Black Flag Rebellion. How well he acquitted himself when faced for the first time with an inquiry into his behind-the-scenes activities is questionable.

*   *   *

The Royal Commissioner appointed to investigate conditions at Kimberley was Colonel Crossman. He arrived at the diamond fields at the end of 1875 and opened his Court of Inquiry in the Kimberley Hall on 2 January 1876. Ostensibly the purpose of Crossman's inquiry was to ascertain the financial situation; in effect it was an investigation of the many grievances that had led up to the Black Flag Rebellion.

The first day of the hearing brought its surprises. Most of the morning was spent in listening to complaints about the administration of the mines. Not until later in the day did Crossman get round to examining specific charges. One of these concerned the flooded claims and the inefficient water-pumping system. A Mr Heuteau, who had charge of the water-pumping machinery at the De Beers mine, was said to have been offered £300 by a speculator if he would stop the machinery by damaging it in some way. On being examined, Heuteau agreed that he had indeed been offered a bribe. He refused, however, to name the speculator concerned. Crossman then threatened that, if this information were withheld, he would take legal action to obtain it. Heuteau suggested a compromise: he had given his word not to divulge the speculator's name, he said, but he was prepared to write the name on a piece of paper. This he was allowed to do and, on being provided with paper, wrote – 'Mr Cecil Rhodes'.

Heuteau's attempt at secrecy proved futile. On reading the name, Crossman asked, in ringing tones, for Mr Rhodes to be sent for. Rhodes was nowhere to be found. Instead, his partner, Charles Rudd, arrived. Rudd told the court that he was prepared to testify to the effect that Heuteau had perjured himself. Cecil Rhodes, he declared, 'was the last man to attempt bribery.' Crossman was not convinced. He summoned both Rhodes and Heuteau to appear before him when the court met the following Friday. If Rhodes showed up before then, he added, he would be prepared to hear what he had to say.

Rhodes arrived shortly before the court rose. He explained that he

33

had been tending his water-pumping equipment at Dutoitspan. He roundly dismissed Heuteau's statement as 'a fabrication' and the following day attended a special meeting of the De Beers Mining Board, where he appealed to members of the Board to help him clear his name. The Board was unhelpful. It was, said the Chairman, simply one man's word against another's. Moreover, Heuteau had told him about the bribe 'some months ago'. The case, it was decided, would be best left to the Court of Inquiry.

Both Rhodes and Heuteau were present when the court met on Friday, 7 January 1876. Rhodes, who had taken legal advice, announced that he intended to charge Heuteau with perjury. This prevented any further investigation and the matter was handed over to the public prosecutor. The affair created a stir in Kimberley. Rhodes was warmly supported by the local press. 'The charge has been made,' thundered the *Diamond News*; 'the character of a respectable citizen has been assailed. If Heuteau can prove that his allegation is true, the Attorney General ought to put the law in force against Rhodes; but if he cannot, then Rhodes ought to have full justice done him.'

But it was not to be as simple as that. During his lifetime Rhodes was to be involved in a number of legal proceedings; more often than not the outcome was to be left in doubt. This first occasion was no exception.

Six days later, the preliminary hearing took place in the Resident Magistrate's Court. The prosecution called witnesses who testified that, before the Inquiry, Heuteau had told them that Rhodes was not the man who had offered him a bribe. Heuteau reserved his defence. There was some doubt about the legality of the proceedings. With Crossman being the only person to see what Heuteau had written, the court had no evidence that Cecil Rhodes was the man named. All the same, a *prima facie* case had been made and Heuteau was committed for trial.

That more or less ended the matter. For, without any reason being given, the case was dropped. At the next hearing the Attorney General announced that he would not prosecute. No more was heard of the bribery charge. Whether there was insufficient evidence, or whether a legal technicality had prevented the prosecution is not known. To all appearances, Rhodes's case against Heuteau seemed better founded than Heuteau's accusation against him. Witnesses had been found to deny Heuteau's charge and, as later transpired, Heuteau stood to lose his job once Rhodes's pumping machines were installed. On the other hand, the Attorney General, Sidney Shippard, was one of Rhodes's few friends in Kimberley and he would undoubtedly have done his best to protect Rhodes's name. Certainly it would have benefited Rhodes to have had the affair thrashed out in public, had there been a reasonable chance of his winning. As it was Heuteau was probably not alone in being relieved that the matter had been so conveniently settled.

*   *   *

One thing is certain: Rhodes did not suffer financially as a result of Heuteau's accusation. The De Beers Mining Board was satisfied with the result and agreed to allow him to operate their machines until his own pumps arrived. All that remained was for him to get his new pumps to the diamond fields. This was a problem with which he had been battling for months. The railway had not reached Kimberley; he had to rely on ox-wagons to bring the machines from the Cape and the recent rains had made the roads pretty well impassable. Nor had the rains improved conditions in the water-logged mines. Work was coming to a standstill and the patience of the De Beers Mining Board was wearing thin. At the beginning of February he was asked to attend a meeting to explain why he was not fulfilling his contract.

He attended the meeting, accompanied by his old friend from Natal, Henry Hawkins. 'I have never forgotten,' Hawkins was to say, 'the way in which he, still quite a youth, handled that body of angry men and gained his point, an extension of time.' But it was not entirely a matter of Rhodes's persuasive personality. A report of the meeting shows that he gave a guarantee to have the pumps at the mine within thirty days or forfeit £100. In giving such a guarantee, Rhodes was pushing his luck. The chances of his meeting the thirty day deadline were exceedingly slim.

He was relying on the vaguest of rumours. He had heard that a farmer in the Karoo (the semi-desert between Cape Town and Kimberley) had brought out a pump from England and was using it for tapping underground water. As the pump was said to be in a shed unused, Rhodes made up his mind to buy it. This was to be a real test of his persuasiveness.

Hiring a Cape-cart and six mules, Rhodes set off for the Karoo immediately. It took him eight days to reach the farm. Here he met with a rebuff. Not only was the farmer – a Mr Devenish – startled by his audacity, but he was quite adamant about not selling the pump. Rhodes, however, refused to be put off. Day after day he returned to the farm, exerting his charm and increasing his offer. But Devenish would not budge. Eventually Rhodes decided to change his tactics. By this time he had become friendly with the entire Devenish family and, having failed to win over the farmer, he turned his attention to the farmer's wife. Mrs Devenish proved far more susceptible. So much so that she joined in the battle to wear her husband down. Finally, attacked from two sides, Devenish was forced to give in. For the exorbitant price of £1,000, plus a further £120 for transport costs, Rhodes bought the pumping engine. Not the least remarkable aspect of the transaction was the fact that Devenish, knowing nothing about Rhodes, agreed to accept his cheques for the entire amount – one of them made out in pencil. That 'every man has his price' was an axiom that guided Rhodes's business career. This deal must have confirmed it.

For an outlay of £1,120, Rhodes had avoided forfeiting £100. But there was more to it than that. He had fulfilled his contract and so secured a monopoly of the water-pumping systems at De Beers as well as at Dutoitspan. This, in turn, took him out of the ranks of the small-time diggers. The Rhodes–Rudd partnership was now on a firm footing and Rhodes was poised for much bigger things.

But first he had his interrupted education to consider. No sooner were the new pumps installed than he left for Oxford. He remained there until the end of the year, returning to Kimberley only for the Long Vacation. 'By all means,' he wrote to Charles Rudd, 'try and spare me for two years: you will find I shall be twice as good a speculator with a profession at my back.'

The two years following his enforced return to the diamond fields – after his first illness at Oxford – is usually regarded as highly important to Rhodes's career. Certainly it contributed to the foundation of his fortune. His deal with Devenish is often quoted (and embroidered upon) to illustrate his pertinacity, his resource and ability to take risks and to wear down opposition. The bribery charge, however, is never mentioned. His early biographers were either unaware of it or have preferred to ignore it. But it is not without significance. For the first time Cecil Rhodes had come under scrutiny at the diggings and he had not escaped unscathed. The charge against him might have been unproven but, as far as the diggers were concerned, he was no longer above suspicion. Rhodes was painfully aware of this. Writing from England, shortly after his return to Oxford, he was to say: 'My character was so battered at the Diamond Fields that I like to preserve the few remnants.'

*   *   *

For the best part of the next two years – 1876 and 1877 – Rhodes was kept busy at Oxford. His studies, like his way of life, were extremely erratic. He had little time for disciplined reading and saw no point in attending lectures. When taxed about his negligence, he was inclined to bridle. 'I shall pass, which is all I wish to do,' he would snap.

All too often, he was preoccupied with his business concerns. He was forever writing to Charles Rudd, discussing the pros and cons of new investments, giving advice on pumping machines, speculating on the effects of a political crisis on the diamond market, describing his interviews with rival companies and telling about his visits to diamond merchants in Hatton Garden. High learning did not sit easily with high finance.

But it was not only his business concerns that demanded his attention. It was during this long spell at Oxford that his life's philosophy took shape, that he conceived his great dream. On 2 June 1877 – the day he was inducted into the Masonic Order – he put these thoughts in writing. 'It often strikes a man,' he wrote, 'to enquire what is the chief good in life; to one the thought comes that it is a happy marriage, to another great wealth, to a third travel, and so on; as each seizes the idea, for that he more or less works for the rest of his existence. To myself thinking over the same question the wish came to render myself useful to my country.'

He then went on to extol the virtues of the Anglo-Saxon race: to argue for the necessity of bringing as much territory as possible under Anglo-Saxon influence, to claim that the more the world was dominated by the Anglo-Saxons the better it would be for the human race.

Scrawled in the quiet of his Oxford lodgings, these high flown sentiments remained in their rough form – with many crossings-out, insertions and rewordings – until he returned to South Africa a few weeks later.

He arrived back in Kimberley on 7 August 1877, having spent the long dusty journey from Cape Town in the company of an officer of the Royal Engineers, Captain (later Sir Charles) Warren. They had got on well together. Warren, a keen Bible student, had been fascinated to find Rhodes working from a divinity cram-book for an Oxford examination. This had led to a friendly argument about religion: a subject on which they agreed to differ. 'He had his views and I had mine,' says Warren, 'and our fellow passengers were greatly amused at the topic of our conversation – for several hours being on this one subject.' Warren had recently been appointed as a special commissioner to Griqualand West for the purpose of investigating land claims. It did not take him long to discover that Rhodes had a reputation in Kimberley for more than his religious knowledge. 'He is,' noted Warren in his diary a few weeks later, 'accredited with a long head.'

Rhodes was kept very busy during this stay in Kimberley. The Rhodes–Rudd partnership now extended far beyond their original claims and the water-pumping contracts. One of the important reforms to result from Colonel Crossman's investigation into the running of the diamond industry had been the lifting, in December 1876, of the restriction which prevented diggers from owning more than ten claims. Those who had the capital were now free to buy claims as they wished, to combine their interests and start company mining in earnest. The day of the small-time diggers was drawing to an end; from now on the fields were open to well-heeled capitalists. Almost overnight mining companies sprouted in the four mines. Rhodes and Rudd were among the first to take advantage of the free-for-all.

It was by cashing-in on the lifting of the claim restrictions and not, as is often assumed, by taking advantage of the 'blue-ground scare' that the partners secured a firm foothold in Kimberley. Starting with a valuable block of claims at Baxter's Gully in the Old De Beers mine (the mine that had developed, not at Colesberg Kopje but around the De Beers farm-house) they increased both their holdings and their influence. When the scramble for claims was at its height, it is said, they had the opportunity of buying the entire De Beers mine for a mere £6,000. This they were forced to decline because, 'they could not afford the capital as well as the licence fees.' If this is true, they were later to regret it. But, at the time, they concentrated on buying as many holdings as they could. By taking others into their partnership they extended their mining interests and emerged as claim-holders of considerable importance. The direct negotiations were handled mostly by Charles Rudd but Rhodes, both by letter and on his visits to Kimberley, was actively involved in every move the partners made.

His visit in 1877 was no exception. Those at Oxford who regarded him as taciturn and stand-offish would have been surprised at the forceful way in which he threw himself into the in-fighting at Kimberley. His shrill, squeaky voice was raised both at board meetings and at public meetings. Diffident was the last thing that anyone on the diamond fields would have considered him. His earlier disgrace was now a thing of the past and he was listened to with respect. He seemed to be everywhere at once.

In fact, he tried to do too much. The strain was more than his weak heart could stand. Sometime during this visit he suffered another heart attack: an attack which left him shaken and frightened. He was staying in his usual bachelor quarters and his behaviour after his heart attack was most strange. 'His friends,' claims Sir Lewis Michell, 'once found him in his room, blue with fright, his door barricaded with a chest of drawers and other furniture; he insisted that he had seen a ghost.'

Incurably superstitious, Rhodes probably believed what he said: but what really scared him was the glimpse he had had of death. This, at least, seems to be the logical explanation of his immediate reaction to his heart attack. Faced with the possibility of dying before he had accomplished his mission – the mission he had recently outlined at Oxford – Rhodes's first thought was to ensure that his work was carried on. He decided that the goals he had set for himself should be openly acknowledged in the form of a will. Later, his critics were to accuse him of using his imperial ideals as a screen for his personal ambitions. His actions on this occasion seem to indicate less selfish motives. He was not so much concerned with his own mortality as he was in the end of his crusade for a far greater cause.

The extraordinary document he had drafted in Oxford was now copied out – not by himself, but in an unknown hand – and formalized in the sweaty heat of a Kimberley shack. He dated it 19 September 1877 (the day he was due to return to England) and described himself as Cecil John Rhodes of 'Oriel College, Oxford, but presently of Kimberley in the Province of Griqualand West, Esquire.' As executors he named Lord Carnarvon, the British Colonial Secretary, and Sidney Shippard, the Attorney General of Griqualand West. The mandate presented to these two unsuspecting gentlemen bordered on the bizarre. After detailing his purpose in making the will, Rhodes entrusted his executors with the establishment of a Secret Society whose aim and object would be 'the extension of British rule throughout the world.' No less. A clandestine and dedicated brotherhood was to bring the entire continent of Africa under its sway and to populate South America, the Holy Land, the seaboard of China and Japan, the Malay Archipelago, the islands of Cyprus and Candia, and any island in the Pacific not 'heretofore possessed by Great Britain,' with British settlers. As if this was not enough for any underground movement to be going on with, the Society was also to recover the United States of America for Britain, consolidate and inaugurate a system of Colonial Representation in the Imperial Parliament for the foundation of 'so great a power as to hereafter render wars impossible and promote the best interests of humanity.'

Having signed this will, and lodged it with a Kimberley attorney, Rhodes returned once more to Oxford.

*   *   *

The lifting of the claim restrictions not only encouraged enterprise, it also opened the way for international financiers. Credit was now more readily available from banks and an opportunity was provided for attracting foreign investors. Groups of diggers were now able to turn over their claims to joint stock companies.

European speculators were slow to rise to the bait of South Africa's diamonds. In the early registered companies the shareholders were mostly Kimberley residents. By 1880, however, at least one company in the Kimberley mine (formerly New Rush) had foreign backing. This was the *Compagnie Française des Mines de Diamant du Cap*, or, as it was popularly known, the French Company. The man responsible for the formation of this company was Jules Porges, head of one of the largest diamond concerns in the world. He launched the French Company with an initial capital of fourteen million francs, divided into 500 franc shares and issued in Paris. Inevitably, the initiative of Jules Porges sharpened interest among the claim holders in the Kimberley mine. Soon other companies were consolidating their holdings and seeking capital abroad. The struggle for supremacy in the Kimberley mine had begun: everyone recognised that, sooner or later, a single company would control the mine. 'Come it will in the end,' warned a local newspaper, 'whether we fight against it or not.'

Nor was the struggle confined to the Kimberley mine. Similar moves were being made in all the mines and nowhere with more success than at Old De Beers. This was largely due to the determined efforts of Cecil Rhodes. His plans to take over Old De Beers were, by this time, well advanced.

After keeping three terms at Oxford in 1878, Rhodes had taken another break from his studies. He spent the whole of the following year in Kimberley and, by the beginning of 1880, the Rhodes–Rudd partnership was well established in Old De Beers. By combining with other claim-holders they had built up a syndicate which controlled an important section of the mine. On 1 April 1880, they were able to announce the formation of the De Beers Mining Company, with an authorized capital of £200,000. This was not Rhodes's only mining interest at this time. By the end of 1880, Rhodes was a director of the Lilienstein Mining Company, which operated in the Bultfontein mine; in January 1881, he became a director of the Kimberley Tramways Company; his name appeared as a director of the International Diamond Mining Company and both he and Rudd were directors of the Kimberley Coal Mining Company.

But it was on the De Beers company that Rhodes focused his ambitions. The mine, it is true, was neither the richest nor the most important, but to control it would place him in a position to match up to any potential rival. While others spent their money and energies jostling for control of the Kimberley mine, Rhodes intended to establish a sound base for any future struggle. And he was convinced that a much tougher struggle lay ahead: a struggle which would involve not merely the control of individual mines but control of the entire diamond industry.

There was no doubt in Rhodes's mind about the enormous potential of the South African diamond fields. 'There is every chance,' he wrote to a friend, shortly after floating the De Beers Mining Company, 'of our prosperity lasting; the old fear of the mines working out is rapidly fading . . . this is now the richest community in the world for its size and it shows every sign of permanency. The present proved depths of our mines alone would take at our present rate of working a hundred years to work out, and of course we cannot tell how much deeper they may go.'

He was wrong in his estimate. The mines were not, as he thought, bottomless; but they were deep enough to give substance to his dreams.

CHAPTER FOUR

Into Politics

From the time diamonds were first discovered in the arid wastes of Griqualand West, the territory's political status had been in dispute. The attempt to administer it as a British Crown Colony had proved far from satisfactory and, in 1877, a bill annexing Griqualand West to the Cape had been passed in the Cape Assembly. Not until three years later, however, was that bill put into effect. At the opening session of the Cape Assembly in 1880, the Colonial Governor, Sir Bartle Frere, had made a formal announcement: 'In redemption of the undertaking given by the Colonial Legislature and confirmed by the Colonial Governor,' he declared, 'we relieve Her Majesty's government of the responsibility of the administration of the affairs of Griqualand West.'

The territory was officially incorporated into the Cape Colony on 15 October 1880.

This change of status meant, of course, that Griqualand West was now entitled to be represented in the Cape Assembly. The Cape Act which proclaimed the new Province of Griqualand West had created two electoral divisions: one for Kimberley and one for the Barkly district – a rural area which included the old river diggings. Each of these divisions was entitled to elect two members. The first elections were announced for March 1881.

There was no immediate rush of candidates for the four seats. Election to the Cape Assembly lacked the attractions of local politics. Not only was the election contest costly but successful candidates would be forced to spend lengthy periods in Cape Town and their businesses might suffer. To the money-conscious inhabitants of Griqualand West this was a serious consideration. While the importance of the diamond industry being strongly represented at the Cape was generally recognized, most local politicians were prepared to hand over this responsibility to others.

From the outset it was acknowledged that, whatever the competition, the Kimberley division was more likely to attract candidates than was Barkly. Kimberley was the centre of the diamond industry, big business was concentrated there, and electioneering in the town was easier than canvassing the widespread rural area. As it happened, there was no contest for the seats at Barkly. Only two candidates presented themselves: one was Frank Orpen, a 57-year-old Irishman whose family had been long active in South African politics; the other was Cecil John Rhodes.

Rhodes's nomination created the biggest surprise. Up until then he had shown little positive interest in politics. A year or so earlier, he had allowed his name to be put forward for a seat on the Legislative Council but had then thrown the election into confusion by withdrawing at the last moment. Even at the time of the annexation he had, at first, appeared as reluctant as the other diamond magnates to forsake Kimberley for Cape Town. But he had changed his mind; or rather, changed his tactics. The allure of the Cape Assembly had proved too much for him. No doubt he recognized that the Cape parliament would provide a better sounding chamber for his grandiose ideas than the Legislative Council of Griqualand West and had consequently accepted nomination for Barkly. Why he chose Barkly rather than Kimberley is something of a puzzle.

When he had first arrived on the diamond fields, the river diggings had been largely abandoned; the constituents he would represent in Barkly were, for the most part, Afrikaner farmers – hardly promising recruits for his imperial crusade. It may have been an atavistic urge – 'My ancestors,' he was fond of saying, 'were keepers of cows' – or he might simply have welcomed the chance of an easy, inexpensive election. Whatever his motives, his choice was wise. Although Rhodes was not opposed at Barkly in this first election, he was later to hold the seat against fierce competition. Even when his reputation in South Africa was at its lowest, nothing could dislodge him from his entrenched position. The way he retained this rural seat against all odds is a striking illustration of his extraordinary ability to command loyalty from the most unlikely of supporters. Rhodes represented Barkly – or Barkly West as it became – until the day he died.

His seat being unopposed, Rhodes held no meetings and delivered no speeches during the election campaign. He made up for this once he took his seat in the Cape Assembly. He was the first of the new members from Griqualand West to make a speech. 'I remember his first appearance in the House,' claimed a political journalist: 'a fine ruddy Englishman, a jovial-looking young squire. His speech was bluff and untutored in style, with no grace of oratory. A candid friend remarked afterwards that he would be a Parliamentary failure.' Others were not so sure. The more discerning appreciated the force of his arguments and the cool, if unspectacular, reasoning of his badly delivered speech. 'I heard several members as well as strangers in the Gallery,' wrote a Kimberley reporter at the time, 'speak highly of his maiden effort, from which they predicted he would make his mark in a quiet unassuming way. In his hands, at least, the dignity of the House will not be lowered.' This was slightly more encouraging, but it was not saying much.

The truth was, as time would show, Cecil Rhodes was not a natural politician. He was far too impulsive and lacked the gravity of manner that distinguishes the statesman; his voice was too uncontrolled for an orator. His habit of sitting on his hands and rocking with laughter was almost as embarrassing as the way his voice was apt to break into a shrill falsetto when he became excited. Reports of his maiden speech confirm that his shortcomings were apparent from the outset. His awkward gestures, his nervous way of speaking, his unkempt appearance – he never bothered much about his dress – and his complete disregard for parliamentary etiquette (the Speaker had repeatedly to remind him to address members by their constituencies, not their names) were hardly compensated for by his obvious enthusiasm. All in all, Cecil Rhodes was not expected to set a continent on fire.

*   *   *

Rhodes did not allow his parliamentary duties to interfere with his business concerns. His immediate aim was a complete take-over of the De Beers mine and this remained his top priority. He had, in fact, made an important advance in the mine before taking his seat in the Cape Assembly.

When Rhodes and Rudd had launched the De Beers Mining Company, in 1880, their most formidable rival was the firm of Stow, English and Compton – a combination of diggers who had been working as a group since 1878. The head of this firm, Frederick Philipson-Stow – a well-known Kimberley lawyer – was to claim that, by the beginning of 1881, his company was much better placed than Rhodes and his partners. They had, he said, 'secured the key to the De Beers Mine. We had succeeded in cutting off the firm of Rudd, Rhodes . . . from the East and West. Besides holding this last position strategically our claims were among the richest.'

This was the first real challenge that Rhodes faced. He met it by bringing his powers of persuasion into play. 'I have never,' he would later boast, 'met anyone in my life whom it was not as easy to deal with as to fight.' This was an exaggeration: his dealings were not always so fortunate. But he did succeed in dealing with Frederick Stow. Precisely how he did so is not certain. The only account of the negotiations is that written by Stow many years later; by that time, Stow had become too disillusioned with Rhodes to elaborate on his methods. All he says is: 'When Mr Rhodes realised the strength of the position acquired by Stow, English & Compton . . . he approached me and made overtures which eventuated in our accepting a portion of his firm's holdings as of sufficient value to justify an amalgamation of the two interests.' The deal was concluded in March 1881 – the month Rhodes was elected as a member for Barkly.

Having gathered Stow, English and Compton into his net, Rhodes set about putting the De Beers Mining Company on a more business-like footing. Until then the management of the company had been somewhat haphazard. For the first year of its existence there had been no regular company secretary; more often than not Rhodes had had to deal with the firm's correspondence himself. One of the first cheques issued by the De Beers Mining Company was drawn by Rhodes in his own favour for £5 'as an advance against his salary as secretary'. Such a happy-go-lucky state of affairs was no longer possible. The company's interests had expanded, Rhodes was now a member of the Cape Assembly and it was obvious that a full-time secretary was needed. As it happened, a suitable candidate for the post was at hand. His name was Neville Ernest Pickering.

Fresh-faced, fair-haired and sunny natured, Neville Pickering was to occupy a more important place in Cecil Rhodes's life than that of secretary of De Beers. This has been acknowledged by all of Rhodes's biographers. Pickering has been described as Rhodes's 'right-hand man'; he is said to have been 'probably the closest friend Rhodes ever had', and the one upon whom Rhodes bestowed 'more confidence than anyone else.' For him, says Basil Williams, 'Rhodes had a romantic affection; he probably never loved anyone so well.' The relationship between Rhodes and Pickering has been likened to that of David and Jonathan.

Where and how Rhodes met Neville Pickering is not certain. They seem to have known each other well before Pickering was appointed secretary of De Beers. It is possible that they first became acquainted when Pickering was transferred to Kimberley by the firm he worked for after leaving school in Port Elizabeth. That firm, Dunell Ebden, had once owned the Vooruitzigt farm upon which the De Beers and Kimberley mines were discovered. They had bought the farm from the De Beers brothers in 1871 for 6,000 guineas and then, four years later, sold it to the Cape Government for £100,000. Neville Pickering had joined the firm in 1875 and, although the farm was resold that year, had been sent to Kimberley where Dunell Ebden retained other interests in the diamond industry. Kimberley was a small place where most business men knew each other: Rhodes's path might easily have crossed that of the young clerk at Dunell Ebden's.

The esteem in which Neville Pickering is held by Rhodes's biographers is, in a way, surprising. They know very little about him and did not bother to find out who he was or even where he had come from. What they have to say about his friendship with Rhodes amounts to little more than a mish-mash of romantic platitudes. The fact that, had fate decreed otherwise, the name of Neville Pickering would have featured prominently, not only in the life of Cecil Rhodes but in the history of a continent, has been largely ignored. One is left with the impression of a mating of rare souls, of two dedicated young men working together in the harmony of high endeavour. 'Pickering,' says J. G. McDonald, 'was delicate and imaginative; and he shared to the full Rhodes's dreams of the future.' It is a touching, idealized picture but one which is open to question. Knowing too little, Rhodes's biographers have assumed too much.

The truth is more humdrum. For, apart from his good looks and engaging personality, Neville Pickering was a very ordinary young man. Intelligent, lively and gregarious, he was, says one who knew him well, 'beloved by both men and women alike.' At the De Beers Mining Company he was considered to be an efficient secretary and the directors praised his 'strict probity and unfailing attention to duty' but, in other respects, he made little impact. He seemed to be happiest working under orders and there was nothing to distinguish his career from a thousand other conscientious young men in similar positions.

The only thing he had in common with Rhodes was that he was a parson's son. His father, the Rev. Edward Pickering, had first come to South Africa with the British army as a young man and had returned in 1857 to take up the appointment of incumbent of St Paul's Church in the Cape coastal town of Port Elizabeth. He had brought with him his wife and four young children: two boys and two girls. Neville, the fifth and last child, was born six months after the family arrived in South Africa.

Together with his two older brothers, Neville was educated at the newly established Grey Institute in Port Elizabeth. He was a bright youngster, with a flair for languages, but his failure to master mathematics prevented him from achieving distinction. When, at the age of eighteen, he was apprenticed to Dunell Ebden's his career seemed set to run a fairly predictable course. And so it might, had he not met Cecil Rhodes. It was this unlikely friendship which lifted him out of the ranks of the routine workers and added a little lustre to his life.

Precisely when Rhodes and Pickering set up house together is not known. It seems to have been at the beginning of 1882, shortly after Rhodes took his degree at Oxford. The two friends shared a corrugated-iron cottage facing the Natal Cricket Ground, but they kept their homelife to themselves. In all written recollections of Kimberley there is no mention of anyone visiting them. If they wished to entertain their friends they did so at the newly-built Kimberley Club. This, to the impressionable young Neville, was the height of elegant living.

46

'Our club,' he wrote to one of his brothers, 'is such perfection. Electric bells wherever you like to touch. Velvet pile and turkey carpets to walk upon and then one loses oneself in a luxurious lounge.' Rhodes, while not so effusive, was equally enthusiastic. From this time on, he was loud in his praises of club living. 'Civilized society,' he once remarked, 'cannot exist without clubs and universities – and if I had to choose between the two I would be tempted to choose clubs. They are the avenues through which man becomes more than a work machine.'

If Rhodes and Pickering were rarely seen at home, they were very much in evidence in the day-to-day life of the town. 'They shared the same office and the same dwelling house,' says the journalist Ian Colvin, 'worked together, played together, shot together.' For Rhodes, this sudden plunge into intimacy with a fellow human being was very much out of character. It was at variance with the aloofness he had displayed both in the Twelve Apostles mess and at Oxford. What makes this sudden friendship more surprising is the fact that the two young men were so dissimilar in status, personality and outlook. By the time they started living together, Rhodes was a business man of considerable standing; Pickering a mere secretary. And where Rhodes was moody, remote and difficult to get on with, Pickering was uncomplicated, sociable and popular. The usual description of Rhodes's young friend as a sickly, sensitive youth is, as far as these early days are concerned, misleading. From the moment Neville Pickering arrived in Kimberley, he threw himself into the social life with gusto. In an account of his early life on the diamond fields, he talks of arriving at church with a girl on each arm, of having to make an effort to fit in all his duty calls and the expense of keeping up with the the ceaseless round of entertainment. 'We have dinners and dances,' he wrote, 'one finds oneself in evening dress every night. It's ruination to health and pocket.' This is a very different person from Rhodes, who went to dances for the exercise and confined his sociability to toasting business deals.

Rhodes's biographers describe Pickering as being much younger than Rhodes. He is referred to as Rhodes's 'young friend' or his 'youthful secretary'. It has even been suggested that Rhodes and Pickering were of different generations. In fact, there was no great difference in their ages. When Pickering was appointed secretary of De Beers, he was twenty-three (an age that was to have a strange significance in Rhodes's later life). Rhodes, on the other hand, was twenty-seven. The difference between them was entirely one of appearance and temperament. The heavily built and grave-faced Rhodes always gave the impression of being ten years older than he was. When his brother Frank had visited Kimberley, the diggers had found it difficult to believe that he was older than Cecil. In the company of the lively Neville Pickering,

Rhodes must, despite occasional outbursts of boyishness, have seemed like an irascible uncle. This is probably what gave rise to the legend of a difference in their ages. It was a difference which helps to explain much of Rhodes's attachment to Pickering.

Neville Pickering was the type of young man whom Rhodes was to admire all his life: a type he was attracted to but could never emulate. A photograph taken in Kimberley shows Pickering to have been an alert-looking youngster, clean cut, open faced and free from guile. There is something almost child-like about him. It fits a contemporary description of him as a 'frank, sunny-tempered young Englishman.' Looking at it one can see why Rhodes placed such trust in this likeable, unassuming young man.

For trust him he certainly did. At no time in his life did Rhodes place greater confidence in any living person than he did in Neville Pickering. This exceptional display of faith manifested itself not, as is often assumed, after years of close friendship, but within a few months of their setting up house together.

On 28 October 1882, Rhodes made a new will. It was short and to the point. In it C. J. Rhodes, 'being of sound mind', leaves his worldly wealth to N. E. Pickering. He handed this in an envelope to Pickering with a covering note: 'My dear Pickering – Open the enclosed after my death. There is an old will of mine with Graham [his attorney] whose conditions are very curious, and can only be carried out by a trustworthy person, and I consider you one.' In a postscript he added: 'You fully understand you are to use the interest of money as you like during your lifetime.'

Rhodes's income at that time is estimated to have been in the region of £50,000 a year. A fortune by any standards, but an enormous fortune in 1882.

Certainly Pickering must have thought so. Only a few weeks earlier he had written to his brother welcoming a windfall of £142 as 'a most undeniable Godsend. I am so grateful, altho I have not been sober since.' As secretary of De Beers he must have had a good idea of what Rhodes earned: he could have had few doubts about the fortune awaiting him.

What he may not have known was just how 'curious' were the conditions of that older will. Had he known that he would have received a more profound shock. For he – Neville Pickering, former clerk at Dunell Ebden's – now replaced the British Colonial Secretary and the Attorney-General for Griqualand West as Rhodes's executor. His was to be the task of extending the British Empire, of recovering the United States of America for Britain, and sending British settlers into the heart of Africa, South America, the Holy Land, the Malay Archipelago, the islands of Cyprus and Candia, the seaboard of China . . . .

48

Shortly after Neville Pickering was engaged as secretary to De Beers –
and before they started sharing a house – Rhodes's shuttlecock life
between Kimberley and Oxford had come to an end. After eight years
of sporadic study, he finally took his degree in December 1881. By that
time his reasons for wanting an academic qualification had, to all
intents and purposes, fallen away.

There was no longer any question of his having to follow a profession. As a successful mining magnate and budding politician, his
degree was superfluous. All the same, he did not feel that his years at
university had been wasted. He was now an 'Oxford man' and that, in
his opinion, placed him among the elite. 'Have you ever thought,' he
once said to a friend, 'how it is that Oxford men figure so largely in all
departments of public life? The Oxford system in its most finished
form *looks* very unpractical, yet, wherever you turn your eye – except in
science – an Oxford man is at the top of the tree.' Cecil Rhodes now felt
himself equipped to scale that tree.

During his last term at Oxford, he was kept too busy to give much
thought to his degree. Frederick Stow, who met him in England at the
end of 1881, found him bubbling over with a scheme he had devised
for amalgamating the four mines of Griqualand West. 'I can see it
now,' Stow remembered, 'Folio after folio of intricate figures . . . The
labour bestowed on this subject must have been prodigious.' Even so,
Stow could not share Rhodes's enthusiasm. He thought it wiser to concentrate on consolidating the De Beers mine before embarking on such
a grandiose scheme. Rhodes was eventually forced to agree. On arriving back in Kimberley, a few weeks later, he dropped his ambitious
amalgamation scheme for a more modest project.

With the help of his Australian partner, William Alderson, Rhodes
approached Baron Erlanger, the international financier, with a proposition for unifying the De Beers mine. News of this approach leaked
out and won the support of the Kimberley press. 'De Beers Mine is the
smallest on the Fields,' observed a local newspaper. 'Many a good thing
has fallen through before now, simply because the promoters were too
precipitate in forwarding it into the market. We hope that mistakes
will not be made with Old De Beers.'

Similar sentiments were expressed by other newspapers. Rhodes's
bold move kept Kimberley in a state of excitement for weeks. It was
seen to herald the end of the ruinous competition which bedevilled the
diamond industry. Rumour had it that the plan to amalgamate De
Beers was merely a beginning and that the Kimberley mine would
follow suit. Rival diamond magnates began to eye each other warily.

Who, it was asked, would emerge as the ultimate victor in the struggle that was about to begin?

Instead of ending competition, Rhodes's proposal intensified it. That, of course, was the trouble. There were too many ambitious men in Kimberley, too many conflicting interests and too much at stake for agreement to be reached among the various companies in the De Beers mine. Just when it looked as though a majority decision was in the offing, some of the companies backed out, demanding a higher valuation of their ground. This infuriated the local press. 'Owing to the silly selfishness of one or two outside and unimportant companies the scheme for the amalgamation of De Beers seems to hang fire,' complained one editor. 'It is absurd, however, for these companies to stand out for long prices, since their ground is by no means essential to the carrying out of the scheme. If the promoters will accept our advice they will leave the contumacious outsiders where they are at present – in the cold – or, the reef.'

The editor could have saved his ink. Baron Erlanger was not looking for advice. He wanted the amalgamation of the entire mine and as long as this was prevented by one or two companies – no matter how small or unimportant they were – he was not prepared to back the scheme. Amalgamation was not to be as simple as some people seemed to think. This was something that Rhodes was beginning to discover.

*   *   *

Although he had now acquired his degree and put Oxford behind him, Rhodes was still forced to lead a double life. In Kimberley he was the mining magnate, working at De Beers and sharing a cottage with Neville Pickering. In Cape Town he was 'the young member for Barkly', attending sittings of the Cape Assembly and sharing a *pied-à-terre* – rooms in Adderley Street – with Captain Penfold, the middle-aged Marine Superintendent of the Docks and Harbour.

Not much is known about Rhodes's friendship with Captain Penfold. It was remembered mainly for the captain's habit of calling his young protégé 'the Old Man' and boasting that he alone was able to ensure that Rhodes kept his engagements on time and was suitably dressed. Just how suitably dressed Rhodes was is questionable. Rhodes was notoriously careless about his appearance. In Kimberley he slouched about in dirty white flannels and a threadbare jacket and in Cape Town his informal dress often shocked conventional members of the House of Assembly. Once, while making a speech, he felt obliged to defend the shabby suit he was wearing. 'I am still in Oxford tweeds,' he announced, 'and I think I can legislate as well in them as in sable clothing.'

Usually he was too preoccupied to bother with such trivialities. He had more important things on his mind. Both inside and outside parliament, he was busily making useful political contacts. At Government House he cultivated the new Governor General and High Commissioner, Sir Hercules Robinson, and the Imperial Secretary, Captain Graham Bower. At the Civil Service Club or at Pooles, where he often lunched, he got to know the leading civil servants and politicians. One of these politicians was Jan Hofmeyr, a moderate Afrikaner and member for Stellenbosch, who was to become his most important political ally for the next fifteen years. In Cape Town, also, were some of his old Kimberley friends: John X. Merriman, his early companion in the veld, who had abandoned the diggings and returned to politics; and J. B. Currey, the former Government Secretary, whose family had nursed Rhodes after his heart attack. New acquaintances and old friends, he had a use for them all. The time had come to put his plans into action: he would need all the support he could muster.

*   *   *

The issue dominating the Cape Assembly when Rhodes took his seat was the future of Basutoland. The Prime Minister of the day, Mr (later Sir) Gordon Sprigg, was trying to restore order in the territory after a rebellion in 1880, precipitated by his attempt to disarm the Basuto. The disarmament question was one of concern to the diamond industry. Africans were attracted to the diggings by the desire to buy firearms. All the candidates in the Kimberley elections had taken a stand on the disarmament question. Rhodes's attitude was – as always on such matters – equivocal. One of his biographers has said: 'Rhodes and the Kimberley people disliked the [Basuto] war, because they had many Basutos working for them in the mines and as one man said, "After all, we sold them the guns; they bought them out of their hard-earned wages, and it *is* hard lines to make them give them up again."' Whether this was Rhodes's view, or whether he was solely concerned with the recruitment of his labour force, it is not possible to say. In his election manifesto he had favoured the Basuto retaining their arms and had stood out against the confiscation of the Basuto territory. On the other hand he had advocated that the power of the Basuto chieftain be broken. Precisely where his sympathies lay was uncertain.

This uncertainty was less in evidence once he arrived in parliament. His clumsy maiden speech had been devoted to the disarmament question and he had emerged, rather surprisingly, as an advocate of the 'imperial factor' – wanting Britain to take over Basutoland from the Cape. Soon, however, he came into direct conflict with the Sprigg administration. Like the rest of the Griqualand contingent, he was critical of the government's delay in pressing ahead with the extension of the railway line to Kimberley – a project which Rhodes rated as a priority – and his opposition proved fatal to the Prime Minister. Sprigg's majority in the House was precarious and he needed the support of the diamond fields' representatives to survive; when this was not forthcoming, his ministry fell. Thus did Rhodes gain his first taste of political power.

He was suitably rewarded. Sprigg was replaced as Prime Minister by Thomas Scanlen, who, in an attempt to pacify the Basuto, appointed a Losses Commission to investigate claims for compensation by 'loyal tribesmen'. Inexperienced as he was, Rhodes was given a seat on this commission, which sat for five months.

While taking evidence in Basutoland – after his return from Oxford – Rhodes came into contact with another controversial Victorian bachelor. That eccentric soldier and mystic, General Charles Gordon – the future 'hero of Khartoum' – had been sent to the territory as a military adviser and was assisting the Losses Commission. Twenty years older than Rhodes, the unpredictable Gordon was not a man who made friends easily. But he warmed to Rhodes. The feeling was mutual. Patriots both, these two sons of Empire had much in common: they served the same ends, even if their methods were different. That difference was illustrated in a scrap of their recorded conversation. Apparently Gordon told Rhodes how he was once offered a roomful of gold by the Chinese government and refused it. Rhodes was unimpressed. 'I'd have taken it,' he snorted, 'and as many more roomfuls as they offered me: it is no use having big ideas if you have not the cash to carry them out.' Later he would say that he liked Gordon but thought him 'cranky in many ways.'

They were not together long enough for their differences to mar their friendship. Gordon, in fact, was so taken with Rhodes that he asked him to stay on: 'We will work together,' he said. But Rhodes had other concerns and, to Gordon's disappointment, he refused. 'There are few men in the world,' complained Gordon, 'to whom I would make such an offer, but of course you *will* have your way. I never met a man so strong for his opinion; you think your views are always right.' They parted after the Basutoland episode and never saw each other again. However, two years later Rhodes received a cable from Gordon. The General was about to set out for the Sudan and he wanted Rhodes to join him. Again Rhodes refused: but this time he regretted doing so. On hearing of Gordon's tragic death in Khartoum, Rhodes was filled with remorse. 'I am sorry I was not with him,' he kept repeating. 'I am sorry I was not with him.'

The combined efforts of Rhodes and Gordon did little to settle the problems of Basutoland. Unrest in the territory continued until it was taken over by Great Britain in March 1884. But Rhodes's debut into colonial politics, lowly as it was, made a lasting impression. He was referring to Basutoland (present-day Lesotho) when he declared that the Cape 'ought to annex land and not natives'. It was a lesson he took to heart.

*　　*　　*

There was a limit to the amount of time Rhodes could give to Basutoland. His more immediate concern was with the affairs of the diamond industry. The failure of his scheme to amalgamate De Beers mine – with the backing of Baron Erlanger – had by no means lessened his determination to control the mine. What that failure had taught him was that he needed to win the confidence of the mining community if he were to carry through such a scheme. It was essential that he establish himself as a trustworthy champion of the diamond industry. An excellent opportunity for him to do so arose shortly after his return from Oxford. The Cape Assembly met in March 1882. It was due to debate important legislation affecting the diamond trade. Rhodes was fully prepared to play his part.

In September of the previous year, he had been appointed as a member of a Mining Commission. The purpose of the Commission was to investigate the state of the diamond industry and make recommendations for improvements. In effect this meant formulating legislation to control the traffic in illicit diamonds. Not everyone welcomed Rhodes as a member of the Commission. The investigation was to be chaired by his old friend, J. X. Merriman and Rhodes's alliance with the intellectual, somewhat cynical Merriman was regarded with suspicion. Merriman was thought to be a disappointed digger, prejudiced against the diamond industry, and his liberal political views were not popular. Some diggers considered him highly unsuitable as chairman of the Commission. 'Mr Rhodes' appointment,' grumbled a Kimberley newspaper, 'appears to be the one most open to objection . . . everyone knows that so long as Mr Merriman is Chairman of the Commission, Mr Rhodes will follow him as a blind man follows a dog.'

These misgivings were to prove unfounded. Rhodes played little part in the deliberations of the Commission. Shortly after his appointment he had departed for his last term at Oxford. It had been left to others to draft the bill that was to be presented in the Cape Assembly.

Prominent among those drafting the bill was the formidable Joseph Benjamin Robinson. Known as the 'Buccaneer', the tall, steely-eyed, morose-looking Robinson was one of the best known and least liked mining magnates of Kimberley. He had arrived on the diamond fields in the early days, was reputed to have made an enormous fortune at the river diggings, and was notorious as a penny-pinching bigot. Unpopular as he was – he thought nothing of publicly horse-whipping newspaper men who offended him – he nevertheless wielded considerable influence. Before being elected to parliament, he had served for a year as Kimberley's mayor and was a board-member of several important financial institutions. In 1881 he had been instrumental in establishing the Diamond Mining Protection Society – an organization dedicated to stamping out IDB. With J. B. Robinson in full cry, there could be little doubt that the draft of the proposed Diamond Trade Act would be as stringent as it was punitive.

Rhodes and Robinson had no love for each other. They rarely met but when they did, they invariably disagreed vehemently. In their first parliamentary session they had clashed over the Basutoland issue – Robinson was in favour of disarmament – and later, at a civic reception in Kimberley, Robinson had denounced Rhodes as a traitor to the electors. When Rhodes rose to reply he was received 'with cries of "rat" and mingled cheers and hisses'. Only when their pockets were threatened could Rhodes and Robinson make common cause: even then they did so in a spirit of rivalry. The debate on the Diamond Trade Act of 1882, in the Cape Assembly, saw them in uneasy harness.

Having lost ground to Robinson during the drafting stages of the bill, Rhodes was determined to make himself heard in parliament. He was given every opportunity. The new legislation had a stormy passage through the Cape Assembly.

'We had great difficulty in passing the Diamond Trade Act,' Robinson was to say. 'This Bill took weeks and weeks – nearly the whole session of 1882.' The mining magnates had to fight for practically every clause. Most times they won. Only Rhodes's attempt to retain flogging as a punishment for buyers, as well as stealers, of illicit diamonds was rejected outright. 'I decidedly objected . . .,' declared one of their opponents, 'to flogging being inflicted for what was not a crime against the person but against property.' Rhodes, however, was to advocate these brutal ideas throughout his life.

For his part, Robinson fought the suggestion that three qualified judges should be appointed to hear IDB cases. In his opinion, knowledge of the diamond industry counted for more in cases involving stolen diamonds than did a knowledge of the law. His objections were only partly met. A compromise was reached whereby one judge and 'two others' were appointed to a Special Court.

There were very few other compromises. Most of the recommendations of the Diamond Protection Society were adopted without modification. They were extremely harsh. Detectives were empowered to search for rough diamonds without a warrant; all diamonds passing through the hands of dealers had to be registered and a monthly return made; any diamond-buyer who was merely suspected of an illicit transaction could be stopped, searched and have his books impounded; the onus of proof of legal possession of diamonds was thrown on the individual in whose custody they were found. The penalty for nearly all these offences was 15 years imprisonment or a fine of £1,000.

It was a remarkable piece of legislation. Visitors to South Africa were shocked by the provisions of the Diamond Trade Act and by the sentiments that inspired it. 'A law of exceptional rigour punished illicit diamond buying, known in the slang of South Africa as IDBism,' wrote Lord Randolph Churchill, when he toured southern Africa. 'Under this statute, the ordinary presumption of law in favour of the accused disappears and the accused person has to prove his innocence in the clearest manner, instead of the accuser having to prove his guilt . . . this tremendous law is in thorough conformity with South African sentiment, which elevates IDBism almost to the level, if not above the level, of actual homicide.' Others saw it as a capitalist charter.

Rhodes is rarely, if ever, associated with the Diamond Trade Act. Unlike J. B. Robinson – who regarded the passing of the act as a personal triumph – Rhodes preferred to forget that he had sponsored this controversial legislation. He had more to boast about in later years and the diamond laws were never universally popular. What is perhaps more important is that they failed in their purpose. There was a short period – immediately after the act was passed – when the ships to Europe were said to be crowded with frustrated IDB agents. But new ways of evading the laws were discovered; IDB continued to be a menace.

However, at the time the legislation was passed, Rhodes did not hesitate to pose as its champion. He firmly believed, he said, 'in his baby the Diamond Trade Act, however unpleasant it might be to a portion of the community.' Both he and J. B. Robinson were given a hearty welcome when they returned to Kimberley in July 1882. At an impressive ceremony in the Kimberley Town Hall, later that year, they were each presented with an 'influentially signed' address. It was a memorable occasion. Never again were these two rich and powerful magnates to share such popular acclaim, under a joint banner. 'By their efforts in the cause of morality and the general well-being of the community,' it was said, 'Messrs Robinson and Rhodes have well earned the mark of regard which is conferred upon them.'

But Rhodes had earned more than that: he had earned a place beside one of Kimberley's most influential citizens. The public now saw him in a different light. He could expect far more support in any move he made to manipulate the diamond industry.

* * *

There was one section of Kimberley's heterogeneous population that had no cause to celebrate the triumph of Rhodes and Robinson. The Diamond Trade Act cleared the way for further restrictions to be imposed on the African mine-workers. Earlier legislators had bowed to the prevailing racialism and debarred black men from owning and working claims; now the labourers were to be shut off from the town completely. Fenced compounds – or barracks – were erected, corrugated iron dormitories and bath houses were built and shops were sited within the fenced-in areas. These prison-like enclosures were designed to house black workers from the day they arrived at the diggings until the day they left.

The excuse given for depriving the Africans of what little freedom they enjoyed, was that, by isolating them, they would not only be prevented from selling stolen diamonds but would be kept away from the notorious 'Kaffir-canteens'. The employer, it was argued would 'get more of his diamonds and his natives [would be] always fit for work instead of being incapacitated by poisonous liquor.' In truth, it simply served to ensure the servitude of the Africans.

Rhodes has often been accused of instituting the infamous 'compound system'. This is not true. Certainly he went along with it, but it was not his idea. The system resulted from a joint decision by the mine owners. Precisely who suggested it is unclear. The first compound was built by the Central Mining Company, headed by Francis Baring-Gould, in April 1885. Rhodes's company did not follow suit until a year later. By that time compounds were a common sight in the four mines.

Most whites in Kimberley welcomed the closed compound system. The opening day of the Central Mining Company's compound was treated as a gala occasion. Visitors flocked to inspect the living arrangements and enthused over the sleeping rooms, the 'magnificent kitchen and pantry, large baths, guard room, dispensary and sick ward'. There could be no doubt, declared one sight-seer, 'that this arrangement will be the means of greatly decreasing the thieving by natives.'

Few could have disagreed. Every precaution was taken to ensure that no stolen stones left the compounds. Not only were the Africans thoroughly searched after each work-shift – made to strip naked and then subjected to the probing of every orifice of their bodies – but, when the time came for them to leave the mine, they underwent further humiliation. One of the most common ways of secreting diamonds was for a worker to swallow them. To guard against this, ritual purgings were introduced. When their contracts expired, the labourers were confined in a tin hut where 'they remained in a perfectly nude condition, save for a pair of fingerless leathern gloves, which were padlocked to their hands' and dosed with castor oil. They remained locked up 'for some ten days'.

Rhodes did not instigate the closed compound system but, by condoning it, he was as guilty as the rest of the mine-owners. He had drifted a long way from the parsonage in Bishop's Stortford.

CHAPTER FIVE

The Road to the North

Rhodes's parliamentary activities enhanced his reputation in the Cape Assembly. His forthright pronouncements, his growing confidence and enthusiasm singled him out as a man to be watched. The doubts expressed after his uninspiring maiden speech gradually gave way to a genuine interest in what he had to say. His performances as an orator were seen to be deceptive. Those who listened to him closely quickly recognized the soundness, as well as the bias, of his arguments: he was logical, he gave the impression of sincerity, and, to those who agreed with him, he could at times be heart-warming.

But political debate was not really Rhodes's *métier*. He found the day-to-day routine of parliament boring and was at times driven to despair. 'Politics to me are perfectly hopeless,' he wrote to J. X. Merriman in 1883. 'I shall stand again and believe I shall be returned but I have not much heart in the matter . . . . I am looking forward to being able to stroll around the world for a couple of years and intend doing so immediately after the next session.' But such moods passed. Rhodes was far more interested in changing the world than in strolling round it. By the end of the next session he was too busy to think of taking a holiday.

On 19 March 1884, the somewhat feeble Treasurer of the Cape Colony resigned and Thomas Scanlen, the Prime Minister, offered the post to Rhodes. A few months earlier, Rhodes had impressed the House with a speech on taxation. He had advocated an income tax and – in conformity with Kimberley sentiments – had proposed a heavy duty on Cape spirits, claiming that the cheapness of liquor was demoralizing the Africans. When he accepted Scanlen's offer and joined the Cabinet, great hopes were held out for his first budget. 'You will see we have taken Rhodes into the Ministry,' J. X. Merriman wrote to a friend; 'he is a man under thirty [actually he was almost thirty-one] but of the greatest talent and originality, and I look upon him as by far the rising man in South Africa.' Merriman's wife was not so sure. She considered Rhodes to be unstable, not able to manage his own financial affairs and lacking in business acumen. Writing to Merriman, who was also in the Cabinet, she said. 'Well! All I can say – the fate of the

Ministry is sealed, and I give you three weeks after Parliament meets. I am *thoroughly* disgusted . . . . The small interest I still had left in your Ministry has vanished with this new introduction, and for the sake of the country I can only hope you may be turned out soon.'

She got her wish – the Ministry fell a few weeks later. The Prime Minister's resignation had nothing to do with Rhodes, but it prevented him from presenting his budget.

Rhodes's next appointment was more fortunate. In August 1884, the British High Commissioner, Sir Hercules Robinson, appointed him to replace the controversial missionary, John Mackenzie, as a Deputy-Commissioner in Bechuanaland. This was a post for which Rhodes had been angling: he saw it as a first step on the road to the north.

'I went down to the Cape,' he was to boast, 'thinking in my practical way, "I will go and take the North."'. For one who had set his heart on winning the world, it was a modest enough ambition. By 'the North' he meant, of course, the continent of Africa; but this, even for Cecil Rhodes, had to be a long-term objective. More immediately, the north was represented by Bechuanaland. This was the vast, largely barren land to the north of the Cape Colony and to the west of the Transvaal. In many respects it was an unpromising and unattractive prize; its fascination for Rhodes lay in the comparatively fertile territory which ran along its eastern border – the border it shared with the Transvaal. Along this strip of land missionaries – such as Robert Moffat and his son-in-law, David Livingstone – traders, hunters and explorers had passed on their journeys into the heart of Africa. And where these trail-blazers had gone, British enterprise could follow; and so, in time, could British settlers. It was known as the Missionaries Road, but Rhodes had more than the conversion of the heathen in mind.

'I look upon this Bechuanaland territory,' he told the Cape Assembly, 'as the Suez Canal of the trade of this country, the key of its road into the interior.' He was determined that Bechuanaland should be annexed to the Cape.

This was easier said than done. By the time Rhodes was ready to make his first move, this vital 'Suez Canal' was blocked. The Bechuana were a quarrelsome people and were inclined to drag outsiders into their quarrels. The tribal squabbling had already caused 'volunteer' Boers from the Transvaal to make advances into the territory and, once having gained a foothold, they were reluctant to move. To Rhodes's intense annoyance, two Boer republics – Stellaland and Goshen – had been established in 1882–3 at the mouth of his 'Suez Canal'. They had the secret support of the Transvaal government and there was an outcry in the Cape about the Boer 'freebooters'. Rhodes made his anger known in the Cape Assembly. 'Is this house prepared,' he stormed, 'to allow these petty Republics to form a wall across our trade route? Are we to allow the Transvaal and its allies to acquire the whole of the interior? Bechuanaland is the neck of the bottle and commands the route to the Zambesi. We must secure it, unless we are to see the whole of the North pass out of our hands.' Now, as a Deputy-Commissioner in Bechuanaland, he was given the opportunity of translating his indignation into action.

The situation was further complicated when Bismarck proclaimed a German protectorate over the ill-defined country west of Bechuanaland which stretched to the Atlantic coast (present-day Namibia). This had awakened British fears. The scramble for Africa among the countries of Europe was under way and Britain had recognized the need to secure an interest in Bechuanaland. Whitehall's response to Bismarck's move was to start negotiations with the Cape, with the intention of declaring a protectorate over Bechuanaland. Earlier the British authorities had wagged a warning finger at the Transvaal by sending an agent to investigate the situation in Bechuanaland and then appointing the Rev. John Mackenzie as a Deputy-Commissioner in the territory. Unfortunately, Mackenzie – an ardent imperialist and rabid anti-Boer – had created so much trouble among the Boers of Stellaland and Goshen that, four months later, he had to be recalled. This is what provided Rhodes with his long awaited opportunity.

Rhodes had become totally disillusioned with British tactics in Africa. Whatever action the British government took seemed to lead to a reversal of British interests. He had no faith in the politics of a government which operated from a distance of 6,000 miles and which appeared to take little cognizance of the opinions of colonial officials. The Bechuanaland problem could not, in his opinion, be left to the vagaries of Whitehall. 'We want to get rid of the Imperial factor in this question and deal with it ourselves,' he declared.

As the new Deputy-Commissioner, Rhodes set off to win over the truculent republics. Years later he was to tell of how his bluff diplomacy had outwitted the Boers of Stellaland. One of the first Boers he interviewed was 'Groot' Adriaan De la Rey, a huge, fearsome-looking ruffian. 'I shall never forget our meeting,' said Rhodes. 'When I spoke to De la Rey, his answer was, "Blood must flow," to which I remember making the retort: "No, give me my breakfast, and then we can talk about blood."' By the end of the week, he claimed, he had become godfather to De la Rey's grandchild and had Stellaland in his pocket. It had not been as simple as that: Rhodes was obliged to make concessions, but he did come to terms with the Stellalanders.

In Goshen things were more difficult. There the situation was complicated by tribal faction fighting. The Transvaal had recently proclaimed a protectorate over the territory and although, in response to a

British demand, they eventually withdrew their claim, Rhodes still felt that a show of force was needed. Unable to get support from the Cape, he was obliged to fall back on the 'Imperial factor'. In January 1885, at Rhodes's request, his old travelling companion Sir Charles Warren, with 4,000 troops, arrived in South Africa and proceeded to Bechuanaland. This unprecedented show of force was meant to impress Bismarck's Germany as much as it was to subdue the freebooters in Goshen.

Rhodes, dressed in his habitual ragged coat, dirty white flannels and a pair of old tennis shoes – and accompanied by J. B. Currey's twenty-one-year-old son, Harry – joined the British troops soon after their arrival. He was present at Sir Charles Warren's meeting with Paul Kruger, a few days later.

The meeting was held at Fourteen Streams on the Vaal River. It was one of the few occasions on which Rhodes came face to face with President Kruger – the man who was to be his greatest adversary. Kruger was then almost sixty, nearly twice the age of Rhodes, and the two had little to say to each other. Rhodes, completely overshadowed by the belligerent Sir Charles Warren, took little part in the discussions. But, if legend is to be believed, he did not escape the eye of the wily old president. 'That young man will cause me trouble,' Kruger is said to have remarked, 'if he does not leave politics alone and turn to something else.'

The Bechuanaland negotiations did not work out as Rhodes had hoped. He wanted part of the territory to be taken over by the Cape, but Sir Charles Warren was determined that the whole of Bechuanaland should be annexed by Britain. Both men were obstinate and self-opinionated and their differences ended with Rhodes resigning as Deputy Commissioner and leaving the country. Warren had won. Bechuanaland was eventually divided into a Crown Colony and a British Protectorate and was thus lost to the Cape. This, for Rhodes, was a blow. Admittedly the area had been safeguarded from the Transvaal and Germany but there was still the 'Imperial factor' to contend with. The obstructionists of Whitehall might well prove antagonistic to Rhodes's future plans. He needed a free hand. His money had started him on his political career but it had not taken him far enough. He was still dependent on politicians and Government officials. Not until he was powerful enough to act on his own initiative could he hope to realize his great vision.

This was something he brooded over when he returned to the diggings. 'When I am in Kimberley,' he told a friend, 'and have nothing much to do, I often go and sit on the edge of the De Beers mine, and I look at the blue diamondiferous ground, reaching from the surface, a thousand feet down the open workings of the mine, and I reckon up the value of the diamonds in the "blue" and the power conferred by them. In fact every foot of ground means so much power.'

Obviously the more blue ground he obtained, the more power he would wield. Every capitalist in Kimberley recognized the need to amalgamate the mines, but for Rhodes it now became a double necessity. In his mind the future of the diamond industry was wedded to the destinies of the British Empire.

*   *   *

Strongly as Rhodes resented the 'Imperial factor', it served his purpose for the time being. With the road to the north now secure in British hands, he was free to give his attention to his long-term plans. The breath-taking scope of those plans in no way lessened his resolve to implement them.

He had two immediate objectives. Politically, he was determined to bring about a federation of the four states of southern Africa – the Cape Colony, the Transvaal, the Orange Free State and Natal – and to make those states the base for his future conquests in Africa. Financially, his aim was, of course, the unification of the four mines of Griqualand West – De Beers, Kimberley, Dutoitspan and Bultfontein – and this would supply him with the money to achieve his ends. In contemplating the two prongs of this attack he faced, as he later acknowledged, similar problems.

'I have always been an amalgamationist,' he was to tell a gathering at De Beers. 'I look on amalgamation as the only thing that can give a really permanent character to our industry. I have also worked at it with a special interest apart from mining, for I have felt that the task of reconciling the various interests in our mine is a very similar one to that which must fall to the lot of some of our politicians in the future, viz., the union of the various States in this country, as they both require great patience, mutual concessions and ample consideration for local feeling.'

These fine words summed up his ambitions as a capitalist and an imperialist: nothing short of outright monopoly in both spheres would satisfy him.

He had already gone a long way towards unifying the De Beers mine. After the failure of his scheme backed by Baron Erlanger, Rhodes had reverted to his original approach – gradual encroachment. With the patience that he advocated, the De Beers Mining Company had succeeded in buying out, or incorporating, the smaller companies in the mine. 'Amalgamation steadily progresses and I think that some day our scrip will be worth something,' Rhodes reported to Merriman in October 1883. The following year, two more important companies fell into the De Beers net. In March 1884 an amalgamation between De Beers and the Baxter Gully Company was announced; in April 1884 De Beers merged with the Independent Company. There was no mystery about how things were shaping in the De Beers mine.

The same could not be said for the neighbouring Kimberley mine. To most people this was the key mine on the diamond fields. Not only was it the largest of the four mines but it was far and away the richest. Whoever controlled the Kimberley mine would, it was thought, eventually dominate the diamond industry. Rhodes was one of the few who did not agree. In his opinion, two shares in the De Beers mine would always be worth three in the Kimberley mine. But he could not ignore the Kimberley mine; nor could he ignore the struggle for supremacy in that mine. The outcome of that struggle was by no means as predictable as it appeared to be at De Beers.

For some years the most important company in the Kimberley mine was that headed by Francis Baring-Gould. More recently, however, this company had undergone significant changes: by the now established process of amalgamation it had expanded, changed its name, and was now the Central Company. Its closest rival was probably the French Company – the company launched by Jules Porges. The growth of this company had been engineered by its Kimberley representative, Julius Wernher – a cool, astute German financier – who, assisted by his partner, Alfred Beit, had gained for the French Company a position of considerable influence. There were other companies in the running, but the Central Company and the French Company were pivotal to any scheme for controlling the Kimberley mine. Rhodes undoubtedly recognized this. It may well have accounted for the alliance he formed with Alfred Beit.

Where and when Rhodes and Beit first met is not certain. Beit played very little part in the civic or political life of the diamond fields. Occasionally he would write a tart letter to the press on mining affairs; he was known as a man of business and a diamond buyer of some importance but he could hardly be regarded as a Kimberley personality. To look at he was singularly unimpressive. Short and plumpish, with bulbous brown eyes, a receding chin and tiny moustache, Beit gave the impression of being weak-willed and not over-bright. He was painfully shy, a mass of nervous mannerisms: he would tug at his collar, twist his moustache and bite the corner of his handkerchief. With strangers he could rarely relax. But his seeming diffidence was deceptive. When it came to business, Alfred Beit was not only extremely gifted but remarkably determined. This was something that Rhodes was quick to spot. A story is told of an early encounter between Rhodes and Beit. It may or may not be true, but it is indicative of their relationship.

One evening, it is said, Beit was working late in his office when

63

Rhodes stopped by to see him. 'What is your game?' demanded Rhodes. 'I am going to control the whole diamond output before I am much older,' replied Beit. 'That's funny,' said Rhodes, 'I've made up my mind to do the same; we had better join hands.'

Join hands they did. They became business partners and they became friends. Rhodes had become more sociable since sharing a cottage with Neville Pickering; now he was often seen about Kimberley with Alfred Beit. They drank champagne and stout together at the Craven Hotel. They played poker (badly) at the Kimberley Club. Occasionally they were to be seen at a Bachelor's Ball: Rhodes vigorously twirling the plainest girl in the room and Beit prancing beside the tallest. The diminutive Beit had a *penchant* for tall women. To watch him dancing was one of the sights of Kimberley. He appeared, it is said, to run round his lofty partners rather than dance with them. In Rhodes, Beit found a dynamic and purposeful hero. From the time of their meeting, Beit devoted his life to Rhodes's interests: nobody surpassed 'little Alfred', as he was called, in his loyalty to Cecil Rhodes.

Rhodes, in turn, came to depend on Beit's financial advice. Those who knew them both refer to Beit as Rhodes's 'financial genius'. Any problem concerning diamonds would invariably be solved by Beit. 'Ask little Alfred,' became a catch phrase among Rhodes's friends. Together they made a formidable team. When they undertook to monopolize the mines, they set the pace of the race towards amalgamation. But they were given a good run for their money. There was no lack of ruthless capitalists in Kimberley.

*　　　*　　　*

It is a mistake to think that Rhodes originated the idea of monopolizing the diamond output of Kimberley. This is what some of his biographers imply but nothing could be further from the truth. The idea of amalgamation was almost as old as the diggings themselves. As early as 1872, a visiting journalist had warned of the dangers ahead. 'You cannot,' he wrote, 'drown the market with an article only appertaining to the highest luxury – you cannot popularize a traffic in such articles – without swift and sudden catastrophe. These things require the most delicate manipulation, they exact the strictest reticence, they need a hand to hold them back or loose them as the occasion asks . . . . By royal monopoly alone, or by means of great and powerful companies, can jewel digging be made a thriving industry. Into the hands of a company all these public fields must fall.'

Several attempts at amalgamation had already been made. In 1875, at the time of the Black Flag Rebellion, the diggers of the Kimberley mine had initiated a scheme of their own. They had pooled the bulk of their claims and appointed a representative to offer the mine for sale in London. But the English lawyers who examined the scheme found that the existing claim restrictions prevented such a sale. As soon as these restrictions were removed, the diggers tried again, only to be thwarted by the crafty J. B. Robinson, who had his own scheme for amalgamation. Rhodes's attempt to enlist Baron Erlanger in the De Beers amalgamation, in 1881, had also fallen through. The following year Rothschilds of London took a hand in the game. They sent a Mr Gansl to Kimberley to investigate the possibility of amalgamation, starting with the Dutoitspan mine. J. B. Robinson, who had got no further with his own schemes, gave Gansl wholehearted support but even this powerful bid had come to nothing. To weld the dissident elements into a prosperous whole was a thankless and frustrating task.

But, somehow or other, amalgamation had to come. This was something that everyone recognised. Until unity and a common purpose were achieved there could be no stability in the diamond industry. The periodic slumps which plagued Kimberley had proved disastrous. Even the occasional attempt to control the diamond output by a 'gentleman's agreement' had failed. One such attempt, in 1883, had been wrecked by a row between J. B. Robinson and Rhodes. Rhodes had wanted the price of diamonds to be fixed so that one company could not undersell the others; Robinson had insisted that the production of diamonds should be regulated so that the market was not flooded. In the end they had handed the matter over to a committee which, needless to say, had failed to reach an agreement. The future of the diamond industry looked gloomy. Politicians, as well as financiers, were aware of the dangers. It was not merely the capitalists who suffered from the slumps: the export of diamonds had become vital to the Cape's economy. The unfettered competition of the market place, while filling a few pockets, was proving ruinous to the long term interests of the colony. What was needed was judicious intervention by the government, but, as this was unlikely to happen, control by a single powerful company seemed the only solution.

That astute politician, J. X. Merriman, had long been toying with the idea of amalgamation. As early as 1883 he had approached J. B. Robinson in the hopes of devising a co-operative scheme. Robinson had been full of suggestions but none of them had proved workable. But Merriman had persisted. The following year he entered into discussions with C. J. Posno, the international diamond merchant, and received the encouragement he needed. In August 1885, Posno sent Merriman details of a syndicate which had been formed in London for the purpose of buying as many properties as possible in the four mines of Griqualand West. Merriman was asked to act as the syndicate's South African representative.

Posno's proposal was hailed by Merriman as a 'message of salvation' for the diamond industry. In January 1886 he went to Kimberley to start negotiations. The first person he contacted was, again, J. B. Robinson. 'Personally I am very anxious to see you take a leading share in the matter,' Merriman wrote to Robinson. There can be little doubt that Robinson was equally anxious to take that share. But this was not possible: to Merriman's amazement, the once-powerful Robinson was forced to confess that he was verging on bankruptcy. A series of financial disasters, failed investments and landslides in the mine had left him up to his neck in debt. This was the first serious blow to Merriman's plan. There were more to come.

On 13 February, the Kimberley newspapers carried advertisements detailing a new plan for amalgamating the mines. In essence it was simplicity itself. The principal mining companies in the four mines were invited to exchange scrip with each other at a commonly acceptable valuation. In this way a joint interest would develop among the various companies and this, in effect, would amount to amalgamation. The plan was sponsored by the De Beers Mining Company and was the brainchild of the company's chairman, Cecil Rhodes.

This new scheme took Merriman completely by surprise. He had already met with hostility from other companies, but had more or less counted Rhodes as one of his supporters. Now, faced by such powerful opposition from a man he had thought to be his friend, he was obliged to admit defeat. He had no alternative but to telegraph C. J. Posno calling off his stillborn plans.

Rhodes's diversionary tactics worked. He had no intention of implementing the plan he advertised: the exchange-of-shares idea was kept alive for a few more weeks and then dropped, never to be heard of again. It was hardly the type of union for which Rhodes was angling. His intention was that the mines should be controlled, not mutually, but by his company – De Beers, with him at its head. His sole intention was to undermine Merriman and Posno and, in that, he was successful.

Merriman's intervention, brief as it was, alerted others besides Rhodes. Not least among them was one of Kimberley's more colourful characters: a flamboyant, garrulous, ex-music-hall performer from the East End of London who had prospered on the diggings and now headed a relatively small but thriving company in the Kimberley mine. His name was Barney Barnato.

*   *   *

Barney Barnato's real name was Barnett Isaacs. He had grown up in Whitechapel and had adopted his more exotic, Italian-sounding name when he and his older brother, Harry, had played the London music-halls as a double act. Harry Barnato was a comedian juggler and Barney was his knock-about assistant. It was Harry who, in 1872, had first tried his luck at the diamond diggings but it was not until the following year that he was joined in Kimberley by the twenty-one-year-old Barney. Dynamic, cocky, with a sharp cockney wit and an eye for the main chance, Barney Barnato had quickly made his mark on the fields. The rise of the Barnato brothers as diamond merchants, claim owners and, it was said, IDB operators, was steady. In 1880 they were well-enough established to found their own company in the Kimberley mine and to open an office in Hatton Garden in London. This was the base from which Barney Barnato was, in time, to pose a threat to Cecil Rhodes's grandiose schemes.

The battle between Barnato and Rhodes for control of the diamond industry is usually depicted as a long-running trial of strength. They are pictured as taking each other's measure for a number of years before finally coming to grips. This fits the popular concept of each side limbering up in preparation for a classic battle. Unfortunately, Kimberley contests were rarely set in a classic mould; the Rhodes–Barnato clash was not like that at all. It was less of a slow trial of strength and more of a mad scramble for supremacy.

Barney Barnato showed little open interest in amalgamation until J. X. Merriman arrived on the scene. It must have been then that he realized that the formidable J. B. Robinson – whose financial plight had been kept secret – was no longer in the running. Even after that Barney made a great show of opposing all plans for unification. This pretended opposition, however, was a matter of tactics. Once he saw how Rhodes had dealt with Merriman, he rose to the challenge. For a while he was forced to keep his hand hidden. He started at a distinct disadvantage.

By 1886 Barney had a large fortune but not much in the way of mining properties. His interests in the Kimberley mine certainly did not equal Rhodes's holdings at De Beers. In fact, at one time he had considered withdrawing from the mine altogether. His claims were buried by a land-slide and only pressure from his shareholders had persuaded him to keep the Barnato Mining Company alive. It was as well that he did. Once Merriman had disappeared from the scene, Barney concentrated his considerable energies on strengthening his position in the Kimberley mine.

The vantage ground he sought was presented to him by the impoverished J. B. Robinson. In 1880, Robinson had founded the Standard Mining Company in the Kimberley mine but his financial collapse had forced him to pledge his shares in this company to a Cape Town bank. Now, so low had Robinson sunk, the bank – which was also in difficulties – had begun to sell off these shares. In the middle of

1886, Robinson had openly accused Rhodes and Alfred Beit of buying up the shares in an attempt to 'squeeze' him out of the Kimberley mine. But he was wrong. At the next annual meeting of the Standard Company it was neither Rhodes nor Beit who emerged as the largest shareholder, but Barney Barnato.

For the first time since the formation of the Standard Company, J. B. Robinson was not in the chair; he was not even at the meeting. The chair was taken by a Mr Pistorius, but this was a mere formality. The longest and most authoritative speech was made by Barney Barnato. He lectured the shareholders on the running of the company and urged them to agree to a merger with the Barnato Company. He met with considerable opposition, but this did not bother him. Another, much larger, meeting was held two months later and Barney packed it with his own supporters. The merger was pushed through and the new concern took the name of the larger of the two companies: it continued to be known as the Standard Company.

This was Barney's belated answer to Rhodes's moves in the De Beer mine. The combination of his own claims and those of the Standard Company put him in a powerful position in the Kimberley mine. And, like many others, he was convinced that whoever controlled the Kimberley mine would eventually control the diamond industry.

*   *   *

How far Rhodes had been aware of Barney's manoeuvring is not certain. At the time he was kept fully occupied by his own concerns. The year 1886 marked a turning point in Rhodes's life. It was also a crucial year in the history of South Africa. But the crisis Rhodes faced had a personal as well as an historic significance.

South Africa was to remember 1886 as the year when there was a startling development in the Transvaal Republic. After years of rumours and false hopes, gold was discovered in an area known as the Witwatersrand, some thirty miles south of the Boer capital, Pretoria. When news of the gold finds first reached Kimberley, the town was sceptical. Stories of gold-bearing reefs were everyday fare and few had grown fat on them. All too often, the quest for gold had proved more trouble than it was worth. Even after a Kimberley merchant returned from the Transvaal, in July 1886, with specimens of gold-bearing rock which he had picked up on the Witwatersrand and gave a public panning demonstration, the cynics continued to scoff. (One of those who did not scoff was the shrewd J. B. Robinson who borrowed money from Alfred Beit and went to the Witwatersrand, where he was one of the first to arrive; as a result he made a second, much larger fortune.)

Rhodes is said to have been among those who witnessed the panning and who remained unconvinced. This is not surprising. He knew only too well how disastrous gold-fever could be. Had not his brother Herbert dissipated his life by chasing after each new cry of gold? Only by keeping faith with Kimberley had Rhodes been able to build his own fortune, and Kimberley, at that time, was demanding all his attention. Not only was he deeply involved in his amalgamation schemes but he was troubled by a private anxiety: Neville Pickering, his heir and closest friend, was seriously ill.

Two years earlier, on 26 June 1884, Neville Pickering – or 'Pickling' as he was affectionately known – had been thrown from his horse while riding in the veld. He fell into a clump of thorn bushes and was badly cut and bruised, 'some of the thorns,' it is said, 'entering below the knees of both legs.' The poison from the thorns added to the after-effects of a recent bout of 'camp-fever', and his lungs had become affected. He was confined to bed for more than a month; when he did get up he was forced to hobble about on crutches. 'It will . . . be some time yet,' reported the *Diamond Fields Advertiser*, 'before he will be able to resume that stately stride of his pedestrianizing.'

In fact, Pickering was rarely seen about the streets of Kimberley again. His health had been permanently impaired; the next two years were spent in moving between Kimberley and the various places of convalescence recommended by his doctors. He seldom went to the De Beers office. His duties were handed over to an 'acting secretary' and it was probably Rhodes who insisted that his name still appeared as the official secretary of the company.

Throughout his friend's long and depressing illness, Rhodes's devotion was constant. He did all that could possibly be done to ease Neville Pickering's suffering. He nursed him, comforted him and obtained the best medical advice that Kimberley could offer. Among the doctors called in to attend young Pickering was a popular and successful Scotsman – Dr Leander Starr Jameson. This short, perky and able physician had arrived on the diggings, aged twenty-five, some eight years earlier. It was widely believed that he had emigrated to South Africa to cure a weak lung, but he may have been spurred on by the lure of diamonds. One of his brothers, who was in South Africa, sent home a rough diamond and young Jameson was so impressed that he refused to have the stone cut. 'I am going to keep it in its present condition,' he wrote, 'till I can afford to make swell affair of it.' He was then a resident medical officer at University College Hospital in London, and when a Kimberley doctor applied to the hospital for a partner, Jameson volunteered and was accepted. He quickly established himself as a leading practitioner on the diamond fields. Boyishly handsome and talented, his success was assured in a community where doctors were desperately needed. He and Rhodes had known each other casually for some years but, according to Jameson's biographer, it was 'Neville's sickbed' that clinched their friendship. For Rhodes it was the beginning of a life-long and fateful relationship.

But nothing could help Pickering. He grew weaker by the month. It became obvious to everyone except himself that his case was hopeless. At the beginning of 1886 he was staying with his family in Port Elizabeth and, against all advice, suddenly decided to return to Kimberley.

He arrived back at the diggings at the time when stories of gold finds on the Witwatersrand were gathering momentum. The local newspapers were full of glowing accounts of the Transvaal discoveries; reports of diggers flocking to the gold fields from all over South Africa, of the opening up of new farm areas and the scramble for claims, appeared every day. There could no longer be any doubt about the importance of the new El Dorado. J. B. Robinson had been followed by a few other Kimberley capitalists and their activities were reported in detail. Within a matter of days several syndicates and companies had been formed. Even so, Rhodes did not seem unduly bothered. Not until the beginning of August did his attitude change.

On 30 July 1886 the *Diamond Fields Advertiser* carried a long report on the doings of Kimberley men on the Witwatersrand. At the end of the report it stated that Dr Hans Sauer had just left for Kimberley 'with lots of specimens of auriferous soil picked up casually from [J. B.] Robinson's ground'. Rhodes may not have noticed this item, but he was soon aware of Dr Sauer's return.

Hans Sauer was well-known in Kimberley for his fight with the authorities during an earlier smallpox epidemic. This had not endeared him to the diamond magnates. His concern with the goldfever, however, placed him firmly in the capitalist camp. Sauer had accompanied J. B. Robinson to the Witwatersrand and, after trailing round the gold fields with Robinson, had become convinced of the area's potential. Unfortunately he lacked the capital to join in the scramble for claims. His return to Kimberley had been prompted by the hope of obtaining financial backing. It was his brother-in-law who suggested that he approach Cecil Rhodes.

Rhodes was still in bed when, early one morning, Sauer arrived at his cottage. Perching himself on the edge of the bed, Sauer launched into his story. '[Rhodes] listened to what I had to say about my journey and the gold deposits on the Witwatersrand without much apparent interest,' says Sauer, 'and when I had finished my tale he simply said: "Please come back here at one o'clock and bring your bag of samples"'. Returning to the cottage, Sauer was surprised to find Charles Rudd and two Australian miners waiting for him. The miners, who had brought gold-panning equipment with them, quickly confirmed that the doctor's samples were indeed gold-bearing. Neither Rhodes nor Rudd seemed impressed. Sauer was simply told to call on Rhodes that afternoon at the De Beers offices.

The afternoon interview was more promising. Rhodes agreed to allow Sauer to act as his agent in the Transvaal and to give him a fifteen per cent interest in any claims he acquired. It was arranged that he should leave for the Witwatersrand the following morning.

Sauer was delighted. Not only had he secured the backing he needed but, it seemed, he had been given a free hand. That, at least, is what he thought. But he was mistaken. On boarding the coach the next morning, he was astonished to find Rhodes and Rudd ensconced in the two best corner seats. 'No explanation was offered,' he says. Had he known more about Rhodes's business methods, he would not have needed an explanation. Circumspect as always, Rhodes obviously had no intention of sparking off another rush from Kimberley by allowing Sauer to broadcast the fact that he and Rudd were about to leave for the Transvaal – his presence in the coach was a *fait accompli*.

Once on the Witwatersrand, Rhodes was completely out of his depth. He had made himself a diamond expert but of gold he knew nothing. Nor was Rudd much help. If anything, Rudd was more wary of buying gold properties than was Rhodes. Dr Sauer, who rushed about securing options for the partners, was driven nearly frantic by their hesitancy. The trouble was, as A. P. Cartwright, the gold-fields historian has pointed out, that 'though they regarded themselves as mining men . . . they were woefully ignorant of geology, the sinking of shafts and the recovery of gold.' They bought a few valuable properties but others – sometimes more promising – they refused to consider.

Even the arrival of Alfred Beit – who came to see how J. B. Robinson was handling their joint syndicate – did nothing to inspire confidence in Rhodes and Rudd. A particularly promising block of claims which Sauer was offered for £500 was snapped up by Beit for £750. On hearing that Rhodes had recently turned the claims down, Beit was distressed. He told Sauer that he was prepared to give Rhodes a half interest in the block at cost price. But still Rhodes was not interested. The claims were then incorporated in the Beit syndicate and later formed part of the Robinson Gold Mining Company – one of the most valuable mines on the Witwatersrand. This was only one of several similar *gaffes*.

Whether things might have been different had Rhodes stayed longer on the Witwatersrand – which he insisted on calling the Witwater – one does not know. As it was, he gave himself little time to study the reef. He arrived in the Transvaal at the beginning of August and left before the end of the month. A message had arrived to say that Neville Pickering had taken a turn for the worse; he was thought to be dying. To Sauer's astonishment Rhodes announced that he was immediately returning to Kimberley. When Sauer protested that his signature was needed to close some important deals, Rhodes refused to listen. 'I'm off,' he declared.

The coach that evening was fully booked. This did not deter Rhodes. 'Buy a seat from someone who has already booked,' he said. 'Get a special coach – anything; I am going tonight.' None of the passengers was prepared to give up a seat but in the end a place was found for Rhodes on top of the coach; he completed the three hundred dust-choked miles propped up among the mail bags. The journey lasted more than fifteen hours.

*　　*　　*

His haste had not been strictly necessary. Neville Pickering lingered on for a few more weeks. Rhodes never left his side. He was, it is said, 'careless of anything but the wants and comforts of his friend.' From time to time he was joined by Neville's brother William, who was then the manager of a bank at Dutoitspan. Together they sat and watched the life ebb from this once virile, active and light-hearted young man.

A legend was to grow up around the vigil that Rhodes kept at his friend's bedside. It was said that he refused to do any business; that frantic telegrams from the Witwatersrand went unanswered; that by neglecting Sauer's options he destroyed his chances of controlling the gold industry. This is only partly true. He had agents in the Transvaal and he kept in touch with them; moreover he had earlier turned down several of Sauer's options. He might have grown more knowledgeable had he stayed in the Transvaal, but whether he would have grown wiser is another matter. 'The chances he missed,' says A. P. Cartwright, 'he would probably have missed anyway.'

All the same, his unquestioned devotion to his dying friend cannot be lightly dismissed. His concern for Pickering was undoubtedly greater than his interest in the Witwatersrand. Rhodes might not have sacrificed a fortune by returning to Neville Pickering's sick bed, but he was obviously prepared to do so. Never was he again to display such genuine concern for a fellow human being; nor, as far as is known, had he done so previously.

The end came on the morning of 16 October 1886. Shortly after midnight, Rhodes became alarmed at the change in Neville's appearance and sent William Pickering for the doctor. Jameson came at once, but there was nothing he could do. It is said that once, before the end, Neville managed to stir himself. Turning to Rhodes, he whispered: 'You have been father, mother, brother and sister to me.' He died, in Rhodes's arms, at seven o'clock that morning.

He was buried the same day. His hearse was followed to Dutoitspan cemetery by 'upwards of fifty carts'. At the short ceremony that followed, all the town's leading citizens were gathered round the grave. 'It might be said of him,' commented the *Diamond Fields Advertiser*, 'that he had not a single enemy and many warm-hearted friends.'

The chief mourner was his brother William, but the most conspicuous was undoubtedly Cecil Rhodes. Dressed in a crumpled old suit, passing from tears to hysterical laughter and burying his face in a large handkerchief, Rhodes hardly seemed to know where he was or what he was doing. As he turned from the grave, he came face to face with the sobbing Barney Barnato. 'Ah, Barney,' he cried, 'he will never sell you another parcel of diamonds!'

Such uninhibited displays of emotion were rare for Rhodes. After Neville Pickering's death they became rarer still. Rhodes prided himself on his cynicism and his toughness, and he took accusations of ruthlessness as compliments. There was no place in his scheme of things for tenderness. He seldom, if ever, spoke of his dead friend. But his grief was genuine and his silence significant.

CHAPTER SIX

The Battle with Barnato

On the night of Neville Pickering's funeral, Rhodes slept in Dr Jameson's wood-and-iron cottage opposite the Kimberley Club. In the years to come this was to be his Kimberley home. He never again lived in the house he had shared with Pickering.

His way of life did not change much. Jameson was a successful doctor and Rhodes was a rich diamond magnate, but they lived the rough and ready life of impoverished diggers. The little cottage they shared was sparsely furnished and always untidy; there were two bedrooms containing make-shift truckle beds, and a sitting room which looked, according to one astonished visitor, 'like that of an undergraduate at college'. Most of their meals were eaten at the Club across the road.

But if his way of life did not change, there was a definite change in his personality. Many years later Sir David Harris, a Kimberley pioneer, told of a strange incident he witnessed shortly after Neville Pickering's death. He was passing the board-room of the De Beers Mining Company and noticed two men sitting at a table. Their attitudes were identical: each supporting his head with one arm, the elbow on the table and the hand covering the eyes, while the other arm lay flat on the table. Between them was a gold watch which they were pushing to and fro. Sir David recognized the men as William Pickering and Cecil Rhodes. As they pushed the watch backwards and forwards, they each shook their heads in turn and said: 'No, you are his brother' and 'No, you are his greatest friend.'

'And I give you my word,' claimed Sir David, 'they were both crying.'

With Pickering's death there died in Rhodes much of the warmth and tenderness that characterized his short-lived friendship. From now on, where personal relationships were concerned, Rhodes was to be a man on his guard. He would have other friends, other young men, but none of them would be as close as Neville Pickering. The change in Rhodes's personality has been remarked upon by William Plomer. 'There seems,' he says, 'to be some reason to think that the shock of losing this young man who had so enchanted him was an emotional one, and it may possibly have had something to do with his tendency to cultivate more and more hardness and even brutality of manner which, it was supposed by some, was not really natural to him but served to hide his susceptibilities.'

This is more than Rhodes's blinkered admirers would allow. Such an assessment of their hero smacks too much of sentimentality; it does not fit their preconceived notions of a man of destiny. To them Rhodes's friendship with Pickering is an embarrassment. They have either dismissed it as irrelevant or have glossed over it with fine words and high-flown phrases. Because it could not be ignored altogether, it has been trivialized – cloaked in clichés. Rhodes's biographers have, for the most part, paid little attention to his personal life. All too often he is seen purely in terms of his career; he is depicted as a man without human weaknesses, an asexual visionary, a political robot. Politics, in one form or another, did indeed dominate his life, but politics alone cannot explain his complex personality.

The trouble is, of course, that his only acknowledged emotional involvement was with a man. Had he displayed the same intense feelings for a woman, his more conventionally-minded biographers would have rejoiced. His frantic departure from the Witwatersrand, together with his possible sacrifice of a fortune, would have been taken more seriously and dealt with in greater detail had he been hurrying to the sickbed of a dying wife or fiancée. But Pickering was a man and the fact that Rhodes loved him raised awkward questions which were best left alone. Even in a more enlightened age, the idea that such Victorian stalwarts as Rhodes – Kitchener? Gordon? – were subject to emotional aberrations is a matter which calls more for hasty excuses than for acceptance. The 'great sons of Empire', it is usually implied, should not be seen as transgressing a conventional code of behaviour. They were not, after all, bohemian, artistic or effeminate; they were virile men of action and therefore do not fit the commonly accepted stereotype. It is a simplistic view but one that, with occasional variations, persists.

But there is no escaping the fact that Rhodes loved Pickering. Why else would he have made this unassuming young man heir to his entire fortune, custodian of his great dream? The attachment was an emotional one and there is no reason to think that it was expressed in any way other than by an obvious and open devotion. The suggestion that 'ugly rumours' concerning their relationship circulated Kimberley seems to have originated from nothing more than salacious gossip. If – as later events appear to confirm – Rhodes had homosexual tendencies, those tendencies were firmly suppressed. Rhodes was very much a child of his times and, not even to himself, would he have acknowledged an unorthodox sexual orientation – to have done so would have undermined his self-image and jeopardised his life's work. Any rumours that may have been spread about his friendship with Pickering must have started much later and were probably coloured by hindsight.

The most pertinent question posed by that friendship is whether it would have endured. There is reason to think that Neville Pickering, had he lived, would have found Rhodes's possessiveness overpowering. For, despite his affectionate loyalty, Pickering could not have viewed the friendship in quite the same terms as did Rhodes. Indeed, the difference in temperament which had first drawn them together might, in the end, have separated them.

There is a legend in the Pickering family that Neville, at the time of his death, was engaged to a certain Maud Christian of Port Elizabeth. The truth of this story is difficult to ascertain. There is no indication that Miss Christian was sent for when Neville was dying and there is no mention of an engagement in Pickering's obituaries. But Miss Christian, who married Sir William Solomon (a future Chief Justice of South Africa), is said always to have worn a ring on her engagement finger which, it is claimed, was given to her by Neville Pickering. When she died she left this ring to Neville's niece. It would seem that if the engagement were indeed a fact, it was not made public. Rhodes may not even have known about it.

Certainly Rhodes found it impossible to contemplate the prospect of his close friends marrying. When obliged to face such a situation, his rage was monumental. One such scene took place some time after Neville Pickering's death. The young man concerned had been Rhodes's companion for a number of years. 'Everyone knew he was engaged – except Rhodes,' says a friend of them both. 'When the news was broken, there followed an amazing scene. Rhodes raved and stormed like a maniac. His falsetto voice rose to a screech as he kept screaming. "Leave my house! Leave my house!" No small schoolboy, or even schoolgirl, could have behaved more childishly than he did.' In this case there was a temporary reconciliation but the friendship was terminated shortly after the young man married.

The same thing might have happened with Neville Pickering. In his case, death intervened. There is also the possibility that (as often happens in relationships such as this) as Pickering matured, he would have lost his attraction for Rhodes; it was towards the qualities of youth, enthusiasm and virility that Rhodes was always drawn. By dying in his twenties, Pickering ensured that his image, for Rhodes, remained untarnished; nothing, not marriage, nor middle-age, nor disillusion, could spoil it now.

Rhodes never found anyone else to replace Neville Pickering. But he spent the rest of his life searching. His more immediate reaction, however, was to throw himself into his work. The affairs of De Beers provided the distraction he needed to blunt his grief.

*　　*　　*

By the beginning of 1887, Rhodes had taken over all the independent companies in De Beers mine except one. The last to fall was the Victoria Company, headed by Francis Oats. This company had withstood all Rhodes's overtures and showed no sign of yielding. It was Alfred Beit who came up with a plan for the final assault. He suggested that his firm should combine with De Beers to buy shares in the Victoria Company in London.

'We felt that if they were bought in the London market,' Rhodes later explained blandly, 'it would excite no remark . . . The result of our arrangement was that we did obtain 6,000 shares in the Victoria jointly.' They bought the shares at the end of 1886 and kept quiet about them. Negotiations with one or two other companies had to be tied up before they were ready to close in on the Victoria. 'However,' said Rhodes, 'in pursuance of our policy of amalgamation we at last thought the time had arrived to inform the Victoria that we were their largest shareholders . . . and that amalgamation was necessary in our interests.'

That was at the end of April 1887. A few days later Rhodes was able to report on their success at a general meeting of the De Beers Mining Company. He was thanked by Alfred Beit.

They had good reason to congratulate themselves. By taking over the Victoria they had achieved what others had dreamed of: De Beers was the first of the four mines to come under the control of a single company. Amalgamation had, in part, become a reality.

The next step, of course, had to be in the direction of the Kimberley mine. This was a much greater challenge. There had been many changes in the Kimberley mine since the departure of J. X. Merriman a year earlier: a new runner had entered the Grand Amalgamation stakes. Now, for the first time, Rhodes found himself faced by the jaunty Barney Barnato. Getting rid of Barney was to prove a very different matter from that of disposing of J. X. Merriman.

*　　*　　*

Barney Barnato had never lacked *chutzpah*. Almost from the day he arrived in Kimberley he had succeeded in attracting attention. Whether strutting down the street or swaggering on the stage of the Lanyon Theatre – where he performed regularly in a variety of roles – he could always be sure of an appreciative audience. His appearance matched his manner. Always a dandy, he was never less than immaculately turned out. The heat might be gruelling but with his pince-nez,

77

starched collars, bow ties, button-holes, checked suits and spats, he cut a lively figure. Special occasions would see him more splendidly groomed still – in top hat, cravat, watch chain and morning suit. It was as impossible to overlook Barney as it was to take him seriously.

That, at least, had been the case until he emerged as the foremost challenger to Cecil Rhodes. Now he was viewed in an entirely new light. Barney's success in capturing the prestigious Standard Company had revealed him as a far from flippant strategist. Once started in the power seeking game, there was no stopping the enterprising Mr Barnato. With the Standard Company under his belt, he lost no time in launching a new attack.

Barney's next target was Baring-Gould's Central Company. This was a company that J. X. Merriman had regarded as vital to his unification scheme. It was his failure to win over the Central Company that had placed him at the mercy of Rhodes. Barney took no chances. Some of the more influential shareholders in this company were former diggers who had left the diamond fields and were now living in great style in London. Immediately the merger with the Standard Company was tied up, Barney and Harry Barnato left for London. One of their nephews, Woolf Joel, was put in charge of things in Kimberley.

It did not take long to bring the powerful Standard and Central companies together. Events were speeded up by Barney's earlier *coup*; there were few people in Kimberley who did not recognise the way things were going. The Barnatos were riding high; they could no longer be ignored. At the end of June 1887, Woolf Joel sent his uncles a cable to say that negotiations in Kimberley were coming to a head. Barney rushed back.

The Standard and Central companies were formally merged at two meetings held on 7 July 1887. By the end of the day the Standard Company no longer existed; a new, enlarged Central Company was in possession of the greater part of the Kimberley mine. Barney attended both meetings. He had obtained all the backing he needed in London and the result delighted him. In little over a year he had accomplished what it had taken Cecil Rhodes six years to achieve. At the beginning of 1886 there had been four important companies in the Kimberley mine: the Central, the French, the Standard and the Barnato. Of these four the Barnato had been the smallest. Now only the French Company and a few minor concerns stood between Barney and complete control of the richest mine in Griqualand West.

Always a showman, Barney knew how to dramatize his latest triumph. At the conclusion of the Central Company's meeting, a series of loud explosions were heard in the vicinity of the Kimberley mine. Passers-by were said to have been startled out of their wits. It sounded, claimed the *Diamond Fields Advertiser*, as if 'the Transvaal Navy [landlocked though the Transvaal was] had suddenly appeared and were bombarding dear old Kimberley. Hundreds of people rushed towards the mine, where cannon, that is dynamite shots, were being fired all round the edge, while the Companies' flags were seen waving from the Central and Standard Companies works. It was an "Amalgamation Salute" and it sounded gay and joyful, but nervous persons did not like it at first.'

One nervous person would not have liked it at all. That was Cecil John Rhodes. Those dynamite shots were aimed right at the heart of his great vision. Fortunately, he did not hear them. He had sailed from Cape Town the day before. He was on his way to England to organize a counter blast. The siege of the French Company – the company whose claims ran across the Kimberley mine, dividing the holdings of the Central from those of the former Standard – was about to begin. So long as these claims remained outside the Barnato net, the amalgamation of the Central and the Standard was, to all intents and purposes, a financial union only. Barney knew this. Rhodes knew this. All Kimberley watched and waited for the next move.

*   *   *

Rhodes had a slight edge on Barney. The French Company was represented by Wernher and Beit, and Beit was Rhodes's ally. It was not much of an edge. Beit only represented the French Company, he did not control it; but at least he was able to keep Rhodes informed of any moves made against him.

It would have been more to the point had Rhodes had a definite foothold in the Kimberley mine. This he lacked. So busy had he been in manipulating moves at De Beers that he had allowed Barney to entrench at Kimberley without any real opposition. Now, all Barney had to do was to snatch the French company, as he had snatched the other companies, and the Kimberley mine was his.

Rhodes realized this. A few weeks before Barney finalized the amalgamation of the Central and Standard companies, Rhodes had made a last minute bid for a block of claims in the Kimberley mine. They stretched into the centre of the mine and, next to the French Company's holdings, they were probably the most important claims outside Barnato's reach. It was some time in May 1887 that Rhodes tried to buy the company that owned these claims, only to find it was too late. He was outbid by a syndicate headed by Sir Donald Currie, the shipping magnate, who also had thoughts of amalgamation.

Immediately after securing the company, Sir Donald left for England. Two of Rhodes's agents joined him on his voyage home. They had instructions to pressure him into re-selling the shares he held. They did a good job. Sir Donald was tempted by Rhodes's offer. However, when the ship reached Lisbon he discovered that the market value of the shares was higher than the price Rhodes was proposing. The negotiations ended abruptly. 'You young thieves,' Currie said to the agents, 'had I listened to you I would have sold at a loss.' Somewhat disconcerted, the young men cabled Rhodes to tell him of Sir Donald's decision. Rhodes sprang into action. By the time the ship reached Plymouth, he had beared the market so effectively that the shares were no longer worth what his agents had offered. Sir Donald had been taught a lesson. Although he held on to his shares for a while longer, he eventually dropped out of the competition.

This little exercise in financial politics did not get Rhodes much further. It was now June and the amalgamation of the Central and Standard was almost complete. He had to move quickly. Only by an outright purchase of the French Company could he hope to block Barnato's take-over. This presented a formidable problem. As the battle for control of the mine had intensified, so had the French Company's shares risen. Rhodes was a rich man but his money was tied up in his holdings; he dare not release his grip on the shares he held. He needed extra capital. He needed to negotiate a large loan.

Once again it was 'little Alfred' who came to his rescue. Beit suggested that they approach Rothschild's of London. As the largest financial house in Europe, Rothschild's had both the name and the resources they needed. Rhodes leapt at the suggestion. Supplied by Beit with the necessary introductions, he set off for London.

On reaching England Rhodes immediately contacted Lord Rothschild. A meeting was arranged and the plan for buying the French Company discussed. Rothschild was cautious but encouraging. 'Well, Mr Rhodes,' he said at the end of the meeting, 'you go to Paris and see what you can do in reference to the purchase of the French Company's property, and in the meantime I will see if I can raise the £1,000,000 which you desire.'

This, from the man who had recently advanced four million pounds for the purchase of the Suez Canal, was good enough for Rhodes.

Rhodes loved to boast of the swiftness with which he pulled off this deal. 'You know the story of my getting on board the steamer at Cape Town, going home and buying the French Company within twenty-four hours,' he used to say. As so often happened, he was taking more credit than was his due. He owed much of his success to Alfred Beit. This was particularly true of his dealings with the directors of the French Company in Paris.

Beit had already paved the way for Rhodes's coming. He had persuaded Jules Porges that amalgamation of the mines was a sound financial move and Porges, in turn, had recommended to his fellow directors that Rhodes's provisional offer be accepted. The French directors agreed to the sale of the company for £1,400,000. Rhodes, confident that with the help of Alfred Beit he could raise the balance, was delighted.

The sale of the company had to be confirmed at a meeting of the French shareholders in October. This, in a way, was a mere formality. The Trust Deed of the company gave the directors power to sell the property, providing their decision was reached with a majority of one. With the majority of directors already in favour, any opposition at the shareholders' meeting could easily be overcome. Or so it was thought. Barney Barnato had other ideas.

*　　*　　*

Barney was aware of Rhodes's every move. He was also suspicious. So suspicious was he that he had already acquired a substantial interest in the French Company. When he heard of Rhodes's Paris deal, he lost no time in countering it. He topped Rhodes's offer by £300,000. The Central Company, he announced, was prepared to pay £1,700,000 in cash for the French Company. This, together with the shares he held, put him in a strong position.

But not strong enough; Rhodes's allies in Paris stood by him. Barnato was told that a provisional agreement had been reached and that he, like the other shareholders, would have to abide by it. Needless to say, Barney was not prepared to do any such thing.

On 21 September he called a meeting of all the French Company's shareholders in Kimberley. It was a mammoth meeting. Barney did most of the talking; he had little difficulty in winning over his audience. With a wealth of facts and figures, he explained how a takeover by Rhodes would harm smaller shareholders. The people who were selling the French Company, he said, had no knowledge of the Kimberley mine. He was loudly cheered. The meeting ended with a cable being sent to Paris protesting against the sale to Rhodes 'as a better offer has already been made by the Kimberley Central Company.'

Rhodes was quick to scent danger. He tried to snuff it out at its source. On his return to Kimberley he arranged a meeting with Barnato in the hopes of calling his bluff. If the Central Company went ahead with their offer to overbid him, he is supposed to have said, he would simply raise his bid. 'You can go on and bid for the benefit of the French shareholders *ad infinitum*,' he warned Barney, 'because we shall have it in the end.'

That, at least, is the story that was later given out. But, like so much that has been said about the 'battle' between Rhodes and Barnato, it smacks more of melodrama than of a cautious jostling for power. The truth about this and later meetings between the two shrewdest capitalists in Kimberley appears, as the detailed researches of Rob Turrell have now revealed, to have been far more conspiratorial than either of them were prepared to admit.

According to the accepted version, this initial clash between Rhodes and Barnato produced an unexpected result. At a later meeting Rhodes is said to have suddenly capitulated. To Barney's surprise he offered to hand over the French Company on easy terms. If, he said, he was allowed to purchase the French Company without interference, he would resell it to Barnato's Central Company for £300,000 cash and the remainder in Central shares. Barney was delighted and the deal was closed. That, it is claimed, was Barnato's greatest mistake. He only discovered how foolish he had been after the French Company had been amalgamated with the Central and new shares had been issued. Then it was that Rhodes emerged as the holder of one fifth of the Central shares and was thus in a position to block Barney's moves in the Kimberley mine, while his rival was powerless against him in De Beer's. Therefore, when the battle between the two mines started in earnest – as it now did – Rhodes was at a distinct advantage.

The battle itself was depicted as a share-grabbing free-for-all. Barney was seen as trying to crush competition from De Beer's, Rhodes as being equally determined to withstand Barnato's onslaught. Production was stepped up. The market price of diamonds plummeted. It appeared to be the worst kind of financial madness.

There was an element of truth in all this. A struggle did ensue and the market was shaken. As more diamonds became available and the price fell, the value of Kimberley Central shares increased out of all proportion. When the conflict began they stood at £14, soon they had risen to £49. Elaborate tricks – most of them deliberately staged – were played by both sides. Stories were told of how Alfred Beit came to Rhodes's rescue with additional cash to keep the battle going and of how Barnato's allies deserted him and sold shares to make a quick profit. Legends were created overnight. The so-called 'duel to the death' between Cecil Rhodes and Barney Barnato was to be remembered as one of the most bitterly fought financial campaigns in the history of the diamond industry.

But it was all a sham; a phoney war designed to ensure that, whatever the outcome, the two main contenders would escape unhurt.

*　　*　　*

The truth was that neither Rhodes nor Barnato could afford to contemplate, let alone embark upon, such a potentially ruinous campaign. Rhodes was stretched to his financial limit and was already having to think of the repayment due to Rothschild's for their loan. Barnato was equally hard pressed. His claim that he would outbid Rhodes in bargaining for the French Company had been pure bluff. The Central Company, in fact, had already applied to the Standard Bank for a loan – similar to that which Rhodes had got from Rothschild's – but had been turned down. Barney had therefore jumped at Rhodes's offer to sell the French Company partly in cash and partly in Central shares. For his part, Rhodes had had no option but to make the offer. Not knowing Central's financial position, and that they had been scratching around for a loan, he could not take chances and ignore Barnato's threats. If the Central proved strong enough to persuade the shareholders of the French Company in Paris to call off the sale which Rhodes had negotiated, then Rhodes would lose the support of Rothschild's. That, of course, would have put Rhodes out of the running. Therefore, with both Rhodes and Barnato desperate, they were forced to come to a settlement before their much publicized 'struggle' began. There was no question of Rhodes obtaining his Central shares by stealth.

Rothschild's were again called in. To sweeten the negotiations they agreed to lend the Central Company £500,000 in addition to Rhodes's offer. And it was their Kimberley agents who assisted Rhodes in winning over Barnato. 'After tense lobbying,' says Rob Turrell, 'and hefty payments by Ludwig Lippert and Carl Meyer for Rothschild's, the deal was clinched.' Rhodes, however, appears to have had little doubt about the outcome.

'The great comfort I feel now,' he wrote to Fred Stow, in October, shortly after his return to Kimberley, 'is that the goal is reached. Barnato who has 8,000 De Beers and 1,500 one hundred Centrals . . . is working in everything with me and has given his pledge to go to the end with me and Baring-Gould [still nominally chairman of the Central Company] though a weak man has made up his mind to go along with the tide . . . I must have the four mines and I will allow no foreign vulture to step in at the end and form a separate mine on the Stock Exchange.'

The details of the agreement, whereby the Kimberley and De Beers mines were to be amalgamated on the basis of the equal value of both mines, were thrashed out by Rhodes, Barnato and Alfred Beit in the Kimberley Club. Barney was not a member of the club and Rhodes is supposed to have invited him as his guest in order to impress him. 'I propose to make a gentleman of you,' Rhodes is reported to have said. They became very friendly and would have reached first name terms had it not been that nobody, apart from his family, called Rhodes, Cecil. Barney compromised by dropping the 'Mr' and calling him Rhodes.

Baring-Gould was in at the start of the negotiations but, believing in the superiority of the Kimberley mine, he refused to accept the 'equal value' basis and backed out at the beginning of November. Barney had no such qualms. He was persuaded to 'desert his company' and allow – or rather assist – De Beers to buy shares in the Central. It was left to Baring-Gould to fight a rearguard action in defence of the other shareholders of the Central Company.

Consequently there was no 'struggle' between Rhodes and Barnato. The so-called battle was fought on a different level, with Beit and Barnato using their influence on the share market, and Rhodes picking up shares from other investors in the Central Company. It was a fierce fight while it lasted but, in the end, De Beers with its powerful backing emerged triumphant. Rhodes may have received financial help from Alfred Beit but he also brought all his other resources into play, diverting funds from his gold concerns (which by then had been extended) and thus ensuring that the fortunes of Kimberley were firmly linked to those of the Witwatersrand. As for Barnato, far from being deserted by his get-rich-quick allies, it was he who cashed in on any profits that were to be made. Not only did he buy shares for De Beers but he sold to De Beers 'at prices far above the going rate'. Later he was to boast to the manager of the Standard Bank of being richly rewarded for his various share transactions. Even so he ended up holding 27,000 out of a total of 178,000 of the Central Company's £10 shares.

The scramble for shares ended in March 1888. Then it was that Rhodes's victory was publicly acknowledged. But the pretence of a duel between Rhodes and Barnato was kept alive and a few embellishments were added to the finale.

Barney was said to have 'surrendered' only after certain conditions of his had been accepted. Popular legend has it that he insisted on Rhodes using his influence to have him elected, first to the Kimberley Club, and then to the Cape Assembly. This, of course, was nonsense. Far from being eager to join the Kimberley Club, Barney did not bother to apply for membership until three years after the deal was concluded. He *was* elected to the Cape Assembly with Rhodes's help but – as he had proved in the past – he was quite capable of winning an election under his own steam. It was simply window-dressing but it was widely believed and the legend lingers on.

So does another, more colourful story. It is said that, after introducing Barney to the Kimberley Club, Rhodes made a request. 'Well, you've had your whim,' Rhodes is supposed to have said; 'I should like to have mine, which you alone in Kimberley can satisfy. I have always wanted to see a bucketful of diamonds; will you produce one?' This is thought to have flattered Barnato. It is claimed that he shovelled all his available diamonds into a bucket and that Rhodes, plunging his hands into the bucket, 'lifted out handfuls of the glittering gems and luxuriously let them stream through his fingers.'

How far Rhodes and Barnato were responsible for such stories it is not possible to say. They were both, in their own way, great showmen and might well have wanted to add a little glamour to their deception. Buckets of diamonds were just the thing to capture the public's imagination: they provided the fantasy upon which both men built their reputations as financial geniuses.

*　　*　　*

In the middle of his bid to control the diamond industry, Rhodes was obliged to attend to some urgent political business. It concerned his plans for central Africa.

With Bechuanaland firmly protected by Britain, he had more or less secured his 'Suez Canal' to the interior. Having achieved this, he was free to contemplate further steps northwards. He turned his attention to Matabeleland, the African ruled territory north of Bechuanaland. This large and fertile country was the home of the Ndebele, an offshoot of the Zulu nation, who had settled there some fifty years earlier. After the subjugation of the Zulu by Britain, in 1879, the Ndebele were the most formidable black race in southern Africa. They had been led to the high plateau which lies between the Limpopo and Zambesi rivers by the leader and founder of their nation, Mzilikazi.

During his lifetime, Mzilikazi – the Path of Blood – had ruled his people in the iron-handed manner of Shaka, the powerful Zulu king whom he had served as a high-ranking young warrior. Mzilikazi's had been a regime of autocratic cruelty and bloodshed, supported by his ability to satisfy the warlike propensities of his followers. For the Ndebele, like the Zulu, were in essence one huge army and their way of life was that of battle and plunder; even their name was derived from their way of fighting – Ndebele, *those who sank out of sight* (behind their long shields). The young men were soldiers who established their manhood in battle; the nation was governed by a hierarchy of warriors, dominated by the paramount chief; the land they occupied was ruled by right of conquest and their defeated foes were treated as inferiors. Leadership was hereditary only in as much as it depended upon the talent for survival of one of Mzilikazi's many contending sons. The fact that Mzilikazi had some three hundred wives and a regettable tendency to rid himself of possible heirs made the right of succession far from predictable.

After Mzilikazi's death – he was buried in the Matopo hills – it was largely power politics that established his son, Lobengula, as leader of the nation. For those who look for some meaning in the workings of fate and the coincidences of history, there may be significance in the fact that the year which brought Lobengula to power, 1870, was the same year that brought Cecil Rhodes to Africa.

In the manner of authoritarian régimes, the Ndebele had imposed a semblance of peace throughout the territory in which they settled. It was the peace which invariably accompanies tyranny: it depended on the absence of effective challenge. The original inhabitants of the country, the comparatively placid Shona, Tswana and Barotse, had been quickly subdued and had, to all outward appearances, appeared to accept their vassalage. The only real threat to the supremacy of the Ndebele was that of the white races to the south and east. Mzilikazi had done his best to safeguard himself against any such threat. In his tempestuous drive northwards from Zululand – he had fled after a quarrel with Shaka, taking a small Zulu force with him and was later joined by the remnants of the clans he defeated – he had clashed with the Boers in the Transvaal; it was not an experience he wished to repeat. His attitude to the white man had been wary rather than hostile; he had remained friendly with the missionaries, particularly the Moffat family, and had been careful to circumscribe the activities of any white visitors to Matabeleland. This was the policy which his son Lobengula tried to continue.

Lobengula, by all accounts, was an impressive man. Over six feet tall, he was bronze, muscular and, despite a considerable paunch, a dignified and undeniably majestic-looking person. 'He walks quite erect,' claimed one of his white visitors, 'with his head thrown some-what back and his broad chest expanded, and he marches along at a slow pace with his long staff in his right hand, while all the men around shout his praises, he looks his part to perfection.' Lobengula is said to have been more intelligent than his father; not so great a warrior, but a shrewd and talented politician. He was also something of a showman.

Certainly he needed to display his majesty to the full. His disputed succession had been followed by fierce faction fighting and echoes of the controversy were to plague him throughout his reign. Nor was he free from outside threats. Not only was there the possibility that the Transvaal Boers would continue their trek northwards but, in the east, the Portuguese – long established in the coastal region – were laying claim to parts of Mashonaland: the ill-defined country which Lobengula regarded as his vassal state.

The extent of the Ndebele overlordship in Mashonaland is difficult to define. Mzilikazi had indeed subdued the surrounding Shona tribes, and Lobengula continued to assert his dominance by periodic raids on those tribes. These raids – involving wholesale slaughter, the burning of kraals and the looting of cattle – had, in fact, become essen-tial to the economy of Matabeleland. But not all of Mashonaland was under Lobengula's sway; not all the Shona chieftains acknowledged Ndebele sovereignty. As Lobengula's reign progressed so did the defiance of the Shona and other neighbouring tribes make itself felt. Having succeeded to his father's kingdom, Lobengula could not be sure of maintaining the 'peace' of Mzilikazi's realm.

There was yet another threat to the new king's supremacy. Shortly after Lobengula assumed the leadership of his people, the mineral potential of southern Africa was confirmed. First came the diamonds at Kimberley, then the gold in the Transvaal: it was inevitable that fortune seekers should look further north. Gold, in fact, had been discovered in Matabeleland, near the Umfuli river, the year before Mzilikazi died. One of Lobengula's first acts as king had been to grant concessions to the representatives of two mining companies, giving them the right to prospect for precious metal. As it happened, the concessions were of no practical value. Little gold was found, mining was expensive, and the excitement created by the earlier finds gradually subsided. For the next few years, Lobengula was not unduly bothered by fortune hunters. But the rumours of hidden gold persisted and in the 1880s the number of prospectors arriving at Gubulawayo – the royal kraal – increased significantly. The more strongly the gold-fever raged in the south, the more demanding did the concession seekers in Matabeleland become.

Lobengula was not interested in the precious metals himself – although he always insisted on a share of any gold that was found – but he knew the dangers of allowing Europeans into his domain. He became alarmed at the unending demands of these newcomers who, he was to tell the British Administrator of Bechuanaland, 'come in here like wolves without my permission and make roads into my country.' The chances of Lobengula's continuing his father's policy of isolation were far from promising.

Rhodes, of course, was fully aware of what was happening in Matabeleland. Preoccupied as he was with his financial concerns, he kept himself informed of events in central Africa. He knew the time would come when he would have to deal with Lobengula and with the concession hunters. But he was not particularly worried. He intended tackling that problem in his own time. First he had to complete the amalgamation of the diamond mines. Not until he had sufficient money behind him could he risk further experiments in territorial advancement. He was sufficiently experienced in manipulating capitalist enterprise to know that, with a divided opposition, he could choose the time to step in and take over. He might have waited longer had he not been challenged by more formidable opponents.

The threat which propelled him into action came, not from the scramble for wealth but from the scramble for Africa. The mineral potential of Matabeleland was proving more than a magnet for private speculators: it had awakened the territorial ambitions of Lobengula's neighbours. To the west the Germans, now firmly established as a colonial power in southern Africa, were showing unmistakable interest in Matabeleland. Then, in 1887, the Portuguese in the east boldly issued a map showing part of Lobengula's territory as a Portuguese possession. In that same year the Transvaal entered the arena by sending an emissary, Pieter Grobler, to renew an earlier treaty of friendship with Lobengula. In itself, the treaty amounted to very little: friendly messages were exchanged, the Transvaal was granted the right to establish a consul at Lobengula's kraal and given jurisdiction over Transvaal subjects living in Matabeleland. More alarming, however, were the rumours that followed the signing of this treaty. It was whispered – and echoed in a Transvaal newspaper – that the Boers were about to declare a protectorate over Matabeleland. Rhodes is said to have had these rumours confirmed by Alfred Beit, who was in touch with a contact close to the Transvaal President, Paul Kruger.

Piet Grobler returned to Matabeleland to present his credentials as Transvaal consul to Lobengula. This time he was given a less than friendly reception. The king's coolness, however, did not prevent Grobler from leaving for the Transvaal to fetch his wife. Unfortunately, on his journey south he was attacked by a band of Ngwato tribesmen and wounded in the leg. Sixteen days later, before medical help could reach him, he died from his wounds. Later it was rumoured that Rhodes's agents were responsible for Grobler's death. But the accusation depends largely on hearsay; the evidence for it is slight. The Boers, not without reason, were willing to believe anything bad about Cecil Rhodes.

There is no doubt about Rhodes's own actions on receiving news of the Boers' plan for Matabeleland. Unable to visit Lobengula himself – the amalgamation battle had reached a crucial stage – he did the next best thing: he appealed to the 'Imperial factor'. He made a quick dash to Grahamstown, in the eastern Cape, where the British High Commissioner, Sir Hercules Robinson, was spending the Christmas holidays. Bursting in upon the startled Sir Hercules, Rhodes demanded that the British forestall the Transvaal by declaring a protectorate over Lobengula's territory. Bechuanaland had been safeguarded in this way and there seemed no reason why the move should not be repeated. But Sir Hercules was hesitant. It was one thing for the impulsive Rhodes to expect nations to fall into his lap at the stroke of a pen but quite another for Her Majesty's representative in South Africa to explain such actions to the British government.

But it was impossible to refuse Rhodes entirely. At times like this, when he set out to get his own way – to win someone over 'on the personal' – Rhodes's powers of persuasion were prodigious. Even the most hard-headed of men could not resist him for long. Sir Hercules was no exception. Although he would not annex Lobengula's country outright, he was prepared to take an option on it. At Rhodes's request he sent a dispatch to Matabeleland asking Lobengula not to enter into any treaty with a foreign power or part with any land without the sanction of the British High Commissioner. To this Lobengula agreed.

On 11 February 1888, a treaty of 'peace and unity' between Victoria, the Great White Queen of England, and Lobengula, the Mighty Elephant of Matabeleland, was signed at Gubulawayo. This was not quite what Rhodes had hoped for, but it was enough. It gave him the breathing space he needed.

On his return to Kimberley, Rhodes set about putting his relationship with Lobengula on a firmer footing. The Transvaal had been warned off, but there were still the concession hunters to contend with. These private speculators had to be cleared from the field; the only way of getting rid of them was for Rhodes to obtain an over-riding concession to mine minerals in Matabeleland. This became his immediate objective. The ever-reliable Alfred Beit threw his weight behind the new venture. Before the treaty between Lobengula and Britain was signed, Rhodes and Beit had despatched John Larkin Fry – a former head of the Kimberley police – to Matabeleland with the object of obtaining a gold-mining concession. Unfortunately Fry was a sick man, suffering from facial cancer; he fell ill and was forced to return without accomplishing anything. But Rhodes was not deterred. He set about organizing a stronger, healthier mission to the Ndebele king. First, however, he had some unfinished business to attend to: the loose ends of the amalgamation deal had to be tied up.

*　　*　　*

The battle for the diamond mines was over: all that remained was to arrange the peace. The unexpected flare-up of the Matabeleland issue gave added emphasis to the terms upon which Rhodes was prepared to settle.

He had always intended to use the amalgamated diamond mines to finance his imperial vision; now the need for financial backing had become imperative. Rhodes insisted that the trust deed of the new company should provide for the accomplishment of his political ambitions. Barney, still the dominating figure in the Central Company, objected. He was a business man and his business was diamonds not politics. They argued for several days. In the end Rhodes got his way.

The last round was played out in the corrugated-iron cottage which Rhodes shared with Jameson. Barney brought his nephew, Woolf Joel, with him; Rhodes was backed by Alfred Beit. The four of them argued throughout the night. They became tired and irritable, but neither side would give in. Rhodes won eventually because he had to win. For him the final stage was the most vital. Amalgamation meant little or nothing if he could not use it for his own ends. He brought all his powers of persuasion to bear on Barnato. He produced facts, figures and maps; he appealed to Barney's business instincts as well as his imagination. There was no telling what riches might be found in central Africa, he contended; Barney owed it to himself as well as to the new company to make provision for exploiting those riches.

'Aren't those just dreams of the future?' asked Woolf Joel. 'Dreams don't pay dividends.'

'No, my friend,' Rhodes insisted, 'they're not dreams, they're plans. There's a difference.'

Night gave way to morning. They were all exhausted. At last Barney, struggling to keep awake, gave in. It was then he made his famous submission. 'Some people,' he shrugged, 'have a fancy for *this* thing and some for *that*; you have a fancy for making an Empire. Well, I suppose I must give it to you.'

And so it was settled. In a dingy, sparsely-furnished Kimberley cottage, the future, not only of the diamond industry, but of an entire continent was decided. The town had been in existence for less than twenty years; the eldest of the four negotiators – Barney Barnato – was thirty-five. If, as Anthony Trollope once said, Kimberley was one of the ugliest places on earth, it was also one of the most remarkable.

The new amalgamated concern was called De Beers Consolidated Mines. It was incorporated in March 1888 with a modest capital of £100,000. The trust deed was drawn up later; it gave Rhodes all he needed. On 31 March 1888, he outlined each stage of the amalgamation struggle (leaving out some of the more interesting sidelights) to the shareholders of De Beers. The speech was one of the longest – it ran to nine thousand words – and one of the most extraordinary he ever made. Speaking without notes, he held his audience enraptured.

Afterwards the shareholders crowded round Rhodes to congratulate him. He was too elated to listen. Pushing his way through the crowd, he beckoned Alfred Beit to follow him. He strode towards the De Beers mine, with little Beit scampering behind him. At the mine they were quickly surrounded by African mine workers. Rhodes asked Beit if he had any money with him and, when Beit handed him a bag of fifty sovereigns, he scattered the gold coins magnanimously among the laughing labourers. Still heady with success, he turned and walked silently towards the Kimberley Club. On the way he suddenly stopped and waited for the panting Beit to catch up with him. 'And tonight,' he remarked cynically of the shareholders, 'they will talk it over with their wives and tomorrow they will sell like hell!' Beit never got his fifty sovereigns back.

There was one last attempt to prevent amalgamation. It almost succeeded. In August 1888, a group of Central shareholders challenged the decision to merge their company with De Beers. They argued that, under their deed of association, such a merger could only be effected with a 'similar company'. The trust deed drawn up by Rhodes showed that, whatever else it might be, De Beers Consolidated Mines was vastly different from the Central Company. They took their case to the Cape Supreme Court.

The action was successful. The Chief Justice of the Cape agreed that the new corporation was an entirely new undertaking. Diamond mining in Kimberley formed only an insignificant part of the powers acquired by De Beers Consolidated Mines. The company, observed the judge, was free to mine anywhere in the world. It could mine diamonds, gold or coal; it could carry on banking operations and undertake financial obligations for foreign governments; it was free to annex territory and maintain a standing army. 'The powers of the company,' he said, 'are as extensive as those of any company that ever existed.' His judgement was in favour of the plaintiffs.

At the same time, he recognized Rhodes's difficulty and suggested a way out. Rhodes acted upon it. He and Barnato held the majority of shares in the Central. They now used this majority to put the company into voluntary liquidation. The shareholders opposed to amalgamation could do nothing, they were very much in a minority. Rhodes and Barnato were now able to buy the assets of the Central. In the course of the Central Company's liquidation, the Kimberley mine had to be tendered for. The highest tender came from De Beers Consolidated Mines. On the 18 July 1889, De Beers issued a cheque in payment for the purchase of the Kimberley mine. The cheque became world famous; for years replicas of it were sold in Kimberley as souvenirs. Made out in favour of the liquidators of the Kimberley Central Diamond Mining Company Limited, it authorised payment of £5,338,650.

The passing of this cheque meant more than the extinction of the Central Company; it marked the end of an era. After almost twenty turbulent years, diamond mining in Kimberley ceased to be an adventure and became a prosaic, soulless industry. Rhodes's victory was complete. He could now concentrate on the more important task of amalgamating Africa.

CHAPTER SEVEN

Good Companions

Cecil Rhodes was well served by his friends. When he needed advice or support, when money had to be raised, strings pulled or pressure exerted, he could always turn to a close associate for help. This was not a matter of luck: Rhodes chose his friends carefully. He liked to boast about his ability to win people over 'on the personal', about his success in converting stubborn opponents into loyal followers. Precisely how he did this is something of a mystery. Men exposed to his blandishments would talk of his bewitching personality, his infectious enthusiasm, his directness and apparent sincerity and the hypnotic intensity of his pale-blue eyes; but none of this fully explains how, after a brief meeting with Rhodes, hard-headed businessmen or politicians could be inspired to give themselves over to a lifetime of service in his interest. It did not always happen like that, of course – not every disciple remained faithful – but it happened often enough to be an important factor in Rhodes's career. He had a discriminating eye and was quick to spot a useful ally, to assess a man's potential and to cultivate a well-placed contact. That was part of what people called his genius. A strange mixture of personal charm and calculation accounted for much of Rhodes's success.

There was, for instance, his life-long friendship with Alfred Beit. That friendship had not come about by accident. When they first met, Beit was practically unknown; there was little to distinguish him from a hundred other Kimberley diamond dealers. Admittedly, he was more successful than most and had a reputation for honesty but, on the diggings, reputations could be deceptive and were apt to crumble overnight. Personality counted for more than success and Beit's personality was far from impressive. But Rhodes had not been deceived by the self-effacing Beit; he recognised financial genius and set out to woo 'little Alfred'. It was one of the wisest moves he made. There can be little doubt that, without Beit's help and influence, the amalgamation battle might have had a very different outcome. Barney Barnato's capitulation was brought about as much by Alfred Beit's timely intervention as by Rhodes's determination.

Every bit as shrewd was Rhodes's earlier decision to team-up with

Charles Rudd. In the diligent, poker-faced and highly capable Rudd – picked from a rag-bag of untried diggers – Rhodes had found the ideal business partner. Some nine years older, and far more mature, than Rhodes, Charles Rudd had not only sympathized with Rhodes's ambitions but had entered whole-heartedly into his schemes. Together they had raised the capital for the De Beers Mining Company, together they had taken over other companies in the De Beers mine, and together they had emerged as challengers for supreme control of the diamond industry. Without the support of Charles Rudd Rhodes's climb to the top of the diamond heap would have been a good deal rougher.

That Rudd was not present during the final stages of the amalgamation battle was unfortunate. He, as much as anyone, deserved to savour the fruits of victory. Savour them he probably did, but he did so from a distance. He no longer lived in Kimberley. While Rhodes was grappling with Barney Barnato, Rudd was coming to grips with a new set of adversaries. To him had fallen the task of extending the Rhodes–Rudd interests on the gold fields of the Witwatersrand.

In their first hurried visit to the Transvaal – the visit confused by Rhodes's sudden departure to attend Neville Pickering's sick-bed – the partners had secured a few valuable properties. The claims they bought were neither the richest nor the best placed but they represented a stake in the new El Dorado. It was not a stake in which Rhodes had much confidence. 'I cannot,' he declared, 'calculate the *power* of these claims.' All the same, he was not one to let a chance slip: he had seen too many fortunes lost by novices in Kimberley to turn his back on an emerging industry.

Unable to return to the gold fields himself, he had persuaded Rudd to represent the partnership on the Witwatersrand. Rudd, at first, had not welcomed the idea. His life was centred on Kimberley, his home and family were there and he considered himself as much a 'diamond man' as Rhodes. There was probably an argument, says A. P. Cartwright, but in the end 'Rhodes won, as he always won in discussions with Rudd.' An agreement was reached by which Rhodes took charge of their diamond interests while Rudd raised the capital for their gold mines and floated a new company. Such were Rhodes's powers of persuasion that Rudd never disputed this decision. He went to the Transvaal and settled in the shanty town of Johannesburg. First, however, he travelled to London to establish the new company – the Gold Fields of South Africa Ltd.

While Rudd was away, Rhodes visited the Witwatersrand for a second time. On this visit he was far more businesslike: he negotiated further deals, secured new holdings and kept Rudd informed of his every move. If gold mining still puzzled him, he no longer doubted the power of his claims. 'The general feeling,' he informed Rudd, before leaving for the Transvaal, 'tends to more faith in the Randt on account of the auriferous deposits.' On arriving in Johannesburg, however, his optimism was tempered. Mining conditions were indeed promising, but, as he quickly discovered, the same could not be said for the political situation.

The discovery of gold in the ochre-coloured hills of the Transvaal – or the South African Republic, as it was officially called – had attracted the usual horde of clamouring opportunists. Prospectors of every nationality, adventurers of every type, had flocked to the Witwatersrand. In September 1886 alone, it is said, some four thousand people had rushed to the Transvaal gold fields. The stampede had completely bewildered the Boer inhabitants of the hitherto isolated territory. They could only watch in amazement as the odd assortment of carts and wagons rumbled across their borders, as camps sprang up and their farms were besieged. Some sold their gold-rich land and trekked away, others remained to sell farm produce to the newcomers. Very few joined in the scramble for gold. The Boers were a puritanical, God-fearing people, deeply suspicious of the working of Mammon.

President Paul Kruger, following these revolutionary events from his homely stoep in Pretoria, regarded the invasion of foreigners – whom the Boers called *uitlanders* – with characteristic shrewdness. Pleased as he was at this staggering godsend to his country's ailing economy, he had no intention of allowing it to corrupt his people. His philosophy was that of the Old Testament: the Boers, like the Israelites, were a chosen race; if they had been sent manna in their wilderness it must be used to further their God-appointed mission. The *uitlanders* were welcome to seek their fortunes in the Transvaal and to add to the country's prosperity, but they must not interfere with the destiny of the Boer nation.

To this end, President Kruger set about hemming in the newcomers with restrictions: he granted them mining rights but withheld concessions for transport and vital mining equipment; he burdened them with heavy taxes but allowed them no say in municipal affairs. Having insufficient burgers to handle the concessions, he granted monopolies to outsiders whom he could trust and left the control of Johannesburg to inefficient appointees. In this way he hoped to regulate the life blood of the mining community, but his grip soon became a stranglehold.

This was how things stood when Rhodes arrived on the Witwatersrand. Already the miners were beginning to chafe under the restrictions, already they were demanding greater control over their own affairs. There were complaints about corruption in high places, about the maladministration of justice and the arrogance of local officials. Each day seemed to bring new examples of Boer truculence, mismanagement and bizarre prejudice. There were even rumours that barmaids were to be forbidden to serve in canteens, that pillar-boxes were to be abolished because they were 'effeminate'. Rhodes listened and sympathized. Wild as some of the talk was, he was left in no doubt about the frustrations of the mining community. He was also becoming increasingly aware of the threat posed by President Kruger and his government not only to the *uitlanders*, but to his own plans for southern Africa.

While he was in Johannesburg, Rhodes met Kruger twice: each meeting was edgy. On the first occasion Rhodes accompanied an *uitlander* deputation to the President, in Pretoria, and made a tactless speech. Kruger listened and answered in Afrikaans. 'Tell him,' he said, pointing his pipe at Rhodes, 'I have heard all these stories before. I am here to protect my burgers as well as the Rand people. I know what I have to do and will do what I consider right.'

Then there was a luncheon in Johannesburg, given in Kruger's honour, at which Rhodes proposed the President's health. This time Kruger made a speech which was more explicit. He attempted to be conciliatory, promised some minor reforms, but was adamant in dismissing the *uitlanders*' claim to the franchise. 'Wealth,' he declared, 'cannot break laws. Though a man has a million pounds he cannot alter the law . . . It is an unthankful people to whom I have given protection, that are always dissatisfied, and, what is more, they would actually want me to alter my laws to suit them.' His audience had been warned.

If Rhodes took this warning to heart, he kept it to himself. He was not, at that time, in any position to interfere in the internal affairs of the Transvaal. The amalgamation of the diamond mines was still far from complete and he had yet to establish himself as a power on the Witwatersrand . In Johannesburg his business concerns took priority over politics: not only was he intent on increasing his gold-mining interests but he needed to consolidate those he already held.

He was helped by Charles Rudd. On 9 February 1887, while Rhodes was in the Transvaal, Rudd registered the Gold Fields of South Africa Limited in London. This company, launched with an authorised capital of £250,000, was the second joint venture of the Rhodes–Rudd partnership. Although it did not equal the gold-mining concerns of Alfred Beit and J. B. Robinson, it gave the partners a firm footing on the Witwatersrand. For Rhodes it proved a highly lucrative undertaking. As a founder he was entitled to one third of the profits and for several years he drew some £300,000 to £400,000 annually from the company. Later he relinquished this privilege for ordinary shares worth, it is estimated, £1,300,000 to £1,400,000. By that time, the success of the company appeared – outwardly, at least – assured. In 1892, when it was renamed The Consolidated Gold Fields of South

Africa, its capital had been increased by a million and a quarter; three years later the dividend had increased to no less than fifty per cent. Rhodes, already immensely rich, became richer still; so rich, in fact, that he was never quite sure of the size of his income.

Was Rhodes a capitalist who used empire building to further his financial ends? This is what some historians claim, but it seems most unlikely. Certainly Rhodes was a capitalist but he was not a worshipper of money for its own sake. In all his financial dealings, his prime aim was to fuel his imperial schemes. Why else should he have argued all night with Barney Barnato? Why else should he have insisted that the trust deeds of his mining companies contain provisions which allowed for the expansion of territorial as well as financial empires? Such provisions entailed risks and certainly did not guarantee profits; they reflect the aspirations of a dreamer, rather than those of a hard-headed business man.

Rhodes's intentions became manifestly clear when the trust deed of De Beers Consolidated Mines was drawn up, but they were also apparent – though less publicized – in the trust deed of the Gold Fields of South Africa Limited. Indeed, the trust deed which Rhodes devised for his gold-mining company could, in some of its provisions, have served as a draft for that which he later imposed on the amalgamated diamond mines. In both cases he ensured that the company was given powers that went beyond the requirements of any ordinary mining concern. The Gold Fields, like De Beers, was empowered to annex and govern territories, to function as a political as well as a financial organization.

*   *   *

Having done all he could in Johannesburg, Rhodes returned to Kimberley to continue the battle for control of the diamond mines. He left the affairs of The Gold Fields of South Africa in the hands of the company's newly appointed secretary, Harry Currey – the son of his old friend J. B. Currey. Rhodes had known young Currey for several years. He was a lively, intelligent young man with a talent for organization and a gift for caustic comment. Having watched him grow up, Rhodes had taken a serious interest in him from the time he was twenty-one. It was Harry Currey who, on leave from the Cape Public Service, accompanied Rhodes to Bechuanaland when he was trying to clear the Boer republics from his 'Suez Canal'. The two of them had become firm friends and two years later – shortly after the death of Neville Pickering – Rhodes decided to employ the twenty-three-year-old Currey full time.

Harry Currey was still working as a civil servant in the Cape when

Rhodes sent for him and offered him the post of secretary of his new gold-mining company. He had no knowledge of the goldfields, no enthusiasm for the Witwatersrand and no real desire to leave the Cape but, when Rhodes offered to pay him three times as much as he was earning as a civil servant, the temptation was too great for him to resist. His change of employment did not please his father. J. X. Merriman, who was in Johannesburg while Rhodes was there, tried, somewhat equivocally, to reassure J. B. Currey. 'I saw Harry . . .' he wrote. 'Don't be too hard on the poor chap – he is suffering the penalty of being the attaché of a wealthy speculator like Rhodes, who of course pooh-poohs everything except the greatest flights and there is no scope for the sort of work a healthy young fellow like Harry might do . . . But it would be foolish of him to throw up a certainty in the present state of the gold-fields.' So Harry Currey – who was never happy with the way the company was run – remained on the Witwatersrand for the next three years. For all his lack of experience, he quickly made his mark on the Rand and won the respect of his associates. His next appointment was to bring him much closer to Rhodes.

Throughout 1887 Rhodes was kept fully occupied with the amalgamation of the diamond mines. His only important distraction came at the end of the year when he was forced to dash to the eastern Cape to persuade Sir Hercules Robinson to negotiate the treaty of 'peace and unity' between Lobengula and Queen Victoria. In arranging for this treaty to be signed, he was helped by his old friend Sir Sidney Shippard, the former Attorney General of Griqualand West. By that time Shippard had left Kimberley and taken up the appointment of Administrator of British Bechuanaland and Deputy Commissioner for the Bechuanaland protectorate – the vast territory which stretched from the northern Cape to the border of Matabeleland. In his dual role he was able to keep Rhodes fully informed of events in Lobengula's domains. It had, in fact, been Shippard's assistant, John Moffat, who had secured the treaty with Lobengula.

Moffat was a member of the famous missionary family and, like his father, Robert Moffat, he had earlier worked in Matabeleland and knew both Mzilikazi and Lobengula well. Such was his influence on the Ndebele king that the agreement between Lobengula and Queen Victoria became known as the 'Moffat Treaty'. After the treaty had been concluded Moffat remained at the royal kraal as the British representative in Matabeleland. Rhodes thus had two important allies – Shippard and Moffat – in his quest for a foothold in the Ndebele territories.

But allies were not enough. When the Moffat Treaty was ratified by the British government, in April 1888, there was an international outcry. Both the Transvaal and Portugal protested against the provisions in the treaty which excluded political interference in Matabeleland by other powers. President Kruger immediately published Pieter Grobler's 'treaty of friendship' with Lobengula, while the Portuguese Consul in Cape Town objected vigorously to the Shona tribes – over whom Portugal claimed jurisdiction – being described as the Ndebele king's 'tributaries'. There was substance in both protests and, not surprisingly, Portugal and the Transvaal refused to accept the British claim that the territories south of the Zambesi were now 'exclusively within the British sphere of influence'. Had they given a little thought to the inhabitants of those territories, they might also have questioned the extent to which Lobengula understood the treaty to which he had affixed his 'elephant seal'. At the time of the signing, Moffat had encouraged the belief that the Ndebele would be given British protection, but there was no mention of this in the treaty. It was very much a one-sided affair and promised Lobengula nothing.

Rhodes must have recognized the danger signals. He must have realized that he would require more than a mineral concession to fend off the mounting opposition. This is probably what decided him to pay a hurried visit to England. The time had come for him to consult 'Grandma' – as he irreverently called the British government.

Not a great deal is known about his visit. In Britain, at this time, Rhodes was looked upon as a petty colonial politician and his activities attracted little attention. He did, however, have sufficient influence to be granted an interview with Lord Knutsford, the recently appointed Colonial Secretary. The interview appears to have been cordial but unproductive. Knutsford had no objections to what Rhodes had to say but he could offer no help. The trouble was, Rhodes later told Shippard, 'I had no concession to work on.' Even more discouraging was the news that two other companies were lobbying the Colonial Office. On this visit Rhodes learned that these companies – The Bechuanaland Exploration Company and the Exploring Company – had recently been formed to obtain and exploit concessions in the Bechuanaland protectorate and Matabeleland. This was a threat that he could not ignore.

The two companies, although ostensibly separate, were in fact allied; their directorships were intertwined and they worked closely together. The men heading these ventures were George Cawston, a London financier, and Lord Gifford, a former colonial servant and soldier who had won the V.C. in the Ashanti War of 1873–74. They were both youngish men, highy respectable and well connected, and it was obvious that the challenge they posed was serious. Getting rid of them would be far more difficult than clearing the field of the motley crowd of concession hunters gathered at Lobengula's kraal. Rhodes's only consolation was the knowledge that their approaches to the

Colonial Office had met with the same non-committal response as his own.

On the voyage back to South Africa, Rhodes was accompanied by his old Oxford friend, James Rochfort Maguire. Two years younger than Rhodes, Maguire was the son of an Irish parson. After leaving Oxford he had entered the Inner Temple but had never practised at the bar: his career was to be fashioned by his friendship with Rhodes. During their days at sea, Rhodes must have discussed his plans for dealing with Lobengula with Maguire – he liked to use his friends as sounding boards for his ideas – and it was probably these discussions which later decided him to involve Maguire in those plans.

Certainly by the time he reached Cape Town, Rhodes's plans were well formulated. This is borne out by the interview he had with yet another old friend: Sir Hercules Robinson, the British High Commissioner. According to a confidential dispatch which Robinson sent to Lord Knutsford, on 21 July 1888, Rhodes was both frank and open about his intentions. After informing Robinson of the powers granted to De Beers Consolidated Mines by its trust deed, Rhodes went on to explain the purpose of such powers. He wanted, said Robinson, to obtain from Lobengula a concession 'of parts of Matabeleland and Mashonaland which are not in the use of the Natives, and to provide for the protection of the Natives in the parts reserved for them, as well as the development of the unoccupied territories surrendered to the Company by a Royal Charter somewhat similar to that granted some years ago to the Borneo Company.'

This was all very vague, as well as predatory. Where were these so-called 'unoccupied territories'? Just how unoccupied were they? and where were the parts 'reserved' for the 'Natives'? Indeed, precisely which 'Natives' had Rhodes in mind? What part was Lobengula, the established ruler of Matabeleland, expected to play in all this? Rhodes appeared to be dividing a country he had never seen, in the most arbitrary fashion, before he entered it. In asking for the co-operation of the British government he was, in fact, seeking an adventurer's licence.

Crude as were Rhodes's plans, Sir Hercules gave them him his backing. His attitude was one favoured by imperialists of the day. Lobengula's domains, he argued, were reported to be wealthy and were therefore bound to attract a 'civilized' power sooner or later; if the country was to be occupied then it was better that it should be occupied by Britain than by a foreign competitor. Rhodes's scheme, he pointed out, would not only ensure the security of the 'Natives', but would allow British capital to develop the 'waste lands' without placing a burden on the taxpayer. Building the empire 'on the cheap' was, as Robinson undoubtedly knew, a proposition that was dear to the hearts of most politicians. The eventual cost to the inhabitants of the largely unknown territories played little or no part in the High Commissioner's calculations.

Robinson's dispatch is revealing in other ways. It shows that, from the very outset, the British authorities were fully aware of Rhodes's intentions. His suggestion that he be granted a Royal Charter – something that Rhodes had long contemplated – made nonsense of his later claims that he was merely seeking a mineral concession. Such charters, although theoretically intended to place a company under close government supervision, in effect gave commercial concerns wide administrative powers over the territories in which they operated. This had certainly been true in the case of the British North Borneo Company and, by referring to this company, Rhodes had signalled his intention of taking over Lobengula's possessions. Obtaining a mineral concession was clearly the means by which he intended to achieve his political ends.

Lord Knutsford's response to Robinson's dispatch was neutral. He found no fault with Rhodes's scheme but pointed out that the government could not favour one company against another. The granting of a royal charter was, he thought, unlikely. As things stood, he could hardly have said more. All the same, it is obvious that the Colonial Office now had a good idea of what was afoot.

*   *   *

Having sounded out officialdom, Rhodes prepared to take action. The first agent he had sent to Lobengula – the sickly John Fry – had returned empty-handed and nothing could be done until he was replaced. Knowledge that George Cawston and Lord Gifford, in London, were planning to send an envoy to Matabeleland added urgency to his arrangements. This time Rhodes was taking no chances. The three men he chose for a new approach to the Ndebele king were healthy, reliable and well-equipped to deal with emergencies: they were also his close friends.

Heading the expedition was the experienced and cool-minded Charles Rudd whose job it would be to negotiate an exclusive, watertight mining concession. To assist Rudd in the negotiations, Rhodes engaged Francis Robert ('Matabele') Thompson, a thirty-one-year-old part-time civil servant who was well versed in African languages and customs and had recently served as compound manager of De Beers. Rhodes had known the Thompson family since his early days on the diamond fields and had employed young Thompson as his secretary during his negotiations in Bechuanaland. The only drawback to Thompson's inclusion in the mission to Bulawayo was the fact that he was married and was not keen to leave his family. Rhodes, however, had anticipated this. 'I must ask my wife,' Thompson protested, when asked to accompany Rudd. 'I knew you would say that,' beamed Rhodes, pulling a letter from his pocket, 'here is her written consent. I got it half an hour ago.'

The third member of the team was Rochfort Maguire. His enlistment appears to have been more a matter of friendship than of necessity. Ostensibly he was chosen because he was a trained lawyer – he was to ensure that the concession was legally worded – but, as Charles Rudd was perfectly capable of drawing up an agreement, Maguire's presence was somewhat superfluous. Not the most practical of men, the dapper, fastidious Maguire was to prove something of an encumbrance to his companions, His 'distaste for life in the wilds,' complained Thompson, 'caused me much trouble.'

The party – which included Rudd's son and another white man, as well as African servants – set out from the Kimberley Club, after dining with Rhodes, on 17 August 1888. Their departure was kept secret and curious onlookers were told they were leaving on a hunting trip. Only Rhodes and a few intimates knew exactly what they were hunting. In Rudd's luggage was £5,000 in specie and a letter from Sir Hercules Robinson introducing him to Lobengula. In this letter, the well-informed High Commissioner described Rudd and Thompson as 'two highly respectable gentlemen who are visiting your country'.

Rudd certainly had no doubts about the purpose of his visit. A couple of weeks before leaving he had written a letter of explanation to Harry Currey. 'After some discussion with Rhodes . . . ,' he confided, 'we have come to the conclusion that our best chance of a big thing is to try to make some terms with Lobengula for a concession for the whole of his country [no mention here of 'unoccupied territories']. Rhodes has arranged for such Imperial support as can be granted and it is thought best that I should start with an expedition at once.' The only doubts he expressed concerned his own role in the negotiations. 'I may or may not go the whole way,' he added. 'That depends on transport and whether mules can go as far as Gubulawayo or not. But Thompson and Maguire will go at any rate with oxen.'

Rudd did, in fact, go the whole way. The journey was not without its hazards, but overcoming the difficulties, the party arrived at Lobengula's kraal six weeks after leaving Kimberley.

*　　*　　*

Gubulawayo – or Bulawayo, as it became known to Europeans – was, given its wild surroundings, an impressive settlement. Roughly oval in shape and almost half a mile across at its widest, the sprawling Ndebele capital housed some fifteen to twenty thousand people. The royal kraal stood on the north bank of a narrow river, hardly more than a stream, and was surrounded by a fence of stout poles. Inside the wooden palisades were a collection of thatched, hive-shaped huts – the living quarters of the king's resident wives – and an enclosure, known as the 'Buck Kraal', where Lobengula performed rain-making ceremonies and other, more gruesome, rituals. Although two brick houses had been built for him (by an English sailor), the king preferred to live and sleep in a covered ox-wagon. This wagon, captured by his warriors on a raiding expedition, provided him with a mobile home and enabled him to divide his time between Bulawayo and his private kraal, Umvutshwa, some seven miles away. Seated on a wooden block in front of the wagon, Lobengula received his subjects and his visitors.

Rudd and his companions had their first audience with the king shortly after they arrived at Bulawayo. It was early evening – Lobengula received nobody after dark – and they were in some doubts about the procedure they should adopt. 'We had agreed,' says Thompson, 'that we should greet the king as an ordinary gentleman, and that by adhering to this line of conduct we could not go far wrong. We had been told that we should have to approach him by crawling on our hands and knees, and remain in a recumbent position while in his presence. This was the custom, and the whites who had thrown in their lot with the natives were wont to observe it. We decided, however, to walk boldly up to him in the ordinary fashion, and this we did, to the evident surprise of his entourage.'

Their audacity did not, however, surprise Lobengula. Far from being offended, he gave them a cordial welcome and listened politely while formalities were exchanged. Both Rudd and Thompson found the king to be very much what they expected. Naked, except for a skimpy loin-cloth and a necklace of animal teeth, he was nonetheless an imposing, decidedly regal figure. Thompson judged him to be a man 'of about twenty stone' – tall, stout and well-built; Rudd was impressed by his beautiful skin and well proportioned body. To both men he appeared to be 'every inch a king', although Rudd was puzzled by his contradictory expressions: at times he seemed friendly and good-natured but he also had a worried look and there was a hint of cruelty in his enigmatic smile.

Conversation was difficult. Not only did Thompson's linguistic abilities fail to match up the intricacies of the Ndebele tongue, but there were constant interruptions from supplicants who crawled, or sidled, up to the king to beg favours. When dealing with his subjects, Lobengula ignored his guests completely. Eventually the audience was brought to an abrupt and inconclusive end when, having ordered his dinner, the king climbed into his wagon, lay down, and covered himself with a blanket.

This first audience had been arranged by John Moffat – now the permanent British representative at Bulawayo – and, over the next few weeks, Moffat was to give Rudd and his party what help he could. But neither Moffat nor Charles Helm, a Cape-born missionary who was sent for to act as interpreter, could bring Lobengula to a decision. The king was not to be rushed. From time to time he would listen attentively to what Rudd had to say but he refused to commit himself. He had his own affairs to attend to, his warriors were growing restive, his *indunas* (head men) were divided in their views of the newcomers and there were other concession hunters at Bulawayo to consider. Shortly before Rudd and his party arrived, Lobengula had in fact granted a comprehensive concession to a group – headed by James Fairbairn, a trusted store-keeper at Bulawayo – and this, together with the more limited concessions he had awarded, undoubtedly weighed heavily against the Rudd group. Not the least of the king's worries, however, was the problem of knowing which of the concession hunters had the backing of the British government. When, in February, he had signed the Moffat Treaty he had been under the impression that he had bound himself to an agreement that promised him the protection of Queen Victoria. Moffat claimed to be the Queen's representative, but how could the unlettered king be sure that this claim was genuine? That Lobengula repeatedly broke off his discussions with Rudd, repeatedly protested that he was too busy to listen, is hardly surprising.

Certainly Rudd and his companions were not welcomed by their rivals. There were, at that time, a great many opportunists at Bulawayo and they were all eager to offer the king advice. Most of these men were simply adventurers from the Cape and the Transvaal who had no real backing, but one, E. R. Renny-Tailyour, was there representing Edward Lippert and a German syndicate. Lippert, well-known as a concessionaire in the Transvaal, was a cousin of Alfred Beit and this, if nothing else, made him a formidable opponent to any group that represented Rhodes. Later an even greater threat was posed by the arrival of Lieutenant Edward Maund, the good-looking and capable agent sent out to Matabeleland by George Cawston and Lord Gifford. Actually Maund had left Kimberley before the Rudd party but had been conveniently delayed in Bechuanaland by Rhodes's friend Sir Sidney Shippard and arrived at Bulawayo too late to hinder Rudd's negotiations. But this was not the last that Rhodes was to hear of the determined Lieutenant Maund.

Faced with Lobengula's indecisiveness and frustrated by the intrigues of their opponents, Rudd, Thompson and Maguire were forced to remain at Bulawayo much longer than they had intended. The weeks of waiting were a trial: alternately boring and tense and, at times, downright frightening. Not only were their living conditions primitive and the food almost uneatable, but there were occasional threats from young warriors who resented their presence at the royal kraal. Throughout their stay, regiments of these young men arrived at Bulawayo to seek Lobengula's permission to kill the older, more compliant *indunas* and drive the white intruders from the country. Luckily the king was able to calm his *impis* and safeguard his visitors but his intervention brought little comfort to the Rudd group. Thompson, who as a young man had seen his own father murdered by marauding tribesmen, found the situation particularly alarming. His fears were not diminished on witnessing the fate of offenders who were denied Lobengula's protection.

'While I was in Matabeleland,' says Thompson, 'I saw many instances of ferocity and the most callous cruelty . . . . I saw the most awful spectacle I have ever seen in my life. I saw crawling on his hands and knees a native, about forty years old, with great lumps of flesh hanging from his face; his nose over his mouth, the ears both suspended by a thread of flesh. Just as I got near I saw a man with a pole hit the crawling man in the small of the back, trying to kill the unfortunate brute. This was all in front of the king. The crime the man had committed was that, while under the influence of liquor, he had drunk some of the king's beer. The king ordered his nose, ears and lips, and the skin of his forehead, to be cut off . . . . Slaves were frequently brought in . . . Two girls aged twelve and fourteen were at the king's kraal . . . . The poor creatures took it in their heads to make a bolt for it and try to get home. Young warriors, about twenty years old, were sent after them, and they caught them near Imshanyani almost dead from hunger. They were brought back and fed for a day, and then thrashed by the 'dog' – twenty boys aged from twelve to eighteen years . . . . A native named Kumalo, whom I knew well, was sentenced to be stoned to death for witchcraft . . . . Hundreds of men were killed in this and other ways. The king suffered from gout, and his doctors put it into his head that the only way to be cured was to "smell out" natives and kill them. The king, unfortunately, had attacks of gout frequently.'

The loyalty which Rhodes demanded from his friends was sorely tested. Fortunately they were not entirely without allies at Bulawayo. Both John Moffat and Charles Helm (the interpreter) did their best to persuade Lobengula that Rudd represented a powerful petitioner and that, by granting his request, the king would be able to send the other concession hunters packing. Their arguments were supported by one of the king's chief *indunas*, Lotshe, whom Thompson befriended and bribed with promises of gifts. Bribes were also offered to Lobengula. On their first meeting, Rudd had presented the king with one hundred sovereigns and, from time to time, this was supplemented by other gifts. But neither arguments nor hand-outs could sway Lobengula. The king remained evasive.

Rudd began to despair. At one stage he wrote to his wife to say that he had repaired his wagon and was about to start for home. Almost two months had passed since he had left Kimberley and in that time he had accomplished nothing. There seemed no point in waiting longer.

The situation was saved, or at least helped, by the timely arrival of a representative of the Great White Queen. It happened that, in the middle of October, Sir Sidney Shippard visited Matabeleland – nominally to conduct an enquiry into the death of Piet Grobler, the unfortunate Transvaal consul – and decided to pay his respects to Lobengula. His arrival could not have been more opportune. A few days earlier yet another *impi* had turned up at Bulawayo asking to be let loose on the whites. Solomon-like, the king had told them that he would not allow such attacks in Matabeleland but, if they wished, they could go to Kimberley and kill all the whites there. It was a witty idea, but not one that guaranteed the safety of the concession hunters.

Shippard was made well aware of the tribal tensions. At first there was some doubt as to whether he would be allowed to travel to Bulawayo. Spies reported to Lobengula that Sir Sidney had been seen taking a bath and was therefore suspected of being a magician. This had alarmed the king and it was only after John Moffat had warned him that it would be unwise to 'refuse the road' to such an eminent official that he relented. His warriors were not so easily won over. On his way up-country, Shippard camped beside a river and discovered he was being dogged by an armed force. 'In passing our encampment,' he later explained, 'they jeered at us, taunting and insulting us, and in their war dances some of them ran out stabbing at us and poising assegais, shouting out that they would soon make an end of us when they came into our camp.' A little later, the warriors returned with reinforcements and the yelling, howling and dancing started up again. This was obviously the army's answer to Lobengula's interdict. Not allowed to attack, the warriors were hoping to provoke the white men into making the first move. But the ruse did not work. 'Our men,' said Shippard, 'behaved throughout with admirable coolness, and looked at the dancing savages with the most stolid indifference.'

On reaching Bulawayo, Shippard lost no time in making his presence felt. Flanked by his police escort and dressed in a bemedalled black frock coat, patent-leather boots, grey gloves and a large white pith helmet, the paunchy little Administrator of Bechuanaland may not have looked impressive but he certainly looked important. When he walked ceremoniously into the royal kraal, Lobengula ordered chairs to be brought so that his distinguished visitor could be seated. As so often happened, the advent of a friendly British official proved beneficial to Rhodes. No record was kept of the talks between Sir Sidney Shippard and Lobengula, but shortly after Sir Sidney's departure the long-awaited concession was granted.

There were several more meetings. At the end of October, Thompson – with Charles Helm interpreting – addressed a huge gathering of *indunas* at a two-day *indaba* and attempted to explain the conditions of the proposed concession. He made little impression and, on the second day, he ended the meeting by threatening to leave Matabeleland. 'Yes, Indunas,' he declared, 'your hearts will break when we have gone.' But, as he was about to stalk from the kraal, he was approached by the ever-attentive Lotshe who told him that the king wished to see him. In the interview which followed, Lobengula indicated that he was prepared to sign the 'fly-blown paper'. Rudd and Maguire were sent for and, on 30 October 1888, Lobengula formally agreed to give Rhodes's agents 'exclusive charge over all metals and minerals' in his kingdom.

The terms of the concession were as comprehensive as Rudd and Maguire could make them. In return for the monopoly they sought, the holders of the concession were to pay the king £100 on the first day of each lunar month and supply him with a thousand Martini-Henry rifles and a hundred thousand cartridges. The promise of an armed steamboat on the Zambesi (this was Rhodes's idea) was thrown in for good measure, but this promise was never fulfilled. The concessionaires were also given the right to expel – with the king's help, if necessary – all other claimants to 'land, metals, minerals or mining rights.' After Lobengula had made his mark, the document was signed by Rudd, Maguire and Thompson; Charles Helm and Rudd's driver, J. F. Dreyer, acted as witnesses.

'Thompson,' drawled Maguire, when the signing was completed, 'this is the epoch of our lives.'

It was to prove an even greater turning point in the life of Lobengula. That the king appreciated the significance of the document he signed is extremely doubtful. Charles Helm explained to him the wording of the concession but he could not have spelt out its implications. As far as can be judged, Lobengula was under the impression that the white men would dig their holes, extract their gold, and that he would be left undisturbed. An end would be put to the constant stream of petitioners to his kraal and he would be free to rule his subjects as he had always done. He is even reported to have expressed the wish that not more than ten men would come and dig as a result of the concession. How wrong he was. But he realized his mistake too late.

Lobengula was given no time to change his mind; the concession was signed at midday and by four o'clock that afternoon Rudd was on his way back to Kimberley. He took his driver, Dreyer, with him and left Thompson and Maguire to look after things at Bulawayo. On his journey south he overtook Shippard's party and then met with near disaster. Separated from his companion, Rudd was lost in the Bechuanaland desert and nearly died of thirst. He was forced to bury the concession, together with £300 in specie, in an ant-hole and recovered it only when he was rescued by some Bushmen. The Bushmen, alerted by the barking of their dogs discovered him lying exhausted close to a dried-out water course, carried him back to their camp and revived him by pouring water into his ear and over his face. Then they went to search for Dreyer whom they eventually found three miles away. For two days Rudd and Dreyer rested at the fly-infested Bushman camp. Dreyer recovered first and set off for the nearest settlement to obtain help. By the time he returned, Rudd felt well enough to continue the journey.

They travelled the rest of the way without any major setbacks. On 19 November – almost three weeks after leaving Bulawayo – Rudd arrived at Kimberley where he met Rhodes. The following morning the two of them left on an express train to Cape Town. Rudd, as he proudly noted in his diary, had completed the journey of almost 1,100 miles in record time. Rhodes, for his part, was delighted at the safe return of his partner and even more delighted to be handed the concession. Once more he could claim that his friends had not let him down.

CHAPTER EIGHT

'Runnymede'

The first step that Rhodes took on reaching Cape Town was to show the concession to Sir Hercules Robinson. According to Rudd, the High Commissioner was 'strongly in favour' of having it published at once. Rhodes was not so sure: there were certain conditions in the concession which he considered unfit for public consumption.

The trickiest clause was that which promised to supply the Ndebele king with guns and ammunition. This, as Rhodes well knew, could prove politically explosive. Much of the opposition to the activities on the diamond fields had arisen from the diggers' connivance in the sale of firearms to African mine workers and there had been repeated attempts to have this 'dangerous practice' outlawed. The idea of arming a tyrannical, independent African ruler with Martini-Henry rifles was a thousand times worse. Not only did it violate the white man's code but it would be seen as a direct threat to white supremacy. Nowhere would the inevitable outcry be louder than in the Transvaal, where the Boers regarded their privileged position as a sacred trust. Rhodes realized this and it weighed heavily with him.

He was not so much worried about the Transvaal Boers, however, as about their influence on their kinsmen in the Cape: those Afrikaners whom he was trying to woo – through an alliance with Jan Hofmeyr and the Cape Afrikaner Bond – as his political supporters. If an outcry in the Transvaal produced hostility in the Cape his long-term plans could be jeopardized. This was something that Rhodes was determined to avoid. All his moves to the north had been influenced by his desire to win over the 'Cape Dutch' and he saw no point in upsetting things now. For this reason he advised caution. It would be wiser, he argued, to wait until the rifles had been smuggled into Matabeleland, when the transaction could be presented as a *fait accompli*.

The High Commissioner also appears to have had second thoughts. Although Rudd claims that Sir Hercules 'raised no difficulty as to the guns', he must have known that he was courting trouble. Supplying arms to Lobengula would contravene the General Act of the Brussels Conference – to which Britain was a party – and this would not go down well in Whitehall. It was in everyone's interest to keep quiet about the details of the concession for the time being.

But an announcement of some sort had to be made. As there were not sufficient guns in South Africa to fulfil the contract, they would have to be imported and this would take time. In the meantime it was essential that Rhodes warn off his rivals. So, having deceived Lobengula about their ends, Rhodes and Rudd decided to deceive the public about their means. It was left to Rudd to draw up the discreetly worded version of the concession which, with the approval of Rhodes and Robinson, was published in the Cape press on 24 November 1888. The rifles were not mentioned. In return for granting the concession, it was claimed, Lobengula was to receive 'the valuable consideration of a large monthly payment in cash, a gunboat for defensive purposes on the Zambesi, and other services.' Put like that, the 'other services' seemed to be little more than a pat on the back.

All the same, the provision of rifles would have to be justified sooner or later. A way of doing this was suggested by Sir Sidney Shippard. Having discussed the matter with missionaries, Shippard had found that some of them were opposed to handing firearms to the Ndebele; Charles Helm, on the other hand, was in favour of it. Helm's reasoning was, to say the least, remarkable. The tribesmen, he argued, had little knowledge of guns, were poor shots, and would be less dangerous with rifles than with assegais. (That the Ndebele's lack of skill was due to lack of experience, and might improve with practice, does not seem to have occurred to him. Nor does the fact, as one of the other missionaries pointed out, that warriors could carry assegais as well as rifles.) Yet tenuous as were Helm's arguments, Rhodes and his cohorts leapt at them. From now on they would maintain that a rifle-toting Ndebele was harmless: he aimed too high, thinking that his bullets would travel farther and hit harder, and invariably missed his target. Why should the white men worry?

Rhodes, in any case, was too preoccupied to worry. He had intended to go straight to Bulawayo himself, but he now decided to postpone his trip until a more important matter was sorted out. With the concession secure, the African chess-board had been simplified. The time had come to think about checkmate: his pawns had cornered the black king and he was ready to bring the white Queen into play. If he could obtain the seal of a Royal Charter his position would be unassailable. To secure the charter became his immediate, most urgent task. It would not be easy. There were still obstacles to overcome; his opponents were still active, he needed friends in England as well as Africa, he would have to enlist politicians as well as financiers. But he did not doubt that he would succeed. He was, after all, a past master of persuasion. Wittily, he dubbed his quest for a Royal Charter 'Runnymede'.

*　　*　　*

Rhodes did not have long to wait for the opposition to show itself. Hardly had Rudd left Bulawayo than a campaign was launched there to persuade Lobengula that he had been deceived by Rhodes's agents. Things were brought to a climax with the arrival of the Cape newspapers containing the bowdlerized version of the concession. This was read to Lobengula by one of the thwarted concession-hunters, who, not surprisingly, interpreted it to suit his own purposes. The king, he claimed, had given away his entire country to the Rhodes group.

Lobengula was furious. That he had been cheated by Rudd now seemed a certainty. The newspaper report confirmed the rumours that had been circulating at Bulawayo for weeks. One after another, the concession hunters had come to him with stories of how Rhodes intended to take over his territories. It had been pointed out that the claim to mineral rights was merely a pretence. How could it be otherwise? Mining operations could not be undertaken, as Lobengula thought, by a handful of white men. They would have to come in great numbers; they would need land to live on, they would have to grow food for themselves and their workers, to build houses and form settlements. Kimberley was a large town, similar towns would arise in the Ndebele domains and the king's authority would be undermined. What doubts Lobengula may have had about such talk were now dispelled. By publishing the concession, Rudd – who had promised secrecy – had broken his trust. Now the king decided to bring the matter into the open himself. He called a meeting of his *indunas*, sent for Charles Helm to act as interpreter and summoned Thompson to answer for Rhodes.

The crisis could not have arisen at a more awkward time for Thompson. He was completely alone at Bulawayo. Some time earlier, Maguire, intent on enforcing the Rudd concession, had left the Ndebele capital with a band of warriors to warn off a new party – headed by Alfred Haggard, the brother of the novelist Rider Haggard – who were reported to be heading for Bulawayo in the hopes of obtaining a mineral concession for yet another London company. Not only had Maguire taken all the remaining mules and wagons with him, but he had also carried away all the cooking utensils. 'I was thus,' bemoaned Thompson, 'left alone, with little or no food in store, to subsist on what I could obtain from the natives. I had a tin of Mortons jam, which I promptly emptied and converted into a cup and teapot combined.' Never had he felt more isolated.

The *indaba* was a lively affair. Besides the *indunas*, a large number of white men crowded into the royal kraal and Thompson was

110

subjected to a close, sometimes bizarre, examination. Did he, asked his interrogators, have a brother named Rhodes 'who eats a whole country for breakfast'? Was not his friend Maguire a magician who rode wolves at night time? Added to the insults of the *indunas* were the accusations of the white men, some of whom threatened to shoot him. Thompson fended off the questions as best he could. He was cross-examined for almost ten and a half hours and felt that, all things considered, he emerged from the ordeal 'satisfactorily'. On one point, however, he was forced to yield. The *indunas* wanted to see the original concession and demanded that it be returned to Bulawayo. Thompson had no option but to agree. He wrote to Rhodes telling him that it was a matter of life and death that the concession should be returned, but some months were to pass before the controversial document reached Bulawayo.

After the *indaba* Thompson went into camp at a place called Umganeng and it was here that Maguire, fresh from his encounter with Alfred Haggard, joined him. The tense atmosphere in the camp reflected the changed circumstances at Bulawayo. Suspicion had turned to outright hostility and Thompson and Maguire were made to fear for their lives. Their every move was watched; they were unable to go for a casual walk without being followed. Eventually, after being warned that they might be attacked in the veld, they decided to forgo exercise and keep close to the camp. This only made things worse. None too happy with each other's company, they became bored, irritable and restless. Maguire found the situation intolerable. Unlike Thompson, he was unable to amuse himself by studying the Ndebele and, to add to his woes, he was plagued with dyspepsia which made it impossible for him to swallow the crude food they were served. At last he could stand it no longer. Being knocked on the head, he told Thompson, would be no worse than dying of indigestion and, if only to break the monotony, he was determined to get a 'clean up'. Petulantly, he snatched up his yellow sponge-bag and set off for the nearest stream.

Unfortunately, there were few streams in the vicinity. The only water to be found was at the king's drinking fountain, some three miles away, and it was to this fountain (or spring) that Maguire strode. Blissfully unaware that he was being watched and not knowing that the fountain was regarded as sacred – it was used only for medicinal purposes and religious rites – he stripped off his clothes and plunged in. Unpacking his sponge-bag, he produced an assortment of brushes, powders and lotions and proceeded to dab himself with eau-de-cologne and clean his teeth with pink tooth-paste. This was apparently too much for the watching Ndebele. Dashing out from their hiding place they seized the sponge-bag and some clothing and ordered the

111

startled Maguire to leave. On arriving back at camp, Maguire told Thompson that something 'very unpleasant' had happened.

Thompson decided to brazen the matter out by going to the royal kraal to complain of the way Maguire had been treated. He did not get far. At the kraal, he was confronted by the guardian of the sacred fountain who accused Maguire of poisoning the water. It was the pink tooth-paste that caused the deepest suspicions. Maguire, the guardian insisted, had been seen to spit blood into the water. This – and the scented eau-de-cologne – was cited as proof positive of Maguire's evil intentions. Lobengula handed the matter over to his *indunas*, who, after some haggling, extracted a heavy fine from Rhodes's agents. They also confiscated all Maguire's toiletries. 'Life for him,' observed Thompson, 'was hardly worth living without them.'

Things had been made worse when, shortly afterwards, Lobengula's mother died. The white concession hunters immediately informed the king that her death had been caused by the poisoned water. Once again there was an outcry. So frightened did Maguire become that, a day or two later, he secretly left the camp and fled south. He intended, he told Thompson, to lay the matter before Rhodes. But Rhodes, when Maguire eventually caught up with him, had other things to worry about. The sacred fountain fiasco was only one of a number of happenings at Bulawayo that threatened his plans.

* * *

Far more serious was an earlier event. Among the trouble makers who had first sown doubts in Lobengula's mind was the smooth-talking Lieutenant Maund. As the agent of Cawston and Gifford's Exploring Company, Maund was determined to undermine the Rudd concession. He had arrived too late to prevent it from being signed but this had not disheartened him. Cashing in on the rumours floating about Bulawayo, he ingratiated himself with the king – whom he had known in earlier days – and made his own contribution to the hostile gossip.

Maund's immediate object was to obtain a mining concession in the Mazoe area of Mashonaland. This was part of the ill-defined eastern territory, already claimed by Portugal, which was rumoured to contain some of the richest gold deposits south of the Zambesi. Other prospectors had obtained concessions from local Shona chieftains in the area and, Rudd or no Rudd, Maund was determined to outwit any potential rival. By playing on Lobengula's resentment of Portuguese claims to Mazoe, Maund was able to make out a case for defying the terms of the Rudd concession which gave Rhodes exclusive right to minerals in Mashonaland.

He was helped also by the anti-Rhodes faction at Bulawayo. One of the most persistent accusations levelled at Rhodes's agents was that they had misrepresented themselves by posing as representatives of the Great White Queen. How, it was asked, could Lobengula know whether they were telling the truth? Indeed, how could he be sure that such a person as Queen Victoria existed? He had never seen her, nor had any of his people. It is even thought that Maund tried to pass himself off as the true spokesman of the British government. The confusion was such that Lobengula was forced to take action. He decided to send two of his senior *indunas* to England·to find out the truth.

Whether the mission to England was Lobengula's own idea, or whether it was suggested to him by Maund, is a matter of dispute. Whatever the truth, there can be little doubt that Maund encouraged the king; for he it was who was chosen to accompany Lobengula's ambassadors. The two *indunas*, Babayan and Mshete, were placed in his charge and he was made responsible for guiding them through the diplomatic maze in London. As an interpreter would be needed, Johan Colenbrander was included in the party. The thirty-one-year-old Colenbrander, son of a Dutch settler in Natal, was a colourful and experienced African adventurer. He had fought in the Zulu war of 1879 and had been brought to Matabeleland by E. R. Renny-Tailyour – the agent of Alfred Beit's cousin, Edward Lippert. Like Maund, Renny-Tailyour was anxious to thwart Rhodes and readily agreed to Colenbrander joining the mission to London.

Before they left, Maund helped Lobengula concoct a letter for delivery to Queen Victoria. In it the king set out his claims to Mashonaland – including the Mazoe river region – and protested against Portuguese encroachments in his domains. 'I send two of my headmen to England,' the letter ended, 'to the Queen, to ask how these things can be. To ask for protection.' At the same time, Lobengula gave secret verbal instructions to his *indunas*. There are various interpretations of these instructions. According to one report, the *indunas* were told: 'There are so many people who come here and tell me they are sent by the Queen; ask her who is the one she has really sent.' It is possible that he also commanded them to deny that he had given away his country to Rhodes and he may even have encouraged them to repudiate the Rudd concession. Certainly when Rhodes learned of the mission, he suspected the worst.

The party left Bulawayo in December 1888 and were away for the best part of a year. They started their journey by travelling south through the Transvaal, so as to avoid being intercepted in Bechuanaland. On reaching Kimberley, Maund met Dr Jameson in the Kimberley Club and was taken to see Rhodes at Jameson's cottage. According to Maund, Rhodes was lying on his bed when they arrived. (This was by no means unusual. Whenever he was at home, Rhodes tended to take to his bed. Notoriously restless – he could never sit at a desk for long – he appears to have welcomed any opportunity to lie down in private. Could this be an indication of his chronic ill-health, evidence of the bouts of exhaustion that result from a faulty heart? For some of his visitors his bedside interviews were an embarrassment, but for Rhodes they were probably a necessity.) Prostrate as Rhodes was, his mind remained alert. Maund was subjected to a lively interrogation.

Why, Rhodes wanted to know, had he travelled by way of the Transvaal? Did he not appreciate that the Rudd concession was unassailable? Maund's replies were evasive and he refused, when asked, to show Rhodes the letter he was taking to the Queen. Failing to bully Maund into submission, Rhodes tried to bribe him. Cawston and Gifford, he hinted, were not to be trusted. The Exploration Company would let Maund down; he would be wise to join the Rhodes group. To illustrate his point, Rhodes cited some of the people who had benefited from his patronage. But Maund refused to be swayed. In the end, Rhodes lost his temper. If Maund is to be believed, he threatened to have the mission stopped at Cape Town. The High Commissioner, he said, would prevent them leaving for England. He was not bluffing. When Maund arrived in Cape Town, he came under pressure from Sir Hercules Robinson who, writing to the Colonial Office, branded him as a liar and an agitator. The *indunas*, Robinson told his superiors, were not royal councillors but merely two 'natives'.

But then things took an unexpected turn. In London, George Cawston and Lord Gifford were having second thoughts. Having failed to get the government's blessing for their enterprise, they recognized that it would be to their advantage to join forces with Rhodes. Urged on by Lord Knutsford, the Colonial Secretary, they decided to start negotiating a merger. In January 1889, shortly after Maund had left Kimberley, George Cawston telegraphed Rhodes suggesting an amalgamation. This was language that Rhodes understood. Not only would it strengthen his chances of obtaining a Royal Charter but it gave him the weapon he needed to deal with Maund. He hurried to Cape Town.

According to Maund, his meeting with Rhodes was highly satisfactory. Bullying tactics were apparently no longer necessary. Maund not only proved pliant but he agreed, at last, to show Rhodes the letter to the Queen. On reading it, Rhodes was both relieved and delighted. He, no less than Lobengula, wanted to halt the Portuguese and the king's request for protection provided him with another argument in favour of a Royal Charter. The letter, he beamed, was 'the very stick' he needed.

Maund's status was upgraded overnight. No longer a 'liar and an agitator', he was now seen as a loyal ambassador accompanying two of

Lobengula's trusted *indunas* to England. With the approval of Sir Hercules Robinson, the party was allowed to continue on their journey. But the verbal instructions, given by Lobengula to Babayan and Mshete, remained secret.

*   *   *

Shortly after Maund's departure, Rhodes also sailed for England. He arrived in London in March 1889 and immediately set to work preparing the ground for the granting of a Royal Charter. His first concern was to eliminate any possible claims by rival concessionaires. Not only did he have to conclude the amalgamation with Cawston and Gifford, but he had to settle with a number of individuals who had secured, or claimed they had been granted, concessions in the Ndebele territories. This he did by the well-tried process of incorporation and, when this was not possible, by outright purchase of all the existing concessions awarded by Lobengula and local Shona chieftains. There were occasional difficulties but these were quickly overcome. Rhodes was a past-master at smoothing the way to an amalgamation and few – not even Cawston and Gifford – had the financial resources to match his.

Next he set about cultivating influential supporters. Among these was W. T. Stead, the editor of the *Pall Mall Gazette* and one of the most powerful journalists of his day. Stead, who had earlier been suspicious of Rhodes's activities, approached their first interview in a cautious mood. He came away completely captivated. 'Mr Rhodes is my man,' he wrote joyously to his wife. 'I have just had three hours talk with him . . . . His ideas are federation, expansion, consolidation of the Empire.' The fact that Rhodes had offered him £20,000 for a share in the *Pall Mall Gazette* might have had something to do with his enthusiasm, but from then on Stead was included among Rhodes's devoted disciples. Although others were not quite so susceptible, Rhodes was able to muster sufficient support in Britain to ensure the success of 'Runnymede'.

During his first few weeks in London, Rhodes was in constant touch with Edward Maund. They were now the best of friends and Maund appears to have made constant reports on his progress. He was moving in the highest circles.

Shortly after their arrival, Maund and the *indunas* had called upon Lord Knutsford. Details of their visit are vague but it is thought that, during the interview, the *indunas* passed on the verbal instructions they had received from Lobengula. How much Maund knew about this is uncertain. The party were then taken to see Queen Victoria. On this occasion, Maund delivered the letter of complaint against the Portuguese and the *indunas* were given presents to take back to their king.

Maund's report of this audience delighted Rhodes. He appears to have regarded the Queen's gifts as a means of 'squaring' Lobengula. 'You go back to him,' he told Maund, 'with your *indunas* and presents from the Queen and keep the old buster [bastard?] happy.'

For the rest of their stay, the *indunas* were treated to the usual round of festivities accorded to visiting African dignitaries. They were lionized by the press, fêted at public functions. One of the highspots was a demonstration of Britain's might at an Aldershot military display. (A few years earlier the Zulu king, Cetshwayo, had been similarly entertained when a 35-ton gun was fired, at Woolwich Arsenal, for his benefit.) Unfortunately the Aldershot manoeuvres were somewhat marred when the machine-guns, which were meant to impress, repeatedly jammed. There was also a gala breakfast, hosted by the Aborigines Protection Society, whose chairman, Sir Fowell Buxton, expressed the specious hope that the day would soon come when the Ndebele and the English would meet 'in the valleys of the Limpopo as happily as they did that day at Westminster'.

But not all of Maund's reports were encouraging. At the end of March he was handed a draft of Lord Knutsford's official reply to Lobengula's letter to the Queen. In it no mention was made of Portuguese encroachment: for the most part it dealt with the importunities of the Queen's subjects. Lobengula was advised to treat the petitioners to his kraal with caution and not to grant exclusive concessions to those who asked first. 'A King,' the letter concluded, in an attempt at African imagery, 'gives a stranger an ox, not his whole herd of cattle, otherwise what would other strangers have to eat?'

The implications of the letter were clear: Lobengula was bound to see it as a warning against the Rudd concession.

This apparent *volte-face* by Lord Knutsford is puzzling. After all, he had known of Rhodes's intentions from the outset, and yet he had encouraged the merger with Cawston and Gifford's Exploring Company and had seemed favourably disposed towards the granting of a Royal Charter. Why was he now putting doubts into Lobengula's head? Why should his public word differ so radically from his private assurances? One explanation is that he had been influenced in some way by Maund. It is possible that Maund was playing a double game and, despite his obligations to the Exploring Company (as well as Rhodes), he may still have had his eye on a concession in the Mazoe region. But it might have been less sinister than that. Could it be that Queen Victoria, who always respected the wishes of indigenous rulers, had been told of Lobengula's instructions to the *indunas* and had advised Knutsford accordingly? The letter was being written in her name and would have to have her sanction. Whatever the truth, Lord Knutsford's draft was bad news for Rhodes.

116

There is only Maund's word for what happened next. He claimed that Rhodes, on being shown Knutsford's letter, angrily demanded that the wording be altered. Maund was told to return to the Colonial Office to try and persuade Knutsford to send a more ambiguous message to Lobengula. This proved impossible. Knutsford explained that the Queen, who had approved his draft, had since gone abroad; he had no authority to tamper with royal correspondence. Rhodes then came up with a more drastic solution. Besides Knutsford's official reply, Maund had been given a letter by the Aborigines Protection Society which likewise warned the Ndebele king against parting with his property; Rhodes now suggested that, on his return voyage, Maund should drop both letters overboard 'by accident'. This Maund refused to do.

Rhodes told a different story. He claimed he was never shown Knutsford's letter. Writing to George Cawston, six months later, Rhodes accused Maund of deliberately deceiving him. Maund was once again demoted and branded a liar. 'If it was not so serious,' fumed Rhodes, 'it would be laughable to think that our own servant should be devoting his brains at our expense to destroy all our plans.'

It is difficult to accept either version. Both Rhodes and Maund had reasons for lying and neither of them was trustworthy. This appears to have been the opinion of the Aborigines Protection Society who, taking no chances, arranged for their letter to be published in a Mafeking paper before it was delivered. Maund therefore had no option but to hand over both letters when he arrived back in Bulawayo. In so doing he sparked off a violent outcry, which did indeed threaten to ruin Rhodes's plans.

*   *   *

If Rhodes knew of the contents of the Queen's letter, he did not allow this to interfere with 'Runnymede'. He had come to London to obtain a Royal Charter and had no intention of leaving until the signing of that Charter was in sight. Too much depended upon his receiving the blessing of the British government for his central African manoeuvrings for him to retreat at this stage of the game.

He pushed ahead with his campaign of wooing influential allies. Besides enlisting W. T. Stead, he received enthusiastic support from Flora Shaw, the respected colonial correspondent of *The Times*, and he was later helped by the arrival in England of his friend Sir Hercules Robinson.

In some quarters Rhodes had already prepared the way. The previous year, when he had visited England to sound out Lord Knutsford, he had been introduced to Charles Stewart Parnell whose

Irish Nationalist party held eighty-five seats in the House of Commons. As a result of his talks and subsequent correspondence with Parnell, Rhodes agreed to donate £5,000 to the Irish party and pledged a further £5,000. To all outward appearances, this donation was made to win Parnell over to the idea of Imperial Federation but there can be little doubt that Rhodes had his own ends in mind. When the time came for him to apply for a Charter, the Irish party – usually opposed to such applications – remained significantly silent.

But the road to Runnymede was by no means smooth. Rhodes had his opponents. Prominent among these was his old antagonist from his Bechuanaland days, the missionary John Mackenzie. With the backing of the Aborigines Protection Society, Mackenzie did his utmost to expose Rhodes as a potential dictator of central Africa, ready to exploit the black inhabitants of Matabeleland. At Westminster there was also the formidable South Africa Committee. This group of eminent parliamentarians included such men as J. Arnold Foster, a future War Minister, Albert Grey, the heir to the 4th Earl Grey, the Earl of Fife – who was soon to be made a Duke when he married the eldest daughter of the Prince of Wales – and the astute and debonair Joseph Chamberlain. Many of them were suspicious of Rhodes and seemed unlikely to support his application. Their doubts were shared by other members of the House of Commons – most notably by that vociferous Radical, Henry Labouchere – as well as by the free-trade champions of the London Chamber of Commerce. It was an odd mixture: odder still considering how little known Rhodes was in London at this time.

Many of the top politicians had only the vaguest idea of who Rhodes was or what he represented. Lord Salisbury, the Prime Minister, for instance, once referred to him as 'rather a pro-Boer MP in South Africa,' Lord Knutsford had earlier confused him with the Imperial Secretary at the Cape, and even the more knowledgeable Joseph Chamberlain was firmly convinced that he was an anti-Imperialist colonial and spoke of him as 'an Afrikander.' But if the British politicians were confused, Rhodes was not. He knew exactly what he was doing. One of the most remarkable things about his bid for the Charter was the way in which he not only out-witted his opponents but won many of them to his side.

An application for the Charter was drawn up on 30 April 1889 in the names of Rhodes, Rudd, Beit and Lord Gifford. By it the petitioners sought powers which would enable them to extend railways and telegraphs to the Zambesi, to encourage colonization and promote trade and to exploit such mineral concessions as they had acquired. The fact that they were asking for a great deal more than had been granted by Lobengula did not seem to bother anyone. Certainly it did not bother Lord Knutsford. In passing the petition to the Prime Minister (who also acted as Foreign Secretary) Knutsford advanced Rhodes's earlier argument: with the grant of a Charter the means would be available for expanding the Empire 'on the cheap'. Or, as he politely put it, 'diplomatic difficulties and heavy expenditure' would be avoided.

Knutsford was also at pains to point out that, Charter or no Charter, the petitioners were perfectly entitled to 'incorporate themselves under the Joint Stock Companies Acts' and that if they did so, their company would not be 'directly subject to control by Her Majesty's government', as would be the case under a Royal Charter. In other words there was no point in opposing the application. Lobengula and his subjects were not mentioned.

The underlying cynicism of Knutsford's recommendation was all too apparent. If Lord Salisbury recognized this cynicism, he did not object to it. Archetypal Tory that he was, the Prime Minister welcomed Rhodes's cost-cutting proposals and did not seem particularly concerned about the rights of an obscure African ruler. But he did doubt the wisdom of granting a Royal Charter to a group of unknown financiers. He hinted that the public would feel more reassured, were the proposed new company to have some men of social standing among its directors. Rhodes took the hint. Equating, in true British fashion, respectability with a title, he widened his search for allies.

Precisely how Rhodes gained the aristocratic support he needed has never been revealed. It is known that he was helped by his friend, Colonel Euan Smith, and that some of the men he first approached turned him down. The secret of his later successes remains a mystery. But succeed he did. His original choice for the chairmanship of the new venture was Lord Balfour of Burleigh who, after accepting, felt obliged to withdraw when he was appointed to a minor government post. The position was then offered to the Duke of Abercorn – the politically experienced owner of large estates – who was apparently delighted to accept. Rhodes then turned his attention to his opponents on the South Africa Committee. Here he scored his greatest triumphs. Not only did he persuade the newly created Duke of Fife to serve as a director, thus forging a link with the royal family, but he set to work on the conscientious Albert Grey who, despite warnings from Joseph Chamberlain, eventually agreed to join the board. Greater prestige – two Dukes and the heir to an earldom – Rhodes could not have hoped for. Now, smiled upon by the government, blessed by the aristocracy and endorsed by two members of the South Africa Committee, Rhodes could discount all other opposition. His charm had not let him down.

The formal application for a Royal Charter was submitted on 13 July. It first passed through the Foreign and Colonial offices for scrutiny. The final draft was then forwarded to the Privy Council for approval. This granted (although not without some objections), the

Charter was sealed under Letters of Patent and signed by Queen Victoria on 29 October 1889.

By that time, Rhodes had returned to South Africa. He saw no point in wasting his time in London. 'I have done all I can,' he told his London lawyer, 'and I will leave you to have the formalities settled.' His distaste for his native land was as strong as ever. Fashionable society bored him and, throughout his stay, he had resisted all attempts to lionize him. Once news of what he was up to leaked out, he was besieged by hostesses trying to lure him to their tables, but he was not to be drawn. 'I see no reason,' he declared, 'to make my interior a dustbin for anyone.' As the social pressure mounted, Rhodes became increasingly impatient and finally decided to book his passage home. He had more important business to attend to in Africa.

*   *   *

The Royal Charter had been granted to the British South Africa Company. This was the company that Rhodes had formed to achieve his aims in central Africa: from now on it was to be known to the public as the Chartered Company. The powers granted to this new and untried company were enormous, far beyond anything adumbrated in the Rudd concession.

Although he failed – temporarily, at least – to have the Bechuanaland Protectorate placed within the Chartered Company's grasp, Rhodes was successful in most other respects. Refusing to be confined to territories south of the Zambesi, he had insisted that no boundary be set for the company's operations in the north. (In agreeing to this, the British government was, in effect, challenging the Portuguese and giving Rhodes a free hand in the heart of Africa.) More specifically, the company's field of operations was defined as 'the region of South Africa lying to the north of British Bechuanaland, and to the north and west of the South African Republic [the Transvaal] and to the west of the Portuguese Dominions.'

The nature of the company's operations in this vast, but still vaguely defined, area was also set out. Rhodes and his fellow directors were authorized to enter into treaties, acquire further concessions, maintain a police force and exercise the 'powers necessary for the purpose of government, and the preservation of public order in or for the protection' of the territories they controlled. They could also build railways, roads and harbours, engage in mining and other industries, establish banks and waterworks, own or charter ships, make land grants and conduct any lawful trade, commerce or business. For its part, the company was obliged to pay due regard to the religion and customs of the indigenous inhabitants, to combat the slave trade and 'domestic servitude' and to 'prevent the sale of any spirits or other intoxicating liquor to any natives'. All the company's activities were subject to the approval of the British government and the right of repeal was reserved for the Queen if 'at any time it is made to appear to Us in Our Council that the Company has substantially failed to observe and conform to the provisions of this Our Charter'.

If Rhodes had been questioned about the discrepancies that existed between the comprehensive powers granted to the Chartered Company and the mining provisions of the Rudd concession, he would have had an answer – but it is doubtful whether he would have produced it. The fact was that the Chartered Company and the Rudd concession were two separate undertakings. The Rudd concession was owned by a body known as the Central Search Association which Rhodes had set up, in April 1889, before he formed the British South Africa Company. Some of the directors of Central Search – including Rhodes, Beit and Gifford – also became directors of the Chartered Company but this in no way altered the financial independence of the two concerns. Not until after the Charter had been granted was an arrangement reached by which Central Search allowed the British South Africa Company to use the Rudd Concession in return for 50 per cent of its profits. In this way, the directors of Central Search were entitled to half the net profits of the Chartered Company without being responsible for any possible failure or debts incurred. This arrangement lasted until July 1890, when Central Search became the United Concessions Company with an increased capital of £4,000,000 – derived from its claim on the profits of the Chartered Company. It was later agreed that the United Concessions Company should be bought out for one million specially created £1 shares in the Chartered Company. As, by that time, the value of Chartered shares had more than trebled – they stood at between £3 and £4 each – and were still rising, the rake-off for Rhodes and his small circle of cronies promised to be enormous.

This financial juggling was typical of Rhodes. So devious was he that, when the Charter was granted, the government was unaware that the British South Africa Company did not own the Rudd concession. Lord Knutsford had not even asked to see this all-important document; which, considering his recommendation, is astonishing. Not until 1892, when the Salisbury government was replacd by a Liberal administration, was the truth revealed.

When Lord Ripon, the new Colonial Secretary, discovered that his predecessor had been 'misled' he was outraged. Angry notes passed between officials in Whitehall and there were suggestions that the Charter be revoked. Rhodes, however, was spared this humiliation. The new government, like the old, could not meet the cost of taking over undeveloped African territories and while, of course, they protested that they could have handled the original negotiations better, they decided to let things stay as they were. Not for the first time, and by no means for the last, had Rhodes cornered the British government into identifying its imperial interests with his own.

It is from this period in his life – the post-Charter years – that the most telling criticism of Rhodes can be dated. His bid for financial and political supremacy in Africa has been described as unscrupulous, callous, shabby and contemptible. He is said to have tyrannized his enemies and deceived his friends. In amalgamating the diamond mines he had resorted to tactics which were less than honest: he tricked his opponents into submission and brought ruin to many of the smaller business men in Kimberley. But even worse was the way in which he bamboozled Lobengula into thinking that he was seeking mining rights when, in fact, his intention was to rob the king of his country. At the same time, Rhodes allowed the British public to assume he had the right to occupy Lobengula's territories. Accompanying his every move there are stories of bribery, double-dealing and sharp practice.

It is easy to appreciate how the theory arose that after the death of Neville Pickering Rhodes became hardened and more ruthless. The time factor supports such a theory. Pickering died towards the end of 1886 and Rhodes's relentless drive northwards started in 1887. To accept such an explanation of the apparent change in Rhodes's personality would, of course, be an oversimplification. Men approaching middle-age cannot change their personalities: they can only, at most, come to terms with life and so reveal their hidden or suppressed characteristics. But, for Rhodes, this process may well have been influenced by Pickering's death. By losing the only person with whom he was emotionally involved he was left without an heir. From now on there would be no chosen individual to whom he could entrust his self-appointed mission in life: his vision of a world inspired by Anglo-Saxon values would be passed on to an impersonal group of trustees. This must have made his own task appear more urgent. And he knew his time was short. 'Everything in the world is too short,' he once told Lord Rosebery. 'Life and fame and achievement, everything is too short.'

But there was more to it than that. Rhodes's dream of extending the British Empire was older than his friendship with Pickering: he would have pursued it whatever happened. It was the nature of the quest rather than the nature of the man that produced the latter-day Rhodes. Empires, as he was the first to admit, are rarely established by philanthropists. 'Pure philanthropy is all very well in its way,' he said, 'but philanthropy plus five per cent is a good deal better.' It was cynicism, but cynicism with a motive. 'Money is power,' was his constant cry, 'and what can one accomplish without power? . . . Ideas are no good without money.' His idea, rightly or wrongly, was to spread British civilization and bring peace to the world. To achieve his Utopia, he needed money and he needed power. But the power he sought can only be obtained at the expense of others; it is rarely wielded by saints.

CHAPTER NINE

The Pioneers

Before leaving for London to negotiate the Charter, Rhodes had taken another important step. By the beginning of 1889, sufficient Martini-Henry rifles had been amassed for him to dispatch the first half of the consignment of arms promised to Lobengula under the Rudd concession. But the business of transporting five hundred rifles to Matabeleland presented problems. With everyone anxious to disguise the fact that the Ndebele were being supplied with arms, it was essential that a trustworthy person be put in charge of the operation. Rhodes's first choice is said to have been Charles Rudd, but unfortunately Rudd was ill and Rhodes had to look elsewhere.

He did not have far to look: he found the man he needed under his own roof. Dr Leander Starr Jameson, the man with whom he had shared a cottage for over two years, seemed to meet all his requirements. Not only was Jameson bright and energetic, but he possessed just the right blend of dash, daring and loyalty to carry off such a tricky undertaking.

According to Ian Colvin, Jameson's somewhat imaginative biographer, Rhodes had some difficulty in talking the dapper little doctor into accepting the assignment. Jameson, he claims, had his Kimberley practice to consider and was reluctant to leave his patients. He knew all about Rhodes's plans for the British Empire and found them exciting and inspiring, but he was a professional man with little taste for exploring the wilds. But Rhodes wore him down. It may have been Rhodes's persuasiveness; it may have been, as Colvin implies, Jameson's sense of duty to his friend or the fact that he could not resist a gamble – for the expedition promised to be a matter of chance – but it seems equally possible that the wily doctor succumbed to the mercenary glint in Rhodes's eye.

'I leave to-morrow morning for Matabeleland,' Jameson wrote to his brother, from Kimberley, on 2 February 1889, 'drive up about 250 miles to catch my wagons which started a fortnight ago. Then about a month's trek to the King's kraal, after that doubtful . . . . Shooting and see the country is the ostensible object of the trip; but possibilities of gold in the future also enter into it.'

124

Jameson was accompanied by a medical colleague, Dr Rutherfoord Harris, whom he described as 'a very nice companion'. Not everyone spoke of the loquacious Dr Harris so favourably. Then thirty-three, Harris had arrived in South Africa some seven years earlier and, like many another medical man, had quickly ingratiated himself with Rhodes. A coarse, ambitious adventurer, he came to be regarded as a loud-mouthed braggart and born intriguer whose penchant for mischief-making caused Rhodes endless trouble. Even the well-disposed Jameson later dismissed Harris as 'really a muddling ass – on the surface a genius but under the crust as thick as they are made'.

But that was in the future. When the two doctors set out for Matabeleland they were the best of friends. Once they had caught up with the wagons, they made their way slowly across the Bechuanaland waste lands and reached the Matabeleland border at the beginning of April. Here they encountered an *impi* of fierce-looking Ndebele whom they succeeded in bribing with an assortment of 'pink beads, brass buttons and blue calico'. Their success, however, was short-lived. On arriving at a frontier post, known as Manyami's kraal, they were stopped and told they could travel no further. The order to halt them had come from Lobengula.

Discouraging as it was, this display of hostility could have come as no surprise. They must, in fact, have been anticipating some opposition. Two weeks before Jameson left Kimberley, a notice had appeared in a Bechuanaland newspaper announcing that Lobengula had suspended the Rudd concession. Although the authenticity of this announcement was disputed – it was said to bear Lobengula's signature but was suspected of being issued by a rival concessionaire – its publication underlined rumours that all was not well at Bulawayo. Indeed, appearing when it did, it may have contributed to Rhodes's decision to dispatch the rifles. For only by persuading Lobengula to accept the rifles could the possibility of the king repudiating the concession be lessened. This thought may well have prompted Jameson to defy Lobengula's order; leaving Harris in charge of the rifles he rode on alone to Bulawayo.

As it happened, the king was not at Bulawayo but at Umvutshwa, his private kraal. This is where he received Jameson. Unfortunately there is no reliable record of the meetings which followed. It is claimed, however, that Lobengula welcomed Jameson's arrival and was captivated by his breezy bedside manner. This is probably true – Jameson's charm was as renowned as Rhodes's persuasiveness – but it is not the entire story. There is every reason to think that, when the purpose of the doctor's visit was discussed, Lobengula was less than friendly. He agreed to allow the rifles to be transported to his kraal but he refused to 'receive' them officially. In other words, he gave a firm indication that he was having second thoughts about the Rudd concession. This was undoubtedly a setback for Jameson. All he could do, in the circumstances, was to arrange for one of the white traders at the kraal, Benjamin Wilson, to act as superintendent of the firearms until a more favourable arrangement was made.

A store was built for the rifles at Umvutshwa. There they remained – together with the second half of the consignment, delivered in May 1889 – unacknowledged by Lobengula for over three years. However, the monthly payment of £100, stipulated in the Rudd concession, continued to be paid. 'I often wonder,' Wilson was to note in his diary, 'if the King thinks these things [the rifles] and a few sovereigns he gets every month, is the price of his country and his throne and maybe his own life. Time will tell.' He was wiser than he knew; time did indeed tell.

Jameson's visit was brief. He stayed in Matabeleland a mere ten days. On his return journey he was joined by the hapless Rochfort Maguire who, after his escapade at the sacred fountain, had chosen this time to flee the country. By the time they arrived back in Kimberley, Rhodes had already left for London.

If, as is claimed, Jameson established a close *rapport* with Lobengula during this, his first, encounter with the king, he made no mention of it on his return. The letter he wrote to his brother, on 14 May 1889, was guarded and not very optimistic. 'Matabeleland was a little rough,' he confessed; 'but I am glad I went, though I don't think financially I shall be any the better.'

*   *   *

Once Jameson had departed, and Maguire had fled, Matabele Thompson – Rhodes's sole remaining agent – was left to face the growing hostility of the Ndebele alone. With only Lobengula standing between him and the rancour of the *indunas* he had every reason to fear for his safety. His nervousness was shared by his Zulu servant Charlie, who, on tucking him up in bed one night, whispered: 'Oh, master, we never come out of this country alive. The Matabili go kill us, I know.'

Time and again, Thompson was summoned by Lobengula to explain his conduct and was invariably accused of being a liar. He could say nothing to convince the king that Rudd and Maguire were not plotting an invasion of Matabeleland. Why, demanded Lobengula, had they left so hurriedly? Why had Maguire tried to steal one of his slaves? Why had Rudd taken the 'fly-blown' concession to the Queen? On leaving the royal kraal, Thompson would be subjected to further questioning by the suspicious *indunas*. That he came to think of himself as the man most hated by the blacks and whites at Bulawayo, is hardly surprising.

The younger warriors, spurred on by the anti-Rhodes faction among the whites, continued to agitate against the Rudd concession. They insisted that, by it, Lobengula had signed away his country. The king, bewildered and alarmed, turned to the local missionaries for advice. Was it true, he wanted to know, that he had been deceived by the 'brothers' of *Ulodzi* [Rhodes]? Why did *Ulodzi* not come to Bulawayo himself? What powers were contained in the concession? Could white men come and dig where they pleased in his domains? How many white men would come and how could he control them? The answers he received brought him little comfort: everyone seemed to interpret events to suit themselves.

Thompson felt more insecure by the day. It was obvious that he could not rely on Lobengula's protection indefinitely. Any incident, however slight, was liable to cause offence and lead to further intimidation. If this happened he was helpless to defend himself. Things were not helped by his inability to meet the *indunas*' earlier demands. They had asked for the Rudd concession to be returned but, with Rhodes having left for London, it took months for that crucial document to reach Bulawayo. Strangely enough, when it did arrive, Thompson seems not to have produced it for inspection. He may have shown it to the *indunas* but if he did he makes no mention of their reaction. All he says is that he buried it in a pumpkin gourd, with some corn seed, and told his servant that if he 'happened to be knocked on the head the growing corn would mark the place where the Concession lay.' The fact that he had received a note from Rhodes warning him not to part with the document until a knife was held to his throat may account for his being so secretive. The *indunas* were later fobbed off with a copy of the concession.

In the meantime, Thompson was forced to live on his wits. From time to time he toyed with the idea of making a bolt for it and leaving things to sort themselves out, but he could not face the risk. Apart from the difficulty in getting away, he says, 'I felt that I must stay and keep the Concession safe for our partnership. This I was determined to do at all costs.'

Things came to a head in August. Then it was that Maund, Babayan and Mshete returned from their mission to London, bringing with them the letters from Queen Victoria and the Aborigines Protection Society. The contents of the letter from the Aborigines Protection Society were already known but the Queen's letter, advising Lobengula not to give away his 'whole herd' to strangers, proved explosive. It confirmed the king's worst fears. By that time Lobengula had made up his mind to revoke the Rudd concession and had written to London to say as much; now, with the Queen's backing, he decided to restate his opposition. After the two letters had been read out to a gathering at the royal kraal – attended by the white men at Bulawayo – Lobengula summoned John Moffat to take down his reply. In this, his second repudiation of the Rudd concession, he emphasized that only his 'servants' would be allowed to dig for gold. This is what he had been told would happen when he signed the concession and he was determined that those verbal assurances should be observed.

But the matter did not end there. Lobengula's wrath was matched by the *indunas'* lust for revenge. It was now clear that they had been deceived by Rhodes's agents and, more seriously, betrayed by Lotshe – the *induna* who had sided with Rudd and his companions. Ndebele justice demanded a rolling of heads. At an *indaba* held at the beginning of September, the process of exacting retribution was set in motion.

Precisely what happened at this harrowing, long drawn-out, meeting is a matter of dispute. Some witnesses say one thing, some another. Thompson, for instance, claims that a copy of the concession was produced and that he, squatting on his haunches in the broiling sun and forbidden to move, was interrogated about its wording for several hours. One of the white men present, he says, tried to trick him into admitting that the concession sought to deprive the Ndebele of their land and only the timely arrival of Lobengula rescued him from his ordeal. Another version has it that the meeting was dominated by Lobengula, who first accused Charles Helm of deceiving him and then attacked Lotshe for 'blinding his eyes'.

Whatever the truth, the outcome was inevitable: Lotshe, the so-called 'prime minister', owner of large herds of cattle and long-hated by the envious *indunas*, was made to pay a traitor's penalty. According to Thompson, he was sentenced to death and executed – killed by a single blow of a knobkerrie – shortly afterwards. (Here again there is an alternative version, which claims he was strangled several days later.) Lotshe's death was followed by wholesale slaughter. On the night of his execution his wives, his kinsmen and all their dependants were rounded up and brutally butchered and his kraal was set alight. The total toll in human lives is estimated to have been upwards of three hundred men, women and children. Queen Victoria could not have foreseen the result of her well-intentioned letter; nor, it is said, did Lobengula welcome the death of his once-trusted adviser. Only the *indunas* rejoiced.

Thompson was not at Bulawayo on the night of the massacre. Earlier, in a state of near-panic, he had decided to seek advice from Charles Helm and had driven over to Helm's mission station at Hope Fountain. On his return journey, he was overtaken by an unknown African riding a grey horse. 'Tomoson,' the man called out as he passed, 'the king says the killing of last night is not yet over.' Knowing Lobengula, Thompson took this as a friendly warning and stopped his

wagon to think it over. As he did so, he spotted a crowd of Ndbele warriors advancing towards him. The sight of them was sufficient for his
nerve to snap. He later hotly denied that he was attacked by 'the funks'
but it is obvious that he was in no mood to take any further risks.
Unharnessing one of his horses, he leapt on it and rode flat out to the
nearest white-owned store. Here he borrowed a saddle and headed for
the border.

Thompson's experiences in the Bechuanaland desert were no less
hazardous than Rudd's had been the previous year. Forced to sleep in
the branches of a tree to avoid prowling lions, weakened by dysentery
and dehydrated by the heat, he ran out of water and almost died of
thirst. By the time he reached Shoshong – the capital of the Ngwato,
ruled over by Lobengula's doughty opponent Kgama (English spell-
ing: Khama) – Thompson was near the point of collapse. Revived by
the missionaries, he staggered on to Mafeking where he telegraphed
his wife, whom he had not seen for fifteen months. Then he sent a wire
to Rhodes.

'Nature,' Rhodes was fond of quoting, 'abhors a vacuum.' He had
just returned from London when he received Thompson's message,
informing him that a vacuum had been created in Matabeleland. His
first reaction was to send a 'frantic' reply to Thompson in Mafeking,
begging him to return to Bulawayo. What appears to have alarmed
him most was the thought of the precious concession lying buried close
to Lobengula's kraal. There had been no time for Thompson to retrieve
the concession and, should it now be discovered, the delicate negotiations of the past year would be seriously impaired. Even worse, the
possible destruction of the concession threatened to undermine the
base upon which the Charter had been granted. This, and the fact that
Lobengula had refused to 'receive' the rifles and was rumoured to have
repudiated the concession, made it imperative that the vacuum at
Bulawayo be filled. It was a matter of urgency, Rhodes insisted, that
the concession be unearthed and shown to Lobengula. 'You know
perfectly well,' he informed Thompson, 'it will not be ratified unless
you are present . . . if we lose the Concession we have nothing for the
Charter.' According to Thompson, Rhodes's pleas were supported by a
telegram from Sir Henry Loch, the new High Commissioner, who had
replaced the recently retired Sir Hercules Robinson.

For the next few days, Rhodes continued to bombard Thompson
with telegrams, letters and messages. He would, he explained, have
liked to have gone to Bulawayo himself but he simply could not spare
the time. Negotiations were then in progress to have the railway and
telegraph lines extended to the Matabeleland border – an extension
which Rhodes was financing; there was also the problem of raising a
police force to guard the northern territories; details concerning the

Charter had still to be settled and Rhodes was trying to talk President Kruger into giving up the Transvaal's claims to Lobengula's domains. Far too much was at stake for Rhodes to think of leaving Kimberley. A firmer hand was needed to deal with the capricious Ndebele monarch, a hand which could both guide and, if necessary, pressure Lobengula into acquiescence. Once again he turned to the man who, above all others, he felt he could trust: the wily Dr Jameson.

They were an incongruous pair, these two friends – the big, bovine-looking Rhodes, with his lumbering gait, flaccid face and heavy-lidded blue eyes, and the slim, doe-eyed and nimble little Jameson. The difference between them, however, was not simply a matter of looks: they were equally at odds in personality and temperament. Where Rhodes was ponderous, calculating and earnest, Jameson was sharp, impulsive and sophisticated. He was easy to get on with, a good mixer and very popular. These were qualities which Rhodes always found attractive. Indeed, this attraction is thought to have played a part in bringing them together, to have cemented their lives and strengthened their affection. Their natures, it is said, complemented each other perfectly and their friendship became 'as strong as a marriage bond'. It is a view which is easy to understand. But there was more to their friendship than a mere attraction of opposites. The two of them had a great deal in common. They were the same age and they came from similar backgrounds; both were products of large middle-class families. They were both life-long bachelors: women played no part in Rhodes's life and, as far as one can gather, very little in Jameson's. Both had been brought to South Africa by vaguely defined ailments and both suffered ill-health for most of their lives. Neither had made much of a mark at school, neither was particularly interested in organized sport; both shunned the company of intellectuals.

For all that it would be a mistake to regard their friendship as the coming together of soul mates. Subsequent events were to highlight the bond between Rhodes and Jameson and their relationship was talked about in dramatic, even romantic, terms. As a result, it is often assumed that Jameson replaced Pickering in Rhodes's life. This is very doubtful. There are many similarities between the two friendships and they were both important in Rhodes's life, but they were conducted on different emotional levels. Rhodes never, for instance, made Jameson his heir and only on his death bed did he include Jameson as one of his trustees. This is very different from the confidence he displayed in making Pickering his legatee. It has been said that Rhodes was wary of handing such a trust to Jameson because he considered him unstable. But this was said only after Jameson had plunged them both into disaster. Had Rhodes not had faith in Jameson's judgement in these early days he would surely never have trusted him with such vital and delicate missions. There is reason to suppose that Jameson had more of the makings of an Empire-builder than did Pickering but the fact remains that Rhodes never made him his heir.

The caution may not have been entirely on Rhodes's side. It could be that Jameson was too independent to allow himself to be taken over completely. He withstood Rhodes's blandishments for longer than most and when he agreed to undertake the first mission to Lobengula, he did so on his own terms. He was quite prepared to come back to his medical practice in Kimberley and even when he had become more deeply involved in Rhodes's plans, he tended to think of himself simply as a doctor on temporary leave. For Rhodes, this was hardly good enough; his demands were inclined to be exclusive. 'I must not only have you, but I must have your heart as well' he was to say to one young man whom he employed. 'If your best is to be given to me, my interests must be your interests.' It took Jameson a long time before he was prepared to go that far. In the often emotive language of Rhodes's critics, Jameson has been described as 'Rhodes's tool'. But Jameson was never a passive instrument; he was quite capable of making his own decisions.

His decision to accept Rhodes's second commission was taken with greater enthusiasm. Although he had recently told his family that he had no intention of returning to Matabeleland, he seems quickly to have changed his mind on being told of Thompson's flight from Bulawayo. 'I will go,' was his instant response, when Rhodes showed him Thompson's telegram. Rhodes was surprised by Jameson's eagerness. 'When will you start?' he asked. 'Tomorrow morning,' grinned Jameson.

This time he took two new companions. One was a Major Maxwell, whom Jameson described as a 'good-natured Guffy'; the other was Denis Doyle, a Natal-born jack-of-all-trades who, in one of his many incarnations, had been employed as the sanitary inspector of Kimberley. On this occasion, Doyle was to act as an interpreter. Travelling in a Cape-cart, the three men went first to Mafeking where they met the still-despondent Thompson. It was not the happiest of meetings but Thompson, declaring that this would be his last visit to Matabeleland, eventually agreed to join them. They arrived at Bulawayo, after the usual delays and uncertainties at the border post, on 17 October 1889.

As always seemed to be the case when Europeans visited the conspiracy-ridden Ndebele capital, there are conflicting versions of the reception given to Jameson's party. Lobengula is said to have been in a bad temper and his mood was suspicious. Apparently he had been drinking heavily – having been supplied with champagne and brandy by the concession-hungry whites – and was suffering from crippling bouts of gout and sore eyes. According to Jameson's biographer, the king's anger was directed mainly at Thompson. 'I don't want to see that man,' he is supposed to have said. 'A man does not doubt what his heart tells him to do, but he ran away without cause, and I do not want to see him any more.' Thompson, of course, disagrees. He claims that not only was he given a warm welcome but that he led the negotiations with Lobengula and was duly honoured by the king and presented with a Ndebele symbol of courage. Both versions were no doubt influenced by self-interest.

Whatever the truth, there can be little doubt that Jameson benefited from Lobengula's ill-health. He may have left his medical practice behind but he had brought along his medicine chest and with this he was able to work the white man's magic. After he had injected Lobengula with morphia and produced some soothing ointment for his eyes, things brightened up considerably. Freed from pain, and flattered by Jameson's banter, the king was easily coaxed out of his sulks. From then on all was sweetness and light.

The concession was unearthed and produced for Lobengula's inspection. Thompson's claim that a reading of this document was sufficient to change Lobengula's attitude, is extremely dubious. (How, one wonders, did it differ from the copy that had been so hotly debated before Thompson fled Bulawayo?) Another account has it that Lobengula scarcely glanced at the concession when it was handed to him and it was only after a lengthy discussion with Jameson and John Moffat that he appeared to capitulate. This seems more feasible. Even so, the picture remains murky.

An agreement was reached but precisely what was agreed is not clear. There were no independent witnesses to the discussion. Lobengula may simply have procrastinated, have told Jameson what he wanted to hear and so given the wrong impression. As Rochfort Maguire once remarked, the king 'had an extraordinary dislike to come to a definite decision upon any subject, coupled with extreme unwillingness to say No.' Significantly, Lobengula still refused to acknowledge the rifles stored at Umvutshwa.

Jameson, however, was convinced that he had broken down Lobengula's resistance. He was to remain in Matabeleland, on and off, for four months. His main concern was to 'clear the road' for the Chartered Company's pioneers, who were then being recruited to occupy Lobengula's domains. As will be seen, various schemes for this occupation were discussed but, for one reason or another, the more drastic means of invasion were abandoned. In the end it was decided that the wisest course would be to secure Lobengula's co-operation. With this in view, Jameson approached the king with a seemingly innocuous request. He sought permission for a group of prospectors to commence

132

digging on the Matabeleland side of the Bechuanaland border. As mining operations had been carried out in this region for several years – mostly in Bechuanaland – Jameson's proposition seemed harmless enough. Permission was eventually given. But all was not as it seemed: this was the first step in what can only be regarded as a cynical manoeuvre. For, as Professor Keppel-Jones has pointed out, 'Jameson did not expect gold to be found there. His tactics were to report failure in that region and then ask for another place – meaning Mashonaland.'

While the pretence of digging went ahead, a somewhat bizarre scene was being played out at Bulawayo. On 27 January 1890 a party of military men – two officers, a corporal-major and a trooper of the Royal Horse Guards – arrived at the Ndebele capital on a special mission. Buttoned-up in their tight scarlet tunics and sporting top-boots, brass breastplates and helmets, these four guardsmen – sweltering in the heat of the African summer – made a splendid, if decidedly incongruous, impression. Such magnificence had never before been seen in Matabeleland. The soldiers were meant to impress. They had been sent as a courtesy gesture from Queen Victoria, in return for the visit of the two *indunas* to London. But they brought with them more than the Queen's compliments. The officers had been entrusted with Lord Knutsford's official reply to Lobengula's most recent letter. In that letter the king had, to all intents and purposes, repudiated the Rudd concession, and Knutsford's dispatch – making no mention of Rhodes – dealt with the king's complaints. Unfortunately, the officialese of the Colonial Office was so convoluted and boring that the dispatch was considered 'unintelligible rubbish'.

That at least was Jameson's opinion. He was in Bulawayo at the time and was shown Knutsford's reply before it was delivered to Lobengula. Never at a loss for a simple remedy, the good doctor promptly tore up the dispatch and 'rewrote it in a style calculated to please a savage monarch'. This version, not surprisingly, gave the Queen's blessing to Rhodes and the Chartered Company and, for good measure, warned the king against possible incursions by the Portuguese and the Transvaal Boers.

Amusing as it appeared at the time, Jameson's cavalier behaviour should not be laughingly dismissed. One of the important points made by Lord Knutsford in recommending that the British South Africa Company be granted a Royal Charter was that it provided the government with the means of controlling the company's activities. Hardly three months had passed between the granting of the charter and Jameson's display of contempt for British authority. By destroying an official communication, bearing the Queen's name, he left no doubt as to who was in control of affairs in central Africa.

Equally ominous is the fact that, unless the officers who delivered

133

the dispatch were completely irresponsible, Jameson's high-handedness must have been reported to Lord Knutsford. If this was the case, it is astonishing that no serious attempt seems to have been made to reassert the Crown's authority in this matter. That Rhodes later took for granted the complaisance of British colonial officials, when he embarked on an even more outrageous escapade, is hardly surprising. Blind eyes have a way of reflecting green lights.

There can be little doubt that Jameson's timely intervention benefited the Rhodes group. It had an 'excellent effect' on Lobengula. Not only was the king dazzled by the guardsmen's sparkling breast plates but he was impressed – if a little bewildered – by the Queen's apparent approval of the Chartered Company. This gave Jameson his opportunity. A day or two after the soldiers had gone clattering off, he again approached Lobengula. This time he explained that the diggers on the border had failed to find gold and were hesitant to move further north. The king suggested that they try somewhere else. 'Where?' asked Jameson. 'Oh, you know,' shrugged the king. That was all the encouragement Jameson needed. Pointing vaguely to the north-east – towards Mashonaland – he asked whether they could explore in that direction. When Lobengula raised no objections, Jameson pounced. He already knew the route Rhodes was planning to take and produced a map to explain how the new 'diggers' would avoid the Ndebele kraal and travel direct to Mashonaland. They would need help to cut a new road, he said, to take out trees and stumps so that wagons could pass through the rough country. Could Lobengula supply men for this work? Once again the king appeared agreeable. He told Jameson to find a place to dig; he would then provide the necessary labour.

Jameson could not have hoped for more. The agreement was merely a verbal one but, as he had recently demonstrated, the doctor set no great store by the written word. He had been 'given the road' and that was all that mattered. His relief offset any misgivings. For four months he had, as he put it, been living a 'funny life . . . in a wagon in the bush with the pure unadulterated savage – which they are. Very healthy, but not very luxurious,' and his one thought now was to get things moving. There was, he told his sister, 'a great probability of ructions in the future' but by that time he expected to be 'out of the country.' Shortly after his conversation with Lobengula, the triumphant Jameson rode south to report his success to Rhodes.

Whether Lobengula saw things in the same light is another matter. When conferring with Jameson, the king had been at his accommodating best: friendly, pliable and ready to fall in with the white man's plans. However, his reaction to – what he thought to be – the Queen's letter seems to belie Jameson's confidence. Perplexed by the contradictory messages he was receiving from London, Lobengula had second thoughts about the Colonial Office's 'recommendation' of Rhodes and the Chartered Company and, when dictating his reply, he was careful neither to confirm nor reject the Rudd concession. Unlike the impulsive doctor, the king obviously appreciated the difference between an official communication and an informal conversation.

*   *   *

While Jameson had been languishing in Bulawayo, Rhodes had been fully occupied in the Cape. On his return from England, he had set about extending the railway from Kimberley to the Matabeleland border, and pushed ahead with his plans to advance into Lobengula's domains. He realized there was no time to spare. Already there were rumours of a *trek* to the north by the Transvaal Boers and, in the east, the Portuguese were actively promoting their claims to large tracts of Mashonaland. It was largely a question of who made the first decisive move. Rhodes, with the Charter as good as in his pocket, was determined to out-manoeuvre his rivals.

His first concern was to recruit the men who would make up the pioneer column. On this score Rhodes had definite ideas. Never losing sight of his ultimate goal of a united South Africa, he stipulated that the pioneers should be politically sound and amenable to the inclusion of the new territories in his all-over scheme. For that reason, he wanted them to be recruited from influential families in the Cape, as well as from other sections of South Africa. (Rhodes was later to point out that, if anything were to go wrong on the march, it would be the fathers of these men who would bring pressure to bear on the 'imperial factor' to rescue them.) The recruits would, of course, have to be young and healthy and they would need to be accomplished in the skills necessary for establishing a civilized community in a primitive, relatively unknown, country. Artisans and tradesmen – butchers, bakers, builders and blacksmiths – these were the men to whom he wanted priority given. He was prepared to offer tempting inducements. All volunteers would be paid seven shillings and sixpence a day while on the march and rewarded with a grant of 3,000 acres of farmland and fifteen gold claims when they reached their destination. The column would be entirely male and, preferably, the men would be unmarried.

Before these conditions could be put into effect, however, the question of organization had to be settled. Rhodes had not only to think of the composition of the pioneer column but, with the uncertainties posed by possible hostility from the Ndebele, he also needed to ensure its safety. Some sort of disciplined, armed guard was required to accompany the would-be settlers. With this in mind, Rhodes approached Colonel Sir Frederick Carrington of the Bechuanaland Police. Carrington was available but only at a price: he estimated that he would need 2,500 men to perform the escort duties. As the cost of paying and equipping such a force promised to be prohibitive, Rhodes was forced to think again. It was at that stage that an enterprising young man named Frank Johnson made a timely appearance.

Frank Johnson was then twenty-three years old. Born in Norfolk, he had come to South Africa four years earlier as a quartermaster-sergeant in Sir Charles Warren's Bechuanaland expedition. Later he joined the Bechuanaland Police and then spent some time prospecting for gold in the Tati region and Mashonaland. Together with three friends – including Maurice Heany, an American – he had formed a syndicate and obtained a mining concession in Bechuanaland. Johnson's hope of being granted a similar concession in Mashonaland, however, was soon dashed. He fell foul of Lobengula, whom he regarded as crafty and treacherous, and he and his partners were obliged to quit the Ndebele territories after being fined £100 for witchcraft. Shortly after this, they merged their Bechuanaland interests with those of George Cawston and Lord Gifford and formed the Bechuanaland Exploration Company, of which Johnson became general manager. He continued to hold this position until Cawston and Gifford linked up with Rhodes when, to his disgust, he was cast aside. Rhodes would not acknowledge the validity of his concession and Cawston and Gifford refused him compensation.

According to Johnson, his next encounter with Rhodes came about by accident. In December 1889 he visited Kimberley and decided one morning to breakfast at the Kimberley Club. He was eating alone in the dining room when Rhodes walked in and, appearing to recognize him, sat down at his table. Without bothering to say good morning, Rhodes ordered bacon and eggs and launched into the story of his troubles. What, he wanted to know, did Johnson think of Colonel Carrington's estimate of 2,500 men? Johnson was flattered to be asked. He had once served under Carrington in the Bechuanaland Police and, at twenty-three, he was still young enough to welcome the opportunity of contradicting his former superior. He decided to cheer Rhodes up. 'Two thousand five hundred men!' he exclaimed. 'Absurd.' With a mere two hundred and fifty men he could walk through the country. Rhodes said nothing. He went on eating his bacon and eggs. Then he looked up. 'Do you mean that?' he asked. Johnson was taken aback. He had hardly given the problem any thought. His suggested 250 men had been an automatic reduction of the 2,500. 'I might just as easily have said twenty-five men as two hundred and fifty,' he later admitted. But, having committed himself, he decided to bluff it out. When Rhodes asked him how much he thought the expedition would cost, he said that if he were given some paper and a room in Rhodes's cottage he would work it out. To this, Rhodes agreed.

The calculation took Johnson four hours. He claims the estimate he produced for Rhodes was £87,500. Rhodes was delighted. Carrington's proposal had been in the region of a million sterling. Knowing next to nothing about Johnson, Rhodes there and then offered to put the young man in control of the expedition. But here Johnson's enthusiasm dried up. He had no wish to be employed by the Chartered Company. Still smarting from the treatment he had received from Cawston and Gifford, he was deeply suspicious of Rhodes's offer and, in any case, he was leaving that night for Cape Town. He turned down the proposal. Rhodes was flabbergasted. Here he was, presenting an unknown young man with the chance of a lifetime – the chance to add a new country to the Empire – and it was being refused. The discussion grew more and more heated until finally Rhodes, in a fit of temperament, slammed out of the room. That same evening, Johnson caught his train to Cape Town.

But Rhodes did not give up that easily. After showing Johnson's estimate to a friend, he cabled the young man and arranged to meet him in Cape Town. They met and for two hours paced up and down under the great oaks lining Government Avenue in the Cape Botanical Gardens, arguing the matter out. Rhodes alternated between bribes, flattery and appeals to duty; Johnson responded with objections to Cawston and Gifford's involvement with the Chartered Company. In the end, Rhodes won. Johnson agreed to accept the job, not as an employee of the Chartered Company but on contract. With the matter settled, they went off to Pooles Club for their second breakfast together. A new country – to be known first as Rhodesia and then as Zimbabwe – was about to be born. Heralded by the clatter of breakfast cups, it was to be delivered by an inexperienced young man who happened to catch the eye of its creator.

That, at least, was Frank Johnson's version of how the occupation of Mashonaland was arranged.

*   *   *

Johnson had an even stranger story to tell. For years this story was suppressed because of its implications and then it was ridiculed because it was thought to be untrue. There is reason to believe, however, that Johnson's interpretation of events was not entirely false. He may have exaggerated certain aspects of the secret agreement he claims to have entered into with Rhodes, but a conspiracy of some sort did exist. Not only are there hints of such a conspiracy in independent contemporary documents but, as will be seen, there is evidence to show that Rhodes was quite capable of the behaviour attributed to him by Johnson.

Was Rhodes prepared to agree to the murder of his opponents? That is the crux of this contentious issue. Johnson not only claims that he was but admits to instigating one of Rhodes's nefarious schemes. It happened, he says, shortly after Rhodes employed him to organize the pioneer column.

At that time – December 1889 – things were still very uncertain in Bulawayo. There was doubt about Lobengula's attitude towards the Rudd concession; it was not known whether he would sanction the arrival of a large body of 'diggers', let alone allow them to settle in his territory. Indeed it seemed likely that an advance by the pioneer column would be fiercely opposed. The news Rhodes was then receiving from his agents was far from reassuring. At the end of October, for instance, that unpredictable weathercock Lieutenant Maund had written to Rhodes suggesting that he bring matters to a head by invading Matabeleland and establishing himself by force. He included a plan of how this could be done. The newly-arrived Jameson, to whom Maund showed this plan, agreed. These were tactics which appealed to the ever-impatient doctor. After making a few enquiries, Jameson added his support to the idea of an invasion. 'I have spoken freely to Helm and Carnegie,' he wrote to Rutherfoord Harris, 'and they with Moffat are convinced that Rhodes is right in his decision that we will never be able to work peaceably alongside the natives, and that the sooner the brush is over the better.'

These suggestions were still fresh in Rhodes's mind when he discussed his problems with Frank Johnson. Once again his impulsive young friend came up with a madcap solution. For a reward of £150,000 and 50,000 morgen of land, he – together with his American partner, Maurice Heany – was prepared not only to organize the pioneer column but to carry out the invasion. He proposed to raise an auxiliary force of 500 men and then make lightning attacks on the principal Ndebele strongholds and so reduce the country to a state in which it could be peaceably occupied. The excuse to be given for these unprovoked attacks was that they would break the Ndebele power and free the surrounding tribes from the barbaric raids carried out by Lobengula's warriors. The king himself was to be captured and held hostage or, if necessary, murdered.

According to Johnson, Rhodes agreed to this plan. A contract was drawn up, signed by Johnson and Rhodes (on behalf of the Chartered Company) and witnessed by the conspiratorial Dr Rutherfoord Harris. Unfortunately, only a copy of this contract has survived. The original is said to have been buried by Johnson, in the garden of his house in Jersey in 1940, and has never been recovered. It is the lack of this original document – evidence of Rhodes's shadier activities had a way of conveniently disappearing – that has helped to cast doubts on Johnson's claims. Some historians have dismissed the plan to capture and kill Lobengula as pure nonsense, nothing more than the crude imaginings of a wild and totally irresponsible young man; others have examined Johnson's proposals and attempted to show that, even if Rhodes had agreed to them, they would have been impossible to implement. Much, of course, depends on the view taken of Cecil Rhodes.

Perhaps the most pertinent question to be asked is whether Rhodes would have compromised himself by signing such an incriminating contract. Would he have risked laying himself open to the political scandal that would have followed had things gone wrong? Would he not have been inviting blackmail in these circumstances? On the surface it would indeed look like a foolish move for Rhodes to have made. He was known to be rash, but would he have been *that* rash? Convincing as such arguments appear, they take little cognizance of Rhodes's cunning.

If Rhodes did enter into an agreement with Johnson, he did so knowing that he was dealing with a raw and extremely gullible young man. He must surely have been aware that the contract, signed or unsigned, was a useless document. How could Johnson have enforced it? Both parties would have been committed to an infamous act, and both would have had to accept the consequences. It would never have stood up in a court of law, even if Johnson had dared to produce it. The chances of blackmail were equally as slight. Rhodes had as great a hold over Johnson – who was actually going to execute the plan – as Johnson had over Rhodes. This could hardly have escaped Rhodes's notice.

The same arguments apply to the feasibility of the plan. It is generally agreed that the contract was hastily drawn up. Johnson's proposals were not presented as foolproof and were obviously subject to adjustment. Something had to be put down on paper – to please Johnson – and Rhodes was never a stickler for the observance of detail where contracts were concerned. Moreover, one does not know what verbal assurances or reservations were given. It was quite in character for Rhodes to allow for deviations from the written word. Why should he have worried when he knew the contract was meaningless anyway?

Rhodes's participation in the more sinister aspects of the plan can also be explained. That he was prepared to sanction the invasion of an independent country was to be dramatically demonstrated later when he instigated the notorious Jameson Raid. In that sorry affair he was assisted by more experienced friends whom he trusted and no contracts were needed. Was he also willing to condone cold-blooded murder? That is a question which has often been asked. He was repeatedly suspected of doing so – most notably so in the case of Piet Grobler, the

Boer emissary in Matabeleland. Invariably his admirers have denied that he was capable of such deeds and pointed to the lack of positive proof. How strong is their case?

The trouble is that most of his accusers have been hostile or irresponsible witnesses and it has been easy to dismiss their charges out of hand. There is, however, evidence of Rhodes's infamy which comes from a far more reliable source. Sir Lewis Michell, who was Rhodes's banker, trustee and official biographer, has given a damning example of Rhodes's readiness to sentence a reputed opponent to death without any lawful justification. Reasons could be advanced to excuse his conduct in this case, but there can be no doubt about his intent.

In his unpublished memoirs (now in the Cape Archives) Michell devotes a few pararaphs to Rhodes's casual attitude towards money. He retells some familiar stories about the great man's generosity and then produces a less heart-warming anecdote. Rhodes, he says, was once overdrawn at the bank and requested a loan of £10,000. He told Michell that he needed the money for use in central Africa. 'I was rather taken aback,' says Michell, 'by his announcing that he proposed to arrange a murder with it. The facts turned out to be as follows: The brother of an intimate friend of his had been killed by a Chief, whose tribal name was Makenjira, and the victim's head was believed to have been placed on a pole in front of the Chief's kraal. Rhodes explained that he intended to make an exchange, i.e. to remove his friend's head and substitute that of Makenjira as a warning to all concerned that an Englishman could not be murdered with impunity.'

In this case the intended victim was killed in a drunken brawl before the hired assassins arrived and Rhodes's commission proved unnecessary. That at least is what Michell claims. It all happened much later – probably when Rhodes was Prime Minister of the Cape – but it says little for Rhodes's sense of justice. The story Rhodes had been told was hearsay; no investigation was requested, Rhodes simply ordered the execution of the man thought to be responsible for the death of his friend's brother. Can there really be any doubt that, with much more at stake, he would not have hesitated in agreeing to the murder of Lobengula – the man whom he and his agents were painting as a bloodthirsty monster?

When dealing with an inexperienced adventurer like Frank Johnson, Rhodes was not over-scrupulous. He was being pressed to launch an invasion and he needed someone to help him. His choice was limited. Anyone he employed would, of necessity, be of doubtful honesty. No self-respecting military man would have volunteered for such a questionable undertaking. Frank Johnson was as good as he was likely to get and, in such cases, Rhodes had ways of safeguarding himself. Precisely what precautions he took it is not possible to say. The whole affair is cloaked in mystery and Rhodes may not have relied entirely on a compromising, unenforceable contract. It is significant that Johnson was careful not to admit to the invasion plan until years after Rhodes's death.

Whatever the details of that plan might have been, it was more than just a figment of Johnson's imagination. Rumours of the conspiracy leaked out. Weeks later, John Moffat reported from Bulawayo that he had received news of some 'aggressive scheme'. References to a small force being raised to invade Matabeleland were also found in the papers of F. C. Selous, the renowned hunter. By the time news reached Bulawayo, however, Johnson had been forced to abandon his madcap plan. Why he did so is not certain. There is reason to think that wiser counsels prevailed. It is said Rhodes was told that he was underestimating the strength of the Ndebele and that any attack would 'lead to disaster'. This resulted in the invasion being called off.

Johnson, however, gave a different explanation. He claimed that his plan was ruined by his partner, Maurice Heany, who got drunk in Shoshong and blurted out the story to a resident missionary. The missionary then informed Sir Sidney Shippard who, in turn, reported to Sir Henry Loch, the High Commissioner. Loch immediately sent for Rhodes who denied all knowledge of the plot, putting the blame squarely on Johnson. Nobly – or so he implies – Johnson accepted responsibility by claiming that he wanted to 'get his own back' on Lobengula for the treatment he had received earlier at Bulawayo. After that Rhodes wanted nothing to do with the plan.

Whatever the truth, the proposed invasion of Matabeleland was abandoned. Fred Selous was employed to find a route to Mashonaland which skirted the Ndebele kraals and Jameson was urged to bring pressure to bear on Lobengula. Then it was that permission was sought for digging to start near the border. When Jameson later produced maps to explain how the diggers would move further north, he was relying on the route already suggested by Selous. His success was a triumph of deception over brute force.

*   *   *

Although Frank Johnson had been prevented from carrying out his more aggressive scheme, this did not affect his earlier agreement with Rhodes. On 1 January 1890, that agreement was formally confirmed. A new contract was drawn up by which Johnson was authorized to raise the pioneer column and conduct it through Lobengula's domains, to Mount Hampden in Mashonaland (a place suggested by Fred Selous, who was to act as guide). In return, Johnson was to be paid £87,500 for expenses and given 40,000 morgen of land and twenty mining claims.

The date stipulated for the completion of the operation was 30 September 1890.

A few days later a conference was held at Government House in Cape Town. It was attended by Rhodes, Sir Henry Loch and various British officials in South Africa. At this conference, Rhodes's plans were explained and it was agreed that Colonel Carrington and 200 of his Bechuanaland Police should escort the column to the border of Lobengula's territories and after that the pioneers would be protected by 250 of the Chartered Company's police. In agreeing to these arrangements, Sir Henry Loch insisted that no advance should be made until Rhodes had reported to him that the preparations were complete and had been approved by Carrington and John Moffat. If all was then considered satisfactory, he would give his permission for the column to embark on its march. Somewhat surprisingly, throughout the discussions, the officials appear to have ignored the implications of the Royal Charter and regarded the expedition purely as a mining venture. Rhodes made no attempt to disillusion them.

The recruitment of volunteers kept Johnson busy for the next couple of months. Shortage of men was not one of his problems. News of the expedition fired the imaginations of adventurous and impoverished youngsters throughout South Africa. Applications poured in from every part of the country. Johnson was left to sort them out. His job was not made easier by the stream of candidates whose only qualification was the influence their families had with Rhodes. This was particularly true of volunteers from Kimberley where a recent slump in the diamond industry had thrown hundreds of young men out of work. Here the cry of 'Go north, young man' promised to solve not merely Rhodes's problems but the problems that the amalgamation of the mines had posed for his defeated rivals.

Recruitment of a sort had, in fact, started in Kimberley as early as November 1889. Once enlistment began officially, however, the number of would-be pioneers applying for a place in the column became almost unmanageable. Johnson, who had extended the qualifications to include professional men – doctors, lawyers and surveyors – as well as artisans, was forced to turn all but the most essential recruits down. This did not please his perverse employer. Forgetting his earlier instructions, Rhodes sent for Johnson and demanded an explanation. 'What,' he thundered, 'is this I hear? You have refused to take so and so. I have promised he *shall* go and you *must* take him.' Johnson, no less angry, told him that to include every place-seeker would cost more than his original estimate and that if Rhodes had additional nominees he would have to pay for them. Rhodes took his point. Calming down, he agreed to meet any extra costs and later handed Johnson a list of twelve men whom he had personally chosen.

These favoured few became known as 'the twelve apostles'. But tl
were also given other names. Sometimes they were dubbed 'Rhod
Angels', sometimes 'Rhodes's Lambs'. Always they were regarded ;
privileged elite. Among them were two youngsters from well-kno
Kimberley families in whom Rhodes took a special interest. They w
Troopers Bob Coryndon and Jack Grimmer.

Bob Coryndon was the son of an influential Kimberley lawyer.
had been born in Queenstown in the Cape, but had spent his early
on the diamond diggings. His selection by Rhodes was to mark
beginning of a spectacular career. Besides becoming one of Rhod
private secretaries, he was to hold high office in various African cou
tries. As Sir Robert Coryndon he was later to serve as Governor
Uganda and then as Governor of Kenya and High Commissioner
Zanzibar.

Jack Grimmer was a great favourite of Rhodes. Born in Colesberg
1867, he was the son of Dr William Grimmer, one of the early pione
of the diamond fields, and had spent most of his life in Kimberley
thick-set, lumbering young man, with an honest, good-natured k
somewhat stolid face, Jack Grimmer – or Johnny, as Rhodes liked
call him – was not particularly good-looking. People meeting him
the first time invariably commented on his lack of animation. H
said to have been 'undemonstrative and phlegmatic', taciturn, a
'seemingly brusque' in manner. But what he lacked in looks and p
sonality was compensated for by his obvious virility and down-to-ea
frankness. Brought up among the rough and tumble of the diggin
his education appears to have been scrappy and he was working a
junior clerk at De Beers when he first came to Rhodes's notice.

Accounts of their first meeting vary, but there can be no doubt tl
Rhodes's interest in the young man was immediate. A short account
Grimmer's life merely states that: 'Mr Rhodes first made his acquai
tance in Kimberley and took a great fancy to him.' There is, however
more romantic version. It is said that Rhodes was one day standing
the veranda of the De Beers office, which looked on the Compan
stables, when he spotted young Grimmer trying to mount a reari
horse. The youngster was thrown to the ground several times but at l
managed to get astride the animal and bring it under control. Rhod
is reported to have been completely fascinated by the struggle an
when it was over, to have turned to a friend and said: 'That boy h
grit, I must speak to him.'

Speak to Grimmer he did. The young horse-tamer was to occupy ;
important place in Rhodes's life. Although no-one ever filled the g;
left by Neville Pickering, Jack Grimmer probably came nearer to doi
so than anyone else. He and Rhodes never lived together, he nev
became Rhodes's heir and he lacked the charm of Pickering, b

Grimmer, more than any other friend, captured Rhodes's affection. He remained a devoted companion until the day Rhodes died.

Jack Grimmer was one of the first young men to volunteer for the pioneer column. He did not bother with Johnson but went straight to Rhodes to offer his services. The story is told that Rhodes teased him at first by refusing to consider his application. 'No,' Rhodes is reported to have said, 'I only want men with beards.' Then, having watched Grimmer's face fall, he laughed and relented. 'I think you will do very well,' he chuckled.

Beard or no beard, there was really never any question of Grimmer being turned down on account of his age. In 1890, when the pioneer column was being mustered, he was twenty-three. This was the age at which Neville Pickering had been appointed secretary of De Beers and the age when Frank Johnson was put in charge of the Mashonaland expedition. Rhodes always favoured raw young men who were approaching maturity.

*　　*　　*

The mustering of the pioneer column created widespread alarm. So worried did Lord Knutsford become that, in February, he cabled Sir Henry Loch to say that the British government could not agree to an advance into Mashonaland unless it was 'specifically sanctioned by Lo Bengula'. His concern was shared by John Moffat in Bulawayo who, on hearing that the 'settlers' were to be accompanied by armed police, feared that such a show of force would result in a collision with the Ndebele. The local missionaries, he reported, were questioning the wisdom of allowing their wives and children to remain in the country. These anxieties were only partly allayed when Jameson obtained Lobengula's verbal consent to the northward march.

Shortly after Jameson's departure, the king again began to display signs of uneasiness. On 17 March, Fred Selous, who was planning the route, arrived at Bulawayo with the intention of confirming the arrangements made by Jameson. He found Lobengula in a highly sus-picious mood. Why, the king wanted to know, was it necessary to cut a new road? Would not this route also be used by the Boers who were threatening to invade his territory? 'There is only one road to Mashona-land,' he insisted, 'and that goes through my country and past Bulawayo.' He wanted, he said, to discuss the matter with 'the big white chief himself'. Why did not Rhodes come to see him? He adamantly refused to supply the labourers he had promised Jameson until he was sure of Rhodes's intent. Selous should go back, said the king, 'and take Rhodes by the hand and bring him here.'

Jameson received a similar response from Lobengula when he

returned to Bulawayo the following month. Once again it was thought that the doctor's 'magical hypodermic needle' would help soothe the king into acquiescence and he had been sent to work his wonders. 'I am going,' he wrote to his brother before leaving Kimberley, 'to try and get things to the point that I left them . . . I feel very uncomfortable at my swagger arrangements being upset.' There are, as usual, conflicting accounts of this, Jamesons's last, visit to Bulawayo. It seems obvious, however, that it was not a success. His last meeting with Lobengula was far from satisfactory. The king was in an angry mood and pointedly refused to answer the doctor's specific requests. In the end, Jameson was obliged to take his silence for consent.

He was wrong, of course. After he left, Denis Doyle – who had remained at the Ndebele capital – was subjected to furious outbursts from Lobengula and the *indunas*. The king sent a formal protest to Sir Henry Loch about the nature of the pioneer column and, according to one account, began summoning his *impis* to Bulawayo. The march north was no longer expected to be peaceful.

But the preparations went ahead. The main assembly point was at Camp Cecil, some eighty miles from Palapye in Bechuanaland. To this isolated, makeshift camp contingents of pioneers and company police were sent after mustering at Mafeking and Kimberley. On 18 April, Rhodes and Sir Henry Loch inspected one of the Kimberley units and at a banquet that evening the High Commissioner gave the enterprise his qualified blessing. 'I feel called upon,' he declared amid great cheering, 'so far as I can legitimately support the interests of a private company, to give my support to that great British South Africa Company.' Only later did he receive Lobengula's protest.

At Camp Cecil things were organized on a military basis and some surprise was caused when it was learned that Sir Henry Loch had 'commissioned' the officers of the private army. (Frank Johnson acquired the rank of major.) Colonel Carrington was placed in charge of the company police until the border was crossed; after that the newly-promoted Lt-Colonel Pennefather, a former major of the Inniskilling Dragoons, assumed command. The pioneers, armed and equipped in brown tunics and slouch hats, were made responsible to Frank Johnson and, included among them, was a small group of civilians. One of these civilians was Archibald Colquhoun, a former civil servant from India, who was to act as the first administrator of the new territories. Jameson, soon to replace Colquhoun – and secretly carrying Rhodes's power of attorney – was to accompany the column in an independent capacity. With Lobengula refusing to supply labour, a force of Africans – mostly Ngwato tribesmen – was hired to carry out the more arduous tasks.

On 27 June 1890, the march began. The column was guided by Fred

145

Selous who, with a small advance party and a team of African labourers, went ahead to cut and clear the road. It was a tough assignment. The most difficult terrain was encountered early in the march, as the column hacked its way through the dense bush and the wagons jolted across the sandy river-beds of the Limpopo valley. Here, not only were they faced with the problems of road making but they were constantly aware that, in such thickly wooded country, they were particularly vulnerable to attack. Selous and his working party were particularly at risk and 'took every precaution to guard against surprise'. Scouting parties, says Selous, 'were always out, and whilst one half of the men walked, and cleared a road through the bush with their axes, they were closely attended by mounted comrades, who led their friends' horses, ready saddled and bridled, and carried their rifles and bandoliers; so that any sudden attack would have been met by the whole troop ready mounted.'

The main column was better armed – equipped with machine guns as well as rifles – but was handicapped by being widely dispersed. With over eighty wagons, following one another in single file, it stretched for more than two miles and this made it impossible to form a defensive *laager* (wagons drawn into a protective ring) in the event of a sudden attack. To remedy this Selous decided, after a few days out, to cut two parallel roads and thus shorten the line. From then on the column went into *laager* at night; a searchlight, mounted in one of the wagons, lit the surrounding bush and explosive charges were positioned around the *laager*. Crude as it was, this demonstration of the white man's magic proved effective. The thud of the searchlight's engine and the intermittent firing of the dynamite charges acted as a warning to any would-be attackers and frightened off wild animals. Nevertheless, the atmosphere remained tense.

Jameson was almost alone in thinking that the Ndebele would not attack. And he was proved right. Although the column was secretly followed and spied upon by a large Ndebele patrol – which sent regular reports back to Lobengula – no attempt was made to interfere with the progress of the pioneers. The apparent lack of hostility boosted Jameson's confidence. 'I have pretty well gone nap on this affair,' he wrote to his brother on 3 August, 'and hope to make a good thing out of it – at all events I don't think it likely I shall do any more practising in Kimberley.' He had at last committed himself to Rhodes. It was a fateful decision.

By that time the column had emerged from the bush and come within sight of the open plains of Mashonaland. 'Here,' wrote Jameson, 'we are in the midst of the grandest scenery I have ever seen, a mass of granite and larger forest – the dense underwood almost disappearing . . . . The end of September ought to see us at the objective

146

point (Mt Hampden).' Selous agreed. Surveying the country that same day, he considered that his task was practically over. He knew that, from there on, he would have no difficulty in 'cutting a good road' and that the march would be completed 'with ease and comfort.'

His confidence was well founded. The column arrived at its destination on 12 September and camped on the plain beneath Mount Hampden. At ten o'clock the following morning the men paraded in full dress, the Union Jack was raised, prayers were offered and a 21 gun salute was fired. Then, without any legal justification whatsoever, the country was casually annexed to the British Empire. The entire company gave three cheers for the Queen.

They named the place Fort Salisbury after the British Prime Minister and an express letter was sent to Rhodes. 'When at last I found they were through to Fort Salisbury,' he said later, 'I do not think there was a happier man in the country than myself.'

CHAPTER TEN

Prime Minister

Rhodes had wanted to accompany the pioneer column but, as usual, was prevented from doing so by his preoccupation with affairs in the Cape. Not the least of his concerns was the extending of the railway line northwards. The need for easy communication with the north weighed heavily with Rhodes. Nothing had hampered the early negotiations with Lobengula more than the delay in travelling to and from Matabeleland. A letter took anything up to a month to reach Bulawayo, the journey by ox-wagon could last from two to four months. Obviously these primitive arrangements had to be improved if Rhodes were to realize his dream of 'expanding the Cape Colony to the Zambesi'. Already he had ordered two hundred and fifty miles of telegraph wire to provide a link with the pioneers; he was determined to strengthen this link by pushing ahead with the railway line. 'The railway,' he was to say, 'is my right hand and the telegraph my voice.' What he had not allowed for was the threat to his plans posed by Cape politicians.

Since his return from England in 1889, Rhodes had not attended the sittings of the House of Assembly. In the general election of the previous year he had been returned as the member for Barkly West but he had been far too absorbed in the Charter negotiations to give attention to his parliamentary duties. In any case, routine politics – the tedious debates and the grind of committee work – bored him; when set against his more exciting activities, such mundane matters seemed incidental, even irrelevant. Only when it looked as if his grand design was in danger did he see the need for action. This happened in May 1890. Then it was that a parliamentary crisis caused him to rush to Cape Town 'without waiting to pack his portmanteau'.

The crisis had been sparked off by the Prime Minister. Once again the Cape government was led by the ever-available Sir Gordon Sprigg (he had been knighted three years earlier) and once again his railway policy brought him into collision with Rhodes. In a desperate attempt to revive the flagging fortunes of his adminstration, Sprigg had decided to court popularity by reforming the existing railway network. Instead of concentrating on the main trunk lines to the north, he proposed to construct branch lines in the south which would serve hitherto neglected districts. Politically this would have been a shrewd move, for not only did it promise to boost the Cape's meagre resources, but it seemed likely to win the votes of isolated farmers. Unfortunately it also put Rhodes's more ambitious schemes at risk. It was estimated that Sprigg's proposed railway bill would cost the taxpayer £7,500,000, thus draining the budget. Rhodes, of course, had no intention of allowing this to happen.

He was not alone. Although there were no political parties, as such, in the Cape parliament, the Afrikaner Bond – mainly Afrikaans-speaking farmers, led by Jan Hofmeyr – formed the largest single group. (In the 1888 general election, Bond members had won almost half the contested seats, but failed to obtain a clear majority.) Rhodes had long recognized the strength of the Bond – which, he claimed, held the 'key of Cape politics' – and had assiduously cultivated the support of Jan Hofmeyr. He had so far succeeded in this that, by 1890, Hofmeyr had emerged as an advocate of the Chartered Company's exclusive claims to the north. Now, in the battle with Sprigg, Rhodes was able to call on the Bond to help him defeat the Prime Minister's 'extravagant' railway proposals. He also had the advantage of popular press support, having secretly bought a controlling interest in the *Cape Argus* some years earlier to promote his financial and imperial schemes.

With this influential backing, Rhodes was able to launch a full-scale onslaught on the hapless Prime Minister. He focused on the expense of Sprigg's proposals, denouncing them as costly, grandiose and impracticable. The Cape's best market, he insisted, was in Kimberley and any railway reforms should be pointed in that direction. So effective were his arguments that, after a stormy debate on 10 July 1890, Sprigg was forced to admit defeat and resign.

Sir Henry Loch, as governor of the Cape, now faced the problem of finding a new prime minister. It was no easy task. The loose groupings and diverse loyalties of the elected members produced so many shifting alliances that to find a minister who could command a majority in the Assembly was a bewildering business. Loch's first choice was J. W. Sauer, a liberal Afrikaner lawyer (he was the brother of Rhodes's friend Hans Sauer) who had once served as Secretary for Native Affairs in an earlier ministry and was generally regarded as the unofficial leader of the opposition. He was not popular with the Afrikaner Bond and this made his chances of forming an effective administration extremely remote. Knowing this, Sauer declined Loch's invitation and recommended Rhodes who, as he knew, was better placed to muster support from the Bond. Loch, whose enthusiasm for the Chartered Company was on the decline, reluctantly accepted Sauer's decision and sent for Rhodes.

Surprisingly, Rhodes was not at all anxious to become Prime Minister. His purpose in defeating Sprigg had been to secure the northward extension of the railway line; now that he had achieved this his interest in Cape politics was diminished. He had far too much on his hands to take on another demanding post. Indeed, his first reaction to Loch's offer was to suggest Hofmeyr for the premiership. He even volunteered to serve in Hofmeyr's cabinet if the Bond leader was prepared to form a government. But Hofmeyr refused. Known as the 'Mole' – 'You never see him at work,' J. X. Merriman observed, 'but every now and then a little mound of earth, thrown up here or there, will testify to his activities' – Hofmeyr preferred to operate behind the scenes. He had no taste for parliamentary office. Hofmeyr did, however, promise Rhodes the support of his followers.

So it was that, two weeks after the pioneer column set off for Mash-onaland, Cecil Rhodes was installed as Prime Minister of the Cape.

By any judgement, this must be seen as an extraordinary feat. What-ever one may think of Rhodes, however much one questions his methods, criticizes his scale of values and deplores his ruthlessness, intolerance and egocentricity, it is impossible not to be amazed at his achievements. Consider what he had done in twenty years – the twenty years when most young men are struggling to find their feet. He had arrived in South Africa an ailing, inconspicuous and, to all outward appearances, unpromising youth. He had neither name nor influence to help him. He had educated himself. He had built one of the largest financial empires in the world. He had organized the occupation of a vast territory. He had become Prime Minister. And he was only thirty-seven years old.

That Rhodes was to become known as the 'Colossus' was, perhaps, inevitable.

*   *   *

As Prime Minister, Rhodes found it necesssary to rearrange his private life. Until this time he had lived a somewhat nomadic existence with no settled base. In Kimberley he had been content to pig it in tin-roofed cottages and on his visits to Cape Town he had been happy enough with temporary accommodation in make-shift lodgings. Meals were eaten at his club and his only servant was Tony de la Cruz, a coloured man from Portuguese East Africa, who served as a valet and general factotum. Now all this was to change. For a long time he had been unhappy with his lodgings in Cape Town (he believed the rooms were haunted and refused to sleep there alone) and in any case, he con-sidered them unsuitable for a Prime Minister of the Cape. He decided to find a more appropriate home.

The place he chose was a rambling old two-storied house, known as 'The Grange'. Built on the lower slopes of Devil's Peak, at Rondesbosch, it lay on the outskirts of Cape Town. It was a place of historic interest, dating back to the days of the Dutch East India Company, when it was a granary. Originally a delightful, whitewashed barn with muscular gables and a high-pitched thatched roof, it had lost much of its pristine charm by the time Rhodes became interested in it. A succession of owners and a series of conversions had effectively camouflaged the dignified simplicity of the original buildings. For the past eleven years it had been owned by the widowed Mrs Hester van der Byl who had rented it to a variety of tenants; including three Cape governors – the last occupant being Sir Henry Loch.

Rhodes also moved into 'The Grange' as a tenant; he was to live there for two years before deciding to buy the property. Then he commissioned Herbert Baker, an unknown architect whom he had met casually at a dinner party, to restore the house to its original architectural character. 'Make it big and simple,' he told Baker, 'barbaric if you like – I'm told my ideas are too big. They would be if I were living in St Helena or Cyprus but we are living on the fringe of a continent.'

Working from a water-colour sketch of the old granary and from his own detailed knowledge of Cape Dutch architecture, Baker faithfully restored the house and, at the same time, founded his reputation as one of the leading architects of his day. Given back its original name Groote Schuur – Great Granary – it was to become one of the show places of the Cape and one of the few personal possessions in which Rhodes took a real delight.

When Rhodes first became a tenant, however, the house was ill-equipped and bleakly furnished. Having neither the time nor the experience to cope with home making, he handed over the domestic arrangements to Harry Currey, the young man who had served as secretary of the Gold Fields of South Africa Limited and was now, since the formation of the Chartered Company, acting as Rhodes's personal assistant. Currey, who was no more experienced in household management than Rhodes, appears to have tackled his domestic duties with more enthusiasm than taste.

The problem of furniture was solved on a visit to London. Told by Rhodes to go to 'some good furniture shop' and order whatever was necessary for the house, Currey went straight to Maples – then the most fashionable store – and asked them to send 'three of a kind' to Rhodes's hotel. When the order was delivered the following morning it included everything from dining room tables and wardrobes to salt-cellars, table napkins and Persian rugs. Laid out in the ballroom of the Westminster Palace Hotel, it was hastily inspected by Harry Currey. 'In about a quarter of an hour,' he was to say, 'I had furnished Groote

Schuur and bought enough of everything to enable Mr Rhodes to have all his guests to stay . . . . I couldn't persuade him even to look at what I selected.' With these expensive but highly unsuitable furnishings, Rhodes was to live until, some years later, he began to take a more discriminating interest in his newly restored house.

For the most part, Currey was left to run the house as he pleased. 'Let's try on £250 a month,' Rhodes suggested at the outset: 'Let me know if you need more'. Generous as it was, this monthly allowance does not seem to have included the stocking of the cellar; this was something which Rhodes organized. He also took a keen interest in the selection of the household staff. Only men were employed at Groote Schuur and they were often personally chosen by Rhodes.

When it came to engaging servants, Rhodes was far from conventional: any personable youngster who happened to take his fancy was likely to be hired on the spot. Harry Currey tells the story of how the butler was acquired for Groote Schuur. One evening, says Currey, he and Rhodes were invited to dine at the nearby Wynberg barracks and were served by a trooper of the Inniskilling Dragoons. Rhodes, 'with his quick eye for a likely lad', was attracted to the young mess waiter and offered him a job. Somehow or other, arrangements were made to have the trooper, J. Norris, released from military service and he became one of Rhodes's most valued servants. Described as 'a young man of gentlemanly manners', Norris not only served as butler but, in time, took over the running of Groote Schuur from Currey. Although Rhodes often shocked his guests by his rough treatment of his devoted housekeeper – he seemed to delight in swearing at Norris in front of visitors – there was no mistaking his fondness for the young man. Eventually, when Norris developed lung trouble, he was pensioned off to a farm in Rhodesia. He lived there for many years on an annuity provided by Rhodes.

The fact that only male servants were employed at Groote Schuur was seen as evidence of Rhodes's dislike of women. This was denied by his more uncritical admirers. One answer given to the accusation is that, at one time, a few servants had been allowed to have their wives living with them but 'the breath of scandal caused Rhodes to clear every woman, white and coloured, off the place.' The truth of this is difficult to ascertain: the source is none too reliable. In any case, as far as most people could remember, Groote Schuur was as free of feminine residents as a monastery. It made staying at Rhodes's house a spartan experience for his more fashionable guests. 'There is no show,' observed one of his female guests, 'no servants in livery or proper butler and no housemaids at all, only black boys upstairs and two nondescript men to wait at table, so of course our maids are furious.'

Fashionable guests were soon very much in evidence at Groote

Schuur. There was hardly an important visitor to South Africa who, over the next few years, did not stay with Rhodes at one time or another. They were attracted not only by his political eminence but by his now widely recognized reputation as a man of destiny. That reputation was confirmed when, in the early months of 1891, he paid a triumphant visit to England. The visit, on which he was accompanied by Harry Currey, marked his return to his native land after the occupation of Mashonaland and his first appearance in London since becoming Prime Minister of the Cape. It was an outstanding success. No longer a relatively obscure colonial financier, Rhodes was hailed as a hero of Empire. He was fêted by London society and given a rousing reception wherever he went. 'Oh yes,' he admitted on his return, 'they have made a Buffalo Bill of me for thirty days.' They were thirty days of wonderment for young Harry Currey.

Rhodes and Currey arrived in London on a bitterly cold winter's night and were met at the railway station by the Duke of Abercorn, the chairman of the Chartered Company. The following morning Lord Rothschild was announced. A few days later, Lord Randolph Churchill arrived to discuss the trip he was proposing to make to Mashonaland. From then on the stream of distinguished visitors to the Westminster Palace Hotel was unending. Currey found his days were divided between warding off the various 'odd fish' trying to gain Rhodes's ear, and amusing the celebrities who crowded the 'great man's' office.

One of the most impressive callers was Charles Stewart Parnell, who came to finalize the second half of the £10,000 donation which Rhodes had promised to make to the Irish Nationalist Party. It was left to Currey to implement payment. The way in which this sizeable sum was handed over is an interesting example of Rhodes's private financial transactions. 'One morning,' says Currey. 'Rhodes said to me, "Make out a cheque for £5,000, go and cash it, and bring the money to me here as soon as you can." I asked to whom the cheque was to be made out and he said "To Bearer" and in the counterfoil insert "For Self". I went off with the cheque to Hoares Bank . . . . Without blinking an eyelid the teller required [*sic*], "How would you like it, sir?" and when a little taken aback I replied, "Well, in hundreds, please," he tossed me a bundle of fifty notes without even troubling to count them. That evening the money was handed to Parnell.'

The highlight of the visit, however, came when Rhodes was invited to dine and sleep at Windsor as Queen Victoria's guest. This was, in effect, a royal command and it created a domestic crisis. Rhodes had no court dress and no idea of what he should wear. There were hurried consultations and, finally, a Bond Street tailor was called in. Not until a few minutes before Rhodes's train was due to leave Paddington Station did a messenger come panting along the platform with a suitcase containing an appropriate wardrobe. Then it was discovered that Rhodes had not enough money to buy his train ticket. This was one of his idiosyncrasies. He would gaily send his secretary to cash a cheque for £5,000 but, like royalty, never carried cash on his person. More often than not, whoever happened to be with him would have to provide him with funds which he invariably forgot to pay back. On this occasion Harry Currey was able to buy him a return ticket and give him a further two sovereigns as pocket money. The story goes that these two sovereigns mysteriously disappeared while he was at Windsor and he had to borrow more money from a fellow guest.

It may have been on this visit to Windsor that the Queen asked Rhodes about his activities in Africa and was told: 'I am doing my best to enlarge Your Majesty's dominions.' Legend records another exchange between Queen Victoria and Cecil Rhodes. Victoria, having heard that he was a woman-hater, asked him if this was true. Rhodes was evasive. 'How,' he replied adeptly, 'can I hate a sex to which Your Majesty belongs?' So charmed was the Queen with this that she later pooh-poohed suggestions that Rhodes was a misogynist. 'Oh, I don't think that can be so,' she would say, 'because he was very civil to me when he came here.'

The London visit came to an end and so, shortly afterwards, did Harry Currey's career as a private secretary. A couple of months after his return to Cape Town, Currey became engaged to Ethelreda Fairbridge. Rhodes was told nothing about the engagement at the time. When, however, Currey plucked up courage and broke the news, all hell broke loose. This was the occasion on which Rhodes stormed up and down the room screaming, 'Leave my house! Leave my house!'

It took a few days for Rhodes to calm down. Then, to Currey's amazement, he appeared to adopt a more philosophic view. Late one evening he drifted into Currey's office for a chat and said that he thought Currey was right. He pointed out, says Currey, that 'we only live once, and that if one met a nice girl who could be a friend and a companion it was the right thing to try and marry her . . . . For himself he said that he would miss me very much, that we always got on "exceedingly well" and that had I not proposed to get married we would doubtless have continued to live together until one or other of us died. He did not know or care whom he would get to succeed me . . .' After going on in this vein for some time, Rhodes suddenly turned the conversation and talked 'a good deal about his income, both present and prospective, and what he intends to do with it.' Currey left with a feeling of bemusement. Reporting the incident to his father the following day, he confessed himself puzzled. 'I feel that neither I nor any living man will ever really "know" him,' he wrote. 'He does not want any living man to know him. His life and interests seem mapped out into squares; and

154

the man who is concerned with Square No.6 must know nothing of Square No.7.'

But was Rhodes's behaviour so inexplicable? Could it not be that he was making one last desperate attempt to win Currey back? First there were the conventional platitudes about marriage. Then came the emphasis on the break in their relationship and Rhodes's own loneliness. This was followed by talk of Rhodes's immense fortune and his grandiose schemes. It was all a matter of comparison. What was the companionship of a 'nice girl' when set against a life-long friendship with an influential man such as himself? Put like that, it seemed ridiculous for an ambitious young man to sacrifice a glittering career for the sake of prosaic domesticity. That, at least, is what Rhodes would have thought.

'I have never met anyone in my life,' Rhodes once said, 'whom it was not as easy to deal with as to fight.' He had tried fighting with Harry Currey and he had failed. Was he now trying to make a deal with him? Rhodes considered every man to have his price and was prepared to 'square' – as he put it – even his most important opponents. ('Can't you square the Pope?' he asked Parnell when he heard that the Irish leader was opposed by the priests.) Money, position and influence; many a young man would have given his right arm for the opportunities that were now being dangled before Rhodes's secretary.

That Rhodes was not sincere in his apparent approval of Currey's marriage, was made startlingly clear on the day of the wedding. The ceremony had just been performed. The guest of honour was Cecil John Rhodes. Chairman of De Beers Consolidated Mines, a managing director of the Consolidated Goldfields of South Africa, Prime Minister of the Cape, founder of a nation, guest of the Queen, host to the famous and one of the world's richest men, Rhodes strode up to the nervous bride and announced: 'I am very jealous of you.' And he was not joking.

After his marriage Harry Currey gave up his post as private secretary but continued in Rhodes's employ. On the surface things seemed to continue much as before. But not for long. There was a final quarrel and the two separated. Currey refused to speak of this last decisive quarrel but it was thought to have been caused by Rhodes's tendency to nepotism. Currey later became active in politics and gave his support to Rhodes's liberal opponents.

On the subject of his relationship with Rhodes, Currey remained silent. 'Rhodes was in many ways a great man,' he wrote half a century later. Then he crossed out 'great' and substituted 'big'. 'But,' he continued, 'has any big man friends? Does he not so give himself to his "cause" that there is no room left in his heart for people?'

There had been room in Rhodes's heart for Harry Currey, but this was something that Currey did not recognize. How could he? It sprang from a deep-seated emotional need which Rhodes himself did not fully appreciate. Only such a need can explain Rhodes's outburst when he heard that Currey intended to marry. He was certainly not worried about losing Currey's services. That was an inconvenience he could quickly have overcome. There were any number of talented, well-qualified civil servants willing to step into Currey's secretarial shoes. Rhodes could have afforded an army of them. Had he not said himself that he did not care who replaced Currey?

No, there was more involved than the loss of a secretary. Trivial as this episode appears, it provides an illuminating glimpse into Rhodes's hidden nature. In the quarrel with Harry Currey, Rhodes's emotions were engaged: frustrated emotions which became violent for want of a conventional outlet. He had come to depend on his secretary for more than his correspondence. He had adopted Currey, shared his home with him, made him part of his life. Currey was always there, could be confided in and he made no demands. In many ways, Harry Currey – at that time – filled the emotional void in Rhodes's life. How could a young man, still in his twenties, know what this implied?

*   *   *

When Rhodes, as Prime Minister, formed his first cabinet he did so with characteristic shrewdness. Resenting all displays of opposition, he attempted to unite the warring factions in the Cape parliament. He started by appointing three of the most prominent liberals in the House of Assembly to key posts. As Treasurer he chose his old Kimberley friend, J. X. Merriman, his Colonial Secretary was J. W. Sauer – the man who had earlier declined the premiership – and the third post went to an enlightened lawyer, James Rose Innes, who became Attorney General. To balance this liberal trio, Rhodes turned to his friends in the Afrikaner Bond. The Scottish-born James Sivewright – a man of questionable probity who acted as go-between in Rhodes's dealings with Jan Hofmeyr – was made Commissioner of Crown Lands and Public Works, and a likeable Afrikaner, Pieter Faure, was appointed as Secretary for Native Affairs.

Popularly known as the 'Ministry of All Talents' it was, in fact, an uneasy alliance. From the very outset, the divisions in Rhodes's cabinet were all too obvious. The liberals, aware of Jan Hofmeyr's influence behind the scenes, were conscious of their vulnerability. 'We have settled down in our Ministerial nests . . . ,' wrote Merriman, shortly after taking office, 'but I cannot say that I feel either proud or pleased . . . . Sauer, Innes and I have a good many things to gulp down. I therefore hardly like to predict a very long life for our craft.' James Sivewright, on the other hand, was so wary of being yoked with Merriman that he had to be coaxed into accepting his ministerial appointment. Rhodes, however, was confident that with the help of Hofmeyr he could sort out any difficulties.

He did not rely entirely on political persuasion. In office, as elsewhere, he was not above squaring any would-be opponents. One of the more notable aspects of his first administration was the blatant way in which he distributed Chartered Company shares among Bond members – including Hofmeyr – at a nominal rate. He was less lucky with the liberal contingent. 'I hope you will not take it amiss,' James Rose Innes replied, when Rhodes offered him 750 shares, 'if I decide not to take them . . . . I shall occupy a sounder political position if I hold no shares . . . . On every ground I would rather keep aloof from any pecuniary connection with the Company.' And Rhodes knew better than even to attempt a bribe with Merriman.

Rhodes's main concern was, as always, with his wider vision of southern Africa united under the British flag. This he hoped to achieve by first establishing railway and tariff agreements with the Boer republics and Natal. He was supported in his aims, with some reservations, by the liberal 'Trinity' – Innes was a loyal imperialist, Sauer admired Rhodes and Merriman was, by and large, sympathetic – as well as by Jan Hofmeyr who, Afrikaner patriot though he was, valued the imperial connection and, despite his misgivings about the extension of British control, favoured closer economic co-operation between the various states of South Africa. Agreement in this respect, therefore, presented Rhodes with no serious problems. A far trickier area was that which involved the rights and treatment of the coloured (mixed-race) and black citizens of the Cape. Here the liberals refused to compromise and this led to clashes with the Bond.

The first crack in Rhodes's ill-assorted cabinet appeared shortly after his return from England in March 1891. The divisive issue on this occasion was the notorious Masters and Servants Act, which was introduced (not for the first time) by a Bond member. Commonly known as the 'Strop Bill' or, more bitingly, the 'Every Man To Wallop His Own Nigger Bill', the proposed legislation was designed to bring the Cape into line with neighbouring states. The most contentious clause of this punitive act was that which entitled an employer to administer corporal punishment to his black labourers. Merriman was so incensed that he thought he might be forced to resign. 'Possibly,' he wrote to his wife, 'this may be a way out of a very ignominious position and with honour too.' His indignation was shared by his liberal colleagues. The Bond, on the other hand, had long been angling for such a measure and – with the notable exception of Hofmeyr – strongly supported its introduction.

Rhodes came out firmly on the side of the floggers. So far had he distanced himself from the paternalism of his youthful Natal days that he now saw nothing wrong with legalized brutality. It was merely an extension of the sentiments he had already publicly expressed. 'Treat the natives as a subject people,' he had earlier advised the House of Assembly, 'as long as they continue in a state of barbarism . . . . Be lords over them and let them be a subject race.' Even the blessing of the Prime Minister, however, was not sufficient to carry the bill. When it came up for a second reading in June, the opposition proved so effective that it had to be withdrawn and the expected cabinet crisis was averted.

But if Rhodes kept his cabinet intact, he lost the sympathy of some of his liberal well-wishers. Prominent among these was Olive Schreiner, the brilliant, complex novelist and one of the outstanding women in South Africa. The stand taken by Rhodes over the 'Strop Bill' ruined the friendship that was developing between them.

Cecil Rhodes and Olive Schreiner had first met in 1890, shortly after Olive had returned to the Cape from England. Rhodes had read Olive's famous novel, *The Story of an African Farm*, and had recognized it as a work of genius. For her part, Olive Schreiner had been so impressed by Rhodes's work and reputation that the prospect of meeting him roused her to an enthusiasm which she rarely displayed for individual South Africans. 'I am going to meet Cecil Rhodes,' she wrote to Havelock Ellis in March 1890. 'the only great man and man of genius South Africa possesses.' For some reason this meeting did not take place. Three months later she was still trying to arrange an introduction. She was forever praising him to her friends. 'The only big man we have here is Rhodes and the only big thing the Chartered Company,' she told W. T. Stead, 'I feel a curious and almost painfully intense interest in the man and his career.' She did, however, express the fear that by accepting premiership of the Cape, he would compromise his work in the north. At last, she could contain herself no longer and, brushing aside convention, wrote to Rhodes asking him to visit her. Rhodes accepted the invitation. Not long after their meeting, however, Olive Schreiner began to have second thoughts about her new-found idol.

Her fear that the politician in Rhodes would eclipse the man of destiny was soon shown to be well founded. By the time they met, Rhodes was already Prime Minister and his administration came under close scrutiny from the increasingly sceptical Olive Schreiner. It was his support for the 'Strop Bill' which brought things to a head. To an ardent humanitarian like Olive Schreiner the idea of flogging defenceless labourers was horrifying. She never forgave Rhodes for condoning such a barbaric proposal. 'The perception of what his character really was in its inmost depths,' she said, 'was one of the most terrible revelations of my life.' From that time on Rhodes was to have no more dedicated and passionate an opponent than Olive Schreiner.

158

*   *   *

In one way, Rhodes did not change. As Prime Minister he remained as careless of parliamentary etiquette as he had been when he first arrived in the House of Assembly. Although he tended to dress more formally, he still forgot to address members by their constituencies and, when laying papers before the House, he was positively off-hand, ignoring all the traditional formulas. On entering and leaving the chamber, he did not bother to bow to the Speaker but gave a casual nod which seemed more like a greeting 'given to a chance acquaintance in the street.'

George Wilson, of the *Cape Times*, retained vivid memories of Rhodes's outlandish manner on the front bench. 'His general behaviour,' says Wilson, recalling his days as a parliamentary correspondent, 'really always struck me as being that of a large, overgrown schoolboy, particularly in debate. He would spring to his feet, deliver a sudden and unexpected attack on some Honourable Member opposite, and then sit down again on his hands and bounce up and down for some seconds, as if he were saying "There's one for you, old boy," chuckling enormously as he did so. Another favourite attitude of his was to extend at full length on the Prime Minister's Bench, and, apparently, go to sleep. At any critical moment, however, he would open one eye, and look searchingly at whoever might be attacking him.'

Unorthodox as this habit of lying down appeared, it might not have been affectation. Just as he took to his bed in Kimberley on every possible occasion, Rhodes probably felt the need to prostrate himself when under stress. It eased his heart. Much as he liked to display his energy, he had very little stamina and any additional strain weakened him noticeably. For the most part Rhodes's biographers have ignored the illness that plagued him throughout his life, seeing it only as the cause of his death, but the symptoms of heart disease can be detected at every stage of his career. They need to be noted. They were a constant reminder to him that his life was under threat, that time was limited, that he had to act speedily if he were to achieve his grandiose ambitions. Sickness, rather than arrogance, may have accounted for much of Rhodes's rashness, his ruthlessness and apparently impulsive actions.

A faulty heart could also have affected his performances in political debates. He was quite capable of making a short, incisive, sometimes witty, speech but he was hopeless when he tried to address parliament. His breathlessness and his inability to control his voice caused him to stumble, to appear jerky and indecisive. This was recognized by everyone. 'Mr Rhodes was certainly not an orator,' says George Wilson.

159

His colleague, George Green – a future editor of the *Cape Argus* – agrees. Green was extremely disappointed when, shortly after his arrival from England, he first heard Rhodes speak. 'My sense of propriety was startled,' he says, 'by his careless, informal style of oratory. While the House listened breathlessly as to the voice of the Oracle, I in my insularity could but marvel at his bald diction and rough, unfinished sentences. At intervals he would jerk out a happy, illumining phrase or apt illustration; but the arrangement of the speech was distressingly faulty, and his occasional lapses into falsetto seemed to belie the well-authenticated story that he had won at school a prize for elocution. At worst indeed his flounderings rather resembled those of a schoolboy trying to repeat an imperfectly learned lesson.'

Rhodes's appearances in the House of Assembly were infrequent and fleeting. Only on the more important occasions would he join in a parliamentary debate. He preferred to govern through private consultations with his ministers. Merriman had taken a house in Rondebosch, close to Groot Schuur, and every morning he would join Rhodes for an early ride when they would discuss the day's business. In most practical matters, Merriman acted as Rhodes's deputy. On the many occasions when Rhodes was away on Chartered Company business, or in Kimberley or England, Merriman more or less took over the running of the government. He was a good deal older than Rhodes and far more experienced in parliamentary procedure. When it came to policy decisions, however, Rhodes kept the outspoken Merriman at a distance and looked to Jan Hofmeyr and James Sivewright for whatever guidance he needed. Tackled about his bias towards the Bond, Rhodes's answer was simple: 'I think,' he said, 'if more pains were taken to explain matters to the Bond party, many of the cobwebs would be swept away and a much better understanding would exist.'

That understanding was more theoretical than real. It did not extend to the liberal 'Trinity'. Merriman, for one, became increasingly suspicious of Bond influence, with the result that divisions in the cabinet widened.

The Bond, however, proved useful to Rhodes: particularly in his dealings with the Boer republics. He had little difficulty, for instance, in arranging with the Orange Free State for an extension of the railway to the Transvaal border. His plan to continue the line beyond the Vaal river and on to Pretoria was not so easily implemented. Here he came up against the hostility of President Paul Kruger. Not only was Kruger opposed to Rhodes's expansionist policies but the Transvaal Volksraad (parliament) resented the high duties imposed on goods imported to their inland republic. These goods had to travel through the Cape and were consequently subject to Cape tax. This made Kruger extremely reluctant to fall in with Rhodes's plans for a South African customs and railway union. He aimed, instead, to link the Transvaal by rail to the eastern port of Delagoa Bay, in Portuguese East Africa, and thus secure the republic's independence. The trouble was that, as a result of a recent gold crisis, the Transvaal could not meet the cost of the rail link and was unable to borrow money from abroad. This is where James Sivewright appeared to prove his worth. He it was who, in December 1891, negotiated an agreement whereby the Cape would provide funds for the Netherland's Railway Company – who were building the Delagoa Bay line – on the understanding that another line would be built from Pretoria to the Vaal river. In this way the Cape was connected to the Transvaal and gained an advantage in the railway race. The agreement was a tremendous success for Sivewright, boosted his popularity and earned him a knighthood.

But the celebrated Sivewright Agreement was not all that it seemed. President Kruger was not so easily ensnared. He did not, as Sivewright implied, promise that the Cape would retain its advantage once the Delagoa Bay line was completed; the shorter line, connecting Pretoria to the Vaal river, continued to be subject to charges imposed by the Netherland's Railway Company. Rhodes himself tried to solve the problem in a different way when, in 1892, he attempted to buy Delagoa Bay from the Portuguese. He was helped in this by Merriman, and was promised the support of Lord Rothschild, but after lengthy negotiations the bid had to be abandoned. Neither political manoeuvring nor high-powered finance could shift the doughty old President. Rhodes would have to seek a more dramatic solution to the problems posed by Paul Kruger.

Failure to come to satisfactory terms with the Transvaal did not prevent Rhodes from pressing ahead with his plans for a united South Africa. Those plans involved more than a railway and customs union. One of the more important political obstacles he faced was the lack of a common 'native policy' in the various South African states. Here the Cape was very much the odd man out. Unlike the Boer republics and Natal, where voting was restricted to white adult males, the Cape franchise was not based on the colour of a man's skin. Any male citizen of the Cape who owned property valued at £25, or who earned £50 a year, was entitled to vote. This was bound to prove an obstruction to any agreement on 'native policy' and therefore threatened to undermine Rhodes's long-term plans. There can be little doubt that Rhodes had this potential threat in mind when, pressurized by the Bond, he agreed to reform (abolition, at this stage, would have been too drastic) the Cape's 'colour-blind' franchise. In doing so he created another cabinet crisis.

The proposed reforms did not seek to deprive coloured citizens of the vote but to raise the voting qualifications. Merriman had long expected such a move. He had expressed his fears in a letter to his wife some six years earlier. 'I remember,' he wrote, 'when Rhodes used to propose to maintain British influence by using the Native vote – now he descants on the theme of the integral race difference between black and white and I should not be surprised to find him an ardent advocate for the restriction of the franchise.'

When the question of reform was first discussed in cabinet there were heated exchanges between the liberals and James Sivewright, who was the strongest advocate of anti-coloured legislation. Jan Hofmeyr was more moderate. He favoured a voting system similar to that which existed in English universities, allowing higher educated electors a dual vote. This suggestion, however, was blocked by Rhodes.

Unfortunately, when the discussions reached a crucial stage, Merriman was absent in England. It was left to his two colleagues to carry on the fight. James Rose Innes was particularly incensed. He warned Rhodes that he would 'retire from the Cabinet and deal with the Bill, when it is brought into the House, as an independent member' if his amendments were ignored. One of those amendments was that provision be made for a secret ballot. This Rhodes, at first refused to consider. 'I object to the ballot *in toto*,' he protested. 'I like to know how a person votes – not, I hasten to say, for any ulterior purpose.' But he rather ruined this argument by adding that he wished to keep his eye on loafers and IDB agents who might vote for 'free liquor and robbery.' He insisted, however, that he would never discharge a person for his vote. Nor would he accept that he was acting out of racial bias: he would never, he claimed, 'disqualify a man on account of his colour.'

In the end a compromise was reached. The Franchise and Ballot Bill of 1892 contained most of Innes's amendments – some of them watered down – when it was passed in the House of Assembly. The property qualifications were raised from £25 to £75, the secret ballot was allowed and an elementary literacy test – voters had to be able to write their name, address and occupation – was included. It was not entirely what the liberals had fought for but at least they had preserved the 'colour-blind' franchise. Rhodes could also claim success, of sorts. He had made a dent in the franchise and he had kept his cabinet together.

How genuine Rhodes was in asserting that he was not motivated by colour prejudice is not possible to say. He was quite capable of saying one thing and ensuring that the opposite would happen. This was certainly the case with the Franchise Bill. Once it was put into operation there were distinct changes in the Cape electoral rolls. The raising of the property qualifications resulted in 3,348 coloured citizens being disenfranchised within a year; the number of white voters, on the other hand, increased by 4,506. This did not, of course, bring the Cape into line with its more bigoted neighbours, but it was a move in that direction.

* * *

It was not, as it happened, 'native policy' that brought about the downfall of Rhodes's first ministry. The split between the liberals and the Bond played its part, but the decisive issue was what became known as the 'Logan scandal'. This unedifying affair involved political jobbery of the most blatant kind and caught Rhodes unaware. At the centre of the rumpus was the newly knighted Commissioner of Public Works, Sir James Sivewright.

On 5 October 1892 Rhodes sailed for England on the *Norham Castle*, taking James Sivewright with him. The day before they left, Sivewright, unbeknown to Rhodes, had authorized a contract giving a railway catering monopoly to his intimate friend and fellow Scot, James Logan. Logan, a former sailor, had started his railway career as a porter on Cape Town station but had risen rapidly and was now established as a well-known hotelier and owner of railway refreshment rooms. In most respects, therefore, he was undoubtedly qualified to handle the catering contract. What created suspicion, however, was the fact that in awarding Logan a monopoly on all railway catering and refreshment rooms for fifteen or more years, Sivewright had highhandedly ignored all the customary procedures. He had not called for tenders, he had not consulted his colleagues and the contract had not been ratified by the Attorney-General. Added to this were the doubts surrounding some of his earlier business deals.

The Attorney-General was, of course, James Rose Innes. He was soon made aware of the disturbing rumours concerning the contract but it was not until he read an informed exposé in the *Cape Times*, on 5 November, that he decided to act. He immediately wrote to Rhodes asking him to obtain a 'satisfactory explanation' from Sivewright. The matter was discussed at a cabinet meeting a few days later and a cable was sent to Rhodes seeking permission to cancel the contract. To this, Rhodes, after consulting with Sivewright, agreed. Logan then announced that he would sue the government for breach of contract. Criticism of Sivewright mounted.

Seemingly unaware of the threat to his ministry, Rhodes made no attempt to hurry back to Cape Town. He did not leave London until the end of December and then, after a short holiday in Egypt, travelled slowly down the east coast of Africa to Delagoa Bay and visited the Transvaal before finally arriving home in March 1893. By that time the situation had worsened. Details of another scandal in which Sivewright was involved had leaked out and Logan had formally instituted his claim for breach of contract. Even so, Rhodes refused to take positive action. Stalling for time – he was preoccupied with Chartered Company affairs and reluctant to face a ministerial crisis – he postponed all discussion of the Logan contract until Sivewright returned in April.

But he could not delay a decision indefinitely. Once Sivewright had returned, on 24 April, the demands of the angry cabinet ministers became more urgent. Innes and Sauer confronted Rhodes with an ultimatum: either he obtain a reasonable explanation from Sivewright or the two of them, and Merriman, would resign. This put Rhodes in an embarrassing position. He had no wish to dismiss Sivewright – who, as well as being a minister he valued, was an agent of the Chartered Company – and Sivewright had publicly announced that he had no intention of resigning. Faced with this dilemma, Rhodes turned to Jan Hofmeyr for advice. The Bond leader told him that, as there was no chance of the government surviving, his best course would be to resign so that a new ministry could be formed.

Rhodes appeared to welcome this idea. So much so that he toyed with the idea of stepping down from the premiership and allowing Sir Henry de Villiers, the Chief Justice, to take his place. De Villiers was fully prepared to become Prime Minister, with Rhodes serving under him as minister without portfolio, but he could not agree to the other appointments Rhodes wanted him to make. They were still debating the composition of the future cabinet when a more agreeable solution presented itself.

At the beginning of May 1893, Rhodes happened to meet his old antagonist Sir Gordon Sprigg on the steps of the House of Assembly and Sprigg offered to join Rhodes's cabinet as Treasurer. This opened up new prospects. Not only would Rhodes be able quietly to drop the controversial Sivewright, who would be replaced by one of Sprigg's supporters, but he would be able to reform his cabinet and thus deny the liberal 'malcontents' the opportunity of resigning on a matter of principle. All things considered, it seemed the most sensible answer to an increasingly ticklish problem.

Two days later Rhodes resigned and brought his first ministry to an end. It was a gamble but it paid off. The newspapers blamed the hostility between Merriman and Sivewright for the break-up. Although Rhodes strongly denied that he had inspired these newspaper attacks – his friend Dr Rutherfoord Harris now controlled the *Cape Argus* – he had reason to be grateful for them. With Merriman under fire, he was given every excuse for not including the liberals in his new cabinet. When, at the beginning of 1894, a general election was held, Rhodes and his supporters won two-thirds of the parliamentary seats and the liberals were forced into opposition.

The long, if shaky, friendship between Rhodes and Merriman had come to an end. There were to be no more early morning rides and swapped confidences. What little restraint Merriman had exercised over Rhodes's more ruthless impulses no longer carried any force. From now on they would face each other from opposite sides of the political fence. In the small white world of South Africa, men of compassion were not easy to come by: in losing Merriman, Rhodes had lost the last vestiges of his youthful idealism.

CHAPTER ELEVEN

Jameson's War

Three months after becoming Prime Minister of the Cape, Rhodes decided that the time had come for him to visit Mashonaland. It was only a matter of weeks since the Union Jack had been hoisted at Fort Salisbury and he was anxious to join the pioneers in the first flush of their success. Adding to his eagerness was the fact that the pioneer column was about to be disbanded and that the men would soon disperse as settlers in the new territory. This, the unfolding of the entire operation, was an event which Rhodes was anxious to witness.

The opportunity presented itself in October 1890. At the beginning of that month Sir Henry Loch, as High Commissioner, set off on a tour of Bechuanaland. Rhodes, accompanied by two Bond members of parliament, joined him. But it was not until later that Rhodes sprang his surprise. He told Loch that he would not be returning with him to Cape Town but that he intended crossing the border and following the road cut by the pioneers. This, he admitted, was the real purpose of his joining the tour. Loch was appalled. Mashonaland was regarded as dangerous territory, there was still talk of a possible attack by the Ndebele who, it was rumoured, were 'spoiling for a fight'. Reverting to his role of Governor of the Cape, Loch firmly vetoed Rhodes's proposal. As Prime Minister, he said, Rhodes had no right to take such a risk. But Rhodes refused to listen. The meeting broke up with 'mutual dissatisfaction' and that same night Rhodes and the two Bond men left to continue their journey.

A couple of days later they crossed the border and pushed on to the Tuli river. Here they were brought to an abrupt halt. A combination of river floods and further ominous reports from Matabeleland finally decided Rhodes to heed Loch – who had sent him an official letter of protest – and retrace his steps. He arrived back in Kimberley, after visiting the Transvaal, on 20 November. Awaiting him was the news that the pioneers had disbanded and were already taking possession of their farms and prospecting for gold. He had missed what should have been a shining hour of his career.

Almost a year passed before Rhodes had another chance to visit Mashonaland. Not until the end of the parliamentary session in 1891 did he feel free to travel north. This time he was determined that neither Sir Henry Loch nor swollen rivers would interfere with his plans. To avoid the uncertainties of the Bechuanaland approach, he decided to sail to Portuguese East Africa and travel inland from the port of Beira. Not only was this safer, but much quicker: he had very little time to spare.

Rhodes regarded the visit as high adventure. The very thought of at last setting foot in his 'promised land' stirred his imagination: there was so much to see, so much to do, so many challenges to be met. His hopes, as well as his excitement, were reflected in a letter he sent to W. T. Stead shortly before leaving. 'I am off to Mashonaland after a very trying session,' he wrote, 'so I feel like a schoolboy about to enjoy his holidays . . . . I quite appreciate the enormous difficulties of opening up a new country, but still if Providence will furnish a few paying gold reefs, I think it will be all right. Please understand it is no personal avarice which desires this, but, as you know, gold hastens the development of a country more than anything.'

Unfortunately, he could no longer be sure that Providence was on his side. The reports from Mashonaland did not inspire faith in 'paying gold reefs'. Only a few weeks earlier an American mining expert, accompanying Lord Randolph Churchill on a tour of the newly opened territory, had issued a damning report on Mashonaland's mineral potential. He admitted that some gold had been found but added that 'neither the extent of the reef, the quality of the ore, nor the general formation of the country, so far at least as judgement can be formed on what has been seen, could justify the formation of large London companies for their further development.' These findings had been summarized by Lord Randolph Churchill in a series of articles he was writing for the British and South African press. 'The truth has to be told,' Churchill concluded. 'Mashonaland, so far as is present known, and much is known, is neither Arcadia nor an El Dorado.' This had come as a blow to Rhodes, who had actively encouraged Lord Randolph to visit Mashonaland in the hopes that his influence, as a leading British politician, would bolster confidence in the Chartered Company and attract emigrants to the country. Although he refused to accept the mining expert's findings, Rhodes could not ignore them. 'I wonder,' he mused, in his letter to Stead, 'if the Supreme Power will help me to this object, for it is certainly a disinterested one, or whether out of pure mischief he dooms it to failure.'

These thoughts must have been on his mind when, on 14 September 1891, he sailed for Beira. He appears to have been in a bad temper for most of the voyage and, according to Frank Johnson who went with him, at one stage he quarrelled openly with the captain. His sullen mood was still very much in evidence when the ship docked at Beira twelve days later. Matters were not helped by the officious behaviour of an armed Portuguese customs official who, at bayonet-point, seized Rhodes's luggage for inspection. Rhodes was outraged. 'I'll take their — country from them,' he shouted as he stormed down the gang plank.

This was no idle threat. Portuguese East Africa featured high on the list of countries he sought to annex.

*   *   *

Rhodes had never regarded the occupation of Mashonaland as anything more than the first step in his plan to spread British influence throughout the world. 'All this to be painted red,' he had once declared, slamming his hand down on a map of Africa. That remained his dream. Red was the cartographical colour which designated British possessions and Rhodes saw it as the colour of success. The railway line he was so busily extending in South Africa was intended to stretch far beyond Mashonaland. In his fantasy world, Rhodes pictured a line of steel linking the Cape to Cairo, running through countries tied to the British Empire. This was one of the reasons why no northern boundaries had been set when the Charter was granted; the less Rhodes was confined, the freer he would be to realize his imperial ambitions. Mashonaland was merely a base, or spring board, from which to launch a more acquisitive, all-embracing northward drive.

The trouble was, of course, that Rhodes was battling against time. Others were already marking out the map of Africa. Mashonaland was rapidly becoming hemmed in: its vaguely defined borders were in danger of being decided by rival powers. Portugal had long held sway on the eastern coast, more recently the Germans had gained a firm foothold in the west, the Boers of the Transvaal posed a threat from the south, and in the north Belgium had, in 1884, been recognized as the controlling power in the Congo and was now about to pounce on the rich province of Katanga. Rhodes recognized what he was up against; he knew that he would have to act swiftly if he were not to be overtaken in the 'scramble for Africa'.

He had, in fact, already begun preparations for clearing the road to the north. As early as 1889, while he was in London negotiating the Charter, he had learned of the financial difficulties of the African Lakes Company – an enterprise founded by Scottish business men and missionaries – which was operating north of the Zambesi in what was to become Nyasaland (present-day Malawi) and had proposed that the Chartered Company take over its business and assist in clearing the region of Arab slave traders. On that same visit he had also met Harry Hamilton (later Sir Harry) Johnston, the newly appointed British

Consul in Portuguese East Africa who shared his vision of extending British influence from the 'Cape to Cairo' – a phrase first coined by Johnston – and had advanced Johnston £2,000 to assist in combating the slave trade in Nyasaland as well as promoting British claims to the north. For the next four years Johnston worked in close co-operation with Rhodes, but they were both too egotistic and self-assertive for such a partnership to last. In 1893 they quarrelled and parted company. By that time Nyasaland had been declared a British protectorate.

Harry Johnston was one of the young men whom Rhodes had summoned to Kimberley in May 1890 – two months before the pioneer column began its march into Mashonaland – to discuss the problems of expansion north of the Zambesi. The terms of the Charter gave the British South Africa Company the right to enter into agreements with local rulers (those not included in the Rudd concession) both within the territory defined by the Charter and 'elsewhere in Africa' and it was this right that Rhodes intended to exploit. The purpose of the Kimberley meeting was to brief the young men – all of whom were experienced Africa hands – on the business of negotiating treaties and obtaining concessions from chieftains in the northern territories. No record appears to have been kept of the discussions but the effect of this meeting soon became apparent.

Hardly had the pioneer column reached Fort Salisbury than Rhodes's emissaries branched out on their appointed missions. They met with varying success. The greatest prize was probably that which was gained in Barotseland (part of present-day Zambia) where one of Rhodes's agents confirmed a concession that had been granted earlier by the Barotse chief, Lewanika. Unfortunately some doubt existed about the validity of this concession – which added 25,000 square miles to the Chartered Company's territory – and it was not until 1897, when Robert Coryndon, one of Rhodes's 'twelve apostles', took up the post of resident commissioner that Barotseland was recognized as part of the company's domains. Less successful was the attempt to grab Katanga, the mineral-rich region south-east of the Congo. Here a series of mishaps and near disasters prevented Rhodes's British agents from reaching an agreement with the formidable Msiri, who dominated Katanga, and they were finally out-manoeuvred by a British army officer who seized the territory on behalf of the King of the Belgians. To Rhodes's intense annoyance, the flag of the so-called Congo Free State was hoisted in Katanga in December 1891, shortly after he ended his first visit to Mashonaland.

But it was with Portuguese East Africa – or Mozambique, as it was known – that Rhodes was most concerned. The acquisition of this strategically important country, which blocked Mashonaland from the Indian Ocean, was vital to his plans. It was more a matter of economics than of politics. At that time it was estimated that it cost £45 a ton to bring goods overland from the Cape to Fort Salisbury and Rhodes had been assured that this cost could be reduced to a mere £11 if goods were transported by way of the Portuguese port of Beira. This made a 'road to the sea', running through Mozambique, appear not merely desirable but essential. To establish such a link had been a top priority with Rhodes even before the pioneers set off for Mashonaland: it had featured prominently in the discussions at Kimberley.

There was little hope, as Rhodes well knew, of cooperation from the Portuguese. Nor, for that matter, was he thinking in terms of cooperation. He had no faith in Portugal as a colonial power. 'They are a bad race,' he was to say, 'and have had three hundred years on the coast, and all they have done is to be a curse to any place they have occupied.' Harsh and arrogant as was this judgement, it was not entirely a matter of prejudice.

The Portuguese, having established themselves on the east coast of Africa in the sixteenth century, had made little effort to develop the hinterland to which they laid claim. Their contacts with the African rulers of the interior had, for the most part, been minimal. They had, it is true, arrived at agreements with some of these rulers, but these agreements were so vague that they could hardly be considered as binding. In the latter years of their occupation the Portuguese had been content to confine themselves to the coastal region and to dream of the day when they would 'cut a swathe across Africa' which would link Mozambique to their Angolan possessions in the west. From time to time they had produced maps supporting their claims but had made no attempt to pursue their ambitions. It was not until British activity in Africa appeared to threaten their dream of an African empire that the Portuguese were aroused from their slumbers.

Rivalry between the British and Portuguese in east Africa had become apparent in the late 1880s. Clashes between the two European powers had occurred before Rhodes began to play an active role. At the beginning of 1890, a particularly serious incident – which resulted in Britain sending gunboats to Mozambique and issuing an ultimatum – had led to the negotiation of a treaty designed to lessen the hostility. This treaty, the Anglo-Portuguese Convention of 1890, was agreed upon shortly after the pioneer column reached Fort Salisbury and was intended to define spheres of influence. Under its terms, Britain secured Nyasaland as well as Mashonaland and Matabeleland while Portugal was recognized as the dominant power in part of Barotseland and in most of Manicaland – the territory which bordered Mashonaland south of the Zambesi. Satisfactory as this seemed to Britain, it did not please everyone. In Lisbon, the

170

Portuguese Cortes was at first reluctant to ratify the treaty and only accepted it provisionally three months later.

Nor, of course, were the Portuguese politicians alone in their objections. Rhodes was even more opposed to what he called 'this wretched treaty'. He bombarded everyone concerned with furious letters of complaint. 'If you have any regard for the work I am doing,' he told the British Foreign Office, 'you will show it by now dropping the Anglo-Portuguese agreement.' For not only did it invalidate his claim to Barotseland but, by placing Manicaland within the Portuguese orbit, it effectively blocked his 'road to the sea'. Manicaland was the territory through which he planned to cut that road and he had no intention of allowing a compromise between politicians in Europe to prevent him from doing so. He welcomed the indecision of the Portuguese Cortes.

His plans in any case were, by that time, already well advanced.

A week or so before the pioneer column arrived at Fort Salisbury, Archibald Colquhoun – the newly-appointed administrator of Mashonaland – had left the marchers and branched off to visit Manicaland. He had orders from Rhodes to negotiate a concession for mineral rights from the 'chief of the Manica country' and to secure a route to the seaboard. (It is also thought that he was secretly instructed to organize a filibustering seizure of the port of Beira.) As far as the concession was concerned, Colquhoun was successful. The ruler of Manicaland, Mtasa, denied that he had signed any agreement with Portugal and, on 4 September 1891, granted exclusive commercial and mineral rights to the Chartered Company.

The treaty with Mtasa was, not surprisingly, immediately challenged by Portugal. That challenge was followed by an attempt to reassert Portuguese authority in the territory. In the resulting confusion, a clash occurred between a small Portuguese force and a detachment of Chartered Company troopers in which the Portuguese were routed and three of their leaders were arrested and packed off to Fort Salisbury. This marked a series of incidents which culminated, six months later, in a more violent confrontation.

On 4 May 1891, a force of Portuguese irregulars – some two hundred white and three hundred black soldiers – took possession of a fortified outpost at Macequece (or Massi Kessi as the British called it) just within the Portuguese border. A few days later a small band of Chartered Company men, commanded by a Captain Heyman, advanced towards the fort. They were immediately attacked by the Portuguese. Although greatly outnumbered, the Chartered Company force repulsed the attack – killing twenty Portuguese soldiers – and frightened their enemy into deserting the fort under cover of night. Heyman, acting on Rhodes's instructions ('Take all you can and ask me afterwards') then despatched a patrol to the coast with the intention of occupying

Beira. Unfortunately for Rhodes, the British authorities decided to intervene and a Major Sapte was sent to warn off the Chartered Company's men. Rhodes was furious. 'But why,' he was to say to Heyman later, 'didn't you put Sapte in irons and say he was drunk?'

This reverse followed a more farcical imbroglio in Gazaland, another territory which bordered Mashonaland south of Manica. Here the prospect of opening a route to the sea had appeared distinctly promising. Not only was Gazaland served by the fast flowing Limpopo river, but the local potentate, Gungunhala – a chieftain of Zulu stock who was related by marriage to Lobengula – was known to be anxious for an alliance with Britain. The fact that Gazaland was widely recognized as being within the Portuguese sphere of influence did not bother Rhodes unduly. He had long considered the territory as a suitable alternative to Manicaland and had actually dispatched an agent to Gungunhala's kraal, some forty miles north of the Limpopo, before the pioneer column began its march.

Rhodes's agent, a burly German doctor named Schulz, had reached Gazaland in June 1890. His negotiations with Gungunhala dragged on for weeks. Not only did he have to overcome Gungunhala's suspicions but he also had to contend with the chief's inability to remain sober: a fatal addiction to the cheap 'trade rum', supplied to him by the Portuguese, invariably left Gungunhala so sozzled that he was incapable of coming to a firm decision. Eventually, however, Schulz managed to obtain a provisional agreement. In return for payment of an annual subsidy, 1,000 rifles and 20,000 rounds of ammunition – as well as the promise of defence – Gungunhala agreed to grant Rhodes mineral and commercial rights in his territory. Signed on 4 October 1890, the agreement was to be ratified on delivery of the rifles. This, of course, entailed further delay. It took some time to amass the firearms and then came the problem of transporting these arms to Gazaland. An attempt to smuggle the rifles up the Limpopo on board a steamer, in February 1891, led to brushes with the Portuguese who, failing to intercept the steamer, sent a force of 150 men to commandeer the contraband weapons. The outcome of this chase up the river bordered on the ludicrous. Instead of seizing the steamer's cargo, the Portuguese officials merely demanded £2,000 customs duty and – as there was no available cash – eventually accepted a signed bond for that amount from the Chartered Company's representative. The denouement of this comic-opera episode came when, under the noses of the Portuguese customs men, the rifles were duly conveyed to Gungunhala's kraal.

But the fun did not end there. Things were further complicated by the unexpected arrival of Dr Jameson. Having survived a gruelling overland trek of almost 800 miles, Jameson and two companions, all on the point of collapse, turned up at Gungunhana's kraal at the beginning of March. By that time Gungunhana had agreed to confirm his provisional concession and, once this was done, Jameson set off for the Limpopo with the intention of sailing to the Cape on the Chartered Company's steamer. But he had reckoned without the Portuguese. On reaching the river he found that a Portuguese gunboat had seized the steamer. He and his companions were then placed under arrest and shipped to Delagoa Bay where they were released and forced to return to Cape Town.

But all was not lost. Before his arrest, Jameson had arranged for a man to take Gungunhana's concession to Delagoa Bay by a land route and, shortly after being released by the Portuguese, he was able to recover it. His eventful mission, it seemed, had not been entirely in vain. Unfortunately, this triumph – important as it seemed at the time – proved to be short-lived. The fate of Gazaland was settled not by Gungunhana, or by Rhodes, but by the politicians in Europe.

Under the terms of a new Anglo-Portuguese Convention, formally ratified on 3 July 1891, Gazaland and most of Manicaland was placed beyond the reach of the Chartered Company. Although Portugal conceded the Manica plateau to Britain, it retained control of the coastal region and reaffirmed its claim to the whole of Gazaland. This, in effect, cut Mashonaland off from the Indian Ocean and put paid to Rhodes's plans for a 'road to the sea'. It was a devastating blow. Nor were things helped by the tardiness of the Portuguese who appeared to be making no effort to build the railway from Beira to Fort Salisbury that had been promised in the first Anglo-Portuguese Convention. The British Foreign Office, Rhodes was later to tell W. T. Stead, had pulled off a 'diplomatic success' but had ignored the practical question of how the pioneers were to be fed. 'The Portuguese Treaty,' he complained, 'stops everything . . . . One clause in the Treaty insisting on the immediate construction from the East Coast of a light train would have saved the situation. But for the sake of European politics, and in order to settle the question, this was not done and we shall have to face great misery through this.'

The second Anglo-Portuguese Convention was signed a mere three months before Rhodes arrived in Beira in September 1891. Its terms were still being digested. Rhodes's anger when confronted by the Portuguese customs official was probably an indication of his difficulty in swallowing his humiliation. According to Frank Johnson, he 'ever afterwards hated Beira'.

* * *

Rhodes's more indulgent biographers describe his first visit to Mashonaland as an idyllic interlude. He is pictured touring the country in a haze of joy and wonderment, revelling in the open-air life, joining in the campfire *camaraderie*, distributing largesse, and being 'greeted with great delight by the settlers'. In fact it was an exhausting and far from carefree sojourn. Rhodes spent most of his time jolting across the veld in a rickety mule cart, or on horseback, often soaked to the skin by the incessant rain, and listening to the interminable complaints of disillusioned pioneers. Far from being the schoolboy holiday he had anticipated, his seven weeks in Mashonaland made considerable demands on his stamina and left him little time for relaxation. He needed all the energy and optimism he could muster to cope with the problems of the 'promised land'.

The pioneers had been settled in Mashonaland for a full year when Rhodes arrived. It had been a year of struggle, hard work, spartan living and, for some, blighted hopes. Things had rarely worked out as planned. Although a primitive township – mostly mud huts, tents and a few corrugaged-iron shacks – had been established at Fort Salisbury (the 'Fort' was soon dropped) there was little else, other than the widely dispersed police outposts and mining camps, to mark the Chartered Company's occupation. For the most part, the pioneers had been too intent on prospecting for gold to undertake the serious business of settlement. Building materials were scarce, transport expensive and unreliable, and the lack of civilized amenities hampered all attempts at domesticity. None of this would have mattered had Mashonaland lived up to the pioneers' expectations. But it had not. Lured to Lobengula's realms by the hope of quick riches, they had found themselves battling for existence in a remote and potentially hostile wilderness.

On setting out, each recruit to the pioneer column had been promised fifteen gold claims in Mashonaland. No time had been lost in pegging out these claims but, as the months passed, the chances of discovering another Witwatersrand appeared less and less likely. Not everyone had despaired – there was constant talk of the need for patience, of the possibility of lucky strikes and overnight fortunes – but considerable fortitude was required to weather the repeated disappointments. The uncertainty which prevailed in the mining camps was reflected in Lord Randolph Churchill's despatches. 'Many months,' he wrote, shortly before Rhodes arrived, 'probably a year or two, must elapse before any certainty can be arrived at as to whether Mashonaland is a gold-producing country or not. Even if it turns out to be a country possessing gold deposits, the payable character of these deposits depends entirely upon whether cheap and easy access to them can be gained.' Many diggers were reluctant to accept such a gloomy prognostication, but it was impossible to refute it with confidence. Indeed, some of them must have echoed the reply given to Rhodes by one of their more forthright spokesmen when he was asked what he thought of Mashonaland. 'Well, if you want my opinion,' the man snorted, 'it's a bloody fyasco.'

Rhodes had been fully aware of the discontent before his visit. The reports from Chartered Company officials were far from encouraging. Not only was he informed of the pioneers' luckless mining ventures, but he knew also of their hardships. Many of the outlying camps were plagued by blackwater fever, several men had died for want of medical treatment, others had staggered back to Fort Salisbury in a state of delirium, their clothes in tatters and their minds deranged. The onset of the summer rains added to the diggers' misery. Swollen rivers made travelling impossible, some camps were completely water-logged and food rotted in the dank tents, provision convoys from the south were unable to get through for three months and the price of basic necessities – always exorbitant – became prohibitive. Essential medicines, such as quinine, were unobtainable and, even worse for some diggers, so was liquor.

New problems and unforeseen difficulties seemed to present themselves daily. Rhodes constantly had to fend off threats to his authority. One ominous challenge arose towards the end of his visit: it involved the right of the pioneers to settle in Mashonaland.

Besides being allocated fifteen gold claims, the would-be settlers had been promised farms of 3,000 acres. While no objection could be raised to the pioneers' mining activities – which had been provided for by the Rudd concession – their right to take over farm land was highly questionable. There was nothing in Rudd's agreement with Lobengula which allowed the Chartered Company to parcel out land to settlers. This lack of entitlement was seized upon by Rhodes's opponents – some of whom were still stationed at Lobengula's kraal – and they were quick to exploit it. In November 1891, E. R. Renny-Tailyour, acting on behalf of Edward Lippert, persuaded Lobengula to grant a concession which gave Lippert land and settlement rights in the Ndebele domains for a hundred years. The validity of this concession was later to be disputed. For, although the Rudd concession made no provision for the distribution of land, it did stipulate that any land grants made by Lobengula would be subject to the consent of Rhodes's company and, as this consent was not sought, the so-called 'Lippert Concession' lacked legal sanction. (It was actually ruled to be invalid by a judicial committee in 1918.) At the time, however, it appeared a shrewd move. Both Lobengula and Lippert had reason to think that they had cornered Rhodes. With Lippert controlling the settlement of Mashonaland, the Chartered Company's operations would be severely hampered.

175

This was what Rhodes had feared. He had long suspected that Lippert and Renny-Tailyour were working in conjunction with German bankers and the Transvaal government and had earlier tried to prevent them from entering Matabeleland. His first reaction, once the concession was signed, was to have it declared invalid. But, realizing that this would involve lengthy legal proceedings, he decided instead to buy Lippert out. This was not easy. Lippert was every bit as cunning as Rhodes and the negotiations that followed were complicated by mutual distrust. In the end, however, Rhodes won. He bought the concession from Lippert – who may have been angling for such a settlement from the outset – for £30,000. It was a price he was willing to pay to rid himself of a dangerous adversary and this made the legal niceties of the issue irrelevant.

The question of farm land was included in a list of complaints presented to Rhodes when he reached Fort Salisbury at the beginning of his visit. A grimly determined 'Vigilance Committee' met him and poured out their grievances, bemoaning the appalling conditions that made life in Mashonaland intolerable. Some of them had not received their promised gold claims, there was no reliable labour force, food prices had soared and, after a year's wait, the allocation of farms was far from certain. Rhodes listened to all they had to say, sympathized and did his best to reassure them. He was adamant that the promise of gold claims would be honoured, that efforts were being made to improve communications and that this would bring down the price of food but – as Edward Lippert had not then been granted his concession – he could give no firm commitment about the distribution of land. The farms, he claimed, would be allocated but it would take time.

In dealing with another contentious issue, Rhodes was more decisive. He firmly turned down all suggestions that the regulations which governed mining operations in the territory should be altered. The diggers' objections sprang from an obnoxious condition which obliged them to share any profits from their claims, on a fifty-fifty basis, with the Chartered Company. This not only reduced their capital but, they insisted, discouraged mineral development. Such arguments, valid though they were, failed to sway Rhodes. Anxious as he was to shine as a founding-father, he balked at playing fairy-godmother with the Chartered Company's income. It was only later – when hopes were further diminished and the protests grew louder – that the division of profits was replaced by a royalty system.

The amazing thing is that, with so little to offer, Rhodes was able to allay the widespread discontent. It says a great deal for his personal magnetism, his indefinable charm and his prodigious powers of persuasion. No matter how hostile his audience, he invariably succeeded in coaxing meetings into rapturous applause. How he did this remains a mystery. When speaking in public his rhetoric was more predictable than inspiring and there was little about his physical appearance – his heavy features and his habitually reserved, calculating and somewhat withdrawn expression – to suggest a dynamic personality. Yet the fact remains that, by his very presence in Mashonaland, he was able to dispel the pioneers' fears and revive their flagging enthusiasm. He was helped, of course, by his readiness to listen, to sympathize, to offer practical advice and to back his word with generous donations to needy causes. Men who approached him face-to-face rarely went away empty handed. Only occasionally did he fail to convince the sceptics. One of these was a tough Scots spokesman from a hard-pressed community who, after listening to Rhodes extolling the virtues of imperialism, remained distinctly unimpressed. 'I would have ye know, Mr Rhodes,' he growled, 'we didna come here for posterity.'

After his short stay at Fort Salisbury, Rhodes went on a tour of the country, making detours to inspect ancient gold workings in the Mazoe and Hartley districts. He was accompanied part of the way by Lord Randolph Churchill, whose newspaper reports, while they were together, became decidedly more optimistic. Rhodes's arrival in Mashonaland, Churchill observed, 'served to stimulate the action of authority, strengthen confidence, reanimate men's minds.' Churchill even went so far as to describe the condition of Mashonaland as 'bright and smiling' and held out hopes of further improvements once the telegraph reached Fort Salisbury. Admittedly his optimism was short-lived but it is an indication of Rhodes's infectious enthusiasm that the disgruntled Churchill changed his tone at all.

The rest of the tour was conducted in haste. It is estimated that Rhodes and his party travelled 625 miles in seven days, mostly on horseback over rough ground. Even so they found time for some 'excellent sport' on the way. This was a rare experience for Rhodes. Hunting wild animals did not feature high in his African pastimes and his knowledge of tracking game was minimal. Frank Johnson tells the story of Rhodes's first encounter with a lion earlier in the trip. It appears that Rhodes had at first been extremely sceptical about the lighting of fires after dark to keep prowlers from the camp. He quickly changed his mind when, after sneaking out one night to answer a call of nature, he was greeted by a call of the wild. Squatting beyond the ring of trees, he was startled by a nearby growl. 'Almost immediately,' says Johnson, 'I saw the strange sight of the Prime Minister of the Cape dashing back towards our tent. "What's the matter?" I asked him. "A lion has been chasing me," was his breathless reply, given with a considerable amount of emotion, while the trousers of his pyjamas were hanging well below his knees.'

There is no record of how Rhodes fared on the hunting expeditions.

He was probably happier when, on their way south to the Bechuana-land border, the party explored the mysterious ruins of the Great Zim-babwe. This huge stone edifice, built without mortar, was the most im-pressive of the many ruins scattered about the territories north of South Africa and has since been identified as a former religious and commer-cial centre of the powerful (Shona) Rozwi empire, probably built in the 13th or 14th century. At the time, however, its origins were unknown – that it was built by Africans was considered impossible – and later legends were to arise associating it with King Solomon, the Queen of Sheba and the Phoenicians. The incurably superstitious Rhodes was fascinated by the aura of mystery surrounding the ruins. His interest in Zimbabwe continued throughout his life and he took great pride in a collection of stone and iron ornaments which, excavated from the ruins, were housed in a cabinet at Groote Schuur. The fact that many of these relics were phallic, and thought to be connected with phallus worship, is said to have scandalized visitors to Rhodes's house and encouraged rumours about his interests and inclinations.

The tour ended when Rhodes reached Fort Tuli, the southernmost outpost, in the middle of November. From there he travelled on through Bechuanaland to Mafeking, reaching Kimberley at the end of the month. For all the complaints, despair and disappointment he en-countered, he could count his visit a success. He had won most of his arguments with the pioneers, raised morale, comforted the faint-hearted, demonstrated his faith in the future and gained first-hand knowledge of the problems that still had to be solved. Of equal impor-tance were the steps he had taken to ensure Mashonaland's economic viability.

Probably the most significant outcome of this visit resulted from the discussions Rhodes had with Dr Jameson. The two friends had met at Umtali, shortly after Rhodes arrived in the country. They had a great deal to talk about. A month or so earlier, Jameson had replaced Archi-bald Colquhoun as administrator of Mashonaland. The appointment had come as no surprise. Officially Colquhoun's resignation was put down to ill-health but it was well-known that he and Jameson – who was acting as Managing Director of the Chartered Company – were unable to work together. Colquhoun's departure had long been ex-pected. Jameson, with new-broom enthusiasm, had his own ideas about running the country and was looking to Rhodes to give him a free hand. He was given it during the discussions which began at Umtali. 'Rhodes,' he reported to his brother, 'will back up everything I think – at all events he has done so up to this – so everything will come right.'

Jameson's reforms began with what he called 'clearing out rubbish' – by which he meant the tackling of the need for retrenchment. Here

Cecil Rhodes as a boy, in a rare
sporting pose.

Rhodes as a student at Oxford.

Cecil Rhodes, aged 27, and Frank
Orpen, the newly elected members
for Barkly.

Jan Hofmeyr, known as 'The Mole'.
Rhodes's close political ally until the
Jameson raid.

The earliest known photograph of New Rush, taken the month Rhodes arrived at the diggings.

Colesberg Kopje in 1873, enmeshed in hauling lines.

An early diggers' encampment; Rhodes seated right, in black hat.

Leander Starr Jameson as a newly arrived doctor in Kimberley.

The doughty Paul Kruger, President of the Transvaal.

Group of De Beers directors. Rhodes is seated centre with Jameson on his right. Standing far left in the back row is the controversial Dr Rutherfoord Harris.

(Above) The famous cheque for £5,338,650 which signified the end of the titanic struggle for control of the diamond industry.

(Left) The dapper Barney Barnato.

Rhodes with Bob Coryndon (left) and
Johnny Grimmer.

Philip Jourdan, Rhodes's devoted
secretary.

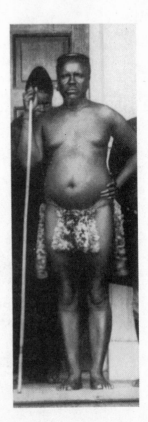

(Above) Neville Ernest Pickering,
the object of Rhodes's deepest
affection.

(Right) Lobengula, last king of the Ndebele.

Encampment in the Matopos during the Ndebele rebellion. Rhodes seated centre, flanked by General Carrington and Mrs Colenbrander. Johnny Grimmer is seated far right.

Rhodes's heart complaint made it necessary for him to lie down at times of stress. Here he takes advantage of a mattress in the veld during the Ndebele rebellion.

Olive Schreiner,
Rhodes's passionate critic.

Princess Catherine Radziwill, at the
time of her meeting with Cecil
Rhodes.

Rhodes seated outside the fortified Sanitorium during the siege of Kimberley.

Groote Schuur, Rhodes's cherished home outside Cape Town.

Rhodes's cottage at Muizenberg, as it was at the time of his death.

Rhodes's coffin arrives at Cape Town station on its way to Rhodesia, where he was buried. Draped funeral train in background.

he had no difficulty in obtaining Rhodes's agreement. The occupation of Mashonaland had proved a very expensive business. So expensive that, within a year, the Chartered Company's original capital of one million pounds had been cut by almost a half. The cost of mounting the pioneer column, of equipping and maintaining a large police force, of extending the telegraph line from South Africa, of buying up concessions and organizing the administration had taxed the Company's resources to the hilt. Once it became apparent that the country was not going to yield quick profits the need to economize had become urgent.

The most obvious target for cost-cutting was the police force. In a speech he later made to Chartered Company shareholders, Rhodes outlined the position in Mashonaland at the time of his visit. He had found, he said, a discontented population of about 15,000 people, protected by a large body of police which had to be fed 'by carting food for 1700 miles from the coast'. This cost the company an estimated £250,000 a year (actually later estimates put it at £150,000 a year). 'Dr Jameson and myself,' Rhodes went on, 'talked matters over, and he said, "If you will give me £3000 a month I can pull through."' This sum was apparently meant to cover the entire administration of Mashonaland; Jameson's promises depended largely on a substantial reduction of the 650-strong police corps.

He was taking a risk. The pioneers were highly critical of the decision to weaken the police garrisons which, however inadequate, were the only armed outposts in the country. Such fears, however, were more theoretical than real. There were few who seriously believed that they were in danger of attack. After a year's occupation, it seemed unlikely that Lobengula would move against them and it was commonly believed that the Shona tribes were poor fighters who looked to the white men to protect them against Ndebele raids. Ill founded as was this thinking, it appears to have been shared by Jameson who, brushing aside all criticism, pushed ahead with his economy drive. By the end of the year, the police were reduced from 650 to 150 and replaced by a volunteer force, recruited from the settlers and known as the Mashonaland Horse, which it was thought would provide adequate protection.

Bold as they were, Jameson's cuts did not solve his economic problems. Two months later he was complaining bitterly that the continual financial worries were 'the hardest part of the whole business.' He had every reason to complain. So low did confidence in the Chartered Company fall that, in March 1892, bankers were refusing to honour its cheques without guarantees. Fortunately, Rhodes was able to call upon the backing of De Beers to help him out, but this was not a strategy he wished to pursue indefinitely. Obviously a more positive approach to Mashonaland was needed.

As administrator, Jameson was popular with the pioneers. Doubts were expressed about his actions from time to time but, by and large, he was seen as a bluff, down-to-earth official who understood the settlers' problems and who could be relied upon to look after their interests. 'It is really extraordinary his popularity here,' wrote his brother Midge, when visiting Mashonaland at the end of 1891, 'especially as the Company with Rhodes . . . have come in for a good deal of criticism, not to give it a stronger name. Many of the Company's laws and mining regulations are much disliked, but somehow or other Lanner [the family name for Jameson] has a way of talking them over and getting the malcontents to agree with him.'

This was an image which the doughty doctor was at pains to cultivate. He prided himself on his bluntness, his lack of pomposity, his earthy language – his favourite expression was 'an abbreviation of balderdash' – and his hearty, no-nonsense method of dealing with disputes. That this was largely an affectation, that Jameson was a little man who liked to act big, a snob whose closest associates were mostly upper-class adventurers, did not seem to register with the gullible diggers. He was taken at face value: it was a face which could charm, inspire trust and radiate confidence. 'Dr Jameson,' observed Fred Selous, 'has endeared himself to all classes of the community by his tact and good temper, and has managed all the diverse details connected with the administration of a new country with a correctness of judgement which amounts to nothing less than genius – and genius of a most rare and versatile order. He was *the* man for the position.'

That is claiming a great deal. Jameson was totally inexperienced, hot-headed and far too easily swayed to be the ideal candidate for a position which called for cool, unbiased judgement. His 'genius' was more a matter of calculated risk than of enlightened management and some of those risks, as time would show, were singularly ill-advised. Friendship with Rhodes – the real reason for Jameson's appointment – was not always the best of recommendations.

Certainly the 'diverse details' with which Jameson had to cope were of a rare order. Not only was he expected to reform the economy, soothe the pioneers and establish law and order – officially he was the chief magistrate of Mashonaland – but he also had to keep a wary eye on the neighbouring Ndebele. Although Lobengula's warriors appeared to be quiescent they could not be ignored entirely. With no outlet to the sea, the pioneers were forced to transport all their supplies through Ndebele territory and the possibility of an attack on the supply routes was a constant source of anxiety. Of even greater concern were the raids which the Ndebele continued to make on their Shona 'vassals'. This was something which the white men – for all their claims to be protectors of the Shona – had failed to stop. Nor, as Professor Keppel-Jones has pointed out, did they possess the authority to interfere in these tribal clashes.

'The country [Mashonaland] belonged to Lobengula,' says Keppel-Jones. 'If it had not the Rudd Concession would have had no force in it. Lobengula had given to Rudd the mineral rights, and to Lippert the right to lay-out, grant and lease farms and townships *on behalf of the king*. Neither concession had given away the land itself or the sovereignty over it. Lobengula could not admit that his authority over his Shona subjects had been in the least affected either by the concessions or by the occupation.'

This, whether acknowledged or not, was the position; Lobengula still looked upon the Shona as his 'dogs' and dealt with them accordingly. Ndebele *impis* were sent to Mashonaland to punish tribesmen accused of defying Lobengula, to confiscate their cattle, to slaughter those who resisted and sometimes to drag off, as captives or hostages, labourers employed by the settlers. So devastating were these raids that the mere rumour of an approaching *impi* was sufficient to send the Shona fleeing to the hills, often remaining in hiding for weeks. The result was – whether the *impi* appeared or not – the settlers were continually being deprived of their workforce. How, it was asked, could the country prosper when the labour needed for its development lived under constant fear of pillage and murder?

It was a question to which there seemed to be no answer. Protests sent to Lobengula, via Jameson, often went unheeded. The Ndbele monarch had his own problems. Not only were the raids essential to his economy but they were the means by which his warriors proved their manhood. To have restrained the plundering would have undermined Lobengula's authority both as the supreme military commander and as a symbol of unity for his people: it might even – as some whites hoped – have led to civil war in Matabeleland and the break-up of the Ndebele nation. Recognizing this, Lobengula remained uncompromising. The Chartered Company, he argued, was in Mashonaland to dig for gold, not to rob him of his subjects.

That the power of the Ndebele would eventually be broken was a cherished belief of the settlers. If it did not come about by internal conflict then, sooner or later, war with Lobengula was thought to be inevitable. Throughout the first year of the occupation there was talk of a 'sudden assault' on the Ndebele. 'They intend snuffing him out next winter,' said one of the few remaining white men at Bulawayo shortly after the arrival of the pioneers. The settlers saw war as the only solution to the threat posed by the Ndebele: it was simply a matter of picking the right time.

Lobengula was not unaware of the danger. His dealings with the white men had left him a wiser, more cautious and far more suspicious man. He kept a close watch on the settlers, was informed by his spies of their discontent and had no wish to provoke them further. For, troubled as he was, he was not prepared to risk a confrontation. His refusal to stop the raids on the Shona was a rare and unavoidable act of defiance. In most other respects his attitude towards the settlers was guarded and, to all outward appearances, placatory. The *impis* sent to Mashonaland were given strict instructions not to harm or challenge the white men and, for the most part, those instructions were obeyed. Occasionally incidents involving settlers or their cattle did occur but they were few and without serious consequences. Lobengula was not looking for trouble.

Nor, for that matter, was Jameson. He had enough on his hands without taking on the Ndebele. There can be little doubt that both he and Rhodes realized that they would have to move against Lobengula one day, but they did not want to rush things. War was expensive and, as Jameson explained, 'from a financial point of view it would throw the country back till God knows when.' This, in the early days, was his main concern. His restraint did not mean, as is sometimes suggested, that he was striving for a peaceful settlement with Lobengula. The fact that he drastically reduced the police force is not, whatever his apologists might say, evidence of his pacific intentions. The police, as Professor Terence Ranger has pointed out, were brought to Mashonaland to help forge a road to the sea – 'they were to deal with the Portuguese rather than with the Ndebele.' Indeed it could be argued that by replacing the police with volunteers of the Mashonaland Horse, Jameson was putting Mashonaland on a more recognisable war footing. The system of arming civilians, who could be called out in time of need, was similar to that employed by Boer commandos, one of the most effective fighting forces in southern Africa. It was the Boers who had defeated the first Ndebele king, Mzilikazi, and driven him from the Transvaal; more recently, in 1881, they had triumphed over the British at Majuba Hill. These events were not lost on Jameson. He had, in fact, already discussed the possibility of a commando raid on Bulawayo with one of the Boer leaders. The police were irrelevant to his plans.

He was not averse, however, to allowing the depleted police force para-military powers in their dealings with the local Shona tribesmen. During Jamesons's term of office the so-called 'police patrols' became notorious for their severity in administering arbitrary justice. Any display of what Jameson called 'impertinent and threatening attitudes' on the part of the Shona was stamped out ruthlessly; men were shot, kraals burnt and cattle confiscated with few questions asked. Rhodes was most impressed. In February 1892 he wired Jameson congratulating him on 'maintaining the dignity of the law'. He had been told, he said, that 'white men travelling in distant parts of Mashonaland were more secure than in most civilized countries'. Whether the Shona were equally secure did not seem to bother him. The following month an incident occurred which demonstrated just how precarious life was for those who defied white authority.

The trouble started when a white trader accused the headman of a local kraal of stealing goods from him. This the headman, Ngomo, denied. He refused to allow his kraal to be searched and subsequently insulted and struck the trader. Jameson was appealed to and sent a senior policeman, Captain Lendy, to investigate. Ngomo, however, remained defiant and Lendy went back to Jameson for further orders. He was told to 'take summary measures'. This Lendy did. Returning with a police patrol, maxim guns and a seven pounder, he proceeded to bombard the kraal. Ngomo and twenty-one of his followers were killed and forty-seven head of cattle were taken. Once again Rhodes strongly approved of this dignified maintenance of the law.

Jameson was more circumspect when the Ndebele were thought to be involved. When, in December, a party of Ndebele were accused of cutting and stealing lengths of telegraph wire, Jameson responded with a show of discretion by sending a letter of complaint to Lobengula. He asked the king to deal with the offenders and warned him – not for the first time – to stop his men crossing into Mashonaland. As it turned out, Jameson was misinformed: the Ndebele were not responsible for the wire cutting and apologies had to be given to Lobengula. A few months later, in May 1893, more telegraph wire was stolen and this time the culprits, who were local tribesmen, were punished and made to pay a fine in cattle. But another mistake had been made. It was discovered that the cattle handed over did not belong to the tribesmen but to Lobengula. The king immediately protested. 'Why,' he asked Jameson, 'should you seize my cattle – did I cut your wire?' Once more apologies were called for and Jameson was forced to return the cattle. Trivial as these incidents appeared, they heralded Lobengula's downfall.

When telling Lobengula to keep his men out of Mashonaland, Jameson pin-pointed the real danger. Border-crossings were transgressions of a vague understanding between Lobengula and the Chartered Company and were therefore a potential *casus belli*. Jameson constantly emphasised the importance of a demarcation line between Mashonaland and Matabeleland and insisted on the pioneers keeping within their own boundaries. Lobengula was, of necessity, less dogmatic. Had he accepted the full implications of Jameson's repeated warnings he would, in effect, have renounced his claim of sovereignty over the Shona and this he was not prepared to do. Consequently the king was careful neither to admit nor deny the existence of a border between the two territories. His evasiveness provided Jameson with a ready-made excuse for moving against the Ndebele when and how he chose. By interpreting Lobengula's silence as agreement, he could plead justification for any retaliatory action he took to safeguard the border.

Why he now decided to take such action is a matter of dispute. The decision may not have been entirely his; it is thought that it was arrived at after consultation with Rhodes and the directors of the Chartered Company. However that might be, there can be no doubt that Jameson chose the pretext and the moment to bring things to a head. There had been several 'incidents' in the past which would have given him an excuse for invading Matabeleland, but he had preferred to keep up the pretence of peaceful co-existence. As late as November 1892, Rhodes was assuring Chartered Company shareholders that: 'We are on the most friendly terms with Lobengula. The latter receives a globular sum of £100 a month in sovereigns, and he looks forward with great satisfaction to the day of the month when he will receive them. I have not the least fear of any trouble with Lobengula.' Jameson was, of course, worried about the expense of a war but that worry now became secondary. Could it have been that, with confidence in the Chartered Company declining, shares on the slide, and discontent among the settlers on the increase, a bold move was needed to restore the company's fortunes?

This is what Rhodes's critics claimed. The invasion of Matabeleland, they argue, gave Jameson the opportunity to demonstrate the Chartered Company's power, widen its sphere of influence and, by removing the threat of Lobengula's *impis*, ensure the security needed for development. Even more important was the tantalizing prospect that Matabeleland would prove to be the promised El Dorado. Stories that King Solomon's legendary mines were buried in central Africa were still firmly believed. Now that it was becoming increasingly clear that those mines were not in Mashonaland, Lobengula's territory took on an added attraction. Capitalism was always the spur to imperial expansion in Rhodes's ventures – or vice versa, as some would say.

Whatever the cause, there is no mistaking the events. First there was the provocation by a Shona clan, living near Fort Victoria, who stole cattle from some tributaries of Lobengula in June 1893. As was to be expected, Lobengula despatched a small *impi* to punish the thieves and recover the cattle. However, shortly after crossing the border the *impi* was intercepted by the ever-vigilant Captain Lendy and ordered

184

to return to Matabeleland. Lobengula was humiliated but unrepentant. Determined to assert his authority, he decided to send a much larger force – some estimates give it as 3,500 warriors – to reclaim his cattle and, while in the area, to avenge the insult of the telegraph-wire-cutters who had made free with his property. As a lesson to the local Shona chiefs, the *impi* was ordered not to bring back captives but to 'sweep them off the face of the earth'. Before the *impi* set off, Lobengula dictated letters to Jameson and Lendy, explaining the reason for the raid and assuring them that no white person would be harmed. Unfortunately these letters – despatched by a roundabout route – were not delivered until after the attack.

The sight of the advancing *impi* dressed in their clipped-feather head gear and jackal-tail kilts, carrying long hide-shields, assegais and knobkerries – created panic among Shona and whites alike. There was a stampede to Fort Victoria, the only place offering security, by the local populace. Although Lobengula's instructions not to harm the whites was obeyed, a number of farms and mission stations were surrounded, property destroyed, cattle seized and Shona labourers were slaughtered in front of their terrified employers. On reaching Fort Victoria, the commander of the *impi* demanded that the Shona refugees in the township be handed over for execution. He promised that they would be killed in the bush, away from the river, so as not to pollute the water. This gruesome request was refused by Captain Lendy and a telegram was sent to Jameson informing him of what had happened.

After some delay, Jameson arrived at Fort Victoria on 17 July. He had not been unduly alarmed by the telegrams and had wired to Cape Town warning against 'exaggerated reports' issuing from the Victoria area. On coming face-to-face with the leaders of the *impi*, however, he was more decisive. He backed Lendy's stand and ordered the Ndebele to depart for the border within an hour. If they did not, he said, they would be driven out by force. This accorded with the telegram he had earlier sent to Cape Town. 'I intend,' he said, 'to treat them like dogs and order the whole *impi* out of the country. Then if they do not go send Lendy out with 50 mounted men to fire into them.'

Lendy followed the *impi* with some forty mounted men and did as instructed. On discovering that the Ndebele had plundered and burnt two kraals *en route*, he launched an attack in which ten warriors were killed. There was no attempt at resistance. The rest of the *impi* fled across the border.

It was this, the so-called 'Victoria incident', which decided Lobengula's fate. Jameson now felt that the time had come to wage an all-out war. He telegraphed Rhodes, who wired back: 'Read Luke xiv 31.' ('Or what king, going to make war against another king, sitteth not down first, and consulteth whether he be able with ten thousand to meet him that cometh against him with twenty thousand?') Sanctioned by holy writ, preparations for war went ahead. There was no difficulty in raising volunteers for the campaign. An agreement signed at Fort Victoria on 14 August promised that recruits would be rewarded with a 6,000 acre farm, twenty gold claims and a share of looted cattle. Rhodes agreed to meet additional expenses by selling some 50,000 of his Chartered shares. Two months later the invasion of Matabeleland began.

It was a short war; hardly a war at all, in fact. Jameson moved his men off in the middle of October and by 4 November the white troops were marching into Lobengula's ruined and deserted kraal. The Ndebele had been unprepared for the attack. Before Lobengula had time to organize his defence, the white army was well into Matabeleland and as, according to Keppel-Jones, the king's force was 'riddled with smallpox . . . only part (perhaps half) of the great Ndebele army was ever brought into action.' Nor were those who did fight – still a large force – equipped to withstand the white man's onslaught. Towards the end of 1892, Lobengula had begun to distribute the rifles stored at his kraal but these weapons proved ineffective on the battlefield. The Ndebele had little experience in handling rifles and tended to set their sights too high, believing that the higher they shot the better their aim would be. The invaders, on the other hand, were armed with Maxim guns (this was one of the first occasions these guns were extensively used in warfare) and their firing power was formidable. No less frightening were the cannon which, it is said, excited superstition in the Ndebele ranks. Some of the warriors – or so the story goes – were convinced that when a shell exploded 'numbers of little white men came out of it and began firing with their rifles.' Small as was the invading army, it was incalculably strengthened by its vastly superior weaponry.

Lobengula recognized the hopelessness of his position from the outset. Shortly before the fighting began, he had despatched his half-brother, with two *indunas* to interview Sir Henry Loch in Cape Town. They were accompanied by James Dawson, a white trader, but only got as far as Tati. Here Major Kenneth Goold-Adams, in charge of a contingent of Bechuanaland police, had established his headquarters. On arriving at the police camp, Dawson went off for a drink, leaving the Ndebele in charge of a mine foreman and giving only a vague indication of who they were. Goold-Adams, hearing that 'three natives' had arrived and thinking they might be spies, ordered their arrest. The two *indunas* put up a fight and were killed and it was only after Dawson had explained the purpose of their mission that Lobengula's half-brother was allowed to return to Bulawayo. Whatever doubts

Lobengula may have had of the white men's intentions were amply confirmed by the muddled Tati incident. He knew his days were numbered. 'The white men,' he declared, 'are fathers of liars.'

As Jameson's troops prepared to converge on Bulawayo, Lobengula prepared to flee north. He had often spoken of leaving Matabeleland, but now flight was his only option. After destroying the remains of his arsenal and burning his kraal, he set off in his bullock wagon with a band of loyal followers. The invaders, he declared before leaving, 'will never catch me. I will throw myself over a height . . . . The white people are coming now. I did not want to fight them.' The pathos of Lobengula's plight was not lost on Rhodes. 'Fancy,' he wrote to Sir Henry Loch, 'the King in the bush in his wagon drawn along by a few Bulawayo boys and deserted by all his royal regiments. It is really very sad.'

By that time Rhodes was in Mashonaland. He had left Cape Town on 18 September, shortly after parliament rose, and sailed to Beira. He was in high spirits and appeared anxious to arrive before the fighting began. On reaching Umtali, however, his mood changed. Instead of pushing straight on to Fort Salisbury he decided to spend several days in camp, allowing his companions to amuse themselves with a little partridge shooting. Not until some soldiers arrived with news that the invasion of Matabeleland had begun did he recover his former zest and continue on to Salisbury. His behaviour was not as eccentric as it first appeared: there was a purpose to his dawdling in the bush. Fearing that a cable would arrive from the Colonial Office, forbidding the invasion, he judged it wise to remain incommunicado until the troops were on the move. Jameson's force was camped amid the charred remains of Bulawayo when Rhodes eventually caught up with it.

Rhodes's arrival coincided with the most tragic event of Jameson's campaign. Earlier a mounted force of some 160 men had been sent in pursuit of Lobengula. The capture of the king was considered essential to the negotiated settlement upon which the imperial authorities at the Cape were now insisting. Already the rains had set in and Lobengula's trail was not easy to follow. By the beginning of December, however, the troops were within a day's march of their quarry who, it was thought, was camped on the opposite side of the Shangani river. But the men were exhausted and their commander decided to send a patrol of fifteen troopers, under Major Alan Wilson, to reconnoitre before proceeding further. The patrol was under orders to return before dusk.

Wilson led his men across the river but then, thinking he might seize the king in a sudden *coup*, sent back for reinforcements. By then it was dark and the commander of the column, fearing a night attack, was reluctant to break camp. Instead he sent a second patrol of twenty-one men to assist Wilson. Neither they nor Wilson's men were seen alive again. At dawn firing was heard from the other side of the Shangani but, so swollen was the river, it was impossible to cross. Later that morning the main column was attacked by a large Ndebele *impi* and forced to retreat to Bulawayo. Not until two months later was the fate of the two patrols confirmed. The bleached bones of the thirty-six men were found on the spot where they had been ambushed and speared to death. They had fired all their cartridges and, according to some reports, died singing the National Anthem. It was an example *par excellence* of the sort of stirring episode by which the history of the British Empire was considered to have been made glorious.

Lobengula's end came shortly afterwards. At the time it was said that he died of smallpox. A later, more sentimental, legend had it that his death was the result of a broken heart. Somewhat more convincing is the account given in 1943 by one of the few survivors among his followers. The king, this old man claimed, sent for a 'small bottle', drank from it and died three or four hours later.

It would be ridiculous to weep over the passing of the bloodthirsty Ndebele regime; on the other hand, there is little to be said for those responsible for its passing. Whatever Lobengula's faults, the 'naked old savage', as Rhodes called him, had not chosen to quarrel with the men who hounded him to death.

On the 19 December, Rhodes addressed the disbanded troops at Bulawayo. Criticism of the invasion was already being voiced by radicals in Britain – led by that *bête noir* of the Victorian establishment, Henry Labouchere – and Rhodes was quick to defend what one of his biographers described as 'the heroic action of the settlers in defending their lives and property against a formidable foe'. The fact that settlers' lives had not beeen threatened and the property they were defending had been acquired by questionable means was obviously beside the point. 'You would have thought,' said Rhodes, 'that Englishmen would have been satisfied. On the contrary, you are called freebooters, marauders and murderers . . . . There are no more loyal people than our colonists in Africa, but persistent misrepresentation will alienate the best of us.' This was the line he invariably took when rebutting criticism of his actions. The assertion of 'loyalty' – mixed with a threat to withdraw it – would always take precedence over moral considerations. For Rhodes patriotism most certainly covered a multitude of sins.

But those who criticized Rhodes were not fooled. Already the mixed motives which inspired the invasion were becoming apparent. Hardly had the fighting started than Chartered shares rose. To those with an eye for such things, other signs of the invaders' predatory intentions were in evidence. Within a month of occupying Lobengula's kraal, the

European settlement of Bulawayo was fully marked out. Originally Rhodes had intended that this settlement should rise from the ashes of old Bulawayo but this scheme was abandoned and a new site chosen, some four miles away. The change of location was neither accidental nor sentimental. Rumour had it that Lobengula's kraal had been built on gold-bearing ground. King Lobengula was dead but the memory of King Solomon was very much alive. No time was lost in searching for the hidden riches of Matabeleland.

CHAPTER TWELVE

Home Affairs

The crisis which led to the invasion of Matabeleland came hot on the heels of the break-up of Rhodes's first ministry. He had only just formed a new government when Jameson announced his intention of moving against Lobengula. This new government was far more to his liking. Having rid himself of the troublesome liberals and dropped the obnoxious Sivewright, Rhodes was able to fill his cabinet with more pliable men. Sivewright's portfolio went to one of Rhodes's newly-converted admirers, John Laing; Sir Gordon Sprigg replaced Merriman as Treasurer, the amenable Pieter Faure took over J. W. Sauer's post as Colonial Secretary and the thirty-five-year-old William Schreiner – a younger brother of Olive Schreiner, who had worked for De Beers – was called in to assume Rose Innes's office as Attorney General. With these men and the backing of Jan Hofmeyr, Rhodes felt himself better placed to pursue his expansionist policies.

The direction those policies were to take soon became apparent. Shortly before leaving for Matabeleland, Rhodes had abolished the office of Secretary for Native Affairs and taken over responsibility for the indigenous population himself. Now, on his return from Bulawayo, he set about implementing his plans for dealing with the 'native problem'. He started by annexing Pondoland to the Cape.

Unrest in this tribal territory, situated between the Cape and Natal, had long been a source of grievance among its white neighbours. Not only were they harassed by Mpondo cattle raiders but, more recently, faction fighting in the territory had tended to spill over the Pondoland borders and cause upheavals in the two white colonies. Annexation had been talked about for years. In 1893 the demand for action had become more urgent when the Mpondo appeared to add insult to injury. Sir Henry Loch, on a tour of the territory, had sent for the paramount chief, Sigcau, to discuss the situation and Sigcau had been three days late in keeping his appointment. There was nothing unusual in this – the Mpondo chiefs were said to be extremely 'dilatory in their attendance at meetings with representatives of the Government' – but for the High Commissioner to be kept waiting in this way was seen as a calculated act of defiance. The fact that Sigcau tried to make amends by offering Loch twelve head of cattle did nothing to lessen the High Commissioner's sense of outrage. The Mpondo, it was thought, should be brought to heel.

But Rhodes had his own reasons for annexing Pondoland. Already concession hunters were busy acquiring land grants in the territory and – a matter of greater concern – Natal's recently elected government was threatening to forestall him with a take-over bid. Faced with these threats, Rhodes moved swiftly. With the help of local magistrates in Pondoland, he brought pressure to bear on Sigcau who, after much heart-searching, agreed to sign a deed of submission on 17 March 1894. Three weeks later Rhodes paid a hasty visit to the territory.

This visit was to give rise to a romantic legend. Almost to a man, Rhodes's biographers have pictured him progressing through Pondoland in great state, travelling in a coach drawn by eight cream horses and accompanied by a police escort armed with machine guns. He was determined, it is said, to teach the Mpondo a lesson. The precise nature of that lesson was revealed when he arranged to meet Sigcau. First Rhodes kept the chief waiting for three days, in retaliation for his impertinence to Sir Henry Loch, and then demonstrated what would happen if the Mpondo gave any further trouble. Taking Sigcau to a field of mealies (maize) Rhodes ordered the policemen to open fire with their machine guns and destroy the mealie crop. When the firing stopped, it is claimed, 'Sigcau noted the lesson, and ceded his country.'

It is a colourful story for which there seems to be no factual evidence. How it originated is a mystery (perhaps the success of the Maxim guns in Matabeleland had something to do with it) but, whatever its provenance, it has become firmly ensconced in the Rhodes mythology. Admirers see it as an example of Rhodes's understanding of the 'native mind', his ability to put would-be rebels in their place. Others regard it as typical of Rhodes's arrogance.

The truth is less picturesque. Rhodes's tour was devoid of any showy gestures. Pondoland had been ceded to the Cape before he set out and there was no need for him to frighten Sigcau with machine guns. Moreover, a detailed account of his visit shows that he had neither the time nor the means to stage such a demonstration. Sir Walter Stanford – the chief magistrate of eastern Pondoland, who accompanied Rhodes – was later to deny the stories that were told of the encounter with Sigcau. 'There was no artillery with the escort,' says Stanford, who kept a day-to-day record. 'At the rate which Rhodes travelled there was no possibility whatever of artillery keeping up with him and at that time Sigcau had given no trouble at all to myself as his Chief Magistrate, nor to the Government. This incident of a mealie field did not occur at all.' Stanford was an honest and reliable witness and there is no reason to disbelieve him. The Pondoland Annexation Bill was formally passed by the Cape Assembly in June 1894.

The following month parliament debated a more controversial measure. Officially known as the Glen Grey Act of 1894, this proposed legislation came up for a second reading on 26 July and was described by Rhodes as his 'Bill for Africa'. So proud was he of it that his introductory speech lasted an hour and forty minutes. He was at pains to explain the compromise he was proposing for an extremely divisive issue. Ostensibly the Glen Grey Act was designed to resolve a dilemma that had bedevilled the Cape Assembly for over a decade, but its implications were much wider. It was Rhodes's answer to the perennial and intractable 'native problem'.

Glen Grey was a district of some 250,000 morgen, near Queenstown in the eastern Cape. Semi-mountainous, overpopulated with refugees from nearby tribal lands, overgrazed by cattle and choked in parts by burr-weed, it had long been a source of contention in the Cape legislature. Most Africans in Glen Grey were squatters with no clear title to land and, despite the urgings of Afrikaner farmers who coveted the region, all attempts to evict them had proved unsuccessful. In the early 1890s a further influx of migrant tribesmen had added to the overcrowding and highlighted the district's problems. It had become obvious that something would have to be done.

But what? To have granted the squatters property rights, improving their economic status, would have created a situation which many white colonists were anxious to avoid. Not only would the migrants be recognized as permanent settlers but, under stable and more prosperous conditions, the number of Africans qualifying to vote in Cape elections would steadily increase. Bondsmen, in particular, were vehemently opposed to such reforms. Parliamentary liberals, on the other hand, were every bit as reluctant to condone forced removals and further homelessness. This, in essence, was the cause of a not unfamiliar deadlock. In attempting to break it, Rhodes looked for a policy which would unite not only the Cape but the whole of southern Africa.

Under pressure from the Bond, Rhodes set things going in 1892 by appointing a commission to investigate the situation in Glen Grey. The most important recommendation of this commission was that African families should be granted individual land tenure of 55 morgen (roughly 110 acres) and that those who received no title to land should be obliged to find work in other parts of the Cape. This recommendation was supported by a majority of Africans in Glen Grey and welcomed, with reservations, by their liberal champions in the Cape Assembly. The liberals, however, wanted land titles to be granted without any surrender of voting rights on the part of the Africans and insisted that white men be prevented from procuring land in Glen Grey. Neither of these conditions were acceptable to the Bond. They favoured earlier suggestions made by Victor Sampson – a Cape lawyer and Bond sympathizer – who, in 1891, had proposed that Africans be granted title to their existing huts and gardens, that land not built upon be treated as commonage and grants be given to poor whites. These much smaller property rights would, of course, have made it difficult for the African landowners to meet the £75 occupancy requirements of the recently amended franchise legislation.

Now, in bringing forward his Glen Grey Act, Rhodes hoped to reconcile the opposing factions. His intentions, he claimed, were those of one 'who loves the natives'. The indigenous peoples of Africa had to be made worthy of their country through discipline and hard work. 'You will certainly not make them worthy,' he said, 'if you allow them to sit in idleness and if you do not train them in the arts of civilization.' He therefore proposed a compromise. The migrant Africans would be granted land titles for four-morgen holdings, not the 55 morgen recommended by the commission. Succession to these holdings would be by primogeniture – as suggested by Victor Sampson – and younger sons, debarred from inheritance, would have to find work elsewhere. The £75 franchise would be abolished in Glen Grey but local councils would be set up to allow elected Africans some say over their own affairs. Whites would not be permitted to settle in Glen Grey. He also proposed a labour tax for all adult males who did not possess land and had not worked outside the district during the previous year. This 'gentle stimulus', as he called it, was intended to force the landless to seek work in other parts of the Cape but, in the event, it was not enforced.

The measures envisaged by Rhodes went some way towards pacifying his critics. The liberals remained strongly opposed to the abolition of the £75 franchise and considered the labour tax as a thinly disguised form of slavery. In answering objections to the tax, Rhodes made one of his more asinine disclaimers. He insisted that he had been more of a slave as a schoolboy. 'I had to work five hours during the day,' he protested, 'and prepared for work next day for three hours in the evening . . . . I was compounded in the evenings and not allowed out after nine o'clock.' The liberals were not impressed. 'And you never went out, I suppose?' shouted Rose Innes. Bond members were also critical, particularly of the restrictions imposed on whites, but both sides recognized the need for concessions and the Glen Grey Act was forced through the Cape Assembly in an unprecedented all-night sitting.

This was Rhodes's 'Bill for Africa'. He hoped it would bring the Cape further into line with the Boer republics and so make for a united white South Africa. 'If the Glen Grey policy is a success,' he declared, 'we shall see the neighbouring states adopting it . . . . I hope we shall have one native policy in South Africa.' His hopes were unhappily realized. It took South Africa many years to arrive at an all-embracing 'native policy' but, when it did, the result appeared to follow a process started by the Glen Grey Act. Rhodes, in fact, has been accused of supplying a blue-print for apartheid.

Perhaps it was inevitable that a later generation should see this first attempt to separate the black and white races by legal enactment in a sinister light and judge Rhodes accordingly. But such judgements are biased, clouded by emotion and hindsight, and must be approached warily. Rhodes was undoubtedly ruthless: he would stop at nothing in his attempts to shape the world to his own liking. But whether he foresaw, and deliberately encouraged, the evil effect of his fanaticism is another matter. *Autres temps, autres moeurs*. When the Glen Grey Act was passed it was not only Rhodes but the most enlightened members of the Cape Assembly who welcomed it as a humane solution to a distressing problem. They may have been divided on detail, but they all accepted the act in principle. Indeed it was liberals like Merriman and Innes who suggested that *all* the tribal lands to the east of the Cape should be declared 'a native preserve' (an important step to this end was taken the following year with the establishment of the Transkeian General Council, or Bunga). And Innes, mindful of the Chartered Company's actions in Matabeleland, later described the Glen Grey Act as Rhodes's greatest legislative achievement.

To hold Rhodes responsible for modern day apartheid is to oversimplify an extremely complicated process. Segregation was an acknowledged fact of life throughout southern Africa long before the arrival of Cecil Rhodes; even in the 'colour-blind' Cape, no coloured man had been elected to parliament and in the other states Africans were prevented by law from rising above their serf-like status. There was nothing remarkably inventive about the Glen Grey Act. The idea of conceding minimal rights to blacks in a defined area had been discussed by others and was adopted by Rhodes as a political convenience. His motives were very different from those which inspired the apostles of apartheid. To think otherwise is to underestimate the strength of Afrikaner nationalism, the determination of a threatened people to retain their identity, and the fervent belief that the separation of the races was God-ordained. Safeguarding the purity of their race was, for most Afrikaners, nothing short of a sacred mission. They made no secret of this and once they gained power in South Africa (1948) they set about enforcing the doctrines they had cherished throughout their history. Some Afrikaner historians have, it is true, spoken favourably of the Glen Grey Act but, in pursuing their own ends, the architects of apartheid needed no blue-print from Rhodes.

Apartheid would have been imposed on South Africa had Rhodes never existed.

Rhodes was a racist, his entire career was based on his belief in the superiority of the Anglo-Saxon race; but the extent of his colour prejudice is debatable. His critics can point to his actions in Matabeleland and Mashonaland, and to some of his speeches in the Cape Assembly, to support their accusations of his hostility towards black men. He has been depicted as a blind bigot who shared to the full the prevailing racial attitudes in South Africa, but such an indictment leaves many questions unanswered. Professor Keppel-Jones, for instance, says that it would be too simple to classify Rhodes 'as a racist in the narrow sense', and points to the stand he made on property rights in Matabeleland. After the Matabele war, the British government stepped in and, after consluting the Chartered Company, proclaimed the Matabeleland Order in Council of June 1894. The purpose of this ordinance was to place both Mashonaland and Matabeleland under the administration of the Chartered Company on certain conditions. One of those conditions was that: 'Natives shall have the right to acquire and hold landed property.' To which, in the original draft of the Order in Council, the Colonial Office had added that any attempt by black owners to 'alienate, mortgage or encumber' their property would require the permission of a land court. But Rhodes had objected. If the 'natives', he said, 'show intelligence or capacity to acquire property of their own, they certainly should not be debarred from doing so; but then I think they should be treated as ordinary citizens.'

His intention was obvious. While favouring 'native reserves' in Matabeleland, he had no objections to Africans owning land outside those reserves or to their being accorded the privileges of citizenship. Land-owning implied responsibility and this was an attribute that Rhodes admired: anyone who was not a 'loafer' was, in his eyes, worthy of respect. Admittedly he shared the assumption of most whites that the majority of Africans were idle and therefore would not qualify as diligent landowners but he was willing to give those who did the opportunity of proving themselves.

It is worth noting that the Matabeleland Order in Council was promulgated a month before the Glen Grey Act came up for its second reading in the Cape Assembly. There can be little doubt that, in his quest for a united 'native policy', Rhodes approached both measures with the same intent. If he did not spell this out in public, it was probably because he did not want to risk alienating his Bond supporters when pushing the Glen Grey bill through parliament. He had no such qualms when writing to the British authorities.

This does not, of course, excuse the ruthlessness with which Rhodes dealt with his opponents. It merely indicates that his actions were not inspired by colour prejudice. He was perfectly prepared – as time would show – to crush anyone who stood in his way, be they black or white. Such was the determination with which he sought to achieve his own ends that he had little time for moral scruples. It was only when those ends were secure that he displayed his so-called Anglo-Saxon virtues.

*   *   *

When he first became Prime Minister, Rhodes let it be known that he did not intend to follow the pattern set by previous governments. He had no intention of confining his attention to the ports and the purely commercial interests of the Cape Colony. Priding himself on the fact that his ancestors were 'keepers of cows', he was careful to pay due regard to the needs of farmers and to promote the colony's natural resources. Not only was this necessary but politically wise. The Bond, on whom he relied, was largely supported by Afrikaans-speaking farmers and keeping his allies happy was one of Rhodes's prime concerns.

He became extremely touchy when accused of being subservient to the Bond. 'I have great sympathy with the Dutch,' he protested on one occasion; 'they have needs and experiences, which we are all, I sincerely think, apt to overlook. I help them as far as I can, instead of opposing them. Is not that the better way? It pleases them and it pleases me.'

But he did not always please the farmers. One of his most controversial measures was the Scab Act which became law during his second term of office. The need for protective legislation to safeguard sheep against the ravages of the scab insect – which it was estimated cost farmers something like £500,000 a year – was widely recognized. Since 1886 a number of acts had been passed by the Cape Assembly in an attempt to enforce sheep-dipping and, where necessary, quarantine but they had been poorly administered and were often undermined by the reluctance of some farmers to countenance government interference in what they saw as a purely domestic matter. Shortly after becoming Prime Minister, Rhodes had set up a Scab Disease Commission to investigate the workings of these earlier acts and it was found that, although the scab legislation was observed in parts of the Cape, there was strong resistance in the north-western areas where a combination of drought and ignorance caused a high proportion of the sheep fatalities. The commissioners therefore recommended a new compulsory act which could, under special circumstances, be suspended in particular districts.

The Bond, some of whose members objected to the compulsory measures, first tried to have the act amended and then opposed it outright. Rhodes tried to placate them by suggesting that the new legislation be given a three year trial, but was met with a demand that a dividing line be drawn which would allow farmers in the west to operate on a voluntary basis. To his credit, Rhodes refused to agree to such a compromise and, by standing firm, sparked off widespread protests. The rumpus continued throughout his premiership. Angry meetings were held, petitions signed, and deputations were sent to Cape Town to harangue government officials. So heated was the controversy that it threatened to split the Bond and destroy the alliance with Rhodes; it may even have contributed to Jan Hofmeyr's decision to resign his parliamentary seat. For all that, Rhodes held fast. By doing so he undoubtedly contributed to the recovery of the Cape wool industry. By 1896 there was a significant reduction in the number of infected sheep and an increase in exported wool.

He was able to claim other successes with less contention. In 1894 he created the first Ministry of Agriculture and took a personal interest in experimental farming in the Cape. By financing a nursery in the Stellenbosch district, under the supervision of Harry Pickstone – a California-trained horticulturist – he encouraged the growing of imported deciduous fruit trees and later established the fruit farms which gave rise to a thriving Cape industry. The story goes that, when selecting the site for these farms, Rhodes instructed his farm manager to buy the entire Drakenstein valley. Startled, the man protested that it would 'cost a million.' 'I don't ask your advice,' retorted Rhodes. 'I want you to buy it. Buy it!' The manager bought whatever land was for sale.

Other experts were called in to improve the methods of fruit growing and to advise on the packing of fruit for export. Australian ladybirds were imported – via California – to clear the orange groves of insect pests; American vine roots were planted to combat phylloxera, the aphid disease which was ruining Cape vines. (A seedless variety of South African grape was named, somewhat ambiguously, Cecily.) Only in trying to persuade the British government to give preference to colonial wines over those imported from France, did Rhodes fail in his efforts to promote the Cape's export trade.

Bond members had reason to be grateful to Rhodes. The furore caused by the Scab Act was partly offset by the benefits of improved farming methods. Never, it was said, had Cape farmers had a Prime Minister 'so solicitous for their interests.' But Rhodes was not motivated entirely by politics. His interest in farming was genuine and displayed itself in many ways. He is credited with importing Arab stallions to improve the breed of Cape horses, with seeking out a special type of Angora goat to cross with the Cape stock and with inspiring the afforestation of large tracts on the lower slopes of Table

Mountain. He donated six acres of land to the newly revived agricultural society and encouraged plant research. 'Sweet pasture grasses,' he would claim, when the mood took him, 'are of more importance to South Africa than all their politics.' It was advice he would have been wise to heed.

Had Rhodes confined his activities to the Cape, had he been content with his role as a colonial Prime Minister, had he sought to create sweet pasture instead of empires, he might not have earned world renown but he would have carved an honourable niche for himself. For there can be no doubt that his love for the Cape was sincere and that sincerity was one of his more endearing virtues. The Cape was the only place Rhodes acknowledged as home: he cherished its institutions, delighted in its natural beauty and was proud of its civilized traditions. Nowhere was that pride more obvious than in his enthusiasm for Cape Dutch architecture.

Until Rhodes undertook the restoration of Groote Schuur, it was considered unfashionable – particularly among the English – to admire the Cape's architectural heritage. Many of the colony's older houses had been allowed to fall into decay or had been crudely modernized: ugly Victorian façades – cast iron balconies, corrugated-iron roofs and brick frontages – had completely disguised the simple, dignified buildings of the early Dutch settlers. Ornately gabled farm houses, with their thatched roofs, broad paved stoeps and whitewashed exteriors, were rapidly disappearing – often replaced by vulgar copies of European mansions. The vogue for pretentious self-display took little account of climatic conditions or of the surrounding landscape and, with a few notable exceptions, houses were built to reflect their owners' affluence rather than to perpetuate a graceful way of life. This, to Rhodes, was an irreverence that had to be remedied.

The transformation of Groote Schuur was not confined to the exterior of the house. Every room was faithfully restored to its original design; paper was stripped from the walls and replaced by plaster, whitewash or plain panelling; solid teak beams were exposed in the living-room ceilings and all traces of 'imported ironmongery' – hinges and metal work in doors and windows – were removed to make way, where necessary, for brass and copper fittings. Only materials available to the early settlers – teak, stinkwood, natural stone and whitewash – were regarded as sacrosanct. This meant, of course, that the house had to be refurnished. The fake 'antiques', acquired at Maples by Harry Currey, were, says Baker, 'one by one cheerfully consigned to "the kitchen"' and the Cape was scoured for replacements. The discovery by Herbert Baker of a 'plain old wardrobe made of stinkwood', in a Cape Town pawnbroker's shop, started the collection of magnificent Cape Dutch furniture which, over the years, became one of Rhodes's most

198

prized possessions. A fire, in 1896, destroyed some of his treasures but, by adding to what was salvaged, he was able to amass one of the finest displays of furniture, china and *objets d'art* in southern Africa. He had, as Sarah Gertrude Millin observed, 'that poignant sense of the appropriate which is taste.'

Rhodes's reverence for tradition – he once toyed with the idea of having no electric light, or oil lamps, in Groote Schuur and of burning only tallow candles to keep the illusion of age – puzzled his friends. (Even his most cultured associate, John X. Merriman, asked Herbert Baker why he had not torn down Groote Schuur and built a 'fine Tudor house' in its place.) And, perhaps inevitably, his opponents saw his passion for Cape Dutch crafts as yet another ploy in his campaign to win the support of the Bond. Herbert Baker denies this. Rhodes, he says, was impelled 'by a deeper feeling of sympathy for the history of the early settlers and respect for their achievements in civilization, in contrast to his dislike of the Victorian art and industrial materialism of his age.'

This view of Rhodes as a lover of beauty, a man of sensibility and aesthetic discernment, is in marked contrast to accounts of him as a grasping capitalist, a scheming business man of malevolent intent, and bears little resemblance to the ruthless conqueror of Matabeleland who was ready to sacrifice the lives of others to gain his own ends. Admittedly Herbert Baker was a biased witness who was in Rhodes's pay and knew nothing of his financial and political machinations but there is no reason to doubt his word. He, perhaps more than anyone, was in a position to know Rhodes's artistic tastes and interests and the results of their cooperation speak for themselves. In any case, there is nothing particularly unusual about Rhodes's dual nature; it was something he shared with other autocrats. Moreover, Rhodes was notorious for dividing his life into separate compartments: he rarely allowed the snare in his hand to frighten the dove on his shoulder.

What is more surprising is that Rhodes's private enthusiasms were not shared by his close associates. There were few of his friends with whom he could discuss his more civilized interests. He appears, in fact, to have regarded any expression of his finer feelings as a weakness: something to be indulged but not spoken about.

His friendships were, for the most part, political and his social life was confined to routine entertainments. He played whist and later graduated to bridge; he enjoyed table talk and banter and often sat late into the night chatting to his guests; he prided himself on drawing other people out and loved scoring debating points; but he was careful to keep the conversation impersonal and shied away from any attempt at intimacy. The slightest hint of familiarity tended to embarrass him. According to Herbert Baker, he even disliked saying good-night or good-bye and discouraged all 'outward show of welcome'. His brother Frank, arriving at Groote Schuur after a long absence, was astonished when, instead of greeting him with the 'expected outstretched hands', the flustered Rhodes rushed him off to inspect a recently decorated room. That was the nearest Rhodes could come to a demonstration of affection.

Only with a small group of male companions did Rhodes seem to unbend. Stretched out on a sofa, his hands locked behind his head, he appeared to become more expansive and to talk openly. But his confidences were deceptive. He revealed only what he wanted his friends to know. In all the memoirs written about Cecil Rhodes, there is nothing to suggest a spontaneous sharing of secrets. Those who claim to have known him intimately can only speak of his dreams of empire; he kept his personal hopes and fears to himself.

* * *

There had been a number of changes in Rhodes's private life since the departure of Harry Currey. He was still without a personal assistant but he had appointed two of his favourite recruits to the pioneer column – Johnny Grimmer and Bob Coryndon – to act as his secretaries. Act was all they did. Essentially young men of action, they were out of their depth when it came to clerical work. Bob Coryndon had reacted strongly to the suggestion that he exchange his saddle for an office chair. 'That's not my job, sir,' he is said to have told Rhodes. 'If you want to use me, think of something I'm suited for.' Grimmer was not happy at being called indoors either; but he was an easy-going youngster and, in his slap-happy way, he did his best to oblige. The result was chaotic. A man of few words, Grimmer's command of language was equally limited when writing letters. An example has been given of the way he dealt with Rhodes's correspondence:

> Dear Sir,
>   In reply to your application Mr Rhodes says no.
>   Yours faithfully,
>   John R. Grimmer.

Rhodes's political associates were outraged and civil servants despaired. How, it was asked, could the Prime Minister of the Cape allow his affairs to be so appallingly mismanaged? But Rhodes refused to listen to complaints. Confronted by one of his secretary's glaring *faux pas*, he was apt to brush it aside with an indulgent chuckle. Once, when an angry politician stormed into his office waving one of Grimmer's tactless letters, Rhodes looked frankly astonished. 'Ah,' he smiled, 'but you've never seen him handle mules.'

200

Amusing as it all appeared even Rhodes came to realize that things could not go on like this indefinitely. There was no question of his dismissing Grimmer, but it was obvious that he would have to get an efficient secretary. His mind was made up for him when a special Prime Minister's department was established in the House of Assembly and a clerk was appointed to handle his personal correspondence. This clerk, who, in effect, became his private assistant was chosen by Rhodes himself. He appointed a junior civil servant named Philip Jourdan, a young man he had long had his eye on as a suitable candidate for the post.

Philip Jourdan came from an old Cape family. Born in the beautiful Hex River Valley, he was of Huguenot descent and was twenty-three when he joined Rhodes's staff. Shy, unassuming and primly efficient, he was very different from the usual run of young men in Rhodes's employ. His appearance matched his manner: with his soft, gentle features, which even a heavy walrus-moustache did little to strengthen, his neatly-buttoned suits, starched shirt-collar and sober tie, he looked every bit the reliable, self-effacing secretary. Never very healthy, he was the type of youngster who arouses the protective instinct in both men and women. It was unusual for Rhodes to be attracted by such refined and delicate qualities but that he was immediately drawn to this modest civil servant there can be no doubt.

Jourdan was first spotted by Rhodes in 1890, shortly after he became Prime Minister. At that time he was working as a clerk in a parliamentary office where Rhodes left his hat and coat before entering the Assembly chamber. 'He seemed to have a liking for young men,' said Jourdan, 'and, although I was only a youngster, twenty years of age, he always had a kind word for me on going into or from the House.' Then, on one never-to-be-forgotten day, Rhodes stopped for a longer chat. He questioned Jourdan closely about his background and private affairs; he wanted to know his age and whether he could speak Dutch and write shorthand. On most points Jourdan could satisfy him but he had to admit to a lack of shorthand. 'You must learn shorthand,' said Rhodes, and disappeared into the Assembly chamber. From then on the daily greetings became increasingly friendly.

To say that Jourdan was flattered would be an understatement. He was ecstatic. The effect Rhodes could have on an impressionable young man has never been more graphically described than in the account given by Jourdan. It was a case of instant hero-worship. 'I was never happier than when I was with him,' says Jourdan, 'even the thought that he was present in the House was a source of happiness to me . . . an uncontrollable desire took hold of me to be his private secretary and to travel the world with him . . . . I delighted to harbour the idea, and sometimes I would lie awake half the night working myself up into a

201

state of delirious excitement, speculating on the joy and pleasure which would be mine . . . . I worshipped him and had an intense desire to work for him and to please him. That was all I wanted.' Completely besotted, Jourdan was forced to endure a year's agony when he was transferred to a magistrate's court in a small village. 'I used to take long solitary walks,' he says, 'sometimes extending over several hours, into the country thinking of nothing else but Rhodes, Rhodes . . . .'

He was put out of his misery when, in March 1894, he was informed of his appointment to Rhodes's staff. 'I suppose you thought I had forgotten all about you,' Rhodes said, when he reported for work. 'Do you know shorthand?' With all his mooning about, Jourdan had neglected to take Rhodes's advice and had to admit as much. 'You are a fool,' laughed Rhodes, 'did I not tell you to study shorthand? . . . Well you must acquire a knowledge of it as soon as possible, because I want you to do my private letters.' Until that moment Jourdan had thought he was simply to be another clerk in the office; now he could hardly contain himself. 'I went out of that room,' he says, 'treading on air.'

Jourdan worked hard to please Rhodes. With the possible exception of Harry Currey, he was the most efficient of Rhodes's secretaries. From the very beginning, Rhodes seems to have placed this ingenuous, doe-eyed young man in a special category. 'I knew he would never abuse my trust or let me down,' he said. In marked contrast to the usual chaff and horseplay which accompanied the initiation of a young man into his service, Rhodes appears to have handled Flippie Jourdan – as he was called by his friends – with exceptional tact. 'He was exceedingly kind and tender towards me,' admits Jourdan. 'He made me draw up my chair quite close to him, and frequently placed his hand on my shoulder.' This for Rhodes, who could not bring himself to shake even his brother's hand, was remarkable indeed. Only with the submissive Jourdan, from whom he did not fear rebuff, did he attempt to express his need for human contact.

Yet, for all the growing affection between them, Jourdan had still not realized his ultimate ambition. He remained a civil servant; his position as clerk in the Prime Minister's department fell short of his dream of living with Rhodes as his private secretary. That post was still held, as something of a sinecure, by the ill-qualified Johnny Grimmer. Nor had the innocent Jourdan reason to think that Rhodes's interest in him was exceptional. He was not the only clerk to enjoy special treatment at the hands of the Prime Minister. Few young men in the parliamentary offices seem to have escaped Rhodes's notice. There was, for example, the occasion when he stumbled upon a youngster shivering with cold in one of the corridors and immediately gave instructions for an overcoat to be bought for him at the government's expense. (The clerk who made out the requisition was so incensed by this extraordinary gesture that his pen spluttered as he wrote.) Not many Prime Ministers can have paid as much attention to the junior clerks in their office as did Rhodes.

Another clerk who was to earn rapid promotion was Gordon le Sueur. Like Flippie Jourdan, he was South African born and worked for a while at the House of Assembly. He, however, was completely unaware of Rhodes's interest in him until he paid a duty call at Groote Schuur. He went, he said, 'looking on it as a terrible bore [and] hoped to get it over as soon as possible.' Much to his surprise, when he sent his card in, a steward came out and said Rhodes wished to see him. He was even more astonished when Rhodes greeted him with. 'Well, I wondered when you were coming to see me.'

This was the start of le Sueur's long association with Rhodes. In time, he too was to be enrolled as a secretary and to accompany Rhodes on his journeys north. Rhodes's pursuit of him – he at first refused Rhodes's offer of employment and had to be badgered and bribed into accepting – was, in some ways, even stranger than the slow enticement of Jourdan. For le Sueur had none of Jourdan's sterling qualities. He is vague about the position he held in the civil service but it could not have been a demanding one. Later evidence shows that he could hardly write English and he had nothing else, apart from good looks and an engaging *insouciance*, to recommend him. Lazy, irresponsible, *gauche* and semi-literate, Gordon le Sueur was the last person any sensible employer would favour, let alone chase after in the way that Rhodes did. But he possessed an attraction that had nothing to do with his capabilities: he, like Johnny Grimmer, was a virile, muscular, outspoken, brash young man, the type of devil-may-care adventurer whom Rhodes found irresistible. Le Sueur was taken on as a 'secretary' but he preferred to describe himself as Rhodes's bodyguard. In time there would be other young men who occupied a similar position and le Sueur was highly amused by Rhodes's insistence on calling them his secretaries. He liked to point out that they were rarely qualified for clerical work and, out of the entire bunch, only Flippie Jourdan knew how to type. 'We were all much more companions than secretaries in the ordinary sense of the word,' says le Sueur.

But they were hardly companions in the ordinary sense of the word. Very little real friendship existed between these young men and Rhodes. They were certainly not his political confidants, nor did they share in his more ambitious schemes. These were matters he reserved for men like Jameson, Beit and Hofmeyr. What did exist between Rhodes and his 'secretaries' was an almost adolescent relationship: banter, horse-play and practical jokes. They provided Rhodes with a means of relaxation rather than companionship. It was in his dealings with these young men that his emotions were most obviously involved

– the tears, the sulks and the tantrums. He treated them rather as another man might treat a skittish mistress. He indulged their whims, pandered to their exuberance, spoilt them, teased them and amused himself with them but he never took them into his confidence.

What private life Rhodes can be said to have enjoyed, revolved around his all-male entourage. Women played no part in his domestic arrangements. There were no female servants at Groote Schuur and he tended to panic if he was left alone with a woman guest for any length of time. The physical attractions of the opposite sex were completely lost on him. His friends delighted in telling stories about his immunity to feminine charms. When, for instance, one of them happened to mention that a female guest at Groote Schuur was very good-looking, Rhodes was taken aback. 'Yes, I suppose she is,' he said, after a pause. 'I never thought of it before.' As in his early days on the diamond diggings, he still sought out the plainest woman in any gathering and excused his preference by saying: 'I like her, she has ideas.' His excuses, however, were not always so polite. 'I have been accused of hating women,' he once told an inquisitive female. 'It isn't true, but I have had no time for them.' On the other hand, he would sometimes admire a woman's dress and was known to blush at any suggestion of 'equivocal talk' in mixed company. His apologists often quoted such refinements to soften his boorish image but, in a more enlightened age, they are open to a very different interpretation.

Asked why he did not marry, Rhodes always had a pat answer. 'I cannot get married,' he would say. 'I have too much work on my hands. I shall always be away from home and should not be able to do my duty as a husband towards his wife.' Precisely what he meant by this is not clear. Was he seriously suggesting that men only marry if they have the time to spare? Did he really look upon marriage as a competing career, rather than a human relationship? His trite evasion has been widely accepted by his biographers but it does not bear close examination.

The destinies of the world have not been shaped by busy bachelors. Marriage, for most men, is a basic need, a means of fulfilment. Rhodes must have known he was talking nonsense. One of his great heroes was Napoleon, who, while carving out an empire, married twice. Had Rhodes married, his wife would have wanted for nothing. Like the wives of other powerful men she would have accommodated herself to his career, travelled with him if necessary, and proved more of an asset than a liability. Moreover, Rhodes was not always away from home and he certainly found time to cosset the various young men he adopted. An intelligent wife would have been more supportive of Cecil Rhodes than some of his more irresponsible protégés.

Rhodes's aversion to marriage is open to a more logical explanation. He did not 'hate women' – that was a Victorian euphemism – but he was not sexually attracted to them and he resented their intrusion into his all-male world. 'I hope you won't get married,' he wrote to a friend, while still an undergraduate at Oxford. 'I hate people getting married. They simply become machines and have no ideas beyond their respective spouses and offspring.' This was to be his attitude throughout life. He was willing to overlook the incompetence of the youngsters he employed, to excuse their mistakes and to ignore their insubordination, but he froze at the very mention of marriage. Any of his hirelings bold enough to take a wife met the same fate as Harry Currey: they were denounced and driven from the fold.

The theory that Rhodes was homosexual has been disputed by both his admirers and his critics: it has either been spurned as a 'fashionable calumny' or dismissed as irrelevant. A combination of prudery and prejudice has stifled serious discussion of Rhodes's complex nature. Even those who condemn his actions, his ruthless pursuit of power and shady business deals, have been reluctant to look too closely into the inner workings of his mind. He has been portrayed as an enigma, an egocentric impostor, even a megalomaniac, without any attempt being made to probe his obsessions. But Rhodes, for all his failings, was not a monster and account should be taken of his human frailties.

The more research that is done into Rhodes's life, the more obvious it becomes that he was sexually maladjusted. He made no pretence to being heterosexual and did little to disguise his true preferences. When a woman once applied to be his secretary, he turned her down with embarrassing frankness: 'I don't want a secretary,' he blurted out. 'Can't you find me a nice English boy?' Surprisingly, one of his biographers quotes this remark as proof that Rhodes was not homosexual. According to J. G. Lockhart, no homosexual would dare to say such a thing unless he was a 'flagrant exhibitionist' and Rhodes, he insists, was not that. He appears to think it would have been out of character for him to behave in such a way. But would it? Much of what he said when talking of his young men is equally revealing. If this unguarded remark seems to indicate innocence, it is probably because Rhodes was not guiltily conscious of his homosexual tendencies.

Rhodes was very much a man of his times. He respected Victorian taboos and observed social conventions. His puritanical upbringing made him reluctant to talk about sex and his ambitions demanded that his private life should be above reproach. Any outward display of unorthodox behaviour would have belied his claims of Anglo-Saxon integrity. The society in which he mixed – both on the diamond fields and during his political career – was male orientated and he prided himself on being a man amongst men. Indeed his horror of effeminacy was so excessive that it might be seen as suspect. 'He liked a man to display the attributes of a man,' says Jourdan, 'and despised indecision, weakness and effeminateness in the male sex.' Careless about his own clothes, Rhodes hated 'anything loud in the way of dress' and was so suspicious of jewellery on a man that he would not even wear a watch. Such traits are not uncommon in repressed homosexuals: they indicate both sexual inhibitions and the attractions of aggressive masculinity. Rhodes paraded his prejudices as evidence of his own virility and he may even have deceived himself.

Never would he have associated with homosexuals. The young men with whom he became involved were, as far as can be judged, ordinary, uncomplicated heterosexuals (Jourdan was prissy but not 'camp'), who were oblivious of anything untoward in Rhodes's feelings for them. On the other hand, they were conscious of his tendency to erect barriers between himself and those for whom he cared. Even the insensitive le Sueur instinctively realized that, shortly after their first meeting, his employer had 'adopted an artificial manner, and that the man who spoke to me was not the real Rhodes.' Only gradually did he come to appreciate that, far from being without feeling, the supposedly brutal Colossus was 'crammed with sentiment to his finger-tips'. But it was sentiment reserved for the chosen few and was always indirectly expressed. Had Rhodes found a physical outlet for his affections, he might have overcome his inhibitions and led a more resolved life. As it was his attachments appear to have been purely emotional.

To be surrounded by young men, to be looked up to and admired by them and to exercise control of their lives was, it would seem, the most that Rhodes could expect in the way of close human relationships. It was hardly satisfactory, but it was a definite emotional force in his life. Women could never arouse similar emotions in him. It would be foolish, without further evidence, to speculate on the effect that Rhodes's repressed sexuality had upon his career but it would be equally mistaken to ignore it entirely. Frustration may not have shaped Rhodes's ends but it could well have contributed to the ruthlessness with which he pursued his goals.

*   *   *

With the occupation of Matabeleland, Rhodes had consolidated his base in central Africa and was now master of the two territories which were to bear his name. The problem of what to call the united Mashonaland and Matabeleland had given rise to a great deal of speculation. Various suggestions had been made. Jameson favoured 'Charterland' but most people thought that the name of the new country should honour its founder: 'Rhodesland' had been considered and so, in all seriousness, had 'Cecilia' but in the end it was agreed to adopt the name which – promoted by journalists – had been in common usage almost from the time that the pioneers reached Mashonaland: Rhodesia.

This was the name which the Chartered Company recognized officially in May 1895 and which was acknowledged by the British government three years later. Rhodes was jubilant when the Chartered Company's decision was announced. 'Has anyone else had a country called after their name?' he crowed. 'Now I don't care what they do to me!' It appeared to mark his greatest triumph and his claim to immortality; but he was mistaken on both counts. Even as he rejoiced he was approaching the downfall from which he never recovered and his bid for immortality was to be decisively rejected when, some eighty years later, Rhodesia was renamed Zimbabwe.

Rhodes did not recognize the flickering danger signals – he was confident that he could match up to any challenge – but he was fully aware that a battle of some sort lay ahead. By 1895, it had become more and more obvious that, for all the optimistic reports of Chartered Company officials, the newly occupied territories were failing to live up to their original promise. The continual disappointments experienced by gold prospectors in Mashonaland were now being repeated in Matabeleland. As early as 1892, the findings of mining experts had cast doubt on the mineral potential of Mashonaland and their prognostications had been given wide publicity by the dismal conclusions reached by Lord Randolph Churchill. Hope had been renewed after the occupation of Matabeleland but the initial enthusiasm had been short lived. Once again the expectations of amateur prospectors had been dampened by the informed judgement of more experienced men. There seemed little chance of a second Witwatersrand being unearthed in the newly-named Rhodesia.

The truth of this had been brought home to Rhodes when, in September 1894, he paid another lightning visit to his promised land. This time he was accompanied by John Hays Hammond, a highly respected American mining expert based in Johannesburg. Together with Dr Jameson, Rhodes and Hammond toured Mashonaland and Matabeleland and two months later Hammond produced his report on the mining prospects of the two territories. It was far from optimistic. Although not as damning as it is sometimes described, Hammond's report made it clear that the possibility of large gold deposits being found in Mashonaland or Matabeleland was extremely remote. Dr Rutherfoord Harris, now secretary of the Chartered Company, had read it with dismay. If, he said, 'we have to depend on Hammond's geological report to raise money for this country, I do not think the outlook is encouraging, for, if he cannot say anything stronger than that, I have not much hope for the future of the Chartered Company.'

Rhodes did his best to hide his disappointment. Addressing the fourth annual meeting of the Chartered Company, a few months later, he so disguised Hammond's findings that he left an impression of 'hundreds of miles of mineralized veins' and had the shareholders' meeting cheering. But privately he was far from confident. Hammond's report, together with similar assessments of Rhodesia's prospects, did not bode well for the Chartered Company. Indeed the shareholders' response to his speech seems to have been inspired partly by their confidence in the mineral wealth of the entire southern African region. At that time the Witwatersrand was on the crest of a boom and its prosperity was seen as an indication of Rhodesia's potential. Geographical assumptions were, in fact, contributing to the distortion of geological truths. Rhodes realized this and must have regretted his lost opportunities in early Johannesburg.

Advanced mining methods were largely responsible for the improvements on the Witwatersrand. First a cyanide process had made it possible to extract gold from pyrite ore and then a deep-level theory had established that the so-called reefs on the Rand were in fact 'tilted layers of conglomerate in vast cakes of sediment' which could be mined to great depths. Deep-level mining had paid off and led to the present boom. The only thing hindering further development was the continuing conflict between the *uitlanders* and President Kruger's government. Just how intense that conflict had become was discussd by Rhodes, Jameson and John Hays Hammond during their camp-fire sessions in Mashonaland and Matabeleland.

It was a subject in which Hammond was well versed. Then a man in his late thirties, he had been brought to Johannesburg to manage Barney Barnato's gold-mining properties but had left six months later and joined Rhodes as a consulting engineer. Through his work with the Consolidated Goldfields of South Africa he had come to know most of the leading personalities in the *uitlander* community. Sympathetic to their grievances and aware of the restrictions placed upon their mining activities, he was able to inform Rhodes of recent developments on the Witwatersrand. 'Unless a radical change is made,' he warned, 'there will be a rising of the people of Johannesburg.'

Whether or not this was the first time Rhodes had entertained the thought, there can be no doubt that the idea of revolution in the Transvaal appealed to him. Not only would it end Kruger's stranglehold on the mining industry but it could solve his mounting financial problems and pave the way for a united South Africa. That at least is the theory later advanced to explain the madcap scheme upon which he now embarked.

CHAPTER THIRTEEN

Jameson's Blunder

In November 1894 Rhodes and Jameson visited England. This time Jameson, the 'conqueror of Matabeleland', shared the acclaim that greeted his friend. There was hardly a newspaper that did not hail their arrival and record their movements; they were fêted, flattered and fussed over throughout their stay in London. Rhodes was again invited to stay at Windsor Castle as a guest of the Queen and later he was made a privy councillor. Jameson, somewhat unexpectedly, was made a Commander of the Bath. This visit is sometimes seen as marking the apogee of Rhodes's career and the guarantee of Jameson's future. It was a time of mutual back-slapping, of statesmanlike posturing and high-flown rhetoric.

Basking in his first taste of fame, Jameson was at his disarming best. Addressing a meeting at the Imperial Institute, with the Prince of Wales in the chair and Rhodes at his side, he gave a fulsome account of his recent achievements. The Chartered Company, he told his audience, had annexed 'a country as large as Europe', a country 'where white men and women can live, where children can be reared in health and vigour.' He saw this as the start of even greater things, the beginnings of 'a commercial union of the different states of South Africa'. The extent to which those developments would entail the acceptance of the Union Jack as a symbol of unity had yet to be decided – the Boer states had their own ambitions – but he had no doubts about the commercial prospects of the region. There were now 50,000 Englishmen in the Transvaal and, he pointed out, 'surely even the Transvaal with its 15,000 Boers and Mr Paul Kruger will within a reasonable time see reason, and join in this much to be desired union of the South African states.' The picture he painted was reassuring; it was aimed at inspiring confidence in the Chartered Company and promised a peaceful and progressive future. Reason and self-interest were to triumph over narrow nationalism and financial rivalry.

But his soothing words were deceptive. Even then – as Jameson must have known – Rhodes was contemplating other, more decisive, measures for bringing Mr Paul Kruger to heel.

Shortly before leaving for England, Rhodes and Jameson had visited the Transvaal. They found things very much as John Hays Hammond had described them. The relationship between the *uitlanders* and the Boer government had indeed deteriorated. To their many complaints of intransigence on the part of President Kruger the mining community had added new charges of corruption, discrimination and obstruction. A deeply felt grievance was Kruger's practice of awarding monopolies to favoured foreigners who used their privileged position to exploit the mining industry. (Edward Lippert, who was granted the dynamite concession, was said to have made a 200 per cent profit on the explosives he imported and sold to the mines.) Every bit as objectionable were the Hollanders who surrounded Kruger, controlled important state departments, and were reputed to be implacably hostile to the *uitlanders*. How, it was asked, could an industry continue to flourish when it was hampered at every turn by graft and injustice?

The *uitlanders* had made repeated attempts to negotiate a peaceful settlement of their grievances. In 1892 they had formed the National Union, under the chairmanship of an accomplished young lawyer named Charles Leonard, to campaign for their rights. But they had failed to move the stubborn old President. Their petitions for an extension of the franchise were scornfully dismissed, their pleas for reform were ignored. Any hope of a democratic solution to their problems was effectively dashed when, in the elections of 1893, Kruger was returned to office with a narrow majority. He was then sixty-eight years old, well set in his ways, but physically as strong as Jameson had judged him to be two years earlier. 'Damn you fellows!' Jameson had complained to some *uitlanders*. 'You have all been telling us he has not another year to live, but he will see us all under – like an old elephant.' And while the old elephant lived there was little chance of the situation improving.

Kruger would not yield because he knew he dare not. He saw himself as the guardian of his *volk* and the land they had carved out of a wilderness. As a young boy he had trekked from the Cape with his parents to escape the British and he had no intention of surrendering that hard-won independence. His attitude was made clear in a reply he once gave to the *uitlanders'* demands. 'You see that flag,' he said when asked to make the concession. 'If I grant the franchise, I may as well pull it down.' There can be little doubt that he was right. The *uitlanders* far outnumbered the Boers in the Transvaal and, given the vote, they would soon have taken over the country. Rhodes also knew this and claimed to sympathize with Kruger's obstinacy. 'If I were President Kruger,' he admitted in a newspaper interview, 'I dare say I might not have given the Uitlanders the franchise, because that might have ended my own power. But I would have made my new population comfortable and given them justice.' The trouble was that the two men had different ideas of justice.

210

There were faults on both sides. Kruger had made things worse when, in May 1894, he commandeered a number of voteless Englishmen to serve in a commando raised to quell a local African uprising. Five of the men, supported by the National Union, refused to obey the order and were arrested. There was an immediate outcry and protests were sent to the British government. It was partly to enquire into this episode that the British High Commissioner, Sir Henry Loch, had visited the Transvaal the following month. His arrival in Pretoria gave the *uitlanders* an opportunity to stage one of their highly provocative demonstrations.

Sir Henry Loch was met at Pretoria's newly-built railway station by President Kruger. There was also a large crowd of Englishmen present. When the High Commissioner and the President climbed into a waiting carriage, the noisy onlookers surged forward and some of the men unharnessed the horses, took their place, and proceeded to drag the carriage to Loch's hotel. One man clambered on to the coachman's seat waving a huge Union Jack which, during the journey blew back and enveloped the unfortunate and distinctly embarrassed President. Arriving at the hotel, Loch got out and was immediately surrounded by the crowd who presented him with an address. Kruger was left stranded. There were no horses to take him back to his house and the men who had pulled the carriage disappeared into the crowd. Not until some Boers came to his rescue was Kruger able to depart. Not surprisingly, the old President was furious and the incident was denounced in the *Volksraad* as a studied insult. This, however, was merely an outward sign of the existing hostility. Far more serious were the complaints made to Loch by the *uitlanders*.

The High Commissioner could hardly have been surprised by what he heard. The Imperial authorities were fully aware of the increased tension in the Transvaal. On returning to the Cape, however, Loch wrote to London expressing his fear of a rising in Johannesburg. He proposed strengthening the Bechuanaland police on the Transvaal border, suggested that reinforcements be sent to the Cape and that he be given the authority to intervene in the event of trouble. This plan was rejected by the Colonial Office but, as events would show, it was not forgotten. Rhodes appears to have heard about it while he was in Johannesburg and it must certainly have been on his mind during his London visit. A rising in Johannesburg, supported by an armed force stationed near the Transvaal border, had, by then, become part of the plot he was hatching.

That plot began to take shape while Rhodes was in London. Then it was that he saw Lord Rosebery, Prime Minister of the tottering Liberal government, and discussed the possibility of the Bechuanaland Protectorate being transferred to the Chartered Company. This was not a new

211

proposal. From the time that the Royal Charter was granted it had been understood that such a transfer would one day be necessary but the timing of the hand-over had been left open. Rhodes had his own reasons for applying for the transfer at this time but how much he told Rosebery is uncertain. There is nothing untoward in the official record of the meetings between the two men; later disclosures, however, show that Rosebery not only knew of Rhodes's plans but offered him cautionary advice. As in all Rhodes's dealings with British officials, the distinction between official innocence and private knowledge tends to confuse the basic issue. But sympathetic as Rosebery undoubtedly was, neither he nor his Colonial Secretary was prepared to act hastily and, for the time being, the question of transferring Bechuanaland to the Chartered Company was left in abeyance.

All the same, Rhodes did not leave London empty handed. On another important score he was able to chalk up success. At the beginning of 1895, Sir Henry Loch resigned. The part played by Rhodes in this convenient resignation is again uncertain but there can be no doubt that he influenced the choice of Loch's replacement. The man chosen to become High Commissioner of South Africa – for the second time – was none other than Rhodes's old friend and confidant, Sir Hercules Robinson. Not only Robinson's age – he was seventy and in poor health – but his association with Rhodes and financial in-volvement with De Beers made his reinstatement extremely suspect; but his appointment was pushed through so swiftly that all attempts at opposition to it proved ineffective. In one stroke Rhodes had rid himself of Loch, whom he distrusted, and gained a far more pliable and self-interested ally.

He needed all the support he could get. Before leaving England, he received news of a development which added urgency to his plans. In Pretoria a banquet, attended by Paul Kruger, had been held to celebrate the Kaiser's birthday and the Boer President had made an ominous speech. After telling the German guests of a cordial visit he had once paid to the Kaiser, he went on to praise the loyalty of his 'German subjects'. 'I know I may count on the Germans in future . . . ,' he said. 'I feel certain that when the time comes for the republic to wear larger clothes, you will have done much to bring it about . . . . The time is coming for our friendship to be more firmly established than ever.' The implications of this speech were not lost on Rhodes. The last thing he wanted was further German interfer-ence in the Transvaal. If his plan was to succeed he would have to move swiftly.

*   *   *

In rough outline Rhodes's plan was as simple as it was bold. Closely following the scenario envisaged by Sir Henry Loch, it was dependent on two dramatic events: first there would be a rising in Johannesburg and then an armed force would cross the Tranvaal border to assist the *uitlanders* in their rebellion. In this way, the Kruger regime would be overthrown and future events would be dictated by the mining community.

Intervention by the military force was seen as essential to the success of the plan. The *uitlanders* were, for the most part, business men and miners with little experience of fighting and, left to themselves, they would be no match for the Boers who were renowned for their marksmanship and guerrilla tactics. Only with the help of trained soldiers who could take advantage of a surprise attack would the rebels succeed. From Rhodes's point of view, the military would also enable him to guard against moves by rival mining magnates. He had no intention, as he put it, of exchanging 'President Kruger for President J. B. Robinson'. Secrecy was, of course, of paramount importance. Nothing must be done to alert the Boers. Arms had to smuggled into Johannesburg for the use of the *uitlanders* and troops had to be mustered on the border in a way that would not arouse suspicion. Simple as was the plan, the dangers involved were obvious.

To overcome those dangers was Rhodes's first concern. He set about tackling his problems on his return to South Africa. One of his first moves was to persuade Alfred Beit – now head of one of the largest mining concerns on the Rand, who had so far kept aloof from Transvaal politics – to join him in actively supporting the National Union. Beit was also let into the plot and agreed to help with finance. Then came the question of arming Johannesburg. Procuring guns and ammunition presented no problems. Bought by Rhodes and Beit, the arms arrived at the Chartered Company's depot in Cape Town as equipment for the company's police. Getting them to Johannesburg was more difficult. First they were sent to Kimberley, stored at De Beers, and then concealed in the false bottoms of oil drums and bags of coke. Thus disguised, they were transferred by rail to a firm in Port Elizabeth – owned by Neville Pickering's brother, Edward – and forwarded to Johannesburg where they were unloaded at various mines and hidden underground.

Stationing troops near the Transvaal border, promised to be a more hazardous undertaking. In applying for the transfer of the Bechuanaland protectorate, Rhodes had hoped to obtain a base for his clandestine activities. Part of the protectorate's border adjoined the Transvaal, close enough to Johannesburg to provide a jumping-off spot, and troops in the region could have been given a legitimate cover. The British government's delay in agreeing to the transfer had complicated matters. However, this obstacle was soon removed. In June 1895, the Liberal government fell and Joseph Chamberlain became Colonial Secretary in the new Conservative administration. The arrival of Chamberlain gave Rhodes new hope.

Until then 'Pushful Joe' Chamberlain had been an open opponent of the Chartered Company but this did not stop Rhodes from renewing his claim to Bechuanaland. The man he sent to negotiate the desperately needed transfer was the foxy Dr Rutherfoord Harris. Ostensibly the negotiations centred on Rhodes's plans to extend the railway line joining the Cape Colony to Rhodesia but, as events were to show, the discussions between Harris and Chamberlain went much further than that. There can now be little doubt that Chamberlain knew about, and encouraged, the plot that was being hatched. But once again the distinction between official and private knowledge tends to cloud the truth, leaving the answers to some questions to guesswork.

In the course of his negotiations, Harris had four interviews with Chamberlain. He and other Chartered Company agents also had discussions with various Colonial Office officials. Exactly what was said at these talks is not known but it is fairly certain that Chamberlain was 'unofficially' informed of Rhodes's intentions. How far the Colonial Secretary committed himself to the plot is a matter for speculation. More would have been known had the contents of certain telegrams which Harris and others sent to Rhodes at this time been revealed but, such was the conspiracy, secrecy prevented this. The coded messages were considered far too incriminating for public scrutiny. Those eventually made available – or later unearthed – were, at best, loosely worded and open to misconstruction; others were suppressed. At least one of the telegrams appears to have disappeared altogether. The mystery of the so-called 'missing telegrams' and Joseph Chamberlain's role in Rhodes's machinations has never been satisfactorily solved. For all that is now known, or guessed at, the evidence remains fragmentary. Heads in high places do not roll easily.

The question of the railway extension is more simply answered. Here Chamberlain proved more amenable than his predecessors. Although he refused Rhodes's request that the Bechuanaland protectorate be divided between the Chartered Company and the Cape Colony – there were strong local objections to this – he did agree to cede a strip of land, flanking the Transvaal border, to accommodate the railway. The rest of the protectorate was to remain, at least for the time being, under British administration for the benefit of the African tribesmen. Rhodes was not happy with this arrangement and considered it 'a scandal' that so much land should be allocated to sixty thousand of 'the laziest rascals in the world'. But he was in no position to argue. He needed a base in Bechuanalandand and this, if nothing else, he now had.

The excuse Rhodes gave for stationing troops at Pitsani – a small village on the Bechuanaland border – was that they were needed to protect the building of the railway line. This was acccepted by Chamberlain, even though there was as yet nó line to protect. As soon as Chamberlain gave the nod, Rhodes sent his brother Frank and Sir Sidney Shippard to negotiate the site for a military camp with two Bechuana chieftains. Shortly afterwards it was officially announced that the Chartered Company had been granted territorial rights in Bechuanaland and authorized to 'appoint and control a force sufficient to maintain peace, order, and good government in the territory'. The announcement was accompanied by a notice stating that the Resident Commissioner at Pitsani would be Dr Leander Starr Jameson, CB.

Rhodes had always intended that Jameson should take charge of the military operation. Who better to deal with Kruger than the man who had defeated Lobengula? A popular hero, with a reputation for bravado, risk-taking, resourcefulness and bold leadership, the swashbuckling little doctor was an obvious choice. Not only would he command the respect of his men and activate the *uitlanders* but, what was more important, he was the one man in whom Rhodes had implicit trust. Once Jameson reached Johannesburg with an armed force there would be no doubt as to who was controlling events. The doctor had been involved in the plot from the outset. While Rhodes was busy negotiating with Chamberlain and arranging for the delivery of arms, Jameson had been rushing around the country preparing for action. He had held discussions with the leaders of Johannesburg's mining community and put the Chartered Company's police on the alert. As soon as the Bechuanaland cession was officially announced, two troops of the Mashonaland mounted police were ordered south and Jameson himself arrived at Pitsani shortly afterwards. He could hardly wait to get started.

Tension in the Transvaal was increased by an unwise move on the part of President Kruger. Determined to make the *uitlanders* use his newly opened railway to Delagoa Bay in Portuguese East Africa, the President had imposed heavy duties on rail freight from the British colonies in the south. In order to evade these duties the Johannesburg merchants had retaliated by unloading their goods at the Vaal river, hauling them across the river drifts (fords) and transporting them to the Rand by ox-wagons. But Kruger was not to be outdone. At the beginning of October he closed the drifts and so sparked off a crisis. His action produced a strong protest from Joseph Chamberlain and troopships bound for India were diverted to the Cape. Secretly the Colonial

215

Secretary informed Rhodes – who was making the most of the crisis – that, if it came to war, the Cape would be expected to bear half the cost and provide 'a fair contingent of the fighting force'. With both sides taking a determined stance, a showdown of some sort seemed inevitable. The apparent *impasse* was eventually broken by Kruger's capitulation. On 5 November 1895 he reopened the drifts, and an uneasy peace returned to South Africa.

For once, the wily old President had played directly into Rhodes's hands. The 'drifts crisis' was raging when Chamberlain ratified the agreement which allowed Rhodes to extend the railway line from the Cape to Rhodesia, and what otherwise might have seemed a suspicious deal, was seen as the outcome of Kruger's obstructive tactics. Rhodes could not have hoped for a better cover-up. Nor was he unaware of the boost which the 'drifts crisis' gave to the propaganda he needed for his next move.

*   *   *

Everything seemed to be going according to plan. The rising in Johannesburg was planned for the end of December. Jameson had been provided with an undated letter calling for him to rescue the 'thousands of unarmed men, women and children of our race . . . at the mercy of well armed Boers'. It was intended that he should date the letter at the appropriate time and ride in. A Reform Committee was set up – to act as an organizing body and possibly a provisional government – and it was proposed that, as soon as trouble started, Sir Hercules Robinson would leave for the Transvaal and arbitrate a settlement. Precisely what form that settlement would take was, however, undecided: different factions had different ideas. This is where things started to go wrong.

The idea of sending the British High Commissioner to the Transvaal was similar to Sir Henry Loch's plan to act as mediator. It was favoured by Joseph Chamberlain, who foresaw the Transvaal becoming a British colony and eventually forming part of a South African federation. Rhodes also wanted Sir Hercules Robinson to arbitrate: the intervention of the High Commissioner would provide the insurrection with a cloak of respectability. But Rhodes was reluctant to commit himself about the future of the Transvaal. Always wary of the 'imperial factor', he did not welcome the idea of handing over his hard-earned gains to Whitehall. The forcible overthrow of Krugerism had been planned by him, he and Beit were largely responsible for financing it and, from the beginning, he had insisted on employing Jameson so that he could control future events.

Some of the *uitlanders*, on the other hand, were suspicious both of Rhodes and of British interference. They were hoping to replace Paul

Kruger with an enlightened President and establish a liberal republic which would accommodate the needs of the mining community. The question of whether victory should be proclaimed under the Union Jack or the Transvaal flag became a matter of vital concern.

Other anxieties followed. As the day for the rising approached, the situation in Johannesburg became more and more confused. Doubts arose as to whether the *uitlanders* were sufficiently prepared. The arms – mostly rifles – that had been smuggled into the Transvaal fell short of what had been expected; a plan to seize the Pretoria arsenal had to be abandoned for lack of recruits; Jameson's force was smaller than had been promised and it no longer looked as if the plot could be kept secret. The telegraph wires between Johannesburg and Cape Town buzzed with frantic, bizarrely coded, messages – the rising was referred to as the 'flotation', the conspirators were the 'subscribers', Jameson the 'contractor' and the High Commissioner became the 'Chairman'. Finally confusion gave way to panic and it was decided to postpone the rising. Attempts were made to stop Jameson: messages were sent to Pitsani warning the doctor not to ride into the Transvaal. Rhodes was contacted and urged to call off the raid but, instead of contacting Jameson directly, he left it to Rutherfoord Harris to sound the alarm. By then it was too late.

Impatient and headstrong, Jameson took little notice of the telegrams he received. He distrusted Rutherfoord Harris and treated the warnings of the *uitlanders* with contempt. 'I received so many messages from day today,' he said later, 'now telling me to come, then to delay starting, that I thought it best to make up their minds for them, before the Boers had time to get together.' That was his chief concern. Already he had heard that news of the plot had leaked out and that the Transvaal government was 'aware slightly'. He had no intention of allowing things to drift further; his long-held fear that someone might 'blab' seemed in danger of being realized. The last straw came when, on 28 December – the day he was due to start – he was shown a Reuter's message that had been published in the South African press. Issued from Johannesburg, it read: 'The position is becoming acute, and persistent rumours are afloat of secret arming of miners and warlike preparations. Women and children are leaving the Rand . . . .' President Kruger and his commandant-general were reported to have returned to Pretoria where, it was said, the 'political situation is the talk of the town'. This should have been a warning, but Jameson took it as a challenge. 'Unless I hear definitely to the contrary,' he wired to Rutherfoord Harris that same day, 'shall leave tomorrow evening . . . and it will be all right.'

He did not hear to the contrary. The telegram was sent on Saturday and Harris – who was away from his office for the week-end – did not get it until Monday. Interpreting the silence for consent, Jameson went ahead with his preparations. On Sunday afternoon, he ordered the telegraph wires to be cut and all communication with the Cape was severed. Unfortunately the same could not be said for the link with the Transvaal. Legend has it that the trooper who was detailed to cut the Transvaal wires got drunk and, blissfully befuddled, snipped off and buried a strand of wire-fencing instead. However it happened, the vital line to the Transvaal remained open.

Later that afternoon, Jameson mustered his men and he and one of his officers addressed them. The faked letter calling for help (now dated) was read out and the troopers were assured that the operation would not entail fighting: they were to make a surprise attack for which the Boers were unprepared. Considering the alarms of the past few days it was, to say the least, a rash assumption.

And so it proved. Once across the Transvaal border, Jameson began to discover how slap-dash his organization had been. The ride proved more gruelling than anticipated, the men had little time to rest and eat and soon they were beginning to droop from fatigue and hunger. The remounts they had been promised turned out to be unsuitable and inadequate and, even more discouraging, they soon became aware that they were being shadowed by small bands of armed Boers. At the first evening halt, Jameson received a message from a Boer commander warning him off. This was one of several similar messages to reach him during the three day ride but he ignored them all and pressed on. Not until New Year's day, when the flagging force was less than thirty miles from Johannesburg, did things take a more serious turn. First Jameson received a letter from the British agent in Pretoria informing him (for the second time) that Her Majesty's government entirely disapproved of his conduct, then came notes from Johannesburg confirming that the rising was off and that the reformers were negotiating with Kruger. Then the inevitable happened: he ran head-on into an ambush prepared for him by the Boers. The raiders put up a brave but futile counter-action. Fighting started at four o'clock that afternoon and lasted, on and off, until shortly after nine the following morning. It ended when a white cloth – some accounts say an apron of an African woman – was hoisted on a wagon whip to signal Jameson's surrender.

The invading party lost seventeen men killed and thirty-five missing; another fifty-five were wounded. Jameson made his formal submission to three Boer commandants at a nearby farmhouse and is said to have been trembling 'like a reed' as he admitted defeat. He and the rest of his force were then taken to Pretoria as prisoners. The troopers sang 'After the ball is over' as they marched to the gaol.

*   *   *

218

Rhodes had made a last minute attempt to stop Jameson. On Sunday, 29 December, he had personally wired to Pitsani advising his friend to stay put but the wires were cut before his telegram could be transmitted. He was shattered when he realized he had acted too late. William Schreiner, who saw him shortly after news of the raid reached Cape Town, was astonished at how deeply he was affected. Only the day before Rhodes had reassured him that nothing was afoot. Now, says Schreiner, he looked a different man, despairing and dejected. 'Yes, yes, it is all true,' he burst out before Schreiner could say a word. 'Old Jameson has upset my apple-cart. It is all true . . . . I thought I had stopped him. I sent messages to stop him . . . . Poor old Jameson. Twenty years we have been friends, and now he goes in and ruins me. I cannot hinder him. I cannot go in and destroy him.'

The blunder was bad enough, failure made things impossible. On hearing that Jameson had surrendered, Rhodes went completely to pieces. He steeled himself to send in his resignation as Prime Minister and then shut himself up in his bedroom. For six days he was 'worried to death', hardly slept and rarely went out. The only person to whom he could turn for comfort, the only person he wanted near him, was Philip Jourdan. 'I took his telegrams straight up to him in his bedroom,' Jourdan was to say, 'and sometimes he would say to me, "Don't go away; stay here for a little while". Sometimes he made me stay in his room for an hour or more, and all the time he paced up and down making frequent efforts to read the telegrams . . . . During one of my visits he said "Now that I am down I shall see who are my real friends."'

This was to be Rhodes's *cri-de-coeur*. Knowing he would need all the moral support he could muster – and believing that the only way to hammer home a point was by repetition – he was constantly to challenge the loyalty of his followers. Once he had pulled himself together, he made straight for Kimberley. Not only was this the centre of his financial empire but it was the only place he could look to for sympathy. He was not disappointed. Despite the fact that the recently-married Olive Schreiner and her husband now lived in the town and had earlier launched a passionate attack there on Rhodes and all his works, the people of Kimberley still trusted their hero. Nothing, not even his resignation as Prime Minister, could convince them that he had acted dishonourably. There was a crowd of 'several thousands' waiting to greet him at the Kimberley station. As he stepped from the train, he was welcomed by 'deafening and repeated cheers'.

Rhodes was highly gratified by the demonstration. 'In time of political adversity,' he declared, when he was able to make himself heard, 'people come to know who their friends are, and I am glad that at this period I can count on so many friends on the Diamond Fields.'

He told the crowd not to listen to rumours that his career was finished. Such things, he knew, were being said, but they were completely untrue. 'On the contrary,' he assured them, 'I think it is only just beginning and I have a firm belief . . . I will live to do much good and useful work on behalf of this community.'

There were more cheers. The crowd cheered Rhodes and they cheered Jameson. They were still cheering as Rhodes drove away. He was headed for the De Beers office. Much as he welcomed the show of loyalty, he had to safeguard his business interests.

Having attended to the affairs of De Beers, Rhodes turned to the trickier problems of the Chartered Company. Here things did not look so promising. The British South Africa Company had been granted a Royal Charter on certain conditions and it could be repealed if those conditions were not met. Underlying the provisions of the Charter was the understanding that the company would do nothing to bring the crown into disrepute. While the specific clauses were open to interpretation, there could be no doubt that the company's police had been engaged in an illegal operation and this could well provide an excuse for the withdrawal of royal patronage. Jameson had ignored the strictures of the British officials and Joseph Chamberlain had publicly repudiated the raid and the raiders. A few days after the raid it was learned that Jameson and his officers were to be shipped back to England to be dealt with by the British authorities. It was obvious that a full enquiry into the fiasco would be called for. What use would Chamberlain make of his power to repeal the Charter, if he were forced to defend his own involvement in the raid? Rhodes was taking no chances. Whatever else happened, he was determined to keep the Chartered Company afloat.

On 15 January 1896, Rhodes sailed for England. He still held a few important cards and he intended to play them.

*   *   *

Before Rhodes left for England, news broke of an ominous development in Johannesburg. On 9 January 1896 – a week after Jameson's surrender – President Kruger proclaimed a general amnesty for the *uitlanders* with the exception of members of the Reform Committee, sixty-four of whom were then arrested. Among those rounded up and taken to Pretoria gaol was Rhodes's brother, Frank. The prisoners expected to be held until they were brought to trial but, within a fortnight, most of them were released on bail. Only the leading conspirators were kept in prison. This distinction between leaders and led was apparent in all Kruger's dealings with the rebels. It was more gruesomely applied when, at the end of April, the reformers were tried for high treason in the Pretoria market hall. The hearing was short but decisive. After clearing the hall of women, the judge sentenced four of the ringleaders – Frank Rhodes and three others – to death by hanging and the rest to two years imprisonment and a fine of £2,000. Fortunately, these sentences were not enforced. Twenty-four hours later, Kruger commuted the death sentences and by the end of May most of those committed for two years had been released. Frank Rhodes and his three companions were also freed in June on payment of £25,000 each. All the fines imposed on the reformers were settled by Rhodes and Alfred Beit who later estimated that the Jameson Raid had cost them each nearly £400,000.

Beit accompanied Rhodes to England. The reformers had then just been arrested and news of other repercussions was still coming in. Lady Sarah Wilson – sister of Lord Randolph Churchill – was staying at Groote Schuur and went to the ship to see the two men off. She was struck by the difference in their appearance. 'Mr Beit,' she says, 'looked ill and worried; Mr Rhodes, on the other hand, seemed to be in robust health, and as calm as the proverbial cucumber.' But, if Rhodes had recovered his composure, he was by no means as confident as he had appeared in Kimberley. When Lady Sarah told him she had bet a friend that he would have regained his former prominence within a year, Rhodes hesitated before he replied. Then he said, 'It will take ten years: better cancel your bet.'

On one score, however, he had few doubts: he fully expected a show of public support when he arrived in London. Opinion in England, though officially frowning, was inclined to be indulgent towards Rhodes and Jameson. This was due, in part, to interference on the part of the German Emperor. When news of the raid had reached Europe, the Kaiser had sent a telegram to President Kruger, congratulating him on maintaining his independence against 'armed bands'. This had so incensed a large section of the British public that, instead of condemning the raiders, they had rallied in support of Rhodes. Some years later, Rhodes was to thank the Kaiser for his timely intervention. 'I was a naughty boy,' he explained archly, 'and you tried to whip me. Now my people were quite ready to whip me for being a naughty boy, but directly *you* did it, they said, "No, if this is anybody's business, it is ours." The result was that Your Majesty got yourself very much disliked by the English people, and I never got whipped at all.'

But no amount of public support could allay Rhodes's fears for the Chartered Company. Here he would need all his skills and cunning, his talent for manipulation, intrigue and double dealing, to overcome official opposition. A lot would depend on how he handled Joseph Chamberlain. As he well knew, the Colonial Secretary's concern would be to protect his own career and Rhodes had to ensure that he was not dragged down in the inevitable political in-fighting and made the sole scapegoat. Chamberlain had almost as much to hide as he did – not only had he known of the plot but, as Rhodes was to say, he was in it 'up to his neck' – and there was no reason for either of them to expect total absolution. Rhodes had no intention of sacrificing his life's work to save a politician's skin. Once in London, he began staking out his ground.

He was reassured about his public standing shortly after he stepped off the train at Paddington station. 'I found all the busmen smiling at me when I came to London,' he said afterwards, 'and then I knew it was all right.' The prevailing anti-German sentiment that provoked those smiles was also on Chamberlain's mind. Rhodes did not see the Colonial Secretary immediately but, through an intermediary, he learned that Chamberlain had suggested that if he could produce evidence of a German–Dutch plot in the Transvaal it would help 'to divert the issue and to share the blame'. The tangled web of deception was already beginning to spread and this must have pleased Rhodes. If nothing else it gave him the measure of the man with whom he was about to deal.

Even so, he moved cautiously. He started the negotiations by sending his London legal adviser, Bouchier Hawksley, to talk to officials at the Colonial Office. Hawksley, a shrewd, forty-five-year-old solicitor, considered himself to be in a strong position. He was already engaged in preparing the defence for Dr Jameson, who was expected to stand trial under the Foreign Enlistment Act, and believed he had an excellent case. The raiders, he intended to argue, had invaded the Transvaal under the impression that they had the consent of the British authorities. This, at any rate, was what Jameson had told his officers before they left Pitsani. The fact that Chamberlain's approval had been conditional on a rising taking place in Johannesburg was either not known to Hawksley or he did not consider it relevant. He was relying on the incriminating telegrams which had been sent to Cape Town by Rhodes's agents and which appeared to sanction Rhodes's plan. These he intended to produce at Jameson's trial.

During his talks at the Colonial Office, Hawksley mentioned the telegrams for the first time. Chamberlain was immediately informed and Hawksley was asked to produce the telegrams. This Hawksley refused to do. Replying to the request, he said that Chamberlain was aware of what he knew and could 'shape his course with this knowledge'. In fact, at that stage, Chamberlain did not know what was in the telegrams and was unaware of the danger they posed. Hawksley's hint, however, was significant: it was the first suggestion of blackmail.

Withholding the telegrams had not been Hawksley's idea: he was anxious for them to be seen and continued to advocate frank and open discussion. The veto had come from Rhodes. For him the telegrams were valuable cards in the game he was set on playing. His immediate objectives were to secure the Charter and, if possible, prevent a full-scale inquiry into Jameson's raid. The Colonial Secretary was the one person who could help him and only by withholding the telegrams and then offering to suppress them could he be sure of Chamberlain's cooperation. Secrecy was essential. If it became known that the Colonial Secretary had been involved in Rhodes's schemes they would both be ruined. Rhodes had to keep a firm hold on Chamberlain and, like most blackmailers, he was obliged to tread warily.

The day after Hawksley's visit, Rhodes had his first official meeting with Chamberlain. Both men were on edge. Rhodes arrived at the Colonial Office looking 'flushed and worried, his face red and his hair rather tumbled'. To Chamberlain's secretary he seemed like a schoolboy who had been summoned to the headmaster's office. Chamberlain, always a dandy – he usually wore a monocle and sported a flower in his buttonhole – was outwardly calm but on his guard. Earlier he had confessed to a friend that he was worried that Rhodes would try to draw him deeper into the plot and that he did not relish hearing 'too much'. But the interview went smoothly enough. Chamberlain's deputy, Lord Selborne, was later to claim that the discussion was 'most satisfactory and that Rhodes had shown a great deal of common sense'. What this meant was that both men were sensible enough to avoid dangerous topics.

Little, if anything, was said about the raid; the conversation centred on the prospects for Rhodesia. On this they were in agreement. Chamberlain explained that, as the Chartered Company's police were now in disgrace, there would be a demand for them to come under Imperial control. Rhodes raised no objections and offered to continue financing the force. For his part, the Colonial Secretary agreed that the Chartered Company should retain the power to appoint civil officials, including magistrates and judges. As far as is known, nothing was said about the Charter being revoked and no mention was made of the telegrams. It was all very amicable, very civilized and very inconclusive. Rhodes returned to his hotel in high spirits.

He did not remain long in London. Running true to form, he had no intention of staying in England – for all its smiling busmen – for longer than was strictly necessary. Once he had met Chamberlain and attended a meeting of the London directors of the Chartered Company, he felt there was nothing to detain him. Before leaving, however, he found time to accept a dinner invitation from Moberly Bell, the energetic manager of *The Times*. This, in a way, was an obligation. No newspaper had been more supportive of Rhodes throughout the recent crisis than *The Times* and its distinguished colonial correspondent,

Flora Shaw – an ardent admirer of Rhodes – had been active in promoting Jameson's raid. Among other things, Miss Shaw had been instrumental in getting *The Times* to publish, on New Year's day, the infamous letter appealing to Jameson to rescue 'women and children' in Johannesburg, a news item which had helped to win sympathy for the raiders in England. Rhodes was deeply indebted to *The Times* and its manager.

But the dinner was not a conspiratorial affair. There were a number of outsiders, including Princess Catherine Radziwill. Then in her late thirties, the dark-haired, vivacious Princess was well known in European society. She was the only daughter of Count Adam Rzewuski, a Polish nobleman who, at the time of her birth, was living in exile in Russia. Christened Ekaterina, she changed her name to Catherine Maria when, at the age of fifteen, she had married Prince William Radziwill. The early years of her married life had been spent with her husband's family living in Berlin. Here she had revealed a fatal flair for political intrigue which, by the time she was twenty-eight, resulted in her being banished from the German court and forced to return to Russia. In St Petersburg she had established a political *salon*, but her influence in the Russian capital diminished after the death of Tsar Alexander III in 1894. The following year the Princess separated from her husband, by whom she had five children, and when she met Rhodes at Moberly Bell's dinner party she was eking out an existence as a freelance journalist. No longer young, her once renowned beauty was beginning to fade, but she was still a striking personality. Her remarkable linguistic abilities – she spoke Russian, Polish, German, French and English – combined with her acid wit and fund of political gossip made her a lively dinner-table companion. Sitting next to Rhodes, and fascinated by the mystery surrounding the Jameson raid, she turned on the charm and did her utmost to win his confidence. Not surprisingly, she failed: Rhodes was later to claim that he hardly remembered her. But the Princess did not give up easily. From now on she was to take a keen interest in the affairs of Cecil Rhodes. When they next met, some three years later, she was to make sure that she was not forgotten.

Rhodes left England on 10 February 1896. He did not return directly to South Africa but travelled across Europe to Italy where he boarded a German ship sailing for Beira. On the way south he visited Egypt and eventually landed at the east African port on 20 March. His arrival could not have been better timed. A few days later, on reaching Umtali in Rhodesia, he received news of an alarming development. On 24 March the Ndebele had begun to attack isolated settlements and murder the white inhabitants. Encouraged by Jameson's defeat, and the depletion of the Chartered Company's police, the Africans of Rhodesia were at last striking back at their conquerors. A full-scale rebellion was in progress.

CHAPTER FOURTEEN

The Ndebele Rebellion

For the Ndebele the coming of the white man had brought nothing but disaster. Their traditional way of life was shattered, their king was dead and their *impis* had been put to flight. The occupation of their country was not a gradual process but a sudden, brutal and devastating take-over. As the white army had advanced on Bulawayo, the surrounding people had scattered, many of them joining the *impis* in their flight to the north. Once the fighting was over the people drifted back to find themselves homeless, their villages destroyed and their land confiscated.

The volunteers in Jameson's army had lost no time in claiming the farms that had been promised them. Not all these farms were occupied immediately – gold prospecting prevented that – but ownership was very quickly established. No sooner were the troops demobilized than they began swarming over Matabeleland, pegging out their ill-gotten properties. It is unlikely, says Professor Keppel-Jones, 'that there was any volunteer who did not know within fifty miles where his farm was.' The dispossessed Ndebele had no right of redress. If they tried to re-occupy their former homes, or were bold enough to complain, they were simply told that they were now living on white men's land and must obey the orders of their overlords. Most of them were allowed to stay, not as home owners but as tenant labourers. Needing a workforce, the new settlers and absentee landlords were prepared to accept the Ndebele as 'native residents' only if they earned their keep. Almost overnight a once proud nation was reduced to serfdom.

Jameson not only condoned the plundering but assisted in it. Surrounded as he was by his aristocratic and army cronies, he found himself well placed to distribute favours. Sir William Milton – who later became administrator of Rhodesia – was amazed by the extent to which 'the Honourable and military elements' had been indulged. 'Jameson,' he complained, 'has given nearly the whole country away to the Willoughbys, Whites and others of that class . . . . It is perfectly sickening to see the way in which the country has been run for the sake of hobnobbing with Lord this and the Honble that. I think Jameson must have been off his head for some time before the raid.'

Rhodes, who was said to be worried about Jameson's toadying, was almost as guilty. His participation in the division of the spoils was equally impulsive and characteristic. Any impecunious young man, to whom he took a shine, was immediately sent to Rhodesia and richly rewarded. One such youngster was Alfred de Fonseca, who, in 1895 – while still a schoolboy – cut his classes and called on Rhodes. He was anxious to go to Rhodesia and demanded an interview. Few prime ministers would have taken the precocious boy seriously but when Rhodes was shown young Alfred's request – marked 'urgent' – he immediately agreed to see him. They spoke together for some time, discussing among other things the possibility of crossing Cape donkeys with Spanish jackasses, and Rhodes was won over. Shortly afterwards the gawky, red-haired Alfred de Fonseca, schoolboy though he was, arrived in Bulawayo clutching a grant for 33,000 acres of Ndebele land. There were other such supplicants, not always so young but every bit as brash, upon whom Rhodes smiled.

Robbed of their land, the Ndebele were also deprived of their cattle. The agreement which Jameson had signed with his volunteer army, before the invasion of Matabeleland, had promised that recruits would be rewarded not only with farms and gold claims but also with a share of any 'looted' cattle. From the very outset it was understood that the Chartered Company would confiscate Lobengula's herds, keep the bulk of them, and distribute or sell off the remainder. This, it was argued, would be the best way to convince the Ndebele that they had been defeated. How a distinction would be made between the royal herds and privately owned cattle was left conveniently vague.

Company agents began seizing cattle as soon as the fighting ended. So widespread was the looting that, when reports of it reached England, there was an outcry. Lord Ripon – then Colonial Secretary of the Liberal government – wrote to Cape Town to protest. Worried that the depredation would leave the Ndebele without the means of subsistence, he was not impressed by the argument that all the cattle being seized belonged to Lobengula. 'Her Majesty's Government,' he insisted, 'attach importance to securing to the Matabele ample cattle for their requirements . . . [and] sufficient cattle should be held in trust, out of any that may have been seized from whatever source, to ensure attaining that object.' Rhodes found this interference 'very annoying'. He considered that he knew more about Matabeleland than did Whitehall and refused to take the Colonial Secretary's objections seriously. 'Lord Ripon,' he told the High Commissioner in Cape Town, 'would be wise not to give credence to every unauthorized telegram which he reads in the English press.' Eventually Ripon was forced to compromise. He accepted that a distinction was being made between Lobengula's cattle and those privately owned but was adamant that the royal herds be regarded as 'state funds' which, if necessary, could be allocated to the Ndebele later. It was agreed that a final settlement would be made by a Land Commission.

For the time being, the worst excesses of the cattle seizure were hidden. There can be little doubt, despite Rhodes's protests to the contrary, that the company collected cattle indiscriminately. Some, it is true, were left in Ndebele kraals, but they were nevertheless regarded as company property. The plundering continued. 'Loot kraals' were established and from them cattle were either distributed to the volunteers or put up for auction. The situation was made worse by a mixed bag of European cattle rustlers who, taking advantage of the confusion, raided Ndebele kraals and made off with any livestock they could seize. Nor were the Shona slow in making the most of the opportunity to recover cattle that had been stolen from them by Lobengula's *impis*. By the time the Land Commission reported a year later, it was impossible to ascertain rightful ownership. Some 76,000 head of cattle had disappeared – probably spirited out of the country – and the Ndebele stock was estimated to be less than a fifth of what it had been before the country was occupied.

The widespread looting shattered the traditional structure of Lobengula's former kingdom. Cattle were vital to the practices of the Ndebele. Not only did they reflect a clan's wealth and status and play a part in ritual observances but they were essential to marriage transactions. Closely following the *lobola* ('bride purchase') of the Zulu, cattle changed hands when a woman left one group for another and were held in custody by her relatives to ensure the stability of the union. In this way intimate links were forged between families and between clans. Cattle, says Philip Mason, 'were one of the strands that bound the Matabele people together.'

Pillage was accompanied by pestilence. By an odd and grim coincidence, the arrival of the white men heralded the onset of hitherto unknown natural disasters. First, in 1892, shortly after the pioneers reached Fort Salisbury, swarms of voracious red locusts descended on southern Africa, attacking crops, stripping bushes and laying bare the veld. Then, early in 1896, came an outbreak of the deadly cattle sickness known as *rinderpest*. Caused by a virus and transmitted by contact, the disease spread throughout Rhodesia. Many cattle died of it; many more were slaughtered, on orders from the High Commissioner, in an attempt to control the contagion. As Lord Grey – the former Albert Grey, who had succeeded Jameson as administrator – wrote to his son, 'all the plagues of Egypt have tumbled at once upon this unhappy country – drought – locusts – failure of crops – total annihilation of the cattle by rinderpest – no milk, no beef in a few days – but lots of lovely smells from dead cattle.' In the nostrils of the Ndebele, that smell was associated with their white overlords: their bitter resentment intensified.

The Chartered Company could not be held responsible for the *rinderpest* – except by the superstitious – but, by slaughtering cattle from the remaining Ndebele herds, its agents added to the growing hostility. The slaughter was seen, not as a method of prevention but as part of the measures employed by a tyrannical administration. In the first year of occupation, Matabeleland was controlled by the Chartered Company's white police. The main aim at that time was to destroy the remnants of Lobengula's military order and the police were authorized to shoot on sight any African seen with a gun. Justice was arbitrary and often cruelly enforced; the Ndebele were regarded as a people 'more or less in a state of war' who had to be rigorously suppressed. Things should have improved when, at the end of the year, a Native Department was created, but in fact there was little change: officials of the department were kept far too busy registering and distributing cattle to attend to the grievances of the oppressed population. Greater reliance was placed on the hastily recruited – they received only a month's training – African police who, as often happens with collaborators, were even more despotic, brutal and untrustworthy than their employers. Later described as 'more like a brigandage' than a police force, they were feared and hated by the majority of the Ndebele.

Opposition to company rule mounted. It led inevitably to a rebellion. Stirred up by the leading *indunas* of the Ndebele hierarchy, the uprising was inspired by the priests and officers of the ancient Mwari cult. Prominent among these priests was a former Ndebele slave called Mkwati whose role in bringing together the disparate groups opposed to the white settlement was of paramount importance to the organization of the rebellion. Mkwati is thought to have been responsible for directing the attacks in which the first whites were murdered.

Details of the early killings are horrific. Isolated farms, mines and trading-stores were stormed, houses were broken into and entire families were massacred. The unsuspecting settlers were taken completely by surprise. At one farmhouse the occupants were just about to sit down to their midday meal when a party of Ndebele burst in and battered them to death. The only survivor was a seven-year-old girl who fled to a nearby river where she was discovered a few days later by some Ndebele women who 'smashed her head with a stone'. A Native Commissioner was seated at his desk, writing a letter, when he was stabbed in the back. Fred Selous later saw the remains of the Fourie family: the father and three children were missing and bodies of a woman and three other children, clubbed to death with knobkerries and axes, had been savaged by dogs or jackals. But, he says, 'the long fair hair of the young Dutch girls was still intact and it is needless to say that the blood-stained tresses awoke the most bitter wrath in the hearts of all who looked upon them, Englishmen, Dutchmen alike vowing a pitiless vengeance against the whole Matabele race.'

There were few women and children in the outlying districts and most of the bodies later discovered, including those of black servants, were those of men. Mutilated and left to rot by the roadside or in river beds, where they had fled to escape, they were evidence of a ghastly carnage. Accurate figures are difficult to ascertain but it is estimated that there were almost two hundred white victims, either murdered or missing. Pent-up anger can be the most deadly of emotions.

*   *   *

Rhodes was in Rhodesia at the outbreak of the rebellion but his presence was not entirely fortuitous. In Cape Town a select committee of the House of Assembly had been appointed to enquire into the Jameson raid and Rhodes wanted to avoid incriminating himself at the hearings of this committee before matters had been settled in London. This was why he had decided to travel via Beira and so delay his return to the Cape: the rebellion gave him a valid reason for absenting himself even longer.

But there can be no doubt that he welcomed the opportunity of playing a part in quelling the Ndebele rising. His career had already been seriously jeopardized by the Jameson raid and he was determined to salvage what remained of his blackened reputation. Above all he wanted to safeguard his precious Charter. So far the question of withdrawing the Charter had been confined to speculation by his opponents: it had not arisen in his interview with Chamberlain. This did not mean that he could rely on the Colonial Secretary's support. As Rhodes well knew, the crisis in Rhodesia could produce pressures which even his blackmailing tactics would be powerless to counter. What was needed was a *grand geste*: a spectacular move which only Rhodes himself was capable of making. His involvement in the rebellion was therefore not only opportune but essential.

Rhodes was on his way to Salisbury when news of the first attacks on the white settlers reached him. A bout of malarial fever prevented him from responding immediately but, once on the mend, he insisted on joining a column that was marching from Salisbury to Bulawayo. He was accompanied by his old Oxford friend, Sir Charles Metcalfe – whom he now employed as his railway engineer – and the burly and ever-faithful Jack Grimmer.

Still suffering the after-effects of his fever, Rhodes was ill equipped, both physically and mentally, for the arduous march. He was not a

230

naturally brave man. This is admitted by the staunchest of his admirers. 'Mr Rhodes,' says one of them, 'as a rule, preferred a sheltered position when danger was about, and would rather escape an ordinary peril than face it.' Referring to this march later, Rhodes himself was to confess that he was 'in a funk all the time' but that, like many another honest hero, he was 'more afraid to be thought afraid.' For all that, he acquitted himself superbly. Armed with only a hunting crop, he led the most dangerous of reconnoitring expeditions; conspicuous in his white flannel trousers, he was to be seen in the forefront of every skirmish.

The object of the march was to relieve the besieged settlers in Bulawayo. This Rhodes hoped to accomplish without imperial assistance, but, as he was quickly informed, there was little chance of success. With only a small, inadequately armed volunteer force at his disposal he could not hope to suppress a full-scale rebellion. This was realized by the authorities in Britain who, appreciating the seriousness of the rising, immediately despatched two hundred regulars to South Africa and arranged for the Assistant Military Secretary in Cape Town, Colonel Plumer, to raise an additional force in the Cape. Under Plumer's command, the Matabele Relief Force – as it became known – was to move north as soon as possible.

In the meantime, Rhodes and his volunteers continued on their march. But even in the wilds of Rhodesia, with a rebellion on his hands, Rhodes could not neglect his political and business affairs and for the next few weeks he was in constant touch with London by cable. The messages he sent at this time reflect his mounting excitement, his bravado and that schoolboyish enthusiasm which was apt to break through in times of high emotion. At the beginning of May, for instance, he received a cable from the Chartered Company concerning a newspaper report that, at Chamberlain's request, he had resigned as managing director. His much quoted reply was flippant. 'Let resignation wait,' he wired back, '– we fight the Matabele to-morrow.' And the cable he sent to the Colonial Office, from Gwelo, a few days later was positively skittish. To resolve a dispute between two officers, neither of whom would serve under the other, Rhodes had high-handedly appointed himself Colonel. 'There is no colonel more unhappy than I am,' he assured Chamberlain; 'obliged to take position to smooth over individual jealousies . . . . The result is I have to go out into the field and be fired at by the horrid Matabeles with their beastly elephant guns, which make a fearful row. It is a new and most unpleasant sensation.'

But his vivacity was deceptive. There was certainly nothing facetious about his attitude toward the Ndebele. As details of the early killings came in, he grew more and more impassioned, vengeful and merciless.

It has been claimed that he was consumed by a 'blood-lust'; the ferocity with which he embarked on the campaign seems to bear this out. During the early stages of the fighting he was obsessed by the need to teach the rebels a lesson. He gave no thought to compromise; even those warriors who threw down their arms and surrendered, he wanted shot. He is said to have told a police officer to show no mercy to the survivors of a battle. 'You should kill all you can,' he advised; 'it serves as a lesson to them when they talk things over at night. They count up the killed, and say So-and-so is dead, and So-and-so is no longer here, and they begin to fear you.' After an action he would sometimes return to count the African corpses simply to settle an argument.

Inevitably Rhodes's callousness has been seen as further evidence of his bigotry towards the black man. But again this appears to be a simplistic explanation of a far more complex attitude.

Professor T. O. Ranger is probably nearer the mark in his summing up of Rhodes's prejudices. 'Rhodes' biographers,' he says, 'have disputed as to whether he regarded Africans as children or as animals, as potential men or predestined objects. In fact the most important thing about Rhodes' views and aims was that he did not really pay much regard to Africans at all.' This is true in as much as Rhodes took little account of people, as such, when pursuing his own ends. His concern was with territory and the wealth it could produce rather than with the inhabitants of any country. Once he had marked out the map and staked his claim, he was prepared to trample on anyone who stood in his way, be they black or white. He would have dealt as ruthlessly with any opposition from the Boers – although perhaps less blatantly – as he now dealt with the Ndebele, had his plan to seize the Transvaal succeeded. 'Rhodes is a splendid enthusiast,' Lord Esher once remarked. 'But he looks upon men as "machines". This is not very penetrating.' The same could be said for many a potential dictator. Lack of human understanding or concern is a weakness often mistaken for a strength; it is only incidentally connected with race.

Rhodes did not retain his military rank for long. In the middle of May, Sir Richard Martin took over as temporary commander, standing in for General Carrington, who arrived from Gibraltar at the beginning of June. (Carrington's attitude was every bit as brutal as Rhodes's. At a public dinner he openly advocated the 'extermination or deportation' of the Ndebele people.) Colonel Plumer and the Matabele Relief Force, advancing from the Cape, also reached Matabeleland in May and, as far as military operations were concerned, Rhodes's participation was no longer strictly necessary. He now had other roles to play.

By the time he reached Bulawayo, on 1 June, the Ndebele *impis* had ceased to be a serious threat to the town. But the inhabitants were still tense. According to J. G. McDonald, the mere sight of Rhodes was sufficient to boost morale. 'No one,' he says, 'ever received a greater welcome. The settlers, who were all laagered up in the Market Square, felt as if their troubles were at an end; men and women united in cheering themselves hoarse, and an air or cheerfulness at once took the place of the depression that had affected everyone for many weeks. "Now that Rhodes is here everything will be all right" was heard on every side.'

Rhodes remained in the town as an onlooker while patrols were despatched to seek out the scattered Ndebele *impis*. On 6 June a clash occurred in which some 300 warriors were killed and the rest put to flight. Many of them took refuge in the Matopo hills where, holed up in a maze of caves and crevices, they prepared themselves for a long defensive campaign.

The tide had turned but the rebellion was by no means ended.

*   *   *

In the third week of June there was a totally unexpected development. The Shona, whom the whites considered 'notorious cowards', began attacking outlying settlers and, in a matter of days, killed an estimated 120 men, women and children. This new rebellion was not an attempt to assist the beleaguered Ndebele but, inspired once again by agents of the Mwari cult – including two 'spirit mediums', one a man known as Kagubi, the other a woman, Nehanda – the Shona, under the impression that the whites were being defeated in Matabeleland, seized the opportunity to settle their own grievances.

The Shona, no less than the Ndebele, had every reason to despise the rule of the Chartered Company. Contrary to the belief of many settlers, they had not welcomed the whites as their 'saviours'. What protection they received, in the early years, from Lobengula's plundering *impis* was more than offset by a new form of servitude: bondage to the white man. T. O. Ranger, the foremost authority on the two rebellions, places the blame for Shona hostility squarely on the shoulders of Rhodes and Jameson. They, he maintains, were responsible for the administration of Mashonaland and their neglect resulted in the oppression of the Shona people.

Jameson, in particular, was contemptuous of what he described as 'the red tape and sealing wax' of a properly organized administration. His decision, shortly after assuming office, to cut costs and drastically reduce the police force crippled what little semblance of officialdom existed in Mashonaland. Large districts, denuded of policemen, were entrusted to hastily enrolled Field Cornets, who were assisted by equally inexperienced 'burghers'. As many of these 'burghers' were local farmers and traders, justice was rarely even-handed: any Shona

233

accused of a crime could have his livestock seized, or some other punishment administered, by his self-interested judges. 'The blacks,' Lord Milner was later to declare, 'have been scandalously used . . . . A lot of unfit people were allowed to exercise power, or at any rate did exercise it, especially with regard to the natives.'

Rhodes's attitude towards the Shona was one of indifference. His intention was to establish an independent colony, loyal to Britain, which would provide him with the means – financially and territorially – of expanding his African empire: all other considerations were, at best, secondary. Not until 1894, when Matabeleland and Mashonaland were united, was the so-called 'Native Department' created and even then the appointed officials, as has been seen, were more concerned with the collection of cattle than with the plight of the indigenous population.

Cattle seizure was not as widespread in Mashonaland as it was in Matabeleland – although cattle recovered by the Shona from the Ndebele was often confiscated on the pretext that the beasts were company property – but tax-collection was rigorously enforced. The Chartered Company had always wanted a hut tax in Mashonaland, similar to that levied in South Africa, and in 1894 their wish was met. Under the terms of the Matabeleland Order in Council every male African was required to pay ten shillings a year for each hut occupied by him or one of his wives. If payment could not be made, either in cash, grain or stock, it had to be worked for and this added to the already widespread practice of pressed labour.

The Shona put up a determined resistance to the new tax. Unlike the Ndebele they were not a conquered people and could not see why they should be taxed for living in a country they had occupied for centuries. There were frequent, sometimes bloody, clashes with the tax-collectors. When, at the end of 1894, the newly created Native Department took over the tax gathering its agents became notorious for their high-handed behaviour and blatant jobbery. 'Even in areas where no armed resistance was made,' says Ranger, 'collection of the taxes . . . was arbitrary and irregular, appearing more like the levy of a tribute than the collection of a civil tax. Almost everywhere the tax was taken in stock; "the kraals are complaining that in some instances they are left without a single beast," wrote the Magistrate of Gwelo.'

Even so the Shona rising took the white settlers completely by surprise. The last thing they had expected was that the reputedly docile Shona would turn on them with such ferocity. Failing to recognize the bitter resentment created by their assumption of power and the injustices of an irresponsible administration, they had thought that a people rescued from the tyranny of Lobengula's *impis* would show them nothing but gratitude. This false view of the Shona was shared by

Rhodes. On his way to Bulawayo, Rhodes had discussed the situation with 'Wiri' Edwards, a native commissioner in Mashonaland, and had appeared satisfied with local conditions. 'He was very worried about the position in Matabeleland,' says Edwards, 'but like many more of us he did not expect the Mashonas would follow the lead given by the Matabele.' Only later did the settlers realize their mistake.

'We had under-rated the Mashona native,' admitted 'Wiri' Edwards. 'They were certainly not a warrior race like the Zulu but they were steeped in superstition, and were cunning and clever, far more so than their late over-lords, the Matabele . . . We were sitting on a smouldering fire and we didn't know it.' This, for all its patronizing overtones, was nearer the mark. Many years would pass before the Europeans in Rhodesia fully appreciated the potential of the Shona people.

Rhodes was only incidentally engaged in the suppression of the rebellion in Mashonaland. He appeared, at first, to regard it more as an irritant than as a serious threat. But again he was wrong. The Shona proved more tenacious than the Ndebele, their spirit-mediums were more successful in fanning the flames of fanaticism and the conflict continued, sporadically, for a full year after peace had come to Matabeleland. The eventual defeat of the Shona rebels was hastened when the white troops resorted to tactics which produced an outcry from humanitarians in Britain.

Like the Ndebele in the Matopos, the Shona sought refuge in the labyrinthine caves of Mashonaland's granite hills; the caves to which they had fled to escape the Ndebele *impis*. When all attempts to starve or smoke then out failed, dynamite was used to blast the seemingly inaccessible strongholds, resulting in wholesale, indiscriminate slaughter. Not only the fugitive warriors, but the women and children who accompanied them were blown to smithereens. There was no escape; those who were not killed outright were maimed beyond recognition.

But Rhodes played no part in these operations. His dealings were with the the Ndebele and they ended, with unexpected success, a few months after the Shona rebellion started.

*   *   *

Precisely why Rhodes decided to change his tactics, exchange his role of avenger for that of peacemaker, is not certain. As in most things his motives were mixed.

He was undoubtedly influenced by the stalemate that had been reached in Matabeleland. By taking refuge in the Matopos, the Ndebele had thwarted any hopes the military might have had of a swift and decisive victory: not only were the *impis* difficult to locate but the semi-mountainous terrain made a direct assault on their sheltered positions almost impossible. So ineffective had attempts to dislodge them proved that, by the end of July – two months after Rhodes arrived at Bulawayo – it had become obvious that a second campaign would be needed: a campaign, entailing reinforcement of the white troops, which would take time to mount and could not be launched until the next dry season. That, at least, was the view expressed by General Carrington.

It was not a view shared by Rhodes. He had his own reasons for not wanting to prolong the fighting. A lengthy campaign would, for one thing, be extremely expensive and, for another, it could prove disastrous to the Chartered Company's hopes of survival. Renewed criticism of the company was already making itself felt and there was a limit to the amount of pressure that Chamberlain could withstand. A drawn out war in Rhodesia would play into the hands of the company's opponents and, if something were not done to end it, could signal the end of the Charter. The spread of the rebellion to Mashonaland had worsened the situation and made the need for action of some sort more urgent. Rhodes was in no position to wait for a military solution.

In any case a blood-stained victory would do nothing to restore Rhodes's reputation. The repercussions of the Jameson raid had still to be faced and, in facing them, Rhodes had to show himself to be a man of stature, a worthy ruler of Rhodesia. If he was now regarded as an irresponsible adventurer who had schemed to overthrow the legitimate government of the Transvaal, would the hammering of primitive tribesmen be considered the act of a prudent and mature statesman? How much better it would be if the instigator of the infamous raid now emerged as the wise and moderate pacifier of the Ndebele. All things considered, Rhodes had no alternative but to change his tactics. The enemy had already been taught a salutary lesson: they had been defeated on all fronts and forced to flee into the hills. The time, Rhodes decided, had come to negotiate an honourable peace.

It would not be easy. Safe in their rocky fastnesses, the Ndebele were wary of exposing themselves to the messengers of the white man. They had been tricked too often. This was the first obstacle that had to be surmounted. It was overcome more by accident than design. A patrol combing the country for loot stumbled on an old woman in one of the deserted kraals. She was taken captive and was discovered to be a widow of Mzilikazi, the founder of the Ndebele nation, and one of her sons, Nyanda, was a leader among the rebels. At first the old woman refused to answer any questions, merely spitting whenever she saw one of her captors. Eventually, however, she relented and agreed to act as a go-between. Too old to walk any distance, she was carried back to her kraal, supplied with a white flag, and instructed to tell the rebels that

236

they should show the flag if they wanted peace. Shortly afterwards, both she and the flag disappeared.

Two or three days later, the flag was seen fluttering in the distant hills. Rhodes recognized it as the signal for which he had been waiting. Moving his camp away from the military, he despatched four Africans – led by John Grootboom, a Tembu scout from the Cape – to sound out the rebels. The negotiations which followed were tentative and protracted. Grootboom's party returned to report that the 'hills were black' with rebels; Ndebele emissaries complained bitterly about the earlier behaviour of the Chartered Company's African police. Finally it was agreed that Rhodes should meet the rebel *indunas*. The date set for the *indaba* was 21 August and Rhodes's party was to be confined to four or five men.

The risks involved were enormous. The failure of the Jameson raid had played an important part in sparking off the rebellion but it had not lessened Rhodes's standing with the Africans; he was still regarded as the most important white man in the land that bore his name. By going unprotected to a secret *indaba* with the rebels, he would be placing himself at their mercy. Although his party was not unarmed – some of them carried concealed weapons – they would be so vastly outnumbered that they could hardly hope to escape a determined attack. Even a more civilized foe would have been prepared to take advantage of such a valuable hostage. But, knowing this, Rhodes did not hesitate to agree to the *indunas'* conditions. 'We must risk it,' he said, 'I believe they mean well.' Rejecting all suggestions of an armed patrol, he chose his companions. He took Johan Colenbrander, the one-time agent at Lobengula's kraal, to act as interpreter and John Grootboom, the Tembu scout, to act as a guide. The two other men in the party were Dr Hans Sauer, the man who had accompanied Rhodes on his first gold-prospecting visit to the Transvaal, and Vere Stent, a well-known Cape journalist who would ensure that the proceedings were well publicized.

They set off on a fine winter's morning. Threading their way through the ochre-coloured grass, they headed towards the Ndebele encampment. 'We talked very little,' says Vere Stent. 'Must I confess it? – we were all a little nervous.' For part of the way they were accompanied by Johnny Grimmer and J. G. McDonald, one of Rhodes's young estate agents. After they had gone a few miles, Grimmer and McDonald off-saddled and the rest of the party rode on towards a small clearing at the foot of the hills. Here, Rhodes gave the order to dismount. Shortly afterwards they spotted the huge white flag which preceded a small procession of Ndebele warriors.

'Yes, yes, there they are,' whispered Rhodes. 'This is one of those moments in life that make it worth living! Here they come!' He seemed, says Stent, 'the calmest man of the five.'

On reaching the white men, the procession halted. The man carrying the white flag thrust the sapling to which the flag was tied into the ground and the rest of the party arranged themselves in a semi-circle, the *indunas* in the centre. Rhodes, prompted by Colenbrander, welcomed them with a peace greeting. 'The eyes are white,' he said in Zulu. A Ndebele spokesman then launched into a long oration. After outlining the history and struggles of his people, he detailed their grievances against the Chartered Company. 'You came, you conquered,' he remonstrated. 'The strongest takes the land. We accepted your rule. We lived under you. But not as dogs! If we are to be dogs it is better to be dead . . . Children of the Stars can never be dogs.'

Rhodes heard him out and then replied. He acknowledged the wrongs the Ndebele had suffered and promised that such things would end. 'But why,' he asked, 'did they kill women and children?' At this the Ndebele became restless: they all started to talk and make angry gestures. One of the *indunas* silenced them and their spokesman replied. The Europeans, he said, had first killed their women and children. 'I shouldn't go on with the subject,' whispered Colenbrander to Rhodes. 'It is quite true. Some women were shot by cattle collectors.'

The sun was setting when the *indaba* ended. As a first step towards peace it could be counted a success. The Ndebele were not yet ready to capitulate but they were clearly willing to negotiate. They accepted that moves would be made to redress their grievances and welcomed Rhodes's promise to disband the company's 'native police'. When the two sides parted Rhodes had every reason to feel optimistic. On returning to camp Hans Sauer and Vere Stent telegraphed to London 'to buy Charters'.

A week later there was a second *indaba*. Some of the *indunas* wished to see Sir Richard Martin, the Queen's representative, but Sir Richard would not move without an armed escort. Rhodes went again. By this time Hans Sauer had left but his place was taken by Grimmer and McDonald. Also in the party were two remarkably brave women. Johan Colenbrander's spirited wife and her sister had ridden into the camp and insisted on attending the *indaba*. This time things were more difficult. Some of the younger warriors who wanted to continue fighting made their voices heard and the talks were repeatedly interrupted. At one stage, Rhodes left his companions and went to sit among the rebels in an attempt to smooth things over. In the end he was forced to make a further concession. 'Where are we to live, when it is all over?' demanded one of the younger warriors. 'The white man claims all the land.' Rhodes's reply was prompt. 'We will give you settlements,' he said. 'We will set apart locations for you; we will give you land.' That merely made the young man angrier. 'You will give us land in our own country,' he snorted. 'That's good of you!' Only with the support of the senior *indunas* was Rhodes's compromise reluctantly accepted.

McDonald claims that this second *indaba* was a glorious triumph for Rhodes. Stent, writing nearer the event, says it ended on a somewhat uncertain note. In either case, there can be little doubt of Rhodes's growing confidence that he could deal with the situation peacefully.

These talks with the Ndebele had an invigorating effect on Rhodes. Outwardly he appeared a changed man. All traces of the fever which had dogged him on the march to Bulawayo vanished; he no longer seemed to suffering the strain of the months following the Jameson raid. Philip Jourdan, who had been summoned from Cape Town, arrived to find his employer bounding with energy. 'Mr Rhodes's physical strength and power of endurance were phenomenal at this time,' he says. 'Sometimes the morning ride extended from five a.m. until twelve noon, and when it is considered that at that time of the year the rays of the sun beat down very fiercely from nine o'clock in the morning, increasing in intensity as the day advanced, some idea can be formed of Mr Rhodes's stamina.' For a man with a heart complaint such a punishing routine was as foolhardy as it was extraordinary.

It was during one of his daily gallops that Rhodes stumbled upon the hill in the Matopos which became known, from his own description, as 'World's View'. By African standards the view was by no means remarkable but it captured Rhodes's imagination. So impressed with it was he that, on the day he discovered it, he rode back to his camp and insisted that his entire party accompany him on a return visit. Walking backwards and forwards on the crest of the hill, he suddenly announced: 'I shall be buried here.' Rhodes was only forty-three at the time and the fact that he named his final resting place at such an early age is not without significance. For all his apparent health and energy, he was still troubled by intimations of his own mortality. He no doubt appreciated that this isolated spot with its sweeping vistas symbolized his lonely, far-seeing life. That the view was not the best which Africa has to offer gives an ironic twist to the symbolism.

After a third inconclusive *indaba* on 9 September – at which Sir Richard Martin, who this time accompanied Rhodes, delivered a tactless lecture to the *indunas* – it was decided that firmer action was needed. Accordingly, an ultimatum was sent to the 'minor *indunas*' – who were seen as the main trouble makers – to the effect that 'unless they surrendered quickly fighting would begin.' It may have been this threat or, as Professor Ranger suggests, the news that the Chartered Company intended to restructure its African administration and employ the senior *indunas* as 'salaried and recognized officials' that brought the prolonged deliberations to a sudden end. Whatever the cause, the Ndebele squabbling ended and Rhodes was soon able to report that the prospects of peace were distinctly promising. 'Things,' he wrote on 21 September, 'are looking really bright . . . . We may say the matter is over as far as these hills are concerned.'

Rhodes attended one last *indaba*, on 13 October 1896. The purpose of this meeting was to settle the remaining grievances of the senior *indunas* who complained of having lost authority over the young warriors. They were told that this would be remedied. The 'loyal' *indunas* were promised that, once they had proved they were worthy of trust, they would be appointed as 'salaried headmen'. This promise was then extended to the rebel leaders, providing they submitted to the government's conditions. Matabeleland was to be divided into twelve districts; the rebel *indunas* – to the disgust of the settler press – were supplied with horses to enable them to contact their followers. Peace – albeit a patched-up peace – had at last become a reality.

Most accounts of Rhodes's career agree that this was his 'finest hour'. It also recognizes that his experiences in Matabeleland transformed his attitude towards the Ndebele. There are sound reasons for thinking this.

That Rhodes was stimulated by his days in the veld there can be no doubt. Between the *indabas* he had spent most of his time visiting the kraals of those *indunas* who refused to attend the discussions, and had been brought into close contact with the people he had conquered. For the first time since his youthful days as a cotton planter in Natal he had mingled freely with the indigenous population of Africa. Old memories were reawakened and he had enjoyed himself enormously. 'It was a great pleasure to watch him while these informal Indabas were going on,' says Philip Jourdan. 'He chaffed and teased the chiefs, and sometimes one fancied he was one of them by the way he adapted himself to their customs and methods of expression. He delighted in chaffing them. His face would beam all over when he thought he had the best of an argument.'

Nor was this merely a passing phase. From now on he was to treat the Ndebele with undisguised respect. While he was roaming the country, he came across the site at Inyanga – some eighty miles from Umtali – which he chose as his Rhodesian home. He instructed J. G. McDonald to buy 100,000 acres of farmland and to construct a dam in order to irrigate them and, in later years, this estate became one his favourite retreats. Here he would entertain huge gatherings of Africans, many of whom travelled miles to attend. One such occasion was the *indaba* he organized on 24 June 1897 to celebrate Queen Victoria's Diamond Jubilee. A white visitor described the way in which Rhodes circulated among the crowd, making each new arrival feel welcome. Speaking to the *indunas* individually, he says, 'Mr Rhodes's manner underwent a startling change, it assumed a boyish exuberance and aspect of pleasure, which was intensely gratifying to the indunas personally known to him, and though the remarks might be the same, still, there was a suggestion conveyed to each of the circumstances under which they last met, which indicated an extraordinary memory.' Paternal, almost royal, as his attitude might appear, it contrasts markedly with his former indifference to the people he had dispossessed. Rhodes may not have changed to the extent which his admirers claim, but he had certainly mellowed.

Satisfied as he was with his peace-making efforts, Rhodes had little time in which to enjoy his success. Since leaving England at the beginning of the year, he had been in constant touch with his political associates and was now aware that attempts to prevent Chamberlain from appointing a Committee of Inquiry into the Jameson raid had failed. On being shown the incriminating telegrams held by Rhodes's London solicitor, the Colonial Secretary had tendered his resignation but Lord Salisbury had refused to accept it. Chamberlain had then made it clear that he intended to defy Rhodes's blackmailing tactics and to set up an official inquiry into the affair. The hearings were due to begin in February 1897 and Rhodes was expected to appear before the committee. The outlook did not look promising. In July, Dr Jameson and his officers had been tried before a special jury in London and Jameson had been sentenced to fifteen months imprisonment. Rhodes was informed of the verdict while he was in camp in the Matopos. His reaction was one of outrage. 'A tribute to the upright rectitude of my countrymen,' he snorted, 'who have jumped the whole world.' Now it was his turn to face his upright countrymen.

Before going to London, it was necessary for Rhodes to pay a flying visit to the Cape. The journey south got off to a bad start. Shortly after setting out, he heard that his beloved Groote Schuur had been gutted by fire. When the news was broken to him by Lord Grey (now installed as the administrator of Rhodesia) the colour is said to have drained from Rhodes's face. Then, with a sigh of relief, he said: 'Is that all? I thought you were going to say that Jameson was dead.'

CHAPTER FIFTEEN

Facing the Music

Rhodes returned to the Cape by sea, stopping off at Durban and Port Elizabeth on the way. Although he had received numerous telegrams and letters asking him to address meetings on his return, he was by no means certain of his reception when he appeared in public for the first time since the Jameson raid. He side-stepped an invitation to speak in Natal by saying that his 'arrangements' prevented him from doing so and it was not until he reached Port Elizabeth that he received an indication of the English colonists' reaction to his downfall. He need not have worried. From the moment he stepped ashore at Port Elizabeth, he was mobbed by his supporters; when he came to address a huge gathering at the Feather Market hall, his impromptu speech was exuberant. He trotted out all his well-tried phrases. 'It is a good thing to have a period of adversity,' he told his cheering audience. 'You then find out who are your real friends.' He went on to denounce the 'unctuous rectitude' of his countrymen, a slighting reference to the proceedings in England. This was later to cause him some embarrassment. So much so that Lewis Michell, his banker, advised him to claim that he had been misreported and that what he really said was the 'anxious rectitude' of his countrymen. But Rhodes refused to climb down. 'I said it,' he insisted, 'and I stick to it.'

From Port Elizabeth he travelled to Kimberley by train. At every station on the way up crowds gathered to welcome him. Far from having to slink back home with his tail between his legs, he found himself making a journey which was said to be like a 'triumphal march'. On his return to Cape Town, at the end of December, his reception was so overwhelming that he was reduced to tears. 'I can only say,' he announced at a private dinner held in his honour, 'that I will do my best to make atonement for my error by untiring devotion to the best interests of South Africa.'

But it was not all jubilation. In Cape Town he was confronted with the charred skeleton of Groote Schuur. The fire, which had started – somewhat mysteriously – in a corner of the thatched roof, had destroyed the interior of the house, leaving only the two rooms habitable. One of these was Rhodes's bedroom but, for the first few nights, he refused to sleep in his own bed. In his unpublished *Memoirs*, Sir Lewis Michell has described the strange sleeping arrangements at Groote Schuur. He went, he says, straight to Rhodes's bedroom but 'found it occupied by one of his secretaries, Jourdan, who was down with fever. Rhodes had placed him there as the only quiet spot, and had vanished amid the blackened ruins of his home. After a search I discovered him in an angle of the passage, curled up in a blanket, but he dressed hurriedly and took me to the glen where his hydrangeas made a riot of colour. There, on a rustic seat, he launched out on politics, finance and the destiny of South Africa. It was very pathetic.'

Michell's account is interesting in its contrast to the glowing accounts of Rhodes's snook-cocking progress through the Cape. Away from the public glare, the returning hero dropped his posturing and allowed his true feelings to show. He was far from confident about his chances of future success. 'Physically,' says Michell, 'he was a wreck and spoke plainly as to his own days being numbered. I came away with the depressed conviction that his strenuous life was practically over.'

The loss of Groote Schuur undoubtedly deepened Rhodes's despair. The house was his most cherished possession, the only real home he had known since leaving the Bishop's Stortford rectory. It was the one acquisition on which he had lavished personal care and painstaking attention; he had nurtured it with genuine pride and rejoiced in its transformation from a Victorian monstrosity to a classic Cape-Dutch mansion. The fact that he had publicly shrugged off the destruction of Groote Schuur, setting it against the possible death of Jameson, was more a matter of self-defence – an unwillingness to allow a personal weakness to be displayed before his uncomprehending friends – than a true reflection of his feelings.

Not only was the house gutted by the fire but the assiduously assembled and discriminately chosen collections of Cape-Dutch and French furniture, rare tapestries, pictures and china were either reduced to ashes or damaged beyond repair. An unspecified number of valuable books were, however, salvaged from the library by the faithful John Norris, the ex-Dragoon who acted as butler. Rhodes's sister – the mannish, domineering Edith Rhodes – was staying at Groote Schuur when the fire broke out but, in the panic which followed, she was forgotten by the servants. Norris's first act, says Lewis Michell, had been 'to throw all the books out of the library window, after which he helped Miss Rhodes to escape.' Later, on being reproached for his neglect, Norris explained his priorities by saying: 'I first saved what I thought the master valued most.'

Rhodes camped out in the ruins of Groote Schuur until he left for

London on 6 January 1897. He was visited by many of his friends and supporters, including a huge crowd who arrived one night in a torch-light procession and cheered him when he appeared on the front balcony. But there were notable gaps in the ranks of those who sympathized with the fallen Colossus. Not the least of the absentees was the sadly disillusioned Jan Hofmeyr. The news of Rhodes's involvement in the Jameson raid had stunned Hofmeyr; he felt, he was to say, 'as though the wife of his bosom had been torn from his side.' He was never able to forgive Rhodes for betraying him.

The feeling was mutual. Rhodes considered that Hofmeyr had deserted him at his time of need and obstinately refused to speak to him again. The Jameson raid effectively ended the alliance between Rhodes and the Bond; from now on he was to look upon Hofmeyr and his followers as his political opponents. He made his feelings clear in a letter he later wrote to Harry Escombe, the Prime Minister of Natal, when discussing his hopes for a federation of the South African states. 'Our great enemy here,' he declared, 'will be Hofmeyr because poor fool he only thinks of Africanderism by which he means Dutch Africanderism and he believes that Federalism will destroy the supremacy of his little clique.' It was a bitter comment from one who had once regarded those whom he called 'My Dutch' as the key to a united South Africa.

For his part, Hofmeyr was soon to join forces with Rhodes's most passionate critic. He it was who encouraged Olive Schreiner to give wider publicity to the gruesome photograph she used as a frontispiece for her book attacking Rhodes's activities in Mashonaland. This book, *Trooper Peter Halket of Mashonaland*, was one of the most telling indictments of Rhodes to appear during his lifetime.

Often described as a novel, the book is an odd mixture of fact and fiction, of mysticism and polemic, and falls into no conventional literary category. In it a lone trooper in Mashonaland encounters a mysterious, Christ-like stranger who, in the course of a long discussion, parades the iniquities of the Chartered Company in harrowing detail. It is a story of theft, murder and torture, behind which looms the sinister figure of Cecil Rhodes. The frontispiece of the first edition – it was removed from subsequent reprints – appears to underline the text by showing three African corpses dangling from a tree, while a group of white men stand smugly below. Both the book and the photograph were soon to achieve notoriety; they were seen – and continued to be cited – as evidence of Rhodes's callous brutality.

While Olive Schreiner's attack can be justified, it should be pointed out, in all fairness, that the photograph is in certain respects misleading. The Africans appear to be the victims of a white lynch-mob, but in fact they were arrested by a group of tribesmen, sent to

244

Bulawayo, tried, found guilty of 'looting and burning property'. It was questionable justice – the death penalty seems excessive for a crime against property – and the attitude of the white spectators is indefensible but the proceedings which led up to the hanging were not without a semblance of legality. Fred Selous, a reasonably civilized witness to the trial, considered that justice had been done. Rhodes was not directly involved in the incident.

Neither the book nor the photograph had been published when Rhodes, accompanied by his sister, Johnny Grimmer, Bob Coryndon and Hans Sauer, sailed for London on the *Dunvegan Castle*. By coincidence Olive Schreiner, armed with the manuscript of *Trooper Peter Halket of Mashonaland*, was one of his fellow passengers. Although they occupied adjoining cabins, they did not speak to each other. The highly suspicious Olive was taking her book to the publishers and was careful to avoid any contact with Rhodes whom she was convinced would try, by some means or other, to silence her. 'I believe,' she had written to her brother before leaving, 'that Rhodes and the Chartered Company will proceed against me.' But Rhodes had other things on his mind. His thoughts were concentrated on the forthcoming hearings of the Select Committee at Westminster where, as he put it, he would have to 'face the music'.

*   *   *

Shortly after arriving in London, Rhodes made a final bid to have the inquiry into the Jameson raid stopped. On 26 January 1897, he had an important meeting with Joseph Chamberlain at the Colonial Office. According to an account given by Lord Selborne, their discussion developed into a battle of wits. Rhodes at one stage, became quite emotional. They should both, he argued, be prepared to make sacrifices. What did either of their reputations matter compared with the harm that would be done by public exposure? 'In twenty years,' he told Chamberlain, 'you will be gone, snuffed out, but the country will remain.' Surely it would be better to call off the inquiry, even at the last minute, than to risk a national scandal. Chamberlain was calmer and more realistic. It was impossible, he insisted, to stop the inquiry, and even if it were possible such a move would 'produce more evil to the country than the inquiry would'. Behind these professions of patriotism lay other, more immediate, pressures: each man was aware of the damage he could suffer at the other's hands – Chamberlain had the power to rescind the Charter, Rhodes held the telegrams that could incriminate the Colonial Office. In the end Chamberlain's advantage proved the more effective. Rhodes was forced to give way. It was agreed that he should appear before the

Select Committee and that the telegrams would be suppressed. As Chamberlain was to be a member of the committee, Rhodes could count on his support. The Colonial Secretary also promised to retain the Charter. They had both gained a little without giving away too much.

While waiting to attend the inquiry, Rhodes busied himself with the affairs of the Chartered Company. Whenever he could spare the time, he went riding in Hyde Park with Johnny Grimmer and Bob Coryndon. The sight of Rhodes and his two young friends became a familiar one to celebrity spotters in Rotten Row. Often they would be followed, and sometimes joined, by enterprising scalp-hunters. One young heiress was particularly attentive and Rhodes liked to joke about the impression she made on Bob Coryndon. 'She used to ride with me in the Park in the morning,' he would say. 'And d'you know, Coryndon thought she came to see him. Of course she didn't. She came to see *me*.'

For another of his friends, however, Rhodes showed a surprising lack of concern. Dr Jameson was in a nursing home when Rhodes arrived in London. Shortly after being taken to Holloway prison to serve his fifteen months sentence, the doctor had fallen seriously ill. In November 1896 he had been operated on for stone and at the beginning of the following month he had been released because of ill health. He had served little more than four months of his sentence. Since his release he had been confined to bed, his sufferings made worse by the thought of the harm he had caused Rhodes. News of Jameson's illness had alarmed Rhodes in Rhodesia but, in London, he made no attempt to see his friend. It was left to Jameson's manservant, Garlick, to bring the two of them together. When, in answer to Garlick's urgent request, Rhodes arrived at the doctor's bedside, he looked down at the sick man and said: 'Both of us have had a rough time, but you have had a rougher time than I.' From then on, it is said, Jameson began to get better.

The Committee of Inquiry held its first public session in Westminster Hall on 16 February 1897. It was attended by a host of sensation seekers, including members of London's fashionable society. Prominent among the more distinguished spectators was the portly Prince of Wales, flanked by the Duke of Abercorn, the Chartered Company's chairman, and Lord Selborne from the Colonial Office. Rhodes, accompanied by Alfred Beit, arrived early and took his place in the witness chair. At first he appeared nervous, but he was soon to get the measure of his interrogators and parry their questions with an aplomb which bordered at times on impudence. His supporters were delighted with his performance.

Rhodes attended the hearings twice a week for three weeks. The committee sat all day, and during the lunch-time sessions Rhodes faced his examiners sipping a glass of porter and chewing a sandwich. It made a good impression: he looked anything but a guilty man cornered by his opponents. In answering questions, he showed no signs of contrition. He freely admitted his responsibility for the raid but went on to lecture the committee on the conditions in South Africa that had led up to it. Playing on the patriotism of his wider audience – there were thirty-three press representatives present – he emphasized the threat which Germany posed to British interests in Africa and his desire for a union of South African states under the British flag. By refusing to answer questions which might incriminate a third party, he was able to side-step issues concerning his dealings with British officials. Nor would he admit to having written instructions to his subordinates prior to the raid. 'I never write letters,' he said when taxed on this point. Both these evasions were obligingly accepted by the committee.

So too, after some pointed questioning, was his stubborn refusal to hand over the controversial vital telegrams which were thought to involve the Colonial Office. Here again, he pleaded a point of honour. 'I consider,' he argued, 'that they were of a confidential nature and should not be produced.' Even a resolute committee member like Henry Labouchere could not bully him into admitting Chamberlain's role in the plot. Asked whether the Colonial Secretary was aware that 'disturbances' might take place in Johannesburg, Rhodes claimed he was in no position to answer. 'I was out in Africa at the time . . . ,' he explained, 'and had never seen the Colonial Office on any of these questions.' Pressed for a more direct answer – did he or did he not tell Chamberlain of his plans? – Rhodes unblinkingly replied: 'I did not.'

Alternating between prevarication and bluster, half-truths and wooden-faced silences, Rhodes sailed through the hearings with relative ease. He was let off lightly. The committee were divided among themselves; some had their own axes to grind, others were fearful of what might be revealed, and much of the questioning was irrelevant to the serious implications of the raid. Nobody appeared overanxious to probe too deeply. Rhodes was helped by the fact that not only he, but national honour, was on trial. Although not openly acknowledged, this was something which even the more radical members of the committee could not entirely ignore: the political consequences of total exposure might well have proved more costly than the truth was worth. Whatever the reason, the failure of the committee to corner Rhodes undoubtedly worked to his advantage. For, by following his example and refusing to supply any significant evidence, Rhodes's accomplices were later to defy all attempts to pin them down. Under the watchful eye of Joseph Chamberlain, witness after witness challenged the committee's authority with remarkable audacity. Thus it was that, at an investigation held in the glare of world-wide publicity, the only facts to emerge were those which Cecil Rhodes chose to disclose.

It is hardly surprising that the long-awaited inquiry into the Jameson raid was described by one of its critics as 'The Lying in State at Westminster'.

Rhodes had every reason to be pleased with his success; he had earned the congratulations of his friends. Only Johnny Grimmer failed to be impressed by Rhodes's performance. Never the brightest or the most conscientious of secretaries, Grimmer had made no attempt to follow his employer's dreary political concerns. 'D'ye know,' Rhodes exclaimed later, 'Grimmer never showed the slightest interest in the inquiry. He never came into the committee-room.' This negligence appears to have amused, rather than annoyed, Rhodes. He was in a jubilant mood and, with the hearings behind him, he set off with Grimmer and Bob Coryndon for a short tour of Europe before returning to South Africa.

*　　*　　*

On his arrival at the Cape, Rhodes was again met with demonstrations of loyalty. When his ship docked in Table Bay, on 20 April 1897, the quayside was lined with hundreds of his supporters. The proceedings in London had done nothing to dampen their enthusiasm and Rhodes was visibly touched by their cheers. Replying to an address presented to him by the mayors of Cape Town and Port Elizabeth, he made a rousing speech. He had come back, he assured the crowd, to 'strive for equal rights for every white man south of the Zambesi'. He was careful to add, however, that this time he would 'fight constitutionally'.

The speech heralded his return to politics. He followed it up, a day later, by attending a sitting of the House of Assembly. This was his first parliamentary appearance since he resigned as Prime Minister and he was given a surprisingly warm reception with 'only one irreconcilable Dutchman uttering a sepulchral groan amid general laughter'. But all was not what it seemed. A few days later there was the possibility of a split in the government ranks – the ever-available Gordon Sprigg had taken over as Prime Minister after Rhodes's resignation – and Rhodes tried to cash in by offering to assist his former liberal colleague, James Rose Innes, to form a new ministry if the government fell. He chose the wrong man. 'I said nothing,' Innes reported to his wife, 'except that I would give my reply after the division; but as there was a tie the necessity did not arise – of course I should have had nothing to do with forming any Ministry in consultation with him.' Rhodes's supporters were thicker on the quayside than in parliament.

For the next few weeks, Rhodes continued to attend the House of Assembly. But, for all his renewed interest in Cape politics, his main concern was with the activities of the Chartered Company and, at the end of May, he left the Cape for Rhodesia where he was to remain until the end of the year. He was accompanied this time by his new 'secretary', Gordon le Sueur, who was amazed at the style in which Rhodes travelled. For the first part of the journey they occupied the luxuriously appointed De Beers directors' railway coach which – with its plush seats, damask-covered dining table, silver cutlery, sleeping compartment, full-length bath and cold-storage chamber – seemed distinctly at odds with its surroundings as it rumbled across the barren veld. At every stop they were met by deputations of local worthies who arrived with 'beautifully engrossed' addresses or invitations to champagne luncheons. Rhodes was left in no doubt that, whatever the world might think, he was still a hero to the English-speaking communities of South Africa.

In Bechuanaland Rhodes met Sir Alfred Milner, the newly appointed High Commissioner who, a month earlier, had taken over from the ailing, seventy-three-year-old Lord Rosmead (formerly Sir Hercules Robinson). The two men already knew each other; they had been at Oxford at the same time in the 1870s and Milner, a passionate imperialist, admired Rhodes's grandiose schemes for Africa. But the Jameson raid still loomed large and the new High Commissioner was wary of committing himself to a close allegiance. 'He is too self-willed,' he wrote of Rhodes, after this meeting, 'too violent, too sanguine, and always in too great a hurry. He is just the same man as he always was, undaunted and unbroken by his former failure, but also untaught by it . . .' Just how much Milner had learned from Rhodes's mistakes and the extent to which he shared Rhodes's faults had yet to be seen. He continued to regard Rhodes as the only 'really *big* man' in South Africa.

For the first few months of his stay in Rhodesia, Rhodes headquartered himself at Bulawayo. Gordon le Sueur was installed in an office of the Consolidated Gold Fields building – part of which was curtained off to act as a bedroom – and here, lying on the bed, Rhodes received the stream of hard-pressed settlers who came to beg for his assistance. Most of them tended to blame their misfortunes on the Jameson raid: had the police not been withdrawn to assist Jameson, they argued, there would have been no rebellion, their farms would not have been looted, the *rinderpest* would have been easier to control and they would not have lost their cattle. Sometimes, says le Sueur, they 'stood twelve deep outside the door, with petitions for all manner of things – one wanted to be set up in business, another a farm, another a span of oxen and a wagon, and yet another to have his claim for compensation revised . . . .' Not all these demands were met and many of the supplicants were turned away. Those who managed to push their way into the office, however, were often richly rewarded. According to le Sueur, Rhodes 'was giving away money during these months at an enormous rate . . . . Numbers of men, whom it was found impossible to get employment for, or who were ill, were, during 1896 and 1897, given free passages home to England by Rhodes; and on one occasion he paid the passage to Cape Town of a whole circus troupe whom he found stranded.'

One unexpected visitor was Dr Jameson. Rhodes had no idea that the doctor had returned to Rhodesia until he was alerted by the sound of cheering outside the office. Even so, he refused to go outside to greet Jameson and when the doctor eventually came in both men displayed more embarrassment than pleasure. Rhodes, it is claimed, simply 'held out his hand and said, "Hullo, Jameson" and Jameson shook hands, but never said a word.' It was a subdued meeting for two friends who had recently been judged as rash, impetuous and uncontrollable.

The same lack of an emotional response was evident when Rhodes received the official report of the inquiry into the Jameson raid.

Other witnesses had been called after Rhodes had given his evidence and the hearings lasted until the end of June. In the later stages further attempts had been made to unravel the mystery surrounding the un-disclosed telegrams and several of them were eventually obtained from the telegraph company and deciphered from the Chartered Company's code books. Significantly, however, eight of them – thought to be those referring to Chamberlain's role in the plot – could not be unearthed and it was the absence of these so-called 'missing telegrams' that prevented the committee from arriving at a decisive verdict. The report, when it was published on 13 July 1897, was in effect as in-conclusive as had been much of the evidence. Condemnation of the raid itself was 'absolute and unqualified' but there was no such cer-tainty about the events leading up to the Jameson's invasion of the Transvaal.

For want of proof to the contrary, the report exonerated Chamber-lain and the Colonial Office. Indeed, the committee – with Henry Labouchere dissenting – concluded that, by withholding the tele-grams, Rhodes must have known that 'any statements in them purpor-ting to implicate the Colonial Office were unfounded' and therefore he had suppressed them simply to minimize his own culpability. About Rhodes's guilt there could, of course, be no doubt. He had admitted his responsibility for the raid and he was severely castigated for abusing his position as Prime Minister of the Cape and managing director of the Chartered Company, for deceiving his cabinet colleagues and – as it was thought – various British officials. (The separate and earlier inquiry by the Cape House of Assembly, which Rhodes did not attend, had reached much the same verdict.) But it soon became apparent that no further action was contemplated. Any doubts on this score were put to rest a few days later, when the affair was debated in the House of Commons and a motion demanding that specific punitive steps be taken against Rhodes was defeated by 304 votes to 77. Winding up this debate, Joseph Chamberlain had coolly announced that 'the Government do not intend to abolish the Charter'. The gamble had paid off and the chief conspirators had met their obligations.

Rhodes was aware of the verdict before he received a copy of the report. He had kept in touch with his London agents throughout the hearings and was informed of the committee's findings before they were published. 'Regret learn report hostile,' he wired to Bouchier Hawksley on 8 July, 'but maintain my position that in public interest matter should rest.' He was to keep to this decision even though some of his associates were pressing him to expose Chamberlain in order to improve his own public standing. The report was delivered to him in Bulawayo. It held no surprises. After reading the letter which accompanied it, he hardly glanced at the report before handing it over to the dumb-struck Gordon le Sueur. 'You see,' he remarked casually, 'how I have to trust my secretary.' With the Charter safe, Rhodes was not unduly concerned about what others thought of him.

He continued to busy himself with the affairs of the Chartered Company. The railway was expected to reach Bulawayo by the beginning of November and arrangements were being made for the new terminus to be opened by Sir Alfred Milner; there was also the problem of having the rest of the Bechuanaland Protectorate transferred to the Chartered Company and the extension of the transcontinental telegraph to be negotiated. But every bit as important was Rhodes's determination to keep his promise to consult with the Ndebele *indunas*; whatever time he could spare was spent in visiting kraals in and around the Matopos.

Le Sueur often accompanied Rhodes on his rides in the veld and was highly amused by his clumsy, sometimes dangerous, performances on horseback. 'One had to be particular about his mounts,' says le Sueur, 'as he rode very carelessly, allowing the reins to lie on the horse's neck and sitting silently thinking, as if he were asleep . . . . I doubt whether he could have sat a horse at a trot.' On more than one occasion the rides were brought to an abrupt halt by Rhodes sliding, or being thrown, from his saddle. But not all his mishaps were the result of bad horsemanship. Riding out from Bulawayo with le Sueur one day, Rhodes suddenly reeled and almost fell from his horse. He had suffered a slight heart attack. He recovered sufficiently to ride slowly back to the town and on the way he told le Sueur that he wanted to provide for him 'in case anything happened.' The young man, then a relatively new employee, protested, but Rhodes insisted. 'Don't be a fool,' he panted; 'you can't go back to the Civil Service at tuppence a year.' He later gave le Sueur an envelope which, when it was opened some years afterwards, was found to contain a bequest of £5,000 (well over £150,000 in today's money).

Death was very much on Rhodes's mind at this time. At least twice during this stay in Rhodesia, he visited the burial site he had chosen at World's View in the Matopos. He took le Sueur with him on the first occasion in the hopes of impressing him. The young man was told to keep his eyes covered until they reached the top of the hill. 'Now look,' exclaimed Rhodes on arriving at the summit; 'what do you think of it?' To the unimaginative le Sueur, the view was disappointing. 'Oh, I don't know,' he mumbled, 'it's rather fine.' Rhodes was furious. 'I suppose,' he snapped petulantly, 'if Jesus Christ was to ask you what you thought of Heaven, you'd say, "Oh, I don't know, it isn't bad".'

The second visit was more rewarding and more significant. This time Rhodes was accompanied by his banker, Lewis Michell, who was paying his first visit to Rhodesia. They arrived early one morning, with Rhodes in a sombre mood. Not only did he point out the exact spot where he would be buried but lay down on it 'to see how it felt'. He was in the process of drawing up a new will and persuaded Michell to act as one of his executors. When Michell pointed out that Rhodes was younger than he was, Rhodes replied that he 'felt like a man under sentence of death'.

*   *   *

Rhodes's gloomy mood lifted once he left Bulawayo. In August he, le Sueur and Lewis Michell travelled to Salisbury by special coach. The leisurely two week journey – 'starting very early every morning, shooting along the road, and sitting late around the camp fire' – did much to revive Rhodes's spirits. So lively was he that Michell found living at close quarters with him a bit of a strain. 'He had a habit,' says the ponderous banker, 'of throwing at one the gravest problems and requiring their instant and intelligent discussion . . . he kept one's faculties at full stretch.'

At Salisbury the party was joined by Johnny Grimmer, now permanently employed on Rhodes's estates in Rhodesia. The change of occupation made no difference to Grimmer's relationship with his employer: he still treated Rhodes in a cavalier manner, and Rhodes still allowed it. This delighted le Sueur who was quick to follow the example set by Grimmer. Between them they were to lead Rhodes a lively dance in the weeks ahead.

From Salisbury they moved on to Umtali. All along the way

252

Grimmer and le Sueur vied with each other in thinking up ways to tease Rhodes – devising practical jokes and telling outrageous stories. Often it took Rhodes a long time to realize that his leg was being pulled. When he did at last tumble to a joke, his tormentors would whoop with delight at his embarrassment. 'I suppose you think you are funny,' Rhodes would growl as they fell about laughing. But he was far too indulgent to do more than wag a warning finger.

Rhodes could not stay angry with young men for long. He relished their company too much, particularly when roughing it in the veld. Fooling around was all part of the *camaraderie* of camp life. Sleeping in the open, eating meals cooked by his coloured servant, Tony de la Cruz, was, for Rhodes, the peak of existence. It brought him closer to his companions. Years later, when claiming intimacy with his employer, le Sueur was to boast that on this trip he had 'shared Rhodes's blankets'.

Only in one respect did Rhodes's camping expeditions differ from those of the Rhodesian pioneers: this was his obsession with hygiene. Notorious for his umkempt appearance, his abhorrence of personal vanity, Rhodes would never let a day pass without shaving and insisted on his slovenly 'secretaries' following his example. 'Grimmer and le Sueur,' he would say, 'hate water. I don't believe they'd wash at all if I didn't make them.' Nor could he bear an untidy camp. He would always choose the camping site himself, making sure it was cleared of all rubbish and well away from debris left by previous wagons. 'His pet aversion,' says Jourdan, 'was to see old provision tins lying about his camp.' So marked was Rhodes's preoccupation with hygiene and personal cleanliness, so at odds was it with his professed contempt for the niceties of civilized behaviour, that it could be psychologically significant: excessive cleanliness is thought to have sexual connotations.

Much as he enjoyed life in his spick-and-span camp, Rhodes was unable to relax completely. When travelling he remained in touch with his political and business associates and this trip was no exception. Not only was he kept abreast of events in London and the Cape and informed about developments in the diamond and gold industries but he received regular reports of the progress being made by Herbert Baker in rebuilding Groote Schuur. His mail followed him in large hampers and was sorted out while the company sat round the camp fire at night. Official letters were dealt with immediately; the more personal correspondence was stacked away to be answered when the party returned to civilization.

The personal letters often made up the bulk of Rhodes's mail. They were a varied collection: requests for work, begging letters and letters from admirers poured in from all over the world. Among them were a great many proposals of marriage. Women wrote from England,

America, Australia, Canada, New Zealand and the Cape suggesting themselves as suitable partners to help Rhodes in his work. They could have saved themselves the trouble. According to J. G. McDonald, such letters were promptly consigned to the fire.

There was one, however, that escaped the flames. This was the letter which Rhodes received from a female correspondent while encamped outside Umtali. Written on the day that he sailed from England, after attending the Jameson inquiry, it was signed 'Catherine Radziwill.'

As far as is known, Rhodes had not heard from the assertive Princess Radziwill since he had more or less cold-shouldered her at Moberly Bell's dinner party some eighteen months earlier. The letter he now received seems to bear this out: it was a curious mixture of outspokenness, flattery and assumed familiarity from a woman who admitted that she was merely an acquaintance. After telling Rhodes that she had once regarded him with suspicion, the Princess went on to explain that since meeting him she had changed her mind. She now recognized his true greatness and wished to bestow her blessing on him and his enterprises. Her one fear was that something would happen to him, a fear heightened by her powers of second sight. A presentiment told her that within the next six months an attempt would be made on his life; to safeguard him she enclosed a small medallion. This talisman, she said, had been given by a gypsy to her kinsman, the Russian General Skobeleff, who had worn it throughout his campaigns. As the unfortunate Skobeleff had died prematurely – of heart disease – at the age of thirty-eight this was not the most auspicious of recommendations, but the Princess nevertheless urged Rhodes to keep the medallion with him as a mascot.

Rhodes appears to have been impressed by this unexpected concern for his welfare. The fact that it was expressed by a princess may, as was intended, have flattered him. Instead of burning the letter, he had it filed and instructed le Sueur to look after the medallion. 'I understand,' the feckless le Sueur was to say later, 'it has since been lost.'

*　　　*　　　*

A few weeks later, Rhodes had cause to doubt the efficacy of Princess Radziwill's good-luck charm. Shortly after leaving Umtali and arriving at his Inyanga farm he was taken seriously ill. The precise nature of his illness was falsified at the time – so that news of it would not disturb the stock market – and this deception was perpetuated by his biographers. Lewis Michell, for instance, says that Rhodes had 'contracted fever, and for a while his life hung in the balance.' Fever may indeed have weakened him but the real cause of his illness was that he had suffered an attack similar to that which killed General Skobeleff: his heart was badly affected.

The attack was as unexpected as it was serious. When Rhodes first arrived at his mountain retreat he appeared to be in the best of health. Inyanga, he liked to claim, was the 'sanatorium' of Rhodesia and he always felt better once he was there. His first week or so was spent in buying more land for his already large estate, riding out each day and often climbing hills on foot as he carried out his inspections. Exuberant and tireless, he seemed to be in the most carefree of moods. But the combination of excessive exertion and the high altitude proved too much for him and he suddenly collapsed.

Grimmer and le Sueur were at a loss to know what to do. At first they thought the attack was the result of Rhodes walking about stark naked and exposing himself to draughts. In their clumsy way, they did their best to nurse him but he was a difficult patient. 'When Rhodes was ill,' says le Sueur, 'he often alternated between periods of peevishness, fretfulness, and loss of temper and periods of despondency; and it was during the latter, when he used to ask one to sit by him and hold his hand, or place one's hand on his fevered forehead, that one's feeling was perhaps most stirred by him; and one had a peculiar sensation as of an inclination to shield and protect him.' It is a sad comment on the essential loneliness of a man who was then one of the world's richest and most powerful bachelors.

Nothing the bewildered young men could do seemed to help Rhodes. At last, frightened by their responsibility, they defied his orders and sent for the local doctor at Umtali who quickly identified the nature of the illness. He prescribed a heart stimulant (digitalis) and Rhodes, who was well aware of his condition, recognized the treatment. 'Ah, yes,' he gasped, 'that's the stuff; make a note of that, le Sueur, and get a supply.' But it was not until the arrival of Dr Jameson, a few days later, that the patient began to recover.

Rhodes survived this time but he had no illusions about his chronic ill-health. He knew that one day his heart would suddenly cease to function and comforted himself with the thought that the end, when it came, would be quick. More than anything he dreaded a long, lingering illness and a painful death. 'You . . .' he once told le Sueur, 'will probably die of cancer in the throat and linger on in agony, but I shall go off suddenly without any pain; I may go off while I am talking to you now; *this*' – thumping himself on his heart – 'will kill me, but I shan't suffer.'

Rhodes's condition was not helped by his eating and drinking habits. His friends strenuously denied that he was a drunkard – a common accusation during his lifetime – but, as Dr Charles Shee has pointed out, 'there can be little doubt that Rhodes in his final years, as he restlessly waited for death, did drink to excess.' He thought nothing of finishing two bottles of champagne at a sitting and, at a public banquet, he was seen to down a whole bottle of kirsch on top of a full tumbler of whisky, becoming so befuddled that he was unable to make his after-dinner speech. A visitor to Groote Schuur, after Rhodes's death, once asked a servant how much whisky his employer drank and was astounded by the reply. 'Baas,' explained the man, 'what was left in the second bottle next morning was not more than I was allowed to drink.' Nor did Rhodes pay any attention to his diet. Even after his heart attacks, he continued to consume huge quantities of red meat, potatoes and starchy foods. He was, claims le Sueur admiringly, 'a valiant trencherman.'

Not only did Rhodes over-indulge himself, but he encouraged his young companions to follow his example. With the exception of Philip Jourdan – who lived to be ninety-one, despite innumerable ailments – they were all overweight, dyspeptic and plagued by mysterious illnesses: both Grimmer and le Sueur were to die prematurely. Rhodes was forever paying le Sueur's doctor's bills and the deceptively sturdy-looking Grimmer frequently had to take to his bed. Most of Grimmer's illnesses were politely referred to by Rhodes as 'a touch of fever' but, more often than not, they were little more than disastrous hang-overs.

Grimmer was the next one to collapse after Rhodes had recovered. This time his illness was genuine. First he was bitten on the face by a spider or a scorpion and then he succumbed to a fever which enlarged his spleen. Dr Jameson had left Inyanga by this time and it fell to Rhodes to look after the patient and devise a cure. He proved a far more competent nurse than either of his companions. The treatment he decided upon was a mixture of his fetish for hygiene and an old wives' remedy. He ordered everything to be cleared out of the sick-room, which was then scrubbed from ceiling to floor with disinfectant, and sat bathing Grimmer's feet from a basin of vinegar. 'Rhodes hardly left his side,' says le Sueur, 'and although he pretended to be chaffing him all the time, he was much upset.'

The succession of illnesses disrupted Rhodes's plans and prevented him from attending the opening of the new railway terminus at Bulawayo. Instead, he and le Sueur left Inyanga for Salisbury in December, and a few weeks later returned to Cape Town. Here Rhodes, still recuperating from his illness, again became embroiled in Cape politics.

A general election was in the offing, and Rhodes's supporters were anxious to enlist him in the ranks of the newly revived, predominantly English-speaking, Progressive Party. He had earlier resisted attempts to get him to stand as leader of the party, but now he was ready to declare an interest by giving his backing to prospective Progressive candidates. An opportunity for him to make his views known came when, in March 1898, seats in the upper house of the Cape parliament, the Legislative Council, were contested. This, in effect, was to be a curtain-raiser for the general election later that year.

Rhodes broke his political silence by giving a forthright interview to the *Cape Times*. He made no secret of his Progressive sympathies and roundly condemned Jan Hofmeyr and the Bond – the main opposition – claiming they were dominated 'by a Continental gang in Pretoria'. But he added that Rhodesia now held greater fascinations for him than Cape politics and he was willing, if necessary, to retire from the local scene. There was little chance of him doing that. His supporters needed him and demonstrated their loyalty when, on 12 March, he addressed an election meeting in the Good Hope Hall. A capacity crowd of some 2,500 attended – including the visiting Rudyard Kipling – and when Rhodes entered the hall the audience rose and the band struck up *See the conquering hero comes*. There was no talk of retirement on this occasion. He was loudly cheered when he attacked Kruger for depriving the *uitlanders* of the franchise and he assured the meeting that he intended to atone for the past by working for a united South Africa. Three days later, he was given another vociferous reception when he spoke to a packed meeting of working men in the Salt River suburb.

Rhodes did not stay in Cape Town long enough to learn the outcome of the election, in which the Progressives did reasonably well. The day after the Salt River meeting he boarded the *Tantallon Castle* and sailed for London, taking Gordon le Sueur with him. 'I propose running home,' he wrote to Harry Escombe, 'for my railway money and to arrange completion of transcontinental telegraph. I wish to work from both ends.' Rhodesia was still uppermost in his mind.

*   *   *

This time the visit to London lasted only a matter of weeks. Rhodes was kept busy with his Chartered Company affairs and Gordon le Sueur was left to amuse himself. It was le Sueur's first visit to England and, like Johnny Grimmer before him, he made the most of it. Given *carte blanche* at fashionable tailors and booksellers, he embarked on a spending spree which startled even his indulgent employer. 'Seems rather a large amount for a secretary,' wrote Rhodes on a copy of the tailor's bill. But he paid it, as well as another £60 for books. Rhodes, however, was getting a little tired of the indolent le Sueur and, as was his habit when he wished to rid himself of an embarrassment, he began to suggest alternative employment for the young man. He tried to persuade him to remain in England and study for a medical degree; failing this, he suggested the Rhodesian civil service. Before a decision could be reached, le Sueur contracted an ear infection and had to be sent to hospital. Once he had settled into his sick bed, Rhodes left him there and returned to South Africa alone.

He arrived back in Cape Town in time to celebrate his forty-fifth birthday. He looked much older. His recent illness had taken its toll, but so had years of strain, worry, overwork and unhealthy living. His hair was greying rapidly. His face, with its network of broken veins, was flushed and bloated. His eyes had the puffy, watery look of a man who does not get enough sleep. His breathing was laboured and his manner an odd blend of energy and lassitude. He was clearly a man who had not much longer to live.

Yet there was still a great deal to be done. Preparations for the general election were going ahead and everything depended on its outcome. It was to be the first trial of Rhodes's political strength since the Jameson raid and he knew that his opponents would show him no mercy. He entered the contest in a determined mood.

The campaigning, on both sides, was bitter and relentless. Mustering all his energies, Rhodes travelled the country, speaking from the platforms of his supporters, vindicating his past conduct and vilifying his former allies. His opponents accused him of perverting his capital to obtain 'objects which conspiracy and violence have failed to compass'. Rhodes retorted by claiming that they were financed by the Transvaal and were little more than tools of Paul Kruger. 'I am determined not to leave the South till I see you clear of the risk of being dominated by Krugerism,' he told the electors of Port Elizabeth. In the midst of the contest vandals broke into the grounds of Groote Schuur, lighting fires, cutting down trees and injuring the animals in his private zoo. Throughout it all Rhodes maintained his resolute stand; he made what are generally considered to be his finest speeches.

He was determined to clear himself of the accusations being levelled against him. 'I have been painted very black,' he told an hostile audience, 'the worst acts and the most evil designs have been imputed to me; but gentlemen, I can assure you, although I have my faults, I am incapable of such things.' He was believed. The meeting ended with a vote of confidence being passed in Rhodes and his policies. 'I honestly believe,' he declared on another occasion, 'that my years of trouble have made me a better man . . . and I am determined to go on with my work of forming a railway junction with Egypt – and the work of closer union in South Africa.' His words were drowned by cheers. Union was the theme of all his speeches; a union which would include Rhodesia.

But for all his bold talk and his predictions of a Progressive party

258

victory, Rhodes was far from confident of success. 'He gave people in England to understand,' James Rose Innes wrote to a London friend, 'he would sweep the board. He is idolized by the English public, excepting only a sane remnant, really, though not avowedly, because he is opposed by the Dutch. The man has no moral courage, and never had. He goes on making big clever clumsy speeches, but always in constituencies where the issue is not in real doubt. He never ventured in his tour to beard a really Bond district.' There was truth in this. The Jameson raid had lost Rhodes the support of the majority of Cape Afrikaners and this weakened his entire campaign. There were even doubts about his personal prospects of election.

Rhodes had stood for his old constituency of Barkly West, but his friends, apprehensive of the Dutch vote in the rural district, had decided to nominate him for a safer seat in Namaqualand. He therefore stood a chance of being doubly elected: but he could just as easily be doubly defeated. Publicly Rhodes appeared to have no doubts, but he must have known that he was taking a chance. He had to look elsewhere for support.

It was probably during this election that Rhodes was approached by representatives of the Cape coloured voters. They wanted to know what he meant by his pledge to secure equal rights for 'every white man south of the Zambesi'. Rhodes tried to reassure them. 'My motto is,' he said, 'equal rights for every *civilized* man south of the Zambesi.' Asked to explain himself further, he defined a civilized man as one 'who has sufficient education to write his name – has some property or works.' It was a crude definition, but it sufficed for an election. Whether, as is sometimes claimed, it reflects Rhodes's democratic convictions is another matter. Politicians invariably say what prospective voters wish to hear.

There can be little doubt of Rhodes's determination to win this election. The idea that he had lost interest in Cape politics is simply not true. His opponents – the liberals as well as the Bond – were convinced that he was financing Progressive candidates and would not hesitate to stoop to bribery. 'I fear,' wrote Rose Innes's brother, early in the campaign, 'attempts will be made to *buy* the native vote and voters. It has *never* been subject to this temptation before . . . It will be an evil day indeed for the native vote, and *their friends* too, when that vote is on the market – this [is] a real danger . . . .' The more heated the campaign became, the greater suspicion grew concerning Rhodes's electioneering tactics.

But however questionable Rhodes's methods may have been, however much money and energy he spent in trying to whip up support, he was unable to rescue his party. The Progressives lost the election. As expected, they polled heavily in the towns but their opponents picked up the country votes and beat them by a narrow margin. Rhodes at least had the satisfaction of winning his Barkly West seat. The fears of his friends proved false and the constituency he had served for almost twenty years returned both him and his running mate with healthy majorities. Rhodes was to continue to represent Barkly West for the remainder of his life.

This was small consolation for the once all-powerful Rhodes. He had no taste for opposition politics and did not relish returning to the back benches of a chamber he had once ruled. His attempted come-back had been made too soon. Memories of the Jameson raid were too vivid for him to hope for electoral forgiveness. He must have realized this when he had earlier hinted at retiring from Cape politics. Now he had little option but to act on his own suggestion. After attending a few sittings of the new parliamentary session, he gave up. Prematurely aged, sickly, and conscious that time was running out, he could not afford to waste the few years that were left to him. All his efforts from now on had to be directed purposefully. That meant concentrating, almost exclusively, on the development of the Chartered Company's territories. With this in mind he again boarded a steamer at the end of the year and sailed for England to continue his negotiations for the extension of the railway in Rhodesia.

This time he was accompanied by the conscientious and decidedly more efficient Philip Jourdan. For young Jourdan, this trip was the fulfilment of a long cherished dream; after years of being pushed aside by Rhodes's more assertive companions, he was at last travelling the world with his hero. It was a role to which he was well suited. Unlike Gordon le Sueur and Johnny Grimmer, he was not to remain idle, squandering his employer's money on frivolous social sprees and leaving letters to be answered on their return. Always the most diligent of Rhodes's 'secretaries', Jourdan was kept fully occupied dealing with the stream of visitors to the Burlington Hotel – where Rhodes occupied a special suite of rooms – arranging interviews and seeing that Rhodes kept his various engagements. Many years later, he was to look back on this visit to London as one of the most rewarding episodes of his career.

They arrived in England in the middle of January 1899. Rhodes was given a pre-Jameson raid welcome. 'Mr Rhodes's presence in England is now becoming a matter of annual recurrence,' commented *The Times*. 'Reverses, obstacles and failures, in which he has openly acknowledged his own share of shortcomings, have but strengthened his determined grip upon the scheme of his life's work. All is not done, but his measure of success has been on the whole remarkable. The end has never been abandoned, and step by step advance is made towards its attainment.'

The Times was not alone in its enthusiasm. All London seemed anxious to show Rhodes that he was not only welcome but that he was still regarded as a jewel in the imperial crown. Twice he was invited to Sandringham as a guest of the Prince and Princess of Wales and society hostesses chased him as never before. 'He was a great favourite with the ladies . . . .,' says Jourdan. 'He received while in London on an average about half a dozen invitations a day to lunch, dinner or to spend the week-end.'

But, for the most part, Rhodes was kept busy with the affairs of the Chartered Company and De Beers. He did, however, tackle one other important task during this visit. His solicitor, Bourchier Hawksley, was then drawing up his new will and Rhodes – in consultation with his confidant, W. T. Stead – devoted a great deal of time and care into putting the final touches to its provisions.

Since leaving his entire fortune to Neville Pickering, in 1882, Rhodes had revised his will four times. The last one had been signed in 1893. Each new version of the will contained variations but Rhodes had clung to his intention of financing a secret society to expand British influence throughout the world. Not until 1893 had a new and more realistic approach been indicated: then it was that provision had been made for thirty-six scholarships to be awarded to 'young colonials'. This scholarship idea had been maturing in Rhodes's mind for some years and, after introducing it in his 1893 will, he had given it more thought. Now, six years later, he set about perfecting his 'great idea'. The results of his deliberations were to be handed down to posterity and form the basis of his greatest claim to immortality.

Rhodes's last will and testament is a curious document. Its simply-worded provisions reflect the lingering idealism of his youth, tempered by experience and political shrewdness. Before coming to the main purpose of the will, Rhodes deals with his personal obligations. He gives specific instructions concerning his burial in the Matopos. He bequeaths his English estate to his family, and his estates in Rhodesia to the people of that country. He requests that Groote Schuur be retained as a 'park for the people' until South Africa is united and then it is to become a residence for future prime ministers of the federated states. He leaves £100,000 to Oriel College, Oxford. He then unfolds his 'great idea'.

Inevitably Rhodes's scheme for instituting scholarships which would enable youngsters of the English-speaking world to study at Oxford has been severely criticized. He has been accused of, among other things, attempting to create an international elite. There is some truth in this, but it is doubtful whether his intentions were as sinister as they are sometimes made to appear. His thinking was very much in tune with that of his contemporaries: the full implications of the *herrenvolk* mentality were not apparent to the late-Victorians and it is highly unlikely that Rhodes consciously set out to pave the way for future tyrants. To think otherwise is to judge him from hindsight. The stated aim of Rhodes's will was to promote a union of English-speaking people by awarding sixty scholarships annually to suitably qualified students drawn from the colonies of the British Empire and to extend these awards by granting similar scholarships to two students from each of the United States of America. By making these awards, Rhodes hoped that the students would return to their own countries inspired by an Oxford education. This would ensure the spread of British influence throughout the world. The members of his 'secret society' were, in fact, to swap their masks for graduates' gowns.

To qualify for a scholarship, a student had to meet certain requirements. According to the terms of the will, selection was to depend on: 'his literary and scholastic attainments; his fondness of and success in manly outdoor sports . . .; his qualities of manhood, truth, courage, devotion to duty, sympathy for the protection of the weak, kindliness, unselfishness and fellowship; and his exhibition during school-days of moral force of character and instincts to lead and to take an interest in his schoolmates.' Again Rhodes was reflecting the thinking of his times. Many a Victorian headmaster could have compiled a similar list.

But the qualities laid down by Rhodes were those expected of a budding head prefect: they were not the attributes of potential leaders of nations. Rhodes, who cynically summed up his requirements to W. T. Stead as 'brutality', 'smugness' and 'unctuous rectitude', should have realized how wide of the mark they were. His own experience of power must have told him that it is rarely the upright, fair-minded, sports-loving paragons who influence history. He had been too involved in political intrigue not to know that, more often than not, the Empire-builders of the world are lonely, egocentric, ruthless manipulators, men who look back on an adolescence marred by their inability to make friends or to adjust to their surroundings. Indeed it is extremely doubtful whether Rhodes, even as a youngster, would have qualified for one of his own scholarships.

The weakness of Rhodes's 'great idea' lay not in any sinister intent but in the championship of the worthy above the unorthodox. Education, alone, was not the answer Rhodes was seeking: he might have been better served by a secret society. But if he had doubts about the scholarships, they were not transferred to the will. The terms defining a student's qualifications were contained in a codicil but apart from this, and six other codicils – including one leaving Johnny Grimmer £10,000 and the use of the Inyanga farm for his lifetime – the last will and testament of Cecil Rhodes remained unaltered.

Oxford was very much on Rhodes's mind at this time. He had never lost his admiration for the university and, earlier, that admiration had been returned when he and Lord Kitchener – recently raised to the peerage after his victorious campaign in the Sudan – received honorary degrees at Oxford. The conferring of a doctorate of law on Rhodes had been vehemently opposed by a pro-Boer faction at the university but this seems to have made no difference to his reception by the under-graduates. According to Lewis Michell, he was awarded his degree 'amid the most enthusiastic scenes'.

Shortly after arriving in London, Rhodes paid a short visit to Egypt. He went to Cairo with his old Oxford friend, Sir Charles Metcalfe – who was now his adviser on engineering matters – to negotiate an agreement by which his transcontinental telegraph line would be con-nected to Egypt. On his return journey across Europe, Rhodes stopped off at Berlin, where he was warmly received by the Kaiser. The two men, temperamental and highly strung though they both were, appear to have overcome their former distrust of each other and got on surprisingly well. They joked about the Kaiser's notorious telegram to Kruger after the Jameson raid and Rhodes came away confident that his telegraph line would be continued through German East Africa. It was probably as a result of this meeting that fifteen German students were later included among those eligible for the Rhodes scholarships.

On arriving back in England, Rhodes was again made aware of the existence of Princess Catherine Radziwill. She wrote to him asking for advice on an investment she wished to make. Jourdan claims that Rhodes had to be reminded of who she was. (Had he forgotten the letter he had received in Rhodesia?) Luckily Rochfort Maguire was at hand to jog Rhodes's memory. 'Yes,' declared Rhodes, on being told they had met at Moberly Bell's; I remember her; she was quite interest-ing; a vivacious talker.' He then scribbled a reply, telling the Princess to buy Mashonaland railway debentures. This was the only letter Rhodes admitted writing to Catherine Radziwill.

But, as he was soon to discover, it was certainly not the last he was to hear of her.

Rhodes was kept so busy in London that his visit had to be extended. He had originally intended to return to South Africa in April but he was obliged to change his booking on five ships before he eventually got away. Not until July was he free to board the s.s. *Scot* at Southamp-ton. Unknown to him, Princess Radziwill had shared his problems at the shipping office. She too was intending to sail to South Africa and, determined to travel on the same ship as Rhodes, she had repeatedly changed her bookings. Philip Jourdan has described how she made herself known to Rhodes on board the *Scot*.

On the first evening out, Rhodes, Sir Charles Metcalfe and Jourdan were seated at their table in the dining saloon when ten minutes after the gong had sounded, the Princess made entry. 'She was gorgeously gowned and got up to captivate,' says Jourdan. 'She tripped along, lightly, only the rustling of her silk garment being audible.' Pretending not to see Rhodes, she appeared overcome with surprise when she reached his table. 'Oh! How do you do?' she gasped. The three men politely rose to greet her. Then, spotting an empty chair, the Princess asked if she could take it. 'Certainly, Princess,' said Rhodes, pulling out the chair, 'you are quite welcome to it.' That was all the encouragement she needed. 'Of course,' sniffed Jourdan, 'she occupied the chair for the rest of the voyage.'

CHAPTER SIXTEEN

'So Little Done'

If Philip Jourdan is to be believed, Princess Radziwill's behaviour on board the s.s. *Scot* was so outrageous that Rhodes took fright. Her determination to ensnare the 'poor Colossus' – as she later called him – was such that she became embarrassingly flirtatious and overplayed her hand. Uncomfortable as he was with women, Rhodes is said to have done his utmost to avoid her.

But if the Princess's tactics were crude, her performance was nothing if not polished. Whatever else might be said about Catherine Radziwill, there is no denying her power to charm. She was a highly accomplished woman: witty and shrewd, intelligent and plausible; she knew how to make the most of her talents. Every evening, seated at Rhodes's table in the dining saloon, she monopolized the conversation, mesmerizing her companions with stories of her experiences in the courts of Europe, with political gossip and scandalous stories of intrigue in high places. There seemed to be few men of importance whom she did not know and even fewer whom she was not prepared to denigrate. She loved to parade her linguistic abilities – her command of English was good but she claimed to be more at home in French and Russian – to display her familiarity with English and French literature and her knowledge of world affairs. She could produce an apt quote to illuminate any subject and was never at a loss for a telling anecdote to underline any point she wished to make.

Young Jourdan was enormously impressed. 'She was quite an acquisition to our table,' he admitted. 'I thought that she was an extraordinarily clever woman.' Only one thing spoiled her conversation. This was her tendency to express herself bluntly on what Jourdan called 'delicate matters'. Not only did the unworldly Jourdan find her frankness disconcerting but, he noticed, there were times when Rhodes 'could not suppress a blush'. It was left to Sir Charles Metcalfe to reassure his sensitive friends. Openness in discussing questionable subjects, he told them, was simply an unfortunate foreign habit.

The Princess appears to have been particularly outspoken about her personal misfortunes. These centred on her disastrous marriage. She had been more or less forced by her family to marry Prince William

Radziwill – by whom she had three daughters and two sons – and had left her home in Russia, at the age of fifteen, to live in the huge Radziwill palace in Berlin. It is highly unlikely that she told Rhodes of the political meddling that had led to her expulsion from Germany but she had no hesitation in denouncing the brutal behaviour of her husband. 'She had suffered at the hands of her cruel husband more than it was possible for her to describe,' says Jourdan. 'She spoke like a martyr sometimes, with a soft, trembling, hesitating voice full of pathos and sadness. She stirred the very blood in my veins.' Whether Rhodes was similarly moved, he does not say. But there can be little doubt that it was Rhodes's blood the Princess was hoping to stir.

Having told her pathetic story, the Princess went on to explain her presence on board the *Scot*. She claimed that she had reached the limits of endurance and was applying for a divorce. The matter was in the hands of her lawyers and, as divorce proceedings in Russia took a long time, she had decided to spend a year in South Africa to allow time for the divorce to be granted. In fact there is no evidence to show that she was then contemplating a divorce and, in any event, the Russian formalities would have taken much longer than a year. But Rhodes was not to know this. He had merely been given the impression that Princess Radziwill would soon be free to marry again. This is what she intended and what she indicated to other passengers. 'I still think,' one of them, a Major Harding, later observed, 'that she was in love with the South African statesman. Often she would speak of him in the most affectionate terms.'

Nor were her expressions of affection confined to casual deckboard conversations. Not only did she adopt a flirtatious tone when speaking to Rhodes (she was far less winsome when arguing with Jourdan or Sir Charles Metcalfe) but she took to following him about the ship, cornering him at every opportunity. This, according to Jourdan, is what infuriated Rhodes. Finally, when the pursuit was accompanied by a pounce, he decided he had had enough. It happened one day when he and the Princess were seated next to each other on the main deck. Having repeatedly complained of palpitations and shortage of breath, the Princess appeared suddenly to have a heart attack. She sat up, gasped, reeled and tumbled into Rhodes's lap. Trying to support her until help came, Rhodes seemed near to fainting himself. 'I shall never forget,' says Jourdan, 'the absolute look of abject helplessness on his face.' Smelling salts were fetched and in no time the Princess was on her feet again. But from that time on Rhodes is said to have avoided the main promenade and to have confined himself to the captain's deck.

Unfortunately there is only Jourdan's word for all this. He was the only one to report the antics of Princess Radziwill on board the *Scot* at any length. On the whole, Jourdan is a reliable witness but it would seem that his account of this voyage was highly coloured. It smacks too strongly of Gilbert and Sullivan to ring true. Later it became necessary for Rhodes's associates to portray the woman they called 'Princess Razzle Dazzle' as a figure of fun and Jourdan, recording his impressions many years later, appears to have written accordingly. The stories he tells constitute the most vividly described episode of Rhodes's strange association with the Princess but, although Jourdan presents them in detail, his memory was not that good. The fact is that when Princess Radziwill's name cropped up shortly after the voyage ended, Jourdan had difficulty in remembering who she was. The mystery surrounding the part played in Rhodes's life by the Princess seems to have started the moment she appeared.

There is certainly reason to question Jourdan's description of Rhodes's persecutor. He says she was 'tall, inclined to be stout, had black hair and black shifting eyes. She could not be called handsome or pretty and was about forty-seven years of age then.' While this would have been partly true of Princess Radziwill a few years later, it does not fit her appearance on board the *Scot*. Lord Frederick Hamilton, who met the Princess in Berlin when she was a young married woman, claims she was 'the loveliest human being' he had ever met. Traces of her remarkable beauty were still evident when she sailed for South Africa. In July 1899 Catherine Radziwill was forty-one, and a photograph taken about that time shows her to have been slim, elegant and still very attractive. No longer in the first flush of youth, she was nevertheless a poised, delicately-featured, striking-looking woman. With her dark hair piled above her broad forehead, her large, heavy-lidded eyes, her aquiline nose and her mobile mouth, she now had a vivacity and a piquancy of expression that counted for more than mere prettiness. But the picture painted by Jourdan was to cling to her and, in later second-hand accounts, she was to be ridiculed as a fat, blowsy, middle-aged *poseur* who hounded the hapless Rhodes on board the *Scot* in the hopes of seducing him. It was run-of-the-mill farce but it does not match up to reality. Princess Radziwill was better suited to her role of a *femme fatale* that her detractors are prepared to admit.

Philip Jourdan was biased and, while there may be a germ of truth in what he says – he acknowledges the Princess's cleverness and her ability to charm – the few mentions made of her by other passengers contradict his more colourful touches. None of them, for instance, recalls the fainting episode on deck, which Jourdan claims caused a sensation. Nor do they remember Catherine Radziwill as a comic character. One man, who was a guest at Rhodes's table, was enchanted by the Princess's 'strange fascination'. And Major Harding and his wife were so impressed by the Princess's friendship with Rhodes that, when they eventually said good-bye, Harding hailed her as 'the future Queen of Rhodesia.' Admittedly these witnesses were not as involved in events as was Jourdan, but surely they would have noticed that something was amiss?

But the most telling comment on the voyage came from Rhodes himself. If he had spent his days at sea trying to avoid his bothersome table companion, he showed no sign of hostility when they parted. Instead he extended an open invitation to the Princess, asking her to visit him at Groote Schuur.

*　　*　　*

There was another tremendous welcome awaiting Rhodes when the *Scot* docked in Table Bay. His supporters had been preparing for his arrival for over a week. The streets of Cape Town were decked with flags and banners, bunting fluttered from the tram wires and every lamp-post, every telegraph pole, was decorated with brightly coloured medallions. Most of the shops and offices had declared a public holiday and the main road, leading to the docks, was packed with people waiting to cheer their returning idol. Rhodes may have lost his election but he could still rely on the loyalty of his hometown. This, says T. E. Fuller, was perhaps the greatest demonstration ever made in his honour.

Throughout the day congratulatory messages poured into Groote Schuur. That night an enormous crowd filled the Drill Hall where Rhodes was presented with over one hundred addresses of welcome. Once again, as he entered the hall he was greeted with a blast of 'See the conquering hero comes' and a prolonged standing ovation. What sparked off these demonstrations is a mystery. Rhodes, after all, had only gone to London to negotiate extensions to his railway and telegraph systems. But, whatever the cause, the effect was regarded as momentous. 'The extraordinary outburst of public enthusiasm with which Mr Rhodes was welcomed . . . ,' observed the *Cape Times*, 'may fairly be taken as marking another epoch in [his] career.' Rhodes's political opponents, however, regarded the 'excitement' as just another attempt by his followers to boost their champion's battered reputation.

Princess Radziwill appears to have missed most of the fun. She must have been aware of the street demonstrations but she did not, like some of the other passengers from the *Scot*, attend the mass meeting at the Drill Hall. On leaving the ship, she had booked in at Cape Town's new and fashionable hotel, the Mount Nelson, and this became her headquarters. Once she had settled in, one of her first moves was to present herself at Government House where she handed over a letter of introduction to Alfred Milner which, she claimed, had been given to her by the British Prime Minister, Lord Salisbury. At first Milner was a little suspicious of her but he was later to discover, from Lord Salisbury's son, that the Prime Minister was indeed acquainted with the Princess and the letter was genuine.

But it was on Groote Schuur that the Princess had set her sights and she lost no time in calling on Rhodes. For the first few weeks of her stay, she was a regular visitor at Groote Schuur and she was cordially received. Not only did Rhodes invite her to lunch and dinner but, on discovering that she was fond of riding, he provided her with horses for her early morning canters. The Princess was delighted with her success. Soon she began dropping heavy hints to guests at the Mount Nelson that her friendship with Rhodes went far beyond casual social visits. The impression she gave was that she would soon be installed in Groote Schuur, not as a guest, but as Rhodes's wife. Among other things, she claimed that Rhodes had taken a particular interest in her eldest son, Prince Nicholas Radziwill, and had written inviting him to South Africa. She even produced a copy of this letter and read an extract from it which seemed to indicate that Rhodes was thinking of marrying her.

This was to become one of Princess Radziwill's more familiar tactics. Reading, and even passing on what appeared to be personal letters was her favourite way of impressing people. Not the least of the Princess's many skills was, as time would show, her remarkable talent for forgery.

Whether Rhodes knew of Princess Radziwill's whispering campaign is not certain. Far more obvious was his reaction to the Princess's continual presence at Groote Schuur. Once she had established herself as a visitor, she dropped all pretence of politeness and began turning up at the house, uninvited and unexpected, at all hours of the day. There was no escaping her. So confident was she of a welcome that she would demand to see Rhodes the moment she arrived and, if he was out or busy, would plonk herself down and wait for him. Not surprisingly, Rhodes found this highly disconcerting. He began to dread the Princess's visits and, at times, became visibly agitated at the very mention of her name. He would go to any lengths to avoid meeting her and even, it is said, kept a horse permanently saddled so that he could make a quick get away whenever she appeared at his gate.

More than anything else, Rhodes hated being alone with the Princess. He gave his staff and his friends strict instructions never to leave his side when she was present and would get extremely flustered at the thought of being trapped in a room with her. It was not, as might be assumed, the Princess's flirtatiousness that alarmed him, but her insistence on talking politics. Later Rhodes would claim that they had never in fact discussed politics but this is difficult to believe. They had very little else in common and were both incapable of holding a conversation without making political observations. What alarmed Rhodes was not the Princess's political chatter but her relentless political prying. Determined as she was to involve herself in Rhodes's career, she was no less determined to probe his political secrets.

The most tantalizing secret was, of course, the mystery surrounding the notorious 'missing telegrams' which Rhodes had refused to produce at the inquiry into the Jameson raid and it seems to have been the Princess's incessant questions on this murky aspect of his career that provoked Rhodes's hostility. Nobody, not even his close political associates, was allowed to push him too far on the subject of the 'missing telegrams'.

But the Princess did not give up easily. No matter how obvious were the rebuffs from Rhodes, she continued to harass him. Eventually she went too far and Rhodes exploded. There was a stormy scene in which he told his importunate visitor that if she did not drop her political interrogations 'she had better not speak to him at all.' After that the Princess's visits to Groote Schuur became less frequent.

One other significant event occurred about this time. It happened on one of Princess Radziwill's visits to Groote Schuur. J. G. McDonald, who was staying at the house, learned about the 'incident' shortly afterwards. It appears that Philip Jourdan had become alarmed by the Princess's habit of wandering into his office and fingering through the papers on his desk. On this particular occasion, however, she went a step further. Jourdan had been obliged to leave her alone in the office for a few minutes and, on his return, he discovered that certain papers were missing. McDonald, writing forty years later and influenced by later events, imagined that the Princess was trying to obtain a copy of Rhodes's signature. But it would seem the theft was more serious than that. It was so serious, in fact, that Jourdan was afraid to tell Rhodes about it. Nor, for that matter, did he mention the theft in his memoirs. Always the most discreet of Rhodes's secretaries, Jourdan may have had good reasons for remaining silent.

There is no way of knowing what the Princess stole. Later, however, Catherine Radziwill claimed to be in possesion of 'papers' that were damaging to Rhodes. These were the papers she used in her attempt to blackmail the 'poor Colossus'. Precisely what these mysterious documents were, or how the Princess obtained them, is a matter for speculation.

*　　　*　　　*

The temporary retreat of Princess Radziwill did not deprive Rhodes of female company. On his return from Europe, he entertained a number of visitors at Groote Schuur, including two women with whom he was particularly friendly. In July one of his house-guests was Lady Sarah Wilson, a sister of Lord Randolph Churchill, and she was later replaced by Lady Edward Cecil, a daughter-in-law of Lord Salisbury. Both these women met Princess Radziwill but neither of them succumbed to her charms. Lady Sarah Wilson could not bring herself to mention the Princess and Lady Edward Cecil dismissed her as a 'vulgar adventuress. A sort of Edgar Wallace Foreign Spy'. They were both far more interested in Rhodes and his house, than in his shipboard companion.

Lady Sarah Wilson's description of Rhodes at this time contrasts vividly with the impression left by his encounters with Princess Radziwill. 'After his morning rides,' she writes, 'Mr Rhodes, if nothing called him to town, usually walked about his beautiful house . . . . I can often call to mind that tall figure, probably in the same costume in which he had ridden – white flannel trousers and tweed coat – his hair rather rough, from a habit he had of passing his hand through it when talking or thinking. He would wander through the rooms, enjoying the pleasure of looking at his many beautiful pieces of furniture and curiosities of all sorts, nearly all of which had a history. Occasionally shifting a piece of rare old glass or blue Delft china, he would the while talk to anyone who chanced to come in.' After dinner they would sit playing bridge, at which Lady Sarah was an expert and Rhodes an enthusiastic learner.

Lady Edward Cecil's impressions were similar. 'I have seen him walk about for an hour with a blue delft pot under his arm,' she says, 'trying it first here and then there, and the best evidence of his taste was that he did not overload his rooms . . . there was no particular feel of money about his house. It was just beautiful and very simple.' Simplicity was also the keyword for Rhodes's hospitality. Lady Edward found the lack of formality enchanting. 'It is the most amusing house to stay in,' she told her mother, 'being the only real Liberty Hall I have ever come across. You get up when you like, breakfast when you like, lunch any time between 1 and 2.30, no one cares whether you are there to meals or whether you are alive or dead . . . . You can ask anyone to a meal that you please and our host's motto is "Don't bother" – he doesn't bother and his guests don't bother and no one bothers at all about anything.' There was no bridge during Lady Edward's stay. Instead the guests would sit on the stoep after dinner, listening to the band that played every evening.

Princess Radziwill apart, these were days of domesticity for Rhodes. He no longer had the energy for a more active life. Lady Edward Cecil remarked on how grey his hair had become and how his florid face 'gave notice of . . . heart trouble.' He would occasionally attend the House of Assembly or deal with some urgent Chartered Company business, but he was far happier pottering about the newly restored

271

Groote Schuur. He never ceased adding to his treasures. The fire had destroyed most of his highly-prized collections of furniture, painting, tapestries and carpets but he had lost no time in replacing them, employing an expert recommended by Herbert Baker to help and advise him. This man, says Baker, 'came to South Africa, lived in the house, and was most successful in his discovery of old things . . . priceless things often unknown and unprized in the lofts and outhouses of farms, or hidden in paint in labourers' shanties.'

But perhaps Rhodes's most cherished possession was his library. The promptness with which his butler rescued as many books as he could when the fire broke out is an indication of Rhodes's bias. Over the years he had lavished a great deal of time and money in amassing his library. The shelves were packed with a motley collection of modern novels, contemporary biographies, travel books and rare volumes of ancient writings which were said to throw 'a singular and most interesting light on Mr Rhodes's literary tastes and studies'. Among the more esoteric works was a set of handsomely bound books which formed part of a literary scheme devised by Rhodes in 1893. After re-reading Gibbon's *Decline and Fall of the Roman Empire* he had been so impressed that he decided to have translations made from the original sources used by Gibbon. He insisted that these translations be 'absolutely unabridged'. The scheme involved hundreds of volumes and is estimated to have cost about £8,000 (well over £200,000 in today's money). Typewritten and bound in red morocco, it was considered 'the most extensive collection of biographies of Roman emperors and empresses'.

Since his Oxford days, Rhodes had been fascinated by the tyrannical rulers of ancient Rome. The power they exercised and the influence they wielded doubtless appealed to his imperial instincts. Nothing flattered him more than to be told that his profile resembled that of a Roman emperor. But his desire to obtain unexpurgated accounts of the lives of these degenerate despots – including the saturnalia, the orgies and bizarre carnal practices of the later Roman courts – seems odd for a man who is said to have blushed at the very mention of sex. For not only were the texts of the books unabridged but they were illustrated by drawings from coins and medallions, some of which, says Gordon le Sueur, were 'of a decidedly erotic nature'. So pornographic were the illustrations that when le Sueur came to catalogue the library, he felt obliged to lock away certain volumes. After Rhodes's death, it was found that the books had been tampered with. 'Despite all precautions the illustrations were cut out and removed,' says le Sueur. 'I have,' he adds, 'a shrewd idea as to the culprit.' The fact that the library also housed the phallic objects taken from the Zimbabwe ruins is said to have encouraged 'ugly rumours about Rhodes's abnormal sexuality', about his bachelor entourage and the fact that no women servants were employed at Groote Schuur. There is no evidence to support this claim, but the books and the phallic collection undoubtedly call into question Rhodes's reputed puritanism.

The presence at Groote Schuur of Lady Sarah Wilson and Lady Edward Cecil was no accident. They were both married to soldiers and had come to the Cape with their husbands in response to the crisis that was then developing in South Africa. The prospect of war between Britain and the Transvaal republic had been threatening for some months and now looked like becoming a reality. Indeed the clamourous reception given to Rhodes on his return may well have been inspired, in part, by the war-fever that was then sweeping the country. Tension was high and people felt a need to let off steam. But Rhodes, seated on the stoep at Groote Schuur and listening to the band, remained surprisingly relaxed. He had been in London during the most critical events of the past few months and was, in any case, not prepared to involve himself in the crisis.

'I keep aloof from the Transvaal crisis,' he told an interviewer, 'so that no one will be able to say that Rhodes is at it again.' He was confident that the furore would die down. 'The notion of the Transvaal being able to trouble Great Britain at all seriously,' he said on another occasion, 'is too ridiculous. I cannot really think about it. It is too ridiculous . . . . There is not the slightest chance of war.' But he was wrong.

*   *   *

When, in 1897, Sir Alfred Milner arrived in South Africa to take up his position as High Commissioner, it was hoped that his appointment heralded a period of peace and reconciliation. He was acknowledged as a man of great abilities and was thought to be fully in accord with the British government's desire for patience and restraint in its dealings with the Transvaal.

And for a while it looked as if Milner would live up to expectations. He started by making all the right noises: he denounced the Jameson raid, prophesied that the dispute between Kruger and the *uitlanders* would be settled internally and was wary of becoming too closely associated with Rhodes. All of which was fine as long as it lasted but, unfortunately, it did not last long. Within nine months of taking office Milner's attitude began to change. It became increasingly obvious that he was simply playing for time. He had never, in all truth, intended doing otherwise. A self-confessed 'British Race Patriot', Milner was every bit as determined as Rhodes to secure the dominance of the English-speaking race throughout southern Africa. He made this perfectly clear in letters he wrote to his contacts in England as well in a 'credo' that was published after his death. 'The British State,' he declared, 'must follow the race, must comprehend it, wherever it settles in appreciable numbers as an independent community.' This is how he saw his mission in South Africa and nothing, not even the prospect of war, was to deter him from fulfilling it. As far as the Transvaal was concerned, the situation remained very much the same. In an increasingly taut game, only the players had changed: Cecil Rhodes, the rash adventurer, had been replaced by Alfred Milner, the deadly diplomat.

The *uitlanders* in Johannesburg were quick to recognize their new champion. With the downfall of Rhodes, they desperately needed a new, unsullied voice to speak on their behalf. They were still without the vote, still frustrated in their attempts to make the gold-industry more efficient and still at the mercy of Kruger's nominees for vital mining equipment. The Jameson raid, far from resolving the stalemate, had merely compromised their cause and added to their resentment. Sir Alfred Milner, clothed in the trappings of officialdom, promised to be a far more formidable combatant than Dr Jameson and his makeshift army. His arrival on the scene not only revived the *uitlanders'* hopes but spurred them into action. Plans were made to increase the pressure on Paul Kruger and his government. An opportunity for the mining community to display their renewed confidence came when, shortly before Christmas 1898, a British workman, living in Johannesburg was accidentally killed in a fracas with the Transvaal police. The *uitlanders* seized upon this incident to stage a demonstration in the Johannesburg market square and afterwards handed a petition of protest to the British vice-consul – which was later published in the *Cape Times* – addressed to Queen Victoria. In any other country the incident would have been regarded as a minor tragedy and quickly forgotten; such was the tension in Johannesburg, however, that it provoked international comment and was to be remembered as a landmark on the road to war.

A far more significant milepost was reached a few months later when a meeting was arranged between Sir Alfred Milner and President Kruger in Bloemfontein, the capital of the Orange Free State. Ostensibly they came together to discuss a means of settling their differences but, as far as Milner was concerned, it was a futile exercise. The High Commissioner arrived at the conference – which lasted from 31 May to 5 June 1899 – determined to force the issue. Convinced that the Boers were arguing from weakness, he intended to call their bluff. When he demanded a prompt and wholesale reform of the Transvaal franchise, Kruger cried: 'It is our country you want!' The President knew that the *uitlanders* far outnumbered his burgers and to give them the vote would be tantamount to his abdicating power. His attempts to bargain, however, were imperiously rejected and, as expected, the conference ended in stalemate. Kruger's attorney-general, the young Jan Smuts, was later to declare that Milner was worse to deal with than Cecil Rhodes.

It was no longer a question of whether or not there would be a war, but of when the fighting would start. Rhodes, still in London at this time, was one of the few who refused to acknowledge this. 'Kruger,' he was fond of saying, 'will bluff up to the cannon's mouth.' His attitude towards the Boer President appears to have undergone a remarkable change. At a London dinner party he had startled his fellow guests by singing Kruger's praises, saying that he was a splendid old man who had 'defended his wicket against all comers'. His sincerity might be doubted, but he remained convinced that Kruger would prefer to negotiate rather than fight.

This was his attitude throughout the crisis. On his return to South Africa, he met Milner from time to time – mostly on social occasions – but there seems no evidence that he tried to influence the High Commissioner. Indeed, what encouragement Sir Alfred received came more from the *uitlanders*, particularly Alfred Beit and his partner Julius Wernher (although the politically gullible Beit, for all his financial shrewdness, was ill-suited to the sinister role in which he is sometimes cast – that of *éminence grise*). Whether Rhodes, as he claimed, deliberately kept himself aloof from Milner's warmongering or whether he was simply not fit enough to involve himself is difficult to ascertain. The fact is that even when, at Milner's request, shiploads of British troops began arriving at the Cape and Natal, Rhodes continued to deny that war was imminent.

Not until the inevitable happened did his attitude change. On 9 October 1899, President Kruger, pressured beyond endurance, issued an ultimatum demanding that British troops be withdrawn from the borders of the Transvaal and all points of difference between the two countries be referred to arbitration. The British were given forty-eight hours to reply. As there was no chance of these terms being agreed to the ultimatum was recognized for what it was – a declaration of war. This was something that Rhodes could not ignore. He was at last stirred into action.

That same evening Rhodes left Cape Town for Kimberley. He was accompanied by Rochfort Maguire and his wife and Philip Jourdan. Before catching his train, Rhodes scribbled a quick note to Lady Edward Cecil and her friend Lady Charles Bentinck. 'I want you to take care of my house, until I return,' he told them, 'and if you don't stay I shall think you are two very small-minded women.' He had no idea how long he would be away but, like everyone else, he knew that Kimberley would be a prime target for the Boers. A telegram he had received from the mayor of the town had made this quite clear. 'Citizens generally,' it read, 'feel that your presence here would serve to induce a rush . . . would ask you to postpone coming in order to avert any possible risks.' But neither this, nor rumours that the Boers intended to capture him and exhibit him in a cage throughout the Transvaal, could stop Rhodes. Kimberley was the cradle of his fortunes, the source of his continuing wealth, the place to which his thoughts immediately turned when danger threatened. He was determined, as Jourdan put it, 'to see what should be done to safeguard the interests of De Beers'.

* * *

The day after Rhodes arrived in Kimberley, Kruger's ultimatum expired and three days later the Boers surrounded the town, cut the telegraph wires and dislocated the railway line. *'Fearful* excitement . . . ,' wrote Constance Scott, wife of one of the town guards. 'We are now quite cut off . . . . We expect an attack any moment. Every one at his post and keeping a keen look out.'

The previous evening Mrs Scott and her husband had dined with Cecil Rhodes at the Sanatorium. This handsome, double-storied, red-brick hotel had recently been refurbished by De Beers to serve as a health resort and was now Rhodes's headquarters. On arriving in Kimberley, Rhodes had made straight for the Sanatorium – which had already been fortified with sandbags, scaffolding and corrugated iron to protect it from the shelling – and installed himself in two small rooms on the ground floor. When the Scotts dined with him, he had settled in and was in high spirits. 'Had a very pleasant evening,' Constance Scott noted in her diary. 'After dinner played fives. Mr Rhodes very excited over it, he was *very* nice and said he did not know why people here did not want him. He did not think he had done much harm in coming. In fact he has sent for more guns and so done a great deal of good.'

This view of Rhodes was shared by a large section of the Kimberley population. The initial resentment of his presence in the town quickly evaporated. For many he seemed the only man capable of solving the problems that faced the civilian population. One of his first moves was to finance a scheme for repairing the streets of Kimberley and so provide work for the thousands of refugees – white, black and coloured – who had poured into the town when war threatened and were then sleeping in the Town Hall. He also arranged for a hoard of weapons that had been hidden in the town in preparation for the Jameson raid, to be handed over – somewhat shamefacedly – to the military. Throughout the siege he was to be seen everywhere, encouraging the faint-hearted, listening to complaints and consulting local officials. So conspicuous was he that his friends feared for his safety. 'He always wore a pair of white flannel pantaloons,' says Jourdan, 'and it was very easy for the Boers to see him for miles on horseback.' When, at the height of the Boer shelling of the town, an American engineer constructed a gun with which to retaliate, the weapon was immediately dubbed 'Long Cecil'. 'I really do not know what we should have done without Mr Rhodes . . .' gushed one young woman, 'his name will ever mean that of a true friend to everyone who was in Kimberley.'

Had Rhodes confined himself to helping civilians all might have been well. But, of course, he did not. Regarding Kimberley as his own domain, he saw no reason why he should not exercise full authority over every aspect of life there, including the town's defences. It was this that brought him into conflict with Kimberley's hard-pressed, and normally mild-tempered, military commander: Lieutenant-Colonel Robert George Kekewich.

Rhodes had a long-standing contempt for army officers. He not only considered that Kekewich was unfitted for his job but was convinced that he could do it better himself. His high-handed demand for more guns, noted by Mrs Scott, was typical of the line he was to take. It was impossible for this demand to be met but this had not prevented him from making it without consulting Kekewich. He clearly had no intention of working with the military. More demands were to follow. A way had been found for smuggling messages out of the town by African runners and soon he was bombarding Cape Town with imperious telegrams, insisting that Kimberley be relieved immediately. If the town fell to the Boers, he argued, it would 'be most disastrous on account of politics'. He was careful not to mention his financial interests nor, of course, did he inform Kekewich that he was in touch with the Cape authorities. Not until two weeks into the siege, when a reply to one of Rhodes's telegrams was mistakenly delivered to military headquarters, did Kimberley's commanding officer discover that his decree prohibiting the despatch of unauthorized messages was being deliberately flouted by Rhodes. Not surprisingly Kekewich found this alarming. Kimberley was then under martial law and it was essential that the authority of the military be upheld. But Rhodes was unrepentant. He angrily refused to listen to Kekewich's firm, but tactful, protests and soon the situation became intolerable. There was an ugly scene at the Kimberley Club (Kekewich's headquarters) from which Rhodes stormed out 'frothing at the mouth'. After that the siege of Kimberley took on a new dimension: to the threat from the Boers was added the battle of the town's two 'commanders'.

Kimberley was besieged for four months. The longed-for relief column did not arrive until the beginning of February 1900. For the inhabitants of the town these months of waiting were nerve-racking. The Boers kept up their bombardment and, after Christmas, food stocks began to dwindle. Soup kitchens were introduced to feed the starving – mostly Africans – and donkeys, mules and even dogs disappeared mysteriously from the streets. An estimated 8,500 shells were fired into the town, but most deaths were caused by disease and malnutrition. Precise figures are difficult to arrive at but it is said that the general death-rate was 49 per thousand for Europeans and 138 per thousand for other races.

Shortly before the arrival of the relief column, the shelling became so intense that Rhodes opened the diamond mines as shelters. Later it was claimed that by doing this Rhodes sparked off a stampede to the mines – it was thought another serious bombardment was expected – and women and children were bundled down the shafts to face chaotic, insanitary conditions. First-hand accounts by those who took shelter, as well as by mine officials, make this claim open to question. It is agreed that there was panic at first but this was overcome and, once underground, people were well looked after and medical supervision was provided. But there can be no denying that Rhodes's hasty, unconsidered actions were responsible for some near-disasters. His refusal to collaborate with the military led to blunder after blunder. One incident speaks for the rest.

Early in the siege, Rhodes, hoping to relieve pressure on the town's food supplies, gave orders for 3,000 labourers to be released from the mine compounds and sent home. This, in itself, was nothing unusual. Africans were to be sent out of beleaguered Mafeking for the same reason. Rhodes's mistake was in not informing Kekewich of his decision. The result was that, when the huge mass of men were spotted moving across the veld, the military – not knowing who or what they were – opened fire. Fortunately the mistake was soon realized and nobody was hurt. But incidents like this made life very difficult for the long-suffering military commander.

If Kimberley, Joseph Chamberlain was to say, 'had had any other British commander than Kekewich, Rhodes would have been in gaol.'

The final humiliation for Colonel Kekewich came on the day Kimberley was relieved. That morning Kekewich decided to ride out of town in order to meet General French, the commander of the approaching relief force. Such was the confusion, however, that the two officers missed each other. General French was welcomed by the mayor of Kimberley and then escorted to the Sanatorium where he met the triumphant Rhodes. By the time Kekewich returned to Kimberley, a champagne party was in full swing at the Sanatorium and he had to battle past Rhodes before he was allowed to speak to

General French. He could have saved himself the trouble. French gave him a very frosty greeting. Rhodes was clearly the hero of the hour.

*　　*　　*

The tenacious Princess Radziwill had not been idle while Rhodes was shut up in Kimberley. Her political impulses had been quickened by the outbreak of war. She was still determined to involve herself in Rhodes's career and his absence from Cape Town provided the opportunity. No longer did she have to rely on hints and rumours to further her plans; she was now free to act boldly, without fear of repudiation.

As she described it later, her aim was simple. 'I understood . . . ,' she claimed, 'that from the bottom of his heart [Rhodes] regretted his quarrel with the Dutch side . . . . I began then to work with all my heart to bring a reconciliation between them.' By doing this she hoped a new political party would be formed in the Cape, a party that would create an atmosphere in which peace could be negotiated. She even had a name for this new party. It was to be known as 'the Anglo-African Party' and it would be led by Cecil Rhodes. Apart from that she was vague about the policies she wished the party to pursue. Such matters, she said grandly, would be decided by 'strong men' who did not allow 'personal considerations' to sway them. It was asking a lot from race-torn South Africa, but this did not appear to worry her. For the time being she had enough on her hands promoting her 'inspired' idea.

She set to work shortly after Rhodes left for Kimberley. Her first move was to contact Rhodes's known opponents, including J. X. Merriman and J. W. Sauer. Both these men were now members of the government – which was led by William Schreiner and supported by the Afrikaner Bond – and through them she hoped to interest the 'Dutch side'. How far she succeeded is not known. Later she boasted to Leo Amery, *The Times* correspondent in South Africa, of having had a secret meeting with Jan Hofmeyr in Cape Town's botanical gardens which ended in pure farce. 'Hofmeyr,' says Amery, 'had shown her a letter of Rhodes's, very damaging from the Bond point of view. She snatched it and ran down the garden path with old Jan in hot pursuit.' The sight of the middle-aged Princess being pursued through the public gardens by a dignified and ageing politician would undoubtedly have delighted passers-by but it is unlikely that anyone witnessed this hilarious event. The story told to Leo Amery was probably nothing more than a product of Catherine Radziwill's lively imagination. Hofmeyr, who was far more honest about such matters, claimed that he had 'declined to hold any political communication with the good lady at all'.

News of Princess Radziwill's activities did, however, filter through to the press. The anti-Rhodes newspapers carried several reports of her overtures to politicians and referred to her as Rhodes's 'political agent'. The Princess was also sending articles, singing Rhodes's praises and pontificating on South African politics, to Europe and before long the suspicions voiced about her in the Cape were being repeated in Europe. 'Everyone in Paris knows that the woman is a Boer agent,' declared Georges Clémenceau.

When Rhodes returned from Kimberley and discovered what had been happening he was furious. He dismissed her proposed political party as ridiculous and refused to have anything to do with it. This did not deter the Princess. Once again she began turning up at Groote Schuur, bustling about, full of her new importance. Years later she was to admit that Rhodes resented her interference. 'What can one do with you, Mr Rhodes?' she once angrily demanded. 'Leave me alone,' was his exasperated reply. This, she claimed, made her afraid that he might 'break out into one of those fits of rage which he so often used as a means to end a conversation'.

But the Princess had other problems on her mind at this time. Her funds were rapidly running out. She had always been short of cash; her earlier claim that she had inherited money which she wanted to invest seems to have been another of her fabrications. Indeed, it was only by going to South Africa that she had escaped facing a summons in a London court for the unpaid bills she had run up in England. Since then she had seriously overspent herself at the Mount Nelson hotel. Her bill there was said to be in the region of £1,000 of which she still owed £160. With the hotel management pressing her for payment, she was forced to turn to Rhodes for help. Hesitant to ask for money for herself, she sent a woman friend to plead on her behalf. Rhodes responded to her request with apparent generosity. He not only agreed to help the Princess but seemed willing to settle her debts in full. His offer, however, was subject to one important condition. 'Well,' he told the Princess's emissary, 'I will instruct my attorney and if she will leave the country I will pay her bills.'

Princess Radziwill had no alternative but to accept Rhodes's terms. She did not want to leave South Africa but was clearly in no position to argue. The hotel bill was duly paid and, after staying with friends for a couple of weeks, the Princess sailed for England at the end of April, 1900.

On arriving in London the Princess booked in at the Carlton hotel. She still had no money and was forced to pawn her jewels, said to be valued at £25,000, for less than half their worth. This was done secretly, but she appears to have been helped by a mysterious 'agent' named Otto. It may have been Otto who persuaded her to have replicas made of her jewels in preparation for her next startling deception. On 11 June 1900, while dining at the Carlton with Sir Harold Gorst, an experienced political journalist, the Princess's meal was interrupted by the arrival of her distraught maid, Francine, who informed her mistress that her valuable jewels had been stolen. This created a sensation. Reports of the theft appeared in most London papers and the Princess lost no time in writing to her fashionable friends bewailing her misfortune.

She also went, two days later, to Vine Street police station and gave an estimate of her loss: her jewels, she claimed, were worth £50,000. This was a bold move and one she quickly regretted. Closely questioned by the police, the Princess became more and more nervous and eventually broke down. The jewels, she confessed, were paste and had cost something like £35 or £40. Then she appears to have panicked. After explaining that she had been too embarrassed to admit, in front of Sir Harold Gorst, that she owned fake jewellery and had thus been forced into lying, she begged the police to let the matter drop. She pleaded her position in society, her circle of respectable friends, and said she was 'engaged to Mr Rhodes, who was assisting her to obtain her divorce, when he intended marrying her.' The police were sympathetic. They agreed to close their file – although they later sent details of the incident to the Cape police – and kept the matter from the press.

At the Carlton hotel, however, the Princess was less fortunate. How much she told the hotel manager is not certain, but it was obviously not enough to convince him of her innocence: she was told to pack her bags and leave. Shortly after this Princess Radziwill decided to cut short her London visit and return to South Africa. She could have had no qualms about appearing to break her promise to Rhodes. The agreement had been that she would leave the country; there was nothing to say that she could not return.

But there was another, more compelling, reason for the Princess's prompt departure from London. She was about to embark on her scheme for blackmailing Rhodes and to do this she needed to return to the Cape. Precisely what this scheme was is not known but an indication of what the Princess had in mind can be gained from an extract of a letter she wrote to the shady Otto. A copy of this extract was later found in the Zimbabwe national archives and, if it is genuine – it has an authentic ring to it but, where the Princess is involved, it is impossible to be *certain* about any written document – there is no mistaking its drift. It seems that Princess Radziwill and her 'agent' Otto had concocted a plan by which they intended to pressure Rhodes into parting with a large sum of money. Whether money was all the Princess wanted is again uncertain, but the extract shows that a demand for cash was her immediate objective.

On the pretext of needing financial help in her 'divorce proceedings' she proposed asking Rhodes for 'at least' £10,000. Otto was instructed to send her letters and telegrams which she could use to back up her request. Should this approach fail, other methods were to be employed. 'Let the letters be on official paper,' she tells Otto. 'Your advice as to bills is an alternative and you are quite right but he will never dispute or even go into court . . . . Be careful with the signature but I hope I shall not have to resort to this.'

Given that this is true, Princess Radziwill must have had more on her mind than a change of location when, accompanied by her son Nicholas, she sailed for Cape Town.

*   *   *

Rhodes had also paid a short visit to London but had left by the time Princess Radziwill arrived in England. Now, on returning to the Cape, the Princess discovered that he had again disappeared: this time he had gone to Rhodesia.

Unable to travel by land – the war was dragging on and the route to the north was barred – Rhodes had sailed to Beira and then journeyed on to Salisbury. He was accompanied by Sir Charles Metcalfe, Johnny Grimmer, Philip Jourdan and his faithful man-servant Tony de la Cruz. A London heart specialist had advised him to take a rest cure and this caused him to remain in Rhodesia for five months. Happy as these five months were, they could hardly be described as restful. Rhodes was incapable of taking things easy. When his companions warned him not to exhaust himself, he brushed their advice aside. 'So long as I can keep going,' he would say, 'let me continue with my work.' Travelling by horse and mule wagon, the party covered an average of thirty miles a day. Only in the towns would Rhodes slow down a little but he did so reluctantly. 'Let us get away, Metcalfe,' he complained irritably, 'and have our chops in the veld.' This was the signal for them to set off again. Once out in the open, seated round a camp-fire, joking with Metcalfe and chaffing Johnny Grimmer, Rhodes was in his element. The physical exertion seems not to have bothered him. Away from the towns, says Jourdan, he was 'like a schoolboy enjoying his holiday after three months confinement at a boarding school'.

Rhodes's absence from Cape Town was a blow to Princess Radziwill's plans. But it was one which she half expected. 'It may be difficult for me to see Rhodes as soon as I should like,' she said in her letter to Otto, 'and I must have money to go on with. I rely on you for this . . .' But even with Otto's help – if help her he did – she needed to economize. There was no longer any question of her staying at the Mount Nelson so, while waiting for Rhodes to return, she again moved in with

282

friends. It was a short-term arrangement but, while it lasted, it suited the Princess admirably.

She found plenty to occupy her. Although her campaign to win over the 'Dutch side' was wearing a little thin, she still championed Rhodes as a potential peace maker. He alone, she claimed, was capable of negotiating with the Boers and unifying South Africa. Such an assertion, after the Jameson raid, must have raised a few eyebrows but the Princess was blind to opposition. While she was in London she had written several articles on the same theme, insisting that Rhodes was at odds with Milner over the conduct of the war and that the High Commissioner resented his interference. This had won her allies, including the influential newspaper editor. W. T. Stead. A friend, writing to Milner, had warned him that Stead had passed 'under the sway of Princess Radziwill' who was 'an active agent in the policy of getting things in a tangle . . . and has obviously succeeded in perplexing his whole mind about you.' The Princess continued to revile Milner on her return to the Cape and her activities were again reported in the opposition press.

But her main aim was to establish herself as Rhodes's friend and confidante. This, it seems, was essential to her plans. She certainly succeeded. Rumour about her relationship with Rhodes began to circulate in Cape Town – among other things, it was said that he had been a regular visitor to her rooms when she was at the Mount Nelson – and a newspaper columnist was inspired to announce that Rhodes was 'about to forsake the state of single blessedness, and will shortly be married to a princess, a lady of very high rank in Europe'. Titbits like this were later to make it difficult to convince the public that the so-called 'Radziwill affair' was a product of the Princess's imagination.

Rhodes returned from Rhodesia on 8 October 1900. He was met by a messenger from the Princess proposing herself for luncheon the following day. Foolishly he gave in and agreed to her coming. It was a grave mistake. After that the Princess began to turn up at Groote Schuur with a regularity that made her earlier invasions seem tame. Often she was accompanied by her son and this seems to have softened Rhodes somewhat. He is said to have taken a great interest in the young man and to have offered him a position at De Beers. But even the presence of Prince Nicholas failed to reconcile Rhodes to his persistent visitor and new stratagems were devised to enable him to avoid the Princess. A servant was posted on permanent look-out and when warning was given of the lady's approach, Rhodes would dart out of the back door and head for the nearby house of his old Kimberley friend, J. B. Currey. There he would stay until the all-clear was sounded.

But flight was not always possible. Shortly after his return to the Cape, Rhodes was struck down with what was euphemistically described as a bout of 'fever', but appears to have been another of his heart attacks. This illness confined him to the house for over a month and placed him very much at the mercy of the Princess. It was probably during this period that she first mentioned a new venture she had in mind. Not content with writing articles she had decided, with breathtaking audacity and complete disregard for her financial position, to start a newspaper of her own. But perhaps her scheme was not as wild as it appeared. By mentioning it to Rhodes, she may well have intended to introduce her need for financial backing. If so, she was unlucky. Rhodes dismissed her suggestion out of hand. 'That,' he said emphatically, 'is your own business; you will find it will give you a lot of trouble.' She was unable to push the topic any further.

But she had no intention of abandoning the idea. By the 3 January 1901, she was ready to embark on her new enterprise. First she bought a second-hand typewriter and then she started a lengthy correspondence with business contacts in South Africa and England. These humble beginnings were sufficient for her purpose. She could now claim to be the prospective owner of a newspaper and, as such, she had the excuse she needed for approaching Rhodes for money. Any idea she may have had of begging him to help her in her 'divorce proceedings' were forgotten. Her new proposition was founded on much firmer ground. The newspaper, she would claim, was intended to support Rhodes's political cause and therefore, by financing it, he would be furthering his own interests. What could be more reasonable? That, at any rate, seems the most likely explanation of the flaming row she had with Rhodes a couple of weeks later.

It happened after a luncheon party at Groote Schuur. Jameson was one of the guests, but the Princess – who loathed the little doctor – managed to shake him off and trapped Rhodes when he was alone. There is only her word for what followed but what she says is revealing. Although she makes no mention of demanding money from Rhodes, she admits there was a 'violent quarrel' which she claims was sparked off by some vague political dispute. 'That was one point,' she said in a statement that was later published – making it clear that there were other 'points' that she had failed to mention.

Her next admission was more significant. 'Then,' she added, 'he wanted me to return certain documents which I possessed, amongst others a copy of a letter from Mr Stead . . . . I utterly refused to return it, as they are documents which Mr Rhodes knew I had in my possession.'

Again she is obviously not telling the whole story. Stead's letter – which she may well have held – changes from singular to plural in one sentence and she omits to say what the other 'documents' were. This is not surprising. Those other 'documents' would have revealed the nature of the hold the Princess had over Rhodes, the hold which she had now for the first time brought out into the open in order to blackmail him. She had apparently had to resort to this when he did not respond to her more diplomatic attempts to extract money from him.

There is another, unpublished, account of this head-on clash between Princess Radziwill and Cecil Rhodes. The Princess told Gordon le Sueur about it many years later. Again she refused to tell the complete story but her graphic description of the row illustrates the importance which both she and Rhodes placed on her mysterious 'documents'. This time she accused Dr Jameson of being responsible for the 'rupture'. 'Jameson,' she told le Sueur, 'had some reason to dislike me. A marriage, *even a liaison*, with Rhodes could not be *otherwise* than prejudicial to me. We therefore had a violent quarrel one day . . . . The first thing to do was to make me return papers which I possessed. I had some which were very compromising for certain reasons and I possessed above all, several which after having been stolen from their legitimate owners had fallen into my hands. It was necessary therefore to force me to give them up. I had on this subject a tragical scene with Rhodes. He insisted that I should surrender to him such letters & papers as I possessed. I refused vehemently. "Very well," said he. "Whatever happens, I will have those papers."'

The mention of Jameson could be a hint as to the contents of the Princess's papers. From this, and other hints she dropped, it would seem that she had somehow got hold of documents connected with the Jameson raid. They might even have been the notorious 'missing telegrams'. But, whatever the papers contained, the Princess refused to part with them. She clung on to her stolen documents throughout the most distressing period of her life, resisting all efforts by Rhodes's agents to make her hand them over. What they were, and what later happened to them, remains a mystery.

*   *   *

The stormy scene at Groote Schuur put an end to all personal contact between Rhodes and Princess Radziwill. A few weeks later he left for Kimberley but there is no evidence of his seeing the Princess again. From Kimberley he travelled on to Rhodesia and by the time he returned to Cape Town, at the beginning of July 1901, any meeting between him and Princess Radziwill was out of the question. Not until some seven months later did they come face-to-face in a public confrontation which proved to be the most dramatic occurrence in their strange relationship.

Far from being crushed by the rebuff she had received from Rhodes, the Princess remained as buoyant as ever. Amazing as it might seem, she was still determined to launch her newspaper and lost no time in springing into action. She rented offices, hired staff and entered into negotiations with a firm of printers. Never modest in her ambitions, she decided to call the new journal *Greater Britain*. It was to be published weekly, priced sixpence and be avowedly imperialist in policy. Her main purpose, she told her staff, was to further the campaign on Rhodes's behalf.

Her next move was every bit as audacious. She decided to leave her lodgings – the lady of the house, she claimed had become over-friendly with Prince Nicholas – and rent a house in a Cape Town suburb. The lease for the house included the use of a horse and trap and the yearly rent of £435 was payable in advance. This, however, appeared to present no problems. Without a flicker of hesitation, the Princess wrote out a cheque for the full amount and handed it to the house agent. It was a grand but futile gesture. A week or so later the house agent informed her that her cheque had been dishonoured and that his firm had issued a summons. This is hardly surprising: the Princess's bank balance then stood at £4. 9s. 9d.

With a summons in the offing, the printers' bill to be met and other newspaper expenses piling up, the Princess was forced to act swiftly. First she employed a lawyer to stall the house agent, claiming that she was expecting money from Russia, and then took the most fatal step of her career. Using the uninspired name of Miss Smith, she pawned a pair of earrings and went to a bookshop and bought a signed photograph of Rhodes. A couple of days later she sent her lawyer a promissory note to cover her rent. It was endorsed by a signature that was later discovered to be an exact replica of that on the photograph: *C. J. Rhodes*.

This crude forgery was soon to be followed by others. The Princess was caught in a vicious circle: as one promissory note fell due and her debts mounted, she was obliged to produce other notes to keep her creditors at bay. Notes made out in Princess Radziwill's favour and endorsed by Rhodes began to circulate Cape Town. As was only to be expected, doubts were voiced about their validity. This, however, did not appear to worry the Princess. Questioned by money-lenders, she airily waved their misgivings aside and assured them that all would be explained when Rhodes returned. She even produced two letters which she claimed had been written to her by Rhodes and bore his signature. Her confidence could only have been inspired by the thought that Rhodes would not dare to move against her.

But she was dealing with the wrong man. Rhodes was in the Matopos when he first heard of the Princess's activities. His bank manager, Lewis Michell, wired him asking whether he had signed a promissory note in favour of Princess Radziwill. 'Rhodes,' says J. G. McDonald, 'was very much annoyed, and requested Sir Lewis to repudiate the document at once.' That was all he did for the moment, but he was too shrewd not to realize that the Princess was trying to corner him. He may even then have started to devise the plan by which he intended to thwart her. Every bit as cunning as Princess Radziwill, and far more experienced in such matters, Rhodes knew better than to act too hastily. Time was needed to prepare a trap which would silence the blackmailer and, at the same time, ensure that no suspicion was attached to himself. He would challenge the Princess only when he was ready.

That was not yet. On his return to the Cape, he spent only two nights at Groote Schuur before leaving for England. The Princess, of course, made no attempt to see him. Instead she cheekily wrote a note to Philip Jourdan, enclosing the latest edition of *Greater Britain*. 'It may amuse Mr Rhodes to read it on the boat . . . ,' she wrote. 'I would so much like to have come over for a moment to Groote Schuur to wish you all goodbye, but my manager is ill and I am alone in the office.' No doubt she was relieved that Rhodes's visit was so short. But if she thought his renewed absence meant that she was in the clear, she was in for a surprise. 'He sailed for Europe in July 1901,' was her puzzled comment some years later, 'and it was *after* his departure that events developed themselves with thundering rapidity.'

While appearing to be indifferent to the Princess, Rhodes had been busy setting his trap. Having learned that she was having difficulty in cashing her promissory notes, he had obligingly arranged for her to negotiate one through a friend of his. The friend was Tom Louw, an Afrikaner he had known since his Bond days. Louw was one of the Bond members who had remained faithful to Rhodes but few people appear to have appreciated the significance of their shadowy alliance. (Indeed, throughout the public proceedings which lay ahead, the connection between Rhodes and Tom Louw remained a secret.) The Princess therefore had no hesitation in accepting Louw's offer to advance £2,000 on the latest of her succession of promissory notes. Payment was made on 8 August 1901, through an attorney who – unknown to the Princess – had recently worked for a law firm employed by Rhodes. Then it was that Catherine Radziwill received the first of many shocks. That same evening the *Cape Argus* carried a boldly printed announcement on its cable page 'MR RHODES: A WARNING: HIS SIGNATURE FORGED:' ran the headline. 'The London *Times* this morning publishes the following in its money column:

'We understand attempts have been made to negotiate certain promissory notes purporting to have been endorsed by Mr Cecil Rhodes. We are requested to state that if any such instruments are in circulation they are forgeries.'

In two decisive, neatly-timed moves, Rhodes had blocked Princess Radziwill. Not only was he in control of her most recent loan but he had effectively prevented her from obtaining any more money. She could not pay Louw back when his promissory note fell due, on 23 September, and would therefore have to face the consequences.

But Rhodes was not interested in having the money returned. He had more important things on his mind. Louw did, in fact, start proceedings against the Princess at the beginning of October and Rhodes signed an affidavit in London denying that he had endorsed any promissory notes. But this was simply a charade. The Princess was made aware of Rhodes's real intention before the case came up for hearing in the Supreme Court.

Now it was that Rhodes began to bring pressure to bear on Princess Radziwill. He started by instructing his lawyers to offer her 'a certain sum of money' if she would return the papers she held. When this attempt at bribery failed, he sent a mutual woman friend to plead with the Princess, hinting that the only way she could escape prosecution was by surrendering the papers. But the Princess was no more amenable to hints than she had been to bribery. By this time, Rhodes – or his agents – must have realized that stronger measures were called for. Alfred Milner was called in and a CID officer was sent to interview the Princess. She was later to claim that this man promised her a 'large reward' if she handed over the papers and that she had refused to listen to 'such a proposition.' Another account of the interview, however, says that she told the officer that the papers were lodged with the German Consul in Cape Town. (Afterwards she changed this story and said that she had sent the papers to a Mrs Violet Hill of 18 Warren Street, Oxford, but this was also a bluff: there was no such street in Oxford.) Having failed to bribe or badger the Princess into submission, Rhodes was forced to give up and allow the law to take its course.

At last Princess Radziwill was made to realize that she had pushed things too far. She had been too confident that Rhodes would not, as she put it, 'go into court'. But there was nothing she could do to stop him. She had no money with which to fight back and most of the friends she had made in Cape Town had, for one reason or another, deserted her. To add to her troubles, she heard about this time that her son Nicholas – who had recently volunteered to serve with the British forces – had been 'dangerously wounded' in the Transvaal. And there was worse to come. On 20 November 1901, one of Rhodes's agents wrote to tell him that the Princess had been arrested. This was not reported in the Cape newspapers and a week or so later Rhodes was informed that she had been released. It would appear that she had merely been held for questioning, following the visit of the CID, but, if this was so, her spell in prison did not produce the result for which Rhodes had been hoping. Whatever happened, the Princess could not be made to give up her precious papers.

The legal proceedings went ahead. As the Princess's promissory notes had been issued in Rhodes's name his presence at the court hearing was essential. He was therefore formally summoned to appear in the Supreme Court at Cape Town on 6 February 1902.

*   *   *

Rhodes's visit to Britain had not been a happy one. He was now seriously ill and it was obvious that, at the age of forty-eight, he had not much longer to live. Shortly after his arrival in London he had again visited a heart specialist, Dr Kingston Fowler, who had found his condition to have deteriorated and advised 'a long rest and constant change of surroundings'. Rhodes, for once, was pleased to obey doctor's orders and leased Rannock Lodge in Scotland for two months' shooting. Accompanied by Jameson, Rochfort Maguire and his wife, and Philip Jourdan he travelled to Scotland in August and invited various English friends to visit him there.

One of his guests was the socialist Lady Warwick – a former mistress of the new monarch, King Edward VII – who had long been one of Rhodes's more fervent admirers. She found him much changed physically but as mentally alert as ever. 'He was already too ill,' she says, 'to join his own shooting and fishing parties, and instead sat on the moors with me. For hours and hours he would discuss world politics, and the British Empire . . . . He would speak of the Empire where another man would have talked of his family life, or his own predilections.' Another guest was the young Winston Churchill, who was then about to leave the Conservative party to join the Liberals. According to Lady Warwick, Rhodes gave him guarded encouragement. 'You have done the right thing,' he told Churchill, 'but you have chosen the rougher path. The fact that you have changed your party views will be a club with which you will be beaten mercilessly.'

Rhodes's cosy chats with Lady Warwick must have been a refreshing change from his political wrangles with Princess Radziwill. But he could not forget the Princess for long. On his return to London, in October, he signed the affidavit denying that he had endorsed any promissory notes. Then he, Jameson, Alfred Beit and Sir Charles Metcalfe left for a tour of the continent. They ended up in Egypt where, on a trip up the Nile, Rhodes became so exhausted by the heat that Jameson advised him to abandon the tour. They arrived back in England at the beginning of January 1902.

His holiday appears to have done him little good. Gordon le Sueur, who met him at the London docks, was appalled at the way in which Rhodes's appearance had worsened since he had last seen him, some four months earlier. 'His face was bloated, almost swollen,' he observed, 'and he was livid with a purple tinge in his face, and I realized he was very ill indeed. I mumbled something about being glad to see him when I shook hands, but I felt too shocked to say much.'

If nothing else, Egypt had proved that he could not hope to survive in a hot climate. He was at that time negotiating to buy a family estate, Dalham Hall, near Newmarket, so that he could 'spin out his life in the cooler breezes of the heath'. He was also toying with the idea of building a house for himself in Johannesburg, where the air was more bracing than at the Cape. Even so, he refused to allow such considerations to interfere with his plan for dealing with Princess Radziwill. The Cape that year was experiencing a stiflingly hot summer and Rhodes's friends were astonished when he announced that he intended returning to the Cape to answer the court summons. Everyone tried to make him change his mind. He was warned by his medical friends that his heart would not stand the strain. Dr Jameson, who was preparing to accompany Rhodes, was told that he was sending his patient to 'his death'. What, Rhodes was asked, was the point of risking his health for a forged promissory note which he could easily afford to write off? He refused to listen. 'It is not the money,' he replied, 'but no risk will prevent me clearing my character of any stain in connection with that woman.' This was his stock answer to all the protests. He was determined, he said, to upset 'the bona fides of the Princess'.

But, of course, it was not his character that he was worried about: it was the Princess's 'papers'. If Catherine Radziwill produced those documents in court, Rhodes wanted to be present. He intended to denounce her as a forger. That, and only that, was why he felt compelled to return to the Cape. Whatever those questionable papers contained, he was willing to gamble with his life rather than allow the Princess to go unchallenged.

Rhodes arrived back in Cape Town on 4 February 1902. His homecoming was unheralded, only a brief notice of his arrival appeared in the local newspapers. There was, however, no shortage of publicity surrounding his appearance, two days later, at the hearing of the Radziwill case. The court was packed. News of the Princess's papers had leaked out and all Cape Town was agog. It was fully expected that the mysterious papers would reveal not political but romantic secrets. Rhodes, the notorious 'woman-hater', it seemed, was at last to be confronted by a woman he had wronged. Everyone was looking forward to a very lively trial. They were to be disappointed. The Princess did not even show up. At the last minute, she took fright and pleaded illness. The hearing was held without her. Rhodes, looking far from well, gave his evidence in a shaky voice. He disclaimed all knowledge of the promissory notes. 'They are all forgeries,' he gasped. 'All absolute forgeries.' His lawyer then pointed out that the signatures on various notes before the court had all been taken from a single copy and could not have been made at intervals. The judge agreed. 'In my opinion,' he declared, 'they are not the signatures of the defendant, and it is clearly an absolute forgery.'

Technically, Rhodes was being sued by Tom Louw for repayment of a loan but the court refused to give a provisional sentence. The case was dismissed. 'We shall probably,' said the judge, 'hear no more about it.'

He was reckoning without Princess Radziwill. Furious at having been described as a forger she decided to hit back. She gave full warning of her intentions in a letter she wrote to Dr Jameson – always the target for her most bitter attacks. She accused Rhodes of repeating 'in the Supreme Court his experiments before the Select Committee of the House of Commons' and threatened to take 'strong measures' to prove this. The 'woman will show she can bite,' she warned.

Once she realized that – although her forgeries had been openly acknowledged in a court of law – no criminal proceedings were to be taken against her, the Princess recovered her nerve. Her first concern was to pay off Tom Louw and recover his promissory note. This she did with the help of one of her few remaining friends in Cape Town, Mr James Flower, a highly respected civil engineer. James Flower had remained loyal throughout the crisis, even sending his two daughters to keep the Princess company at the time of the court proceedings. Now he went further and agreed to advance the money needed to settle with Tom Louw, by taking a second mortgage on the Princess's Russian estate. His offer was accepted by the Princess, who suggested that the transaction be witnessed by the Russian consul in Cape Town and promised faithfully to repay the loan. (She never did. Neither Flower nor his family received a penny from Princess Radziwill in the years to come.) Having thus eliminated Tom Louw, the Princess felt free to embark on her 'stronger measures'.

This she did by sueing Rhodes for the £2,000 bill which she claimed he had endorsed. Rhodes was flabbergasted. 'Damn that woman!' he exploded when his secretary handed him the summons. 'Can't she leave me alone?' He had no alternative but to take the only step open to him. Sending for his lawyer and a magistrate, Rhodes drew up an affidavit accusing Catherine Radziwill of forgery.

On 28 February 1902 the Princess was formally charged with uttering a forged document. During the preliminary hearing of the case, she and Rhodes came face to face for the last time. Too ill to attend the court, Rhodes had his evidence taken by a magistrate at Groote Schuur. The Princess was present with her attorney. She sat at the back of a small circle of people, gathered in front of the magistrate's desk, and never took her eyes off Rhodes who pointedly refused to meet her gaze. Seated on a sofa, he was coughing badly. The proceedings lasted only a matter of minutes. In a prepared statement, which was read out

291

and handed to the magistrate after Rhodes had signed it, the Princess's promissory notes were formally repudiated. Rhodes then staggered to his feet and made for the door. Before he left the room, however, the Princess was asked whether she had any questions to put to him. Her lawyer said she had not. 'But I will speak,' protested the Princess, half-rising from her chair. 'No, no,' hissed the lawyer, 'sit down.' Reluctantly, she did as she was told.

What the Princess intended to say will never be known. She was not given another opportunity to confront Rhodes. The sight of his stooped back, as he shuffled through the living-room door at Groote Schuur, was the last she saw of the man she called 'the poor Colossus'.

Two months later the Princess faced a charge of fraud and forgery, on twenty-four counts, in Cape Town's Supreme Court. The outcome of her trial was a foregone conclusion. With both sides anxious to avoid any embarrassing disclosures, there was no question of the background to the case being properly explored. The Princess undermined her defence by obstinately refusing to produce her ill-gotten 'papers' and her lawyer was left to flounder about as best he could. This gave the prosecution a clear field. All that was necessary to secure a conviction was to show that the signatures on the promissory notes had been traced from the signed photograph which hung in the offices of *Greater Britain*. So easily was this done that the jury had no hesitation in finding the Princess guilty as charged. She was sentenced to two years imprisonment in a 'House of Correction'. Her humiliation brought her little sympathy. Even one of her daughters later told a friend in London that she thought her mother had been let off too lightly.

As things worked out, the sentence proved less severe than the judge had intended. The Princess served only sixteen months in gaol before being released and deported from South Africa. Such was her talent for trouble-making that the prison authorities were said to be relieved to see the back of her. Remission, however, was not accompanied by repentance. No sooner had the Princess arrived back in Europe than she started proceedings against the Rhodes trustees. She now claimed £1,400,000 on the grounds that Rhodes was the father of a 'female child' delivered to her in December 1897 and that he had employed her as his political representative. The summons was issued, on 2 November 1903, after her attempts to negotiate a private settlement had failed. It was pure bluff. There was no evidence to support her claim and she dropped it before it came to court. No more was heard about the child. For the last twenty years of her life, Princess Radziwill lived in America. When she died in New York on 12 May, 1941, at the age of eighty-four, the only daughters she acknowledged were those from her marriage to Prince William

Radziwill. She rarely mentioned Rhodes in her old age and was quickly forgotten in South Africa.

Rhodes never knew whether or not he had silenced his wayward tormentor. He died a month before the Princess was brought to trial.

*   *   *

'So it came to pass,' wrote W. T. Stead, after Rhodes's death, 'that he who had never harmed a woman in his life met his death in clearing his name from the aspersions of a woman whom, out of sheer good-heartedness, he had befriended in time of need.'

This was journalistic hyperbole. Stead knew there was more to Rhodes's association with Princess Radziwill than could be explained by the betrayal of a casual friendship. He must also have known that Rhodes's precarious heart condition was threatening to shorten his life long before the Princess started her mischief-making. But there is an element of truth in what he says. There can be no doubt that, by ignoring all medical advice and returning to the Cape at the height of an African summer, Rhodes diced with death. He might have lived longer had he remained in Europe. As it was, the score was settled by the stifling heat of the Cape.

For the first few weeks of his return, Rhodes spent his days roaming Groote Schuur, desperately trying to ease his breathing. He would stand panting at an open window, hoping to catch a fleeting breeze, or lie stretched out on a couch in a darkened room, his shirt unbuttoned, his hair plastered to his forehead, his chest heaving. In the evenings he would be driven – he was one of the first motor-car owners in South Africa – to his sparsely furnished, coastal cottage at Muizenberg, a few miles from Cape Town. Here, propped up in bed and fanned by the cooler sea air, he sometimes managed to sleep. But not often. 'He was most comfortable,' says Philip Jourdan, 'in an erect position, and it was most heartrending to see him sit on the edge of his bed . . . at one moment gasping for breath, and at another with his head sunk so low that his chin almost touched his chest.'

As the weeks passed, he grew worse. After his confrontation with Princess Radziwill at Groote Schuur, he was ordered to remain at his Muizenberg cottage and rest as much as possible. Dr Edmund Sinclair Stevenson, who attended him every evening, witnessed his rapidly deteriorating condition. Soon, he says, Rhodes was 'unable to leave his bed, and owing to him being unable to breathe when lying down . . . a contrivance was made which kept him suspended. Then to help the breathing, a double ceiling was made, into which oxygen gas was pumped.' Ice was packed into the ceiling to help cool the room and a hole was knocked into the wall to allow a through draft, but nothing seemed to ease the pressure on Rhodes's lungs. He continued to pant and sweat until his swollen face turned purple. Even in the early morning, when it became 'quite chilly' and those attending him were in overcoats, he would lie on his bed uncovered and beg for more fresh air.

His friends took it in turns to sit with him. Charles Metcalfe, Lewis Michell, Gordon le Sueur, Philip Jourdan and Rhodes's younger brother, Elmhirst, were constant visitors to the cottage – which was too small to sleep them all – and Dr Jameson rarely left the sick-room. He was 'indefatigable,' says le Sueur, 'and one marvelled at his endurance.' For some time, the only one missing was Johnny Grimmer, whom Rhodes refused to have summoned from Rhodesia. It was le Sueur who, recognizing that the end was near, finally plucked up courage and wired for Grimmer to come. He never doubted that he had done the right thing. 'Not long before Rhodes died,' he says, 'he expressed a wish to see Grimmer, and then I told him that Grimmer would arrive the following day. Always devoted to Grimmer he was as pleased as possible, but pretended to be annoyed at my wiring on my own initiative. Until his death he hardly allowed Grimmer out of his sight.'

Other friends wrote and asked to see Rhodes for the last time. One of those allowed to see him was James Rose Innes. Earlier Rhodes had written to Innes asking him to take on the Radziwill case, but the former Attorney General had been too busy to accept the brief. Disappointed, Rhodes nevertheless seized upon the opportunity to renew his links with an old political colleague. 'I shall not regret the worry over the case,' he wrote, after receiving Innes's refusal, 'if it accidentally is the cause of our meeting again. As one gets older I feel how foolish I am – little odds and ends are allowed to separate us.' They were reunited shortly before Rhodes died. But Innes was an exception. There were some friends with whom Rhodes was not permitted to make his peace. When J. X. Merriman and Harry Currey – who had joined the ranks of Rhodes's political opponents – tried to visit the cottage, they were turned away. 'Jameson,' says Currey's son, 'with whom all decisions now lay, was obdurate in his refusal . . . . So the quarrel was not to be made up in this world.'

For the last three days of his life, Rhodes was more or less unconscious. Friends came and went but he hardly stirred and seemed oblivious of what was happening around him. The end came suddenly at three minutes to six on the evening of 26 March 1902. Accounts of his final hours are muddled and contradictory. The men who stood around his bed – Sir Charles Metcalfe, Edgar Walton, Dr Thomas Smartt, Colonel Elmhirst Rhodes, Johnny Grimmer and Dr Jameson – were to give different versions of the vigil they kept that afternoon.

There is one story, however, which is more believable than some of the later, more fanciful recollections of Rhodes's friends. Just before he died, it is said, Rhodes roused himself and spoke to Johnny Grimmer. 'Turn me over, Jack,' he said and then fell silent.

Later that evening Jameson formally announced Rhodes's death to the crowd waiting outside. Some of them had been there for days. Almost from the time Rhodes took to his bed, the road outside the cottage had been thronged with people intent on witnessing the last stages of his life. Philip Jourdan had been driven to despair trying to keep them out of the tiny garden and away from the window. But now they were to be rewarded. Standing on the veranda, Jameson solemnly read from a prepared statement. Rhodes's last coherent words, he claimed, had been: 'So little done, so much to do.' It was a fitting valediction for a man who had died three months before his forty-ninth birthday. But, like so many sayings passed on by Rhodes's disciples, it conceals more than it reveals.

L'Envoi

On the night Rhodes died a mask was taken of his face, and his body, in a coffin of Rhodesian teak, was taken by moonlight to Groote Schuur. During the next two days, messages of sympathy, tributes and wreaths, including one from Queen Alexandra, poured in from all over the world. Flags were flown at half-mast throughout the Cape and a never-ending stream of people filed past the coffin in respectful silence. The coffin was then taken to the House of Assembly where, for another full day, it lay in state.

On Tuesday, 1 April 1902, Frank and Arthur Rhodes arrived from England – they had learned of their brother's death from a passing ship on their voyage to South Africa – and two days later an impressive funeral service, conducted by the Archbishop of Cape Town, was held in St George's Cathedral. Afterwards the coffin, covered by a Union Jack, was placed on a gun-carriage and, escorted by troopers of the Cape Police, trundled through the crowded city streets to the railway station where a special train was waiting in a siding to take the funeral party to Bulawayo.

The long journey north took five days. At all the larger stations the train stopped and people crowded the platforms while military bands played the Dead March from *Saul*; at the wayside halts buglers sounded the Last Post and as the train chugged past the recently built blockhouses in the Karoo groups of soldiers, with their guns reversed, stood silently to attention. But by far the most impressive display of mourning was staged at Kimberley. Here a guard of honour from the Kimberley Regiment lined the entire length of the platform and when, at six o'clock in the evening, the train arrived, the Brigade Band took up a position next to the purple-and-black draped funeral coach. Then, to the strains of the Dead March, a procession headed by the mayor began slowly to file past the carriage where, through a lowered window, 'the massive coffin surmounted by a Union Jack and various wreaths was plainly visible'. For over four hours the crowd continued to shuffle along the platform: men and women were in tears, bewildered children were held up to peer at the coffin. Over 15,000 people of all races – black, white and coloured – are said to have paid homage to Rhodes that evening.

There was another 'very large crowd' waiting when the train reached Bulawayo three days later. A second funeral service was held in the Drill Hall, this time conducted by the Bishop of Mashonaland, and then the instructions laid down in Rhodes's will were faithfully observed. On 10 April, his coffin was taken to his Matopo farm, where it was housed in a thatched hut for the night, and early the following morning a team of oxen hauled it to the top of 'World's View'. Some two thousand five hundred Ndebele had gathered on the hillside and, as the gun-carriage carrying the coffin passed them, they rose to their feet and gave a royal salute. It was the first time that such an honour had been accorded to a white man.

Rhodes's grave had already been hewn out of the rock on the summit of World's View and was waiting to receive him. Close to it lay the stone slab – onto which had been riveted a brass plate inscribed 'Here lie the remains of Cecil John Rhodes' – that was to seal his tomb. He was buried as he wished.

The ceremony was simple but, to the crowd of white settlers standing beneath the huge round boulders at the crest of the hill, extremely moving. The men were grim-faced and moist-eyed, many of the women sobbed openly. After the Bishop of Mashonaland had delivered a eulogy and read a poem – written for the occasion by Rudyard Kipling – the coffin, still covered by a Union Jack, was silently lowered into the ground. Then, as the grave was covered by the granite memorial slab, a hymn was sung. There the funeral rites should have ended: but there was an unexpected sequel.

Among the Ndebele who now began to file past the grave was Mtshana, the *induna* who had commanded Lobengula's *impis* during Jameson's war, and he asked to be allowed to recite the praises of the dead. As he did this, standing beside the grave, the rest of the warriors passed in silence. No further sound was heard from them until they reached the bottom of the hill. 'Then,' it was reported, 'arose the most wonderful chattering as they made their way up the radiating valleys and gorges leading to their camps, their high pitched voices reaching the ears of the mourners lingering on the top of the mountain.'

*   *   *

Rhodes's body will lie in the Matopos for, one presumes, all eternity. Tourists still clamber up the rocky slope to gaze at the unadorned slab and to read the simple inscription. There are no dates on the brass plate, no details. At the time, it was believed that his name alone would suffice. That name would live, it was confidently assumed, forever.

There are other tangible reminders of Cecil Rhodes. In street names, on plaques, in statuary, in the houses in which he lived and the institutions which he endowed, in the name of a South African university, his memory is perpetuated. Groote Schuur is now a museum. Beyond it, on the slopes of Devil's Peak, rises the Rhodes Memorial, impressive in its Grecian simplicity and adorned by Watts's famous statue, 'Physical Energy'.

But what of Rhodes's less tangible legacy – his dreams and his ideals? 'The immense and brooding spirit,' wrote Kipling on Rhodes's death, 'still shall quicken and control.' In fact, far from quickening and controlling, Rhodes's 'spirit' did not long outlast his body. Even at the time of his death, the appreciation of his achievements was by no means universal. Cecil Rhodes, observed *Le Temps*, a leading French newspaper, 'lived only for his schemes and enjoyed life only as a cannon ball enjoys space, travelling to its aim blindly and spreading ruin on its way. He was a great man, no doubt – a man who rendered immense services to his country, but humanity is not much indebted to him.'

And, before long, even these 'immense services' which he is said to have rendered to Britain, were being nullified. So many of the schemes to which he had devoted his life came to nothing. The Cape to Cairo railway was never built. Within fifty years of his death the British Empire was crumbling. Indeed Britain, from being a dominant nation in the world, gradually lost its pre-eminence. Shorn of its power and prestige, it is now simply another European nation.

The map of Africa, which Rhodes had dreamed of painting red, altered out of all recognition as one by one the various states won their freedom from the mother country. What should have been Rhodes's most lasting memorial, the two great countries of central Africa that bore his name – Northern and Southern Rhodesia – gained independence and changed their names to Zambia and Zimbabwe. With almost as much alacrity, Rhodes's triumphant statue was removed from the heart of Salisbury, itself renamed Harare.

In South Africa, where Britain had won the Anglo-Boer War, the defeated Boers eventually won the peace. In time, they broke with Britain and declared the country an independent republic. The men who now rule South Africa have no time for Rhodes or his grandiose dreams; and the men who will take over from them will have even less time.

Rhodes's belief in racial superiority, although understandable in the context of his time, has manifested itself with great cruelty in the years since his death. Planted in the soil of patriotism, it has brought forth some very sinister fruits indeed. It has been enshrined not only in Nazi dominated Europe, but in South Africa itself. Whether or not Rhodes would have approved of apartheid is impossible to say: his moral attitudes apart, one can be sure he would have recognized it as economic madness.

In the end, Rhodes's most durable memorial will probably be the Rhodes scholarships. But even they no longer serve to perpetuate his dream: the fashioning of a stream of upright, unselfish, sports-loving paragons who will enlighten the world with Oxford-inspired, Anglo-Saxon ideals. It is arguable that no Rhodes scholar, however bright, has ever made the sort of outstanding contribution to the destinies of mankind that Rhodes envisaged.

In many ways what Rhodes, for all his idealism, effort and ruthlessness, had built was no more than an elaborate house of cards; a house that has been blown away by the winds of history.

Bibliography

Amery, L. S. *Days of Fresh Air* London 1939
Baker, Sir Herbert *Cecil Rhodes by his Architect* Oxford 1934
Blake, Robert *A History of Rhodesia* London 1977
Boyle, F. *To the Cape for Diamonds* London 1873
Brett, M. V. (ed.) *Journals and Letters of Reginald, Viscount Esher* (3 vols) London 1934
Buchanan-Gould, Vera *Not Without Honour* London (n.d.)
Cartwright, A. P. *Gold Paved The Way* London 1967
Cary, Robert *Charter Royal* Cape Town 1970
Chilvers, H. A. *The Story of De Beers* London 1939
Churchill, Lord Randolph *Men, Mines and Animals in South Africa* London 1892
Cloete, Stuart *African Portraits* London 1946
Choen, Louis *Reminiscences of Kimberley* London 1911
Colvin, Ian *The Life of Jameson* (2 vols) London 1922
Currey, Ronald *Rhodes: A Biographical Footnote* Cape Town (n.d.)
Davenport, T. R. H. *The Afrikaner Bond 1880–1911* Cape Town 1966
Dawborn, Charles *My South African Year* London 1921
Doughty, O. *Early Diamond Days* London 1963
Fitzpatrick, Sir Percy *South African Memories* London 1932
    Selected Papers 1888–1906 (ed. A. H. Duminy & W. R. Guest) Johannesburg 1976
Flint, John *Cecil Rhodes* London 1976
Fort, G. S. *Dr Jameson* London 1908
    Alfred Beit London 1932
Froude, J. A. *Two Lectures on South Africa* London 1880
Fuller, T. E. *The Right Honourable Cecil John Rhodes: A Monograph* London 1910
Furness, H. *Some Victorian Men* London 1924
Garvin, J. L. *Life of Joseph Chamberlain* (3 vols) London 1932–3
Green, G. A. L. *An Editor Looks Back* Cape Town 1947
Green, J. E. S. *Rhodes Goes North* London 1936
Gross, Felix *Rhodes of Africa* London 1956
Guthrie, Frank *A Frontier Magistrate* Cape Town (n.d.)

Hamilton, Lord Frederic *The Vanished World of Yesterday* London 1950

Hammond, John Hays *Autobiography* (2 vols) New York 1935

Harding, Colin *Far Bugles* London 1933

Headlam, C. (ed.) *The Milner Papers* London 1933

Hensman, H. *Cecil Rhodes: A Study of a Career* Edinburgh 1901

Hutchinson, G. S. *Cecil Rhodes: The Man* Oxford 1944

'Imperialist' *Cecil Rhodes: With a Personal Reminiscence by Dr Jameson* London 1897

Jackson, Stanley *The Great Barnato* London 1970

Johnson, Frank *Great Days* London 1940

Jourdan, Philip *Cecil Rhodes: His Private Life by His Private Secretary* London 1910

Keppel-Jones, Arthur *Rhodes and Rhodesia: The White Conquest of Zimbabwe 1884–1902* Kingstone & Montreal 1983

Kiewiet, C. E. de *The Imperial Factor in South Africa* Cambridge 1937

Kruger, Rayne *Goodbye Dolly Gray* London 1959

Le May, G. A. L. *British Supremacy in South Africa* Oxford 1965

Le Roux (ed.) *Groote Schuur* Cape Town 1970

Le Sueur, Gordon *Cecil Rhodes: The Man and His Work* London 1913

Leveson Gower, Sir George *Years of Content* London 1940

Lewsen, Phyllis *J. X. Merriman: Paradoxical South African Statesman* New Haven & London 1982

Longford, Elizabeth *Jameson's Raid* (Panther ed.) London 1984

Macmillan, Mona *Sir Henry Barkly* Cape Town 1970

McDonald, J. G. *Rhodes: A Life* London 1941
    Rhodes: A Heritage London 1943

Markham, Violet *The South African Scene* London 1913

Marlowe, John *Cecil Rhodes: The Anatomy of Empire* London 1972

Mason, Philip *Birth of a Dilemma* Oxford 1958

Matthews, J. W. *Incwadi Yami* London 1887

Maurois, André *Cecil Rhodes* London 1953

Merriman, J. X. *Correspondence 1870–1924* (4 vols) (ed. P. Lewsen) Cape Town 1960/69

Michell, Sir Lewis *The Life of the Right Hon. Cecil John Rhodes* (2 vols) London 1910

Millin, Sarah G. *Rhodes* London 1933

Milner, Viscountess *My Picture Gallery 1886–1901* London 1951

O'Meara, W. A. J. *Kekewich in Kimberley* London 1926

Payton, Charles *The Diamond Diggings of South Africa* London 1872

Pakenham, Thomas *The Boer War* London 1982

Plomer, William *Cecil Rhodes* London 1933

Poel, Jean van der *The Jameson Raid* Oxford 1951

Ponsonby, Sir Frederick *Recollections of Three Reigns* London 1951

Radziwill, Catherine *My Recollections* London 1904
  Memories of Forty Years London 1914
  Cecil Rhodes: Man and Empire Maker London 1918
Ranger, T. O. *Revolt in Southern Africa 1896–7* London 1967
Raymond, E. T. *Portraits of the Nineties* London 1921
Rorke, Melina *Autobiography* Johannesburg (n.d.)
Rose Innes, Sir James *Autobiography* (ed. B. Tindall) Oxford 1949
  Selected Correspondence 1884–1902 (ed. H. M. Wright) Cape
  Town 1972
Robertson, Marian *Diamond Fever* Cape Town 1974
Rouillard, Nancy (ed.) *Matabele Thompson: His Autobiography*
Johannesburg 1953
Rudd, Alan *Charles Dunell Rudd* Privately printed 1981
Sampson, Victor *My Reminiscences* London 1926
Sauer, Hans *Ex Africa* London 1937
Selous, F. *Travels and Adventures in South East Africa* (Century ed.)
London 1984
Schreiner, Olive *Letters* (ed. S. C. Cronwright-Schreiner) London 1924
  Trooper Peter Halket of Mashonaland London 1897
Scully, W. C. *Reminiscences of a South African Pioneer* London 1913
Shaw, Gerald *The Garrett Papers* Cape Town 1984
Stanford, Sir Walter *Reminiscences* (2 vols) Cape Town 1958–62
Stead, W. T. *The Last Will and Testament of Cecil John Rhodes*
London 1902
Stent, Vere *A Personal Record of Some Incidents in the life of Cecil
Rhodes* Cape Town 1925
Stevenson, E. Sinclair *Adventures of a Medical Man* Cape Town 1925
Trevor, G. T. *Forty Years in Africa* London 1932
Trollope, Anthony *South Africa* (abridged edition) London 1938
'Vindex' *Cecil Rhodes: His Political Life and Speeches 1881–1900*
London 1900
Warren, Sir Charles *On the Veldt in the Seventies* London 1902
Warwick, Lady Frances *Afterthoughts* London 1931
Wheatcroft, Geoffrey *The Randlords* London 1985
Whyte, F. *The Life of W. T. Stead* London 1925
Williams, A. F. *Some Dreams Come True* Cape Town 1948
Williams, Basil *Cecil Rhodes* London 1921
Williams, G. F. *The Diamond Mines of South Africa* London 1902
Wilson, G. H. *Gone Down The Years* Cape Town 1947
Wilson, Lady Sarah *South African Memories* London 1909
Wrench, J. E. *Alfred Lord Milner* London 1958

ARTICLES

Hoste, Captain *Some Recollections of Rhodes* African Observer: A Review of Contemporary Affairs July 1934

Jarvis, Sir Weston *Cecil Rhodes and the Raid* United Empire: Journal of the Royal Empire Society October 1934

Phimister, I. B. *Rhodes, Rhodesia and the Rand* Journal of South African Studies January 1974

Shee, Charles *The Ill Health and Mortal Sickness of Cecil John Rhodes* The Central African Journal of Medicine April 1965

Turrell, Rob *Rhodes, De Beers and Monopoly* The Journal of Imperial and Commonwealth History May 1982

Worsfold, W. Basil *The Birthplace of Rhodes* United Empire: The Royal Colonial Institute Journal July 1926

NEWSPAPERS

Magazines and Pamphlets

The Times (London); *The Independent* (Kimberley); *Diamond News* (Kimberley); *Diamond Fields Advertiser* (Kimberley); *The Friend* (Bloemfontein); *Eastern Province Herald* (Port Elizabeth); *Cape Times* (Cape Town); *Cape Argus* (Cape Town); *South Africa* (London); *Rhodesiana Magazine*.

The Trial of Princess Radziwill (*Cape Times* Supplement) May 1902.

Rhodesia's Last Tribute to its Founder Pub: F. Norris, Advertising Agent, Bulawayo 1902

References

Unpublished Sources.
The Library of Rhodes House, Oxford.
Cape Archives, Cape Town, South Africa.
Natal Archives, Pietermaritzburg, South Africa.
South African Library, Cape Town, South Africa.
Kimberley Public Library, Kimberley, South Africa.
McGregor Museum, Kimberley, South Africa.
Privately held papers.
Letter by Neville Pickering: Mrs Judy Hoare, Cape Town, South Africa.
Constance Scott's Diary: the late Mrs D. Pitchford, Grahamstown, South Africa.

(When the source of a quote is indicated in the text, no reference is given.)

Chapter One
p. 1   London club. Leveson Gower p. 175
         'I contend that we . . .' Flint pp. 248–50
p. 2   'When all is said . . .' Raymond p. 40
p. 3   Rhodes and cricket match. Michell Vol I p. 20
p. 4   'My mother got through . . .' McDonald p. 4
p. 5   'not the custom . . .' B. Williams p. 8
         'dressed like a man . . .' Furness p. 86
p. 6   'the nice agreeable . . .' Michell Vol. I p. 18
         'My father frequently . . .' McDonald pp. 7–8
p. 7   'Why did I come . . .' Maurois p. 26
p. 8   Rhodes's illness. Shee: *Central African Journal of Medicine* April
            1965 pp. 89–93
         'When I have been . . .' Michell Vol. I pp. 19–20
p. 12   'Shouldn't do that . . .' B. Williams p. 40
p. 13   'Mr Rhodes came close . . .' *Natal Advertiser* 30/5/1936
         'Of course there is . . .' Colvin Vol. I p. 41
         'I heard of . . .' *Ibid*
p. 14   'Mr Rhodes of Natal . . .' Payton p. 215

Chapter Two
p. 15 'An uglier place . . .' Trollope p. 177
p. 16 'Just fancy . . .' *The Friend* 21/9/1871
       'Imagine a small mound . . .' B. Williams p. 27
       'Holding to one . . .' Boyle p. 173
p. 18 'A tall gaunt youth . . .' B. Williams p. 33
p. 22 'Mr Merriman praises . . .' McDonald p. 23
p. 24 'He belonged to . . .' Michell Vol. I p. 81

Chapter Three
p. 28 Naming of Kimberley. J. B. Currey's *Autobiography* (typescript in
       South African Library, Cape Town)
p. 31 'Great injustice . . .' Macmillan p. 209
p. 32 'It was apparent . . .' A. Williams p. 191
p. 33 Crossman inquiry. *Diamond News* 6/1/1876
p. 35 'I have never forgotten . . .' Michell Vol. I p. 64
p. 36 'By all means try . . .' B. Williams p. 39
       'My character . . .' G. Beet: *History of the Diamond Fields* (typescript
       in Kimberley Library)
p. 38 'they could not afford . . .' B. Williams p. 46
p. 39 Rhodes's will. Michell Vol I pp. 68–9
p. 40 'There is every chance . . .' Lewsen Correspondence Vol. I p. 81

Chapter Four
p. 43 'I remember his first . . .' Michell Vol. I p. 91
       'I heard several . . .' *Independent* 10/5/1881
p. 44 'secured the key . . .' F. Stow: *Memoir of Formation of De Beers*
       (typescript in McGregor Museum Library)
       'When Mr Rhodes . . .' *Ibid*
p. 47 'Civilized society cannot . . .' Quoted: *Cape Times* 15/11/1985
       'We have dinners . . .' N. Pickering: *Letter* (mss.)
p. 48 'My dear Pickering . . .' Michell Vol. I p. 137
       'a most undeniable . . .' Pickering *op cit*
p. 49 'Have you ever thought . . .' B. Williams p. 42
       'I can see it now . . .' F. Stow *op cit*
       'De Beers is the . . .' *Independent* 14/3/1882
p. 50 'Owing to the . . .' *Ibid*
       'I am still . . .' B. Williams p. 58
p. 51 'Rhodes and the Kimberley . . .' *Ibid*
p. 52 Rhodes and Gordon. Lockhart & Woodhouse p. 89; B. Williams
       pp. 64–6
p. 53 'Mr Rhodes appears . . .' *Independent* 19/9/1881
p. 54 'We had great difficulty . . .' *South Africa* 23/12/1893
       'I decidedly objected . . .' Matthews p. 216
p. 55 'A law of exceptional . . .' Churchill pp. 45–6
       'in his baby . . .' *Independent* 4/2/1884
       'By their efforts . . .' *Ibid*
p. 56 'They remained in a perfectly . . .' Wheatcroft p. 67

Chapter Five
p. 59 'I look upon this . . .' B. Williams p. 73
       'Is this House . . .' Michell Vol. I p. 193
p. 60 'I shall never . . .' B. Williams p. 82

p. 61   'That young man . . .' *Ibid* p. 86
         'When I am in Kimberley . . .' Sauer p. 119
p. 62   'I have always been . . .' *Diamond Fields Advertiser* 15/3/1886
p. 64   'What is your game . . .' Fort: *Beit* p. 72
         'You cannot drown . . .' Boyle pp. 376–7
pp. 70–1   Rhodes and Sauer. Sauer p. 111
p. 72   'I'm off . . .' Colvin Vol. I p. 81
         'Buy a seat . . .' Fitzpatrick p. 88
         'careless of anything . . .' Colvin Vol. I p. 81
         'You have been . . .' *Ibid*
p. 73   'Ah, Barney . . .' *Ibid*

Chapter Six
p. 74   Rhodes and William Pickering. Cloete p. 143
p. 76   'Everyone knew he . . .' F. Johnson p. 105
p. 77   'We felt that . . .' *Diamond Fields Advertiser* 7/5/1887
p. 80   'You young thieves . . .' B. Williams p. 99
         'Well Mr Rhodes . . .' G. F. Williams p. 287
         'You know my story . . .' 'Vindex' p. 750
pp. 83–4   Rhodes and Barnato deal. R. Turrell: *Rhodes, De Beers and Monopoly* Journal of Imperial and Commonwealth History: May 1982
p. 86   'He walks quite erect . . .' Plomer pp. 58–9
p. 90   'Aren't those just . . .' Lockhart & Woodhouse p. 120
         'And tonight . . .' Fitzpatrick p. 32
p. 91   Supreme Court judgement. Michell Vol. I pp. 185–6

Chapter Seven
p. 93   'The general feeling . . .' Cartwright p. 27
p. 95   'Tell him I have heard . . .' B. Williams pp. 111–2
         'Wealth cannot break . . .' *Ibid*
p. 97   'I saw Harry . . .' Cartwright p. 41
p. 99   'of parts of Matabeleland . . .' Keppel-Jones p. 64
p. 101   'I must ask my wife . . .' Rouillard p. 49
         'distaste for life . . .' *Ibid* p. 51
         'After some discussion . . .' Cartwright p. 46
p. 102   'We had agreed . . .' Rouillard p. 55
p. 104   'While I was in . . .' Rouillard p. 59
p. 105   'In passing our . . .' Keppel-Jones p. 67
p. 106   'Yes, Indunas . . .' Rouillard p. 68
         'Thompson this is . . .' *Ibid*
p. 107   Rudd and Bushmen. Rudd pp. 40–1

Chapter Eight
p. 108   'raised no difficulty . . .' Rouillard p. 70
p. 110   'I was thus . . .' *Ibid*
p. 113   'I send two of . . .' Keppel-Jones p. 85
         'There are so many . . .' *Ibid* p. 84
p. 114   'the very stick . . .' Lockhart & Woodhouse p. 150
p. 115   'Mr Rhodes is my man . . .' Whyte p. 248
p. 116   'You go back to him . . .' Lockhart & Woodhouse p. 150
         'in the valleys of . . .' Blake p. 50
p. 117   'If it was not so serious . . .' Lockhart & Woodhouse p. 151

p. 156 'We have settled . . .' Merriman Vol II p. 13
p. 157 'I hope you will not . . .' Rose Innes: *Correspondence* p. 82
p. 158 'Treat the natives . . .' 'Vindex' p. 159
'I am going to . . .' Plomer pp. 119–20
'The only big . . .' Schreiner p. 890
'The perception of what . . .' Plomer p. 121
p. 159 'given to a chance . . .' G. A. L. Green p. 40
'His general behaviour . . .' G. H. Wilson pp. 50–1
p. 160 'My sense of propriety . . .' G. A. L. Green p. 38
'I think if more pains . . .' Lockhart & Woodhouse p. 200
p. 162 'retire from the Cabinet . . .' Rose Innes: *Correspondence* p. 96
'I like to know . . .' Lockhart & Woodhouse p. 197

Chapter Eleven
p. 167 'I am off to Mashonaland . . .' Lockhart & Woodhouse p. 247
'neither the extent . . .' Churchill p. 245
p. 168 'I'll take their . . .' F. Johnson p. 206
p. 170 'They are a bad . . .' Lockhart & Woodhouse p. 221
p. 171 'If you have any . . .' B. Williams p. 168
p. 172 'But why didn't you . . .' Colvin Vol. I p. 205
p. 173 'The Portuguese Treaty . . .' Lockhart & Woodhouse p. 284
p. 174 'Many months probably . . .' Churchill pp. 208–9
p. 175 'Well, if you want . . .' Lockhart & Woodhouse p. 248
p. 177 'I would have ye know . . .' Colvin Vol. I p. 216
'Almost immediately, I saw . . .' F. Johnson p. 207
p. 178 'Rhodes will back . . .' Colvin Vol. I p. 207
p. 180 'It is really extraordinary . . .' *Ibid*
'Dr Jameson has endeared . . .' Selous p. 355
p. 181 'They intend snuffing . . .' Keppel-Jones p. 236
p. 182 'from a financial point . . .' Colvin Vol. I p. 249
p. 183 'maintaining the dignity . . .' Ranger p. 65
'Why should you seize . . .' Keppel-Jones p. 235
p. 184 'We are the most . . .' 'Vindex' p. 303
p. 185 'sweep them off . . .' Keppel-Jones p. 237
'I intend to treat . . .' Ranger p. 93
'Read Luke xiv 31 . . .' Colvin Vol. I p. 259
p. 186 'numbers of little white . . .' Keppel-Jones p. 270
p. 187 'The white men are . . .' Lockhart & Woodhouse p. 259
'will never catch me . . .' Keppel-Jones p. 285
'Fancy the king . . .' Ranger p. 98
p. 188 'You would have thought . . .' Michell Vol. II p. 89

Chapter Twelve
p. 190 'dilatory in their . . .' Stanford Vol. II p. 151
p. 191 'There was no artillery . . .' *Cape Argus* 17/8/1929
p. 193 'You will certainly not . . .' 'Vindex' pp. 371–90
'I had to work . . .' *Ibid*
'If the Glen Grey . . .' *Ibid*
p. 195 Rhodes and Matabeleland Order in Council. Keppel-Jones p. 336
p. 196 'I have great sympathy . . .' B. Williams p. 193
p. 197 'I don't ask your advice . . .' Millin p. 151
p. 198 'Sweet pasture . . .' B. Williams p. 193
pp. 198–9 Rhodes and Groote Schuur. Baker pp. 19–34

p. 200   'That's not my job . . .' McDonald: *Heritage* p. 121
           'Dear Sir, in reply . . .' Le Sueur p.195
           'Ah, but you've . . .' Guthrie p. 125
p. 204   'Yes, I suppose she is . . .' Dawborn p. 183
           'I have been accused . . .' *Ibid*
           'I cannot get married . . .' Jourdan p. 165
p. 205   'I hope you won't get . . .' G. Beet: *History of Diamond Fields*
              (typescript in Kimberley Library)
           'I don't want a secretary . . .' Lockhart & Woodhouse p. 27
p. 207   'If we have to depend . . .' Michell Vol. II p. 119
p. 208   'hundreds of miles . . .' Phimister: *Rhodes, Rhodesia and the Rand*.
           Journal of South African Studies Jan 1974
           'Unless radical . . .' McDonald: *Rhodes* p. 178

Chapter Thirteen
p. 209   'a country as large . . .' Colvin Vol. II pp. 18–9
p. 210   'Damn you fellows . . .' Lockhart & Woodhouse p. 288
           'You see that flag . . .' *Ibid*
           'If I were President Kruger . . .' Michell Vol. II pp. 127–8
p. 212   'I know I may count . . .' *Ibid*
p. 214–5   'a scandal . . . the laziest rascals . . .' Lockhart & Woodhouse p. 305
p. 216   'thousands of unarmed . . .' *Times* 1/1/1896
p. 217   'I received so many . . .' Lady S. Wilson p. 35
           'The position is becoming . . .' Colvin Vol. II pp. 54–5
           'Unless I hear . . .' *Ibid* p. 52
p. 219   'In time of political . . .' *Eastern Province Herald* 6/1/1896
p. 221   'Mr Beit looked ill . . .' Ly S. Wilson pp. 29–30
           'I was naughty . . .' B. Williams p. 274
p. 222   'up to the neck' Lockhart & Woodhouse p. 336
           'I found all the busmen . . .' Longford p. 233
           'to divert the issue . . .' Brett Vol. I pp. 194–7
           'shape his course . . .' Garvin Vol. III p. 109
p. 223   'most satisfactory . . .' Lockhart & Woodhouse p. 337

Chapter Fourteen
p. 226   'Jameson has given . . .' Ranger p. 104
p. 227   Alfred de Foncesco. Rorke pp. 112–3
           'Her Majesty's Government attack . . .' Ranger p. 107
           'Lord Ripon would be wise . . .' *Ibid*
p. 228   'all the plagues of Egypt . . .' Blake p. 123
p. 231   'There is no colonel . . .' Keppel-Jones p. 456
p. 232   'You should kill all . . .' Lockhart & Woodhouse p. 349
           'Rhodes is a splendid . . .' Brett Vol. I p. 149
           'extermination or deportation' Ranger p. 172
p. 233   'No one ever received . . .' McDonald p. 210
p. 234   'The blacks have been . . .' Ranger p. 53
p. 235   'He was very worried . . .' *Ibid*
p. 237   'We must risk it . . .' Stent p. 31
p. 238   'You came, you conquered . . .' *Ibid* p. 39
           'I shouldn't go on . . .' *Ibid* p. 46
           'Where are we to live . . .' *Ibid* pp. 59–60
p. 239   'unless they surrendered . . .' Ranger p. 257
p. 240   'Things are looking . . .' *Ibid*

'Mr Rhodes's manner . . .' Keppel-Jones p. 528

p. 241   'A tribute to the . . .' Michell Vol. II p. 177

'Is that all? . . .' Millin p. 317

Chapter Fifteen

p. 242   'It is a good thing . . .' Michell Vol. II p. 180

'I said it . . .' *Ibid*

'I can only say . . .' Fuller p. 209

p. 244   'as though the wife . . .' Lockhart & Woodhouse p. 324

'Our great enemy . . .' *Natal Archives* A159 Vol. XVI

p. 245   'I believe that Rhodes . . .' Buchan-Gould p. 164

'In twenty years . . .' Garvin Vol. III pp. 117–9

p. 246   'She used to ride . . .' Le Sueur p. 193

p. 247   Rhodes before Select Committee. Longford pp. 258–71

p. 248   'D'ye know, Grimmer . . .' Le Sueur p. 195

'strive for equal rights . . .' Michell Vol II p. 202

'Only one irreconcilable . . .' *Ibid*

'I said nothing . . .' Rose Innes *Correspondence* pp. 209–10

p. 249   'He is too self-willed . . .' Wrench p. 187

p. 250   'Hullo, Jameson . . .' Le Sueur p. 154

p. 251   'Regret learn report . . .' Lockhart & Woodhouse p. 380

p. 252   'to see how it felt' Michell Vol II p. 210

'starting very early . . .' *Ibid* p. 211

p. 253   'I suppose you think . . .' Le Sueur p. 165

'shared Rhodes's blankets' *South Africa* 11/10/1913

p. 254   'contracted fever . . .' Michell Vol. II p. 215

p. 256   'there can be little doubt . . .' *Central African Journal of Medicine*
      April 1965

'Baas what was left . . .' Trevor p. 105

p. 257   'by a Continental gang . . .' *Cape Times* 9/3/1898

'I propose running . . .' Natal Archives A159 Vol. XVI

p. 258   'I am determined not . . .' Michell Vol. II p. 240

'I have been painted . . .' *Ibid*

'I honestly believe . . .' *Ibid* p. 235

p. 259   'My motto is . . .' *Ibid* p. 276

'I fear attempts . . .' Rose Innes *Correspondence* p. 242

p. 260   'Mr Rhodes's presence . . .' Michell Vol. II p. 248

pp. 261–2   Rhodes's last will. *Ibid* pp. 313–33

Chapter Sixteen

p. 271   'vulgar adventuress . . .' (and other comments by Lady Edward
      Cecil) Milner *My Picture Gallery*

p. 272   'a singular and most interesting . . .' Fuller p. 133

'ugly rumours about . . .' Gross p. 248

p. 273   'I keep aloof . . .' Fuller p. 220

'The notion of . . .' McDonald pp. 312–3

p. 274   'The British State must . . .' *Times* 20/7/1925

p. 275   'defended his wicket . . .' Pakenham p. 58

p. 276   'Citizens generally feel . . .' Michell Vol. II p. 268

p. 277   'be most disastrous . . .' Pakenham p. 159

p. 279   'I understood that . . .' Statement to le Sueur: Rhodes House
      Library, Oxford.

p. 280   'political agent' *South African News* 14/1/1900

p. 280   'What can one do . . .' Radziwill *Cecil Rhodes* p. 108
           'Well, I will instruct . . .' *Cape Argus Weekly* 12/2/1902

pp. 280–2   Princess Radziwill in London. *Rhodesiana Magazine* Dec. 1969
           and Flint: *Cecil Rhodes*

p. 282   'Let us get away . . .' Jourdan p. 135
           'It may be difficult . . .' *Rhodesiana Magazine op cit*

p. 283   'an active agent . . .' Headlam p. 326
           'about to forsake . . .' *South African News* 25/7/1900

p. 284   'That is your own . . .' *Cape Argus Weekly op cit*
           'That was one . . .' *Cape Times* (supplement) May 1902
           'Then he wanted me . . .' *Ibid*

p. 285   'Jameson had some . . .' Statement to le Sueur *op cit*

p. 287   'He sailed for Europe . . .' *Ibid*

p. 288   'such a proposition . . .' *Ibid*

p. 289   'He was already . . .' Warwick pp. 82–4

p. 290   'It is not the money . . .' Stead *Last Will and Testament*
           'They are all . . .' *Cape Times* (7/2/1902)

p. 291   'We shall probably . . .' *Ibid*
           'in the Supreme Court . . .' *Cape Times* (supplement) *op cit*
           'Damn that woman . . .' Le Sueur *Rhodes* p. 312

pp. 291–2   Confrontation at Groote Schuur *Cape Times* 29/2/1902

p. 293   'So it came to pass . . .' Stead *Last Will and Testament*
           'Unable to leave his bed . . .' Stevenson p. 85

p. 294   'I shall not regret . . .' Rose Innes *Correspondence* p. 338
           'Jameson with whom . . .' Currey p. 23

p. 295   'Turn me over . . .' Millin p. 351

L'Envoi

p. 296   'the massive coffin . . .' *Diamond Fields Advertiser* 9/4/1902

p. 297   'There arose the most . . .' *Rhodesia's Last Tribute*

Index

313

315

317